FDR AND THE HOLOCAUST

THE WORLD OF THE ROOSEVELTS

Published in cooperation with the Franklin and Eleanor Roosevelt Institute
Hyde Park, New York

General Editors:
William E. Leuchtenburg, William vanden Heuvel, and Douglas Brinkley

FDR AND THE HOLOCAUST

Edited by
Verne W. Newton

palgrave
macmillan

FDR AND THE HOLOCAUST
Copyright © Franklin and Eleanor Roosevelt Institute, 1996.

First published in hardcover in 1996 by PALGRAVE MACMILLAN® in the United States – a division of St. Martin's Press LLC, 175 Fifth Avenue, New York, NY 10010.

Where this book is distributed in the UK, Europe and the rest of the world, this is by Palgrave Macmillan, a division of Macmillan Publishers Limited, registered in England, company number 785998, of Houndmills, Basingstoke, Hampshire RG21 6XS.

Palgrave Macmillan is the global academic imprint of the above companies and has companies and representatives throughout the world.

Palgrave® and Macmillan® are registered trademarks in the United States, the United Kingdom, Europe and other countries.

ISBN: 978–0–230–61948–7

Library of Congress Cataloging-in-Publication Data is available from the Library of Congress.

A catalogue record of the book is available from the British Library.

Design by Newgen Imaging Systems (P) Ltd., Chennai, India.

First PALGRAVE MACMILLAN paperback edition: December 2009

10 9 8 7 6 5 4 3 2 1

Printed in the United States of America.

Transferred to Digital Printing in 2009.

CONTENTS

ACKNOWLEDGMENTS

Several individuals contributed significantly to the creation of this volume: John Ferris, Karen O'Keefe, and Karen Casey.

Unless noted below, all contributions were written expressly for this work.

"Allied Knowledge of Auschwitz-Birkenau in 1943-1944," by Richard Breitman (paper given at a symposium entitled "The Bombing of Auschwitz: Should the Allies Have Attempted It?" at the National Air and Space Museum at the Smithsonian Institution, 30 April 1993, Washington, D.C.).

"The Bombing of Auschwitz Reexamined," by James H. Kitchens III, *Journal of Military History* 58 (April 1994), 233-265.

"Bystanders to the Holocaust" (Review Essay of Penkower/Wyman books), by Michael R. Marrus, *Studies in Contemporary Jewry* 3 (1987), 212-221.

"Courage First and Intelligence Second: The American Jewish Secular Elite, Roosevelt, and the Failure to Rescue," by Henry L. Feingold, *American Jewish History* 72 (June 1983), 424-460.

"Did FDR Betray the Jews? Or Did He Do More Than Anyone Else to Save Them?" by Arthur Schlesinger, Jr., *Newsweek,* 18 April 1994, 14.

"The Failure to Provide a Safe Haven for European Jewry," by Richard Breitman (World War II Studies Conference, Washington, D.C., May 1993).

Review Essay of David Wyman's *The Abandonment of the Jews: America and the Holocaust, 1941-1945,* by Henry L. Feingold, *Jewish Social Studies* 48 (winter 1986).

"Roosevelt and the Holocaust," by Richard Breitman, from *American Refugee Policy and European Jewry: 1933-1945,* by Richard Breitman and Alan Kraut, copyright 1987 by Indiana University Press.

"Roosevelt as Foreign Policy Leader" (Epilogue from *Franklin D. Roosevelt and Foreign Policy, 1932-1945,* by Robert Dallek, copyright 1979 by Oxford University Press, Inc. Reprinted by permission.

Transcript of the Summary of the Conference on "Policies and Responsibilities of the American Government toward the Holocaust," Franklin D. Roosevelt Library, 11-12 November, 1993.

"Was There Communal Failure? Some Thoughts on the American Jewish Response to the Holocaust," by Henry L. Feingold, *American Jewish History* 81 (autumn 1993), 60-80.

PREFACE

The genesis of this volume was a conference on "Policies and Responses of the American Government toward the Holocaust" held at the Franklin D. Roosevelt Library on 11-12 November 1993. The conference was chaired by John Morton Blum and sponsored by the Franklin and Eleanor Roosevelt Institute. This book consists of materials from three different sources: (1) a summary of the participants' remarks prepared by rapporteur J. Garry Clifford; (2) articles, chapters, and essays submitted by participants following the conference; and (3) essays and articles by historians who were not participants at the conference, but whose contributions are relevant to the issues discussed.

In convening the gathering at Hyde Park, New York, the organizers were responding to the opinion expressed with growing frequency during the preceding 25 years that Franklin D. Roosevelt personally, as well as individuals and institutions within his administration, failed to rescue the Jews of Europe from the Holocaust and, therefore, bear some responsibility for the death of six million Jews.

One conference objective was to determine to what extent the controversy over the Roosevelt administration's responses to the Holocaust endures because the issues themselves have defied scholarly resolution. To this extent, could such issues be defined and a course of action leading to resolution be chartered? Or, do the issues persist outside the framework of scholarship, kept alive by debates between nonscholars who are either unaware of, or unconcerned with, the historical record?

To tackle these questions the organizers brought together a group of distinguished Roosevelt and Holocaust scholars. To assure the most candid scholar-to-scholar exchange, the conference was not open to the press or the public; it was not recorded; and no papers were commissioned. A rudimentary agenda was divided into three broad topics: (1) Refugee Policies, 1933-1942; (2) Rescue, 1942-1945; (3) Where Do We Go From Here? Future Research and Analysis.

Once the sessions had concluded, participants thought important ground had been covered, including solid ideas for further research. Upon reading through J. Garry Clifford's remarkably thorough summary, the organizers and many of the participants believed it should be published. Each participant was provided a copy and in some cases made minor clarifications or corrections. Additionally, each participant was invited to submit articles or other writings that he or she thought illuminated the points made at the conference.

THE CONFERENCE

Karen J. Greenberg's bibliographic essay attributes much of the impetus for Holocaust history to "questions about who exactly is guilty and conversely who escapes condemnation." The historians who attended the conference were more concerned with trying to place people and events in the context of the times than with searching for the guilty (though, to be sure, as the reader will see in some of the essays included in this volume, many have also taken up the question of guilt).

Henry L. Feingold emphasized that those who attribute guilt to American Jewry for its alleged failure to influence policy in Washington, D.C., exaggerate greatly the unity and power of the prewar and wartime American Jewish community. Robert Dallek, in turn, juxtaposed the limitations on Roosevelt's powers to act during both the refugee period and the war. Dallek, Michael R. Marrus, and Richard Breitman all stressed the need for those wishing to make moral judgments to first understand the options and perceptions that confronted U.S. policymakers. Breitman pointed out the need to remember that there was no Holocaust in the 1930s, only Nazi persecution.

On the subject of refugees, Marrus, Greenberg, and others noted that until 1938—the year of the Anschluss and Kristallnacht—the exiles (as they were then considered) assumed they would be returning to Germany once Adolf Hitler's regime had collapsed. Indeed, many had returned in 1935 *after* the Nuremberg Laws were promulgated.

For some conferees the doomed Wagner-Rogers Bill of 1939 symbolized an insensitivity by Roosevelt to the plight of European refugees. This not surprisingly led to repeated criticisms for allowing Assistant Secretary of State Breckinridge Long to exercise too much discretion—discretion that seemed to be directed at increasing the misery and perils of European refugees.

The issue of bombing Auschwitz eluded resolution. Breitman pointed out that many Jewish leaders either flat out opposed bombing Auschwitz or gave it a very low priority, and he and Feingold agreed that to hold up Auschwitz as the centerpiece for the case against Roosevelt was unwise. Still, Breitman, along with several other participants, expressed the judgment that Auschwitz should have been bombed, just as FDR should have publicly endorsed the Wagner-Rogers Bill even if he could not have won on it.

Bernard Wasserstein suggested that issues like the Wagner-Rogers Bill and the scheme to bomb Auschwitz were more symbolic than real, and he contended that it was unreasonable to expect the leaders of one sovereign nation to intervene on behalf of the citizens of another nation. The Jews, he observed, were not FDR's responsibility.

Much of the search for the guilty has to do with purity of intentions. Feingold's criticism of the Allies for refusing to engage in "retaliatory bombing" led to a fascinating exchange between Wasserstein and Feingold. But Breitman and Wasserstein pose this haunting specter: Fire Breckinridge Long, bomb Auschwitz, pass the Wagner-Rogers Bill, endorse every rescue plan no matter how implausible—and what difference would it have made?

Wasserstein replied that much of the moralizing has to do with *intentions* rather than *results.* All of the good intentions may not have saved one more Jew. On the other hand, one man unknown for humanitarian impulses may have saved more Jews than anyone else. Joseph Stalin shipped thousands of Jews to Siberia because he considered them suspect. They survived while millions of others perished.

Reference to the present conflict in Bosnia with its "ethnic cleansing" was invoked throughout the conference as a reminder of how—especially in the absence of a global war—a morally offensive campaign aimed at an ethnic group can be carried out in full view and yet little is done. Breitman, among others, suggested it may be a sobering reminder of just what constraints policymakers in the 1940s faced.

Breitman also suggested a number of topics needing further research. These included America's resettlement policies; a major study of the War Refugee Board; Congress's role in the refugee policy; biographies of Avra Warren, who oversaw U.S. consular activities in Europe in 1939-1940, and Raymond Geist, consul-general in Berlin and an early Cassandra in predicting the Holocaust; and studies on the activities of Jewish organizations and leaders.

AFTER THE HYDE PARK CONFERENCE

Several months after the conference, in April 1994, "America and the Holocaust: Deceit and Indifference" was aired on public television as part of the *American Experience* series. Based largely on the views of historian David

Wyman, the program, as the title suggests, was highly critical of Americans in general and of President Roosevelt and his administration in particular. This condemnation ignited a whole new round of letters, newspaper articles, op-ed pieces, and talk-show debates.

Greenberg in her essay observed with some irony that Holocaust history had come full cycle with works that seem to blame the Jews themselves. But as Arthur Schlesinger, Jr., who has written a book on the cycles of American history, wrote in a column in *Newsweek* in response to the TV documentary, Holocaust victims are not the only ones to have the historical tables turned upon them. FDR, Schlesinger pointed out, was a man considered by the Jews of his day as their greatest champion. And Hitler, the greatest enemy of the Jews, considered Roosevelt his most fierce, implacable, and, finally, his most dangerous foe. Yet many American Jews today dismiss FDR's defeat of Hitler and insist he must instead be remembered for failing to stop Hitler from murdering Europe's Jews.

The column generated an outpouring of letters to *Newsweek* raising issues from the voyage of the SS *St. Louis* to the bombing of Auschwitz. Schlesinger and William vanden Heuvel, president of the Franklin and Eleanor Roosevelt Institute, composed a letter responding to the most frequently raised issues, which is also included.

The Hyde Park Conference

1

Transcript of the Summary of the Conference on "Policies and Responses of the American Government toward the Holocaust," 11–12 November 1993

FIRST SESSION: 9:00–10:30 A.M.

Michael Marrus began by observing that his first reaction to being invited was to think the topic dealt with *contemporary* U.S. reactions to the Holocaust. He did not think that the Roosevelt administration had policies toward the Holocaust as we have understood the term since the 1960s, but rather that it developed policies toward a series of events that were recognized as the Holocaust only afterward.

In terms of the 1933-1942 period, Marrus pinpointed 1938 as a critical juncture. Most refugees who left Germany before 1938 remained in Europe and contemplated returning. Refugees in France—Marrus's research specialty[1]—expected to go back when Adolf Hitler's regime collapsed, as many thought it would. Marrus recalled John Hope Simpson's[2] comment in 1937 that the refugee situation was serious but manageable. Simpson cited the "potential problem" of Jews from Eastern Europe's authoritarian regimes also leaving and having to find refuge. This was before the Anschluss. The United States could accommodate more refugees from Germany, but what Simpson feared was a cascade of new refugees from Hungary, Poland, Romania, and the like.

Marrus also cited the four elements that weighed most heavily on immigration policy contained in Richard Breitman and Alan Kraut's study of U.S. refugee policy in this period[3]—(1) the constraints of public opinion; (2) FDR's reluctance to take political risks in the face of congressional and public opposition; (3) the pressures and momentum of orthodoxy regarding immigration restriction; and (4) an entrenched State Department bureaucracy with a restrictionist viewpoint.

The issue, Marrus suggested, is to assess the proper weight that should be given to each of these constraints. In response to Charles Maier's request that he make such an assessment, Marrus said that in order to do so, the response of the United States must be assessed within a global context. Canadian restrictionism, for instance, was even greater than that of the United States. Should the United States's performance be judged on the total number of refugees who came to the United States or in terms of the numbers of refugees as a percentage of the total population, or in terms of the total area? One could argue, Marrus pointed out, that at least in terms of numbers admitted, U.S. policy was more generous than many other nations described by Raul Hilberg as "bystanders," to use his designation.[4]

Henry Feingold suggested several more ways to assess U.S. performance in this period. He raised the issue of "sufficiency." What could have reasonably been expected of FDR? What really was possible? What essential role could—and should—the state have played? Feingold referred to the debate between David Wyman and Lucy Dawidowicz on the alleged failures of American Jewry[5] to do more than it did in terms of refuge and rescue. Looking back, what could reasonably have been expected from government and private groups within the given historical context?

At the heart of his second question, Feingold emphasized, are the issues of power and influence. How much power to effect change did FDR have? To underscore his point, Feingold recalled the story of two Jews in Vienna being followed by two Nazi thugs. One Jew says to the other: "There are two of them and we are all alone." This illustrates that at times the perception of power matters as much as the reality of power.

Feingold voiced concern that it is too easy to ascribe too much power and responsibility to American Jewry in the 1930s. To attribute such power to American Jewry would be to overlook the splits within the community, the real constraints of anti-Semitism, as well as self-imposed cultural constraints. Ironically, it is possible American Jewry itself may have overestimated the strength of American anti-Semitism because of what happened in Germany. If it could happen in Germany, many American Jews admonished, it could easily happen in the United States. He recalled Hilberg's description of the "paralytic reaction of European Jewry."

Feingold wondered aloud how much the 1924 Immigration Act was the result of anti-Semitism and pointed out that restrictionism came from many

American impulses, not simply anti-Semitism. Yet the restrictions contained in that law—whatever their motive—made for a pattern of reaction that constrained American Jewry's perception of its own power by raising the specter of an anti-Semitic reaction.

Bernard Bellush asked, in effect, was it possible to refer to "an American Jewish community," or in fact were there many voices and, therefore, many communities?

Henry Feingold responded that the question contained a paradox. The isolationists, most notably Charles Lindbergh in his 1941 Des Moines, Iowa, speech,[6] invented a monolithic Jewish community with enormous power, money, and influence. The recent revisionist criticism of the alleged Jewish failure during the Holocaust seems to accept the anti-Semitic model of Jewish unity and power. But the fact is that American Jewry *was* divided and thus often incoherent. Divided, Jews had less power and thus less responsibility for what failures there were. This lack of unity frustrated Roosevelt, who once lamented that there was "no Jewish pope" who could forge unity.

Carl Schorske pointed out that the Jewish refugees who came to the United States after 1938 tended to be professionals, doctors, academics, and the like; they looked to their professional networks to help them enter the United States. Quite often they were also Social Democrats who were highly politicized and who did not think they would be returning to Germany or Europe. Was this attitude and composition different from that of other European refugees who came before 1938? Did those who came earlier also view themselves as temporary?

In response Michael Marrus asserted that, in general, the earlier the emigration the more likely that it was politically driven and that those emigrating were politically active. And because they had been politically active they were confident in their perceptions of German politics. Many could and did say: "Hitler can't last." There is a tendency today to project the post-1938 period too far backward. It took time for the emigration to take on the character it did after the events of 1938.

John Blum confirmed that the early refugees to the United States did not plan to go back. Yet, ironically, they never left Germany in their own minds. They remained quintessential Germans.

Michael Marrus pointed out that Karl Jaspers had written about precisely that sort of emigre/refugee. As a way of illustration, Marrus recalled the anecdote of the Jewish refugee in New York with the picture of Hitler on his wall—to remind himself daily why he won't go back. To underscore the political nature of the early refugees Marrus described how the early Jewish emigres in France during 1933-1934 associated in Paris with anti-Fascist Italian refugees. It was part of the political dynamic in France. The early refugees came precisely because they *were* anti-Nazi. But as to their own mind-set, Marrus cited George Mosse's[7] estimate that some ten thousand refugees returned to Germany in 1935; the Nuremburg Laws, bad as they were, at least provided a certain legal status. Charles Maier expanded on the extent to which many pre-1938 refugees even to America were part of the longer story of exile and return. He recalled the case of a Cleveland textile manufacturer related to his family who returned to Germany in 1937. Many emigres who came to the United States joined emigre family units already here and with them could keep contact and assist those still in Germany. Again, 1938 was the demarcation point. Everyone knew the events were profound. But it was unclear exactly how they would affect the movement of refugees. European refugees in Prague, for instance, waited to see how the political climate would be affected.

Karen Greenberg offered insights from her extensive research on early refugees. Her findings indicated that if those early refugees came to the United States intending to return eventually to Europe, they did not talk or write about that intention at the time. They were well aware that there would be difficulties when it came time to go back. But they made the final decision *not* to return only at a later date. Those later decisions are documented and can be found in their papers.

These people could also come here more easily; they were not restricted by the immigration laws. Most had been in the United States before. They were not considered refugees; they were exiles; the designation had considerable political connotations. Use of one phrase or the other mattered. More could be done for the exiled scholars.

Richard Breitman reminded us that those who came in the early 1930s were not merely following some abstract rules of supply and demand. The German immigration quotas during the Depression were unfilled; this was deliberate. Many tried to get out and go to the United States in 1933-1934 but were denied entry. Sixty thousand left Germany but were, in effect, barred from the United States. Those who came in 1933-1934 were more political, but they could also get in more easily because of their connections. The immigration policy did serve as a filtering mechanism. By manipulating administrative devices during the 1930s (without changing the law), the FDR administration could cause refugee inflow to fluctuate, depending on which way it was manipulated.

Breitman also pointed out that FDR could calibrate immigration policy at the margins in response to changing external conditions. In short, there was always scope to do more. He cited the victory of the Labor Department over the State Department in winning the Justice Department's verdict on interpreting the "public charge" clause. Consuls had been using the "public charge" clause[8] to deny visas, primarily because of the unemployment issue, since 1930. The Labor Department wanted to get around the strict interpretation by making it possible to approve visas of applicants who had relatives who would guarantee support. Charles Wyzanski[9] was the key person in overturning State Department procedures. Yet once this victory was achieved, the Labor Department backed off because of the political climate. There followed a tacit compromise wherein the Labor Department backed off but the State Department instructed consuls to loosen up on interpreting the public charge clause.

Robert Dallek suggested it was important to expand the conversation beyond the executive branch to consider the congressional attitudes on changing the immigration law. When FDR asked the congressional leadership about making changes, they told him, "No way." This confirmed Roosevelt's political intuition about how sensitive the issue was on the Hill. Dallek also mentioned that it was not just German exiles but seasoned diplomats that misread Hitler's staying power. He reminded the group that George Messersmith, a veteran foreign-service officer who was a fiercely anti-Nazi diplomat, confidently assured everyone that the Nazi regime wouldn't last, that it would blow up.

As further evidence of how hardened attitudes were on Capitol Hill, John Blum pointed out that four of six Jewish congressmen voted against immigration reform.

Robert Dallek observed that were FDR at this conference, he would be surprised and pained at all the recrimination and anguish that has been expressed over the years toward his refugee policy. It is important that as historians we have a sense of proportion and context. In terms of FDR's priorities, refugee matters ranked way down the list. This is true in both the prewar and the wartime period. During the war, keeping the alliance together was a much higher priority than pushing to open the gates to massive Jewish immigration to Palestine, which would have put the United States in direct conflict with Britain.

FDR knew which myths he was promulgating, especially the Wilsonian ideals—not because he thought the postwar world would conform to Wilsonian prescriptions, but because this was the only way to lead isolationist public opinion toward postwar participation in a balance-of-power contest. In this instance, invoking Wilson was done to meet FDR's chief goal of assuring U.S. involvement in global politics. All else ranked lower on his list. We need to keep in mind these competing goals and priorities.

Doris Kearns Goodwin responded that it was still necessary to pinpoint when and where FDR might have been able to do more. She cited figures: In 1939 the quota was filled. Altogether the United States accepted two hundred thousand refugees between 1933 and 1941. We can take some pride in this size.

Yet, Goodwin emphasized, there were moments when FDR could have done more.

She cited the summer and fall of 1940 when Congress did make an exception to permit British children to enter on temporary visas. Eleanor Roosevelt and her organizations wanted to extend the principle to German Jewish children, as in the 1939 Wagner-Rogers Bill. FDR would not agree. Goodwin also mentioned the confrontation between Eleanor and Franklin over Assistant Secretary of State Breckinridge Long. Eleanor called Long a fascist, and FDR told her never to call him that again. ER said she would not call Long a fascist, but it would not change what he was. Goodwin wanted to say "bravo" for ER, and wondered why there were no visas for Jewish children.

Goodwin cited Long and FDR's obsession with the Fifth Column danger as proof that by the fall of 1940 FDR was already thinking like a war president. FDR's switch to a national-security set of priorities meant, whether intended or not, that a window of opportunity closed prematurely.

Henry Feingold injected a number of questions into the discussion. He wondered whether FDR used the national-security psychosis cynically, to do what he intended to do anyway. He asked what motivated FDR to call for the Evian Conference.[10] Was he really interested in the resettlement solution?

Resettlement, Feingold noted, put Zionists in a ticklish spot since they wanted Palestine to be *the* homeland. The seriousness with which Americans pursued resettlement, he stressed, is reflected by the fact that—according to David Wyman—there were 666 resettlement plans. Feingold also pointed out that the Schacht-Rublee talks[11] envisaged what amounted to a ransom of German Jews by the Germans. FDR may have shared the imagination of Jewish control of "international finance" or banking. Zionists would have nothing to do with such a scheme. The story of the abortive Schacht-Rublee plan forms a bookend to the effort at the end of the war by the War Refugee Board to ransom the Jews of Hungary.

Michael Marrus responded to the question of the Fifth Column issue. He suggested that these paranoid reactions were not peculiarly American. Each country, as war approached, followed a pattern of "rounding up the usual suspects." Winston Churchill's response to enemy aliens in Britain was: "Collar the lot." Marrus emphasized that FDR was not cynical in his belief in the Fifth Column. Because of this apparently insurmountable barrier, the only large-scale feasible solution during this period *was* resettlement.

Marrus pointed to the example of Dorothy Thompson, the leading advocate for refugees in the 1930s. She did not think a quest for higher quotas or new immigration laws was practical. Instead, she backed a "super transfer agreement," outlined in her *Foreign Affairs* article in 1938.[12] It had similarities to the Schacht-Rublee plan; she at least thought resettlement was possible.

Charles Maier discussed the way in which historical questions are rationalized. We tend to be Olympian about it. He felt uncomfortable with any suggestion that FDR should be admired for his ability to maneuver at the margins. The problem with the Schacht-Rublee approach was the "free rider" notion, as put forward in "rational choice" theory. Would not agreeing to ransom simply abet indefensible behavior by Nazi Germany? Wouldn't this have made refugees a public goods problem? At the same time Maier said it was necessary to gain further insight into why the State Department seemed so unmoving on the refugee issue. He cited as an example George Kennan's reaction to a Jew trying to get out of Prague in 1939: "Let him face the music." Could FDR have interfered more than he did? Why did he not fire Long?

Robert Dallek asserted that FDR was hardly intimidated by the State Department; this was not a case of kowtowing by the emperor. Dallek reminded us that there was a recession in 1938 and that the president was walking a fine line. His priorities after Munich were to rearm and revise the neutrality laws so as to permit cash-and-carry sales to allies in the event of war; to him there was no point in stirring the opposition on what wasn't yet a priority. FDR had a personal connection with, and confidence in, Breckinridge Long. As for the Evian Conference, it would at least air the issue, perhaps buy some more room to maneuver.

Arthur Schlesinger, Jr., agreed with Dallek about priorities. And to illustrate that not all foreign-service officers were indifferent, he quoted from a letter written in 1938 by John Wiley from Vienna.[13] The quintessential conservative foreign-service officer, Wiley wrote in graphic terms to George Messersmith describing the plight of Jewish refugees after the Anschluss and predicted it would get even worse. He pleaded for no reductions in staff, as had been proposed. In fact, he emphasized, more staff was needed to process refugee applications. He described German policy toward Jews as "utterly lunatic." Yet Wiley was not proposing changes in immigration laws; he wanted to keep the State Department aloof and to encourage voluntary efforts to assist refugees. Schlesinger suggested that Wiley's informed response to what he called this "heartrending misery" is an indication of how restricted were the options even among those who were empathetic to what was happening in Europe.

Verne Newton, responding to Feingold's speculation about the degree of FDR's true concern for the Fifth Column threat, emphasized that there was nothing contrived about Roosevelt's attitude. He deeply *believed* that the existence of a Fifth Column was the only way to explain France's complete collapse and surrender. In fact, his concern bordered on an obsession; FDR eagerly sought information about it. His fears were reinforced by the State Department and the Federal Bureau of Investigation (FBI), and it might be more legitimate to question whether they were merely feeding these fears or whether they actually believed such threats. As for Breckinridge Long, FDR would have expressed surprise at the claim that Long had real power. He relegated Long to purgatory quickly enough when Henry Morgenthau, Jr., secretary of the Treasury, confronted FDR with Long's duplicity. Roosevelt stripped Long of his authority, and within months Long was out of government altogether.

As for whether FDR could have done more, **Richard Breitman** pointed out that it was possible to do more in the 1930s, and that during that period the Roosevelt administration imaginatively invented ways of stretching quotas. Washington's signals to consuls at critical points were mildly positive. Yet even with this, more could have been done. There was no Holocaust in the 1930s, only Nazi persecution. Moral standards of judgment must consider the different contexts.

He also agreed that with the advent of war, the Fifth Column was no ruse for FDR. Breitman further cautioned historians against blaming the State Department alone as a bureaucratic obstacle; the FBI and the military contributed their share of obstruction. The total effort serves to underline the fact that, in Breitman's judgment, there were not many humanitarians in the government.

Trude Lash pointed out that Morgenthau, Jr., was the one high-level person who knew FDR best, and she asked about his role during the early period.

John Blum responded that prior to 1942 Morgenthau's involvement was much less than it would be after the reports of Nazi atrocities made their way to Washington. Morgenthau did regard resettlement as an evasion of the central issue. Though Morgenthau and Roosevelt had been friends and neighbors for years, Blum pointed out that Morgenthau was not always perceptive with respect to FDR.

Doris Kearns Goodwin returned to the question of when and where FDR could have done more. If FDR did better in 1940, he didn't do enough. She cited the meeting in October 1940 in which Breckinridge Long suggested ways to postpone action on rescuing those with transit visas. And after the dilatory approach of various American consuls leaked to the press, Freda Kirchway wrote a blistering piece in the *Nation*.[14] When Eleanor pushed that more be done for those in peril, FDR had a key meeting with Sumner Welles, undersecretary of state, and Long on 3 October 1940. Long argued that the so-called refugees were not refugees at all, but potential saboteurs. Goodwin insisted that admirers of FDR would serve him best by looking hard at his failures. The question remains, what could have been done in 1940 to push Long?

William Korey observed that to him it was inconceivable that FDR's obsession with the Fifth Column blocked a proper response to the refugee problem. Did this fear really constrain his actions, or was the Fifth Column raised to simply permit FDR to do what he wanted to do anyway? The question remains, did FDR have a commitment on behalf of refugees?

As the first session came to a close, **Henry Feingold** expressed concern about the revisionist arguments that the Holocaust was not preplanned, but evolved. In view of this, resettlement in the 1938-1941 period needs to be examined as a viable alternative to the Holocaust, a point Feingold had made in his article on FDR and resettlement.[15]

SECOND SESSION: 10:45 A.M.–12:30 P.M.

Bernard Wasserstein suggested that, as an approach to the 1942-1945 period, it would be more productive to avoid the counterfactual question of what might have been done and concentrate on what happened, the choices available, and what constraints affected the choices taken. He further proposed examining three categories: (1) the small numbers who were rescued or escaped in the 1942-1945 period—compared to the large numbers that had escaped prior to 1942, only a small trickle did so after that year; (2) schemes for relief, alleviation, and mitigation, including such efforts as sending aid in through the blockade, shipping food parcels, and the like; and (3) schemes such as bombing Auschwitz or responding to ransom appeals. Given the huge numbers being exterminated, the scope offered by such schemes was quite small, and such proposals were more symbolic than real.

Wasserstein also suggested there were, in effect, three competing scenarios for U.S. policy:

1. A hidden-hand/Adam Smith scenario in which everyone looked to their own and let others face the music. Isolationists found this approach most appealing.
2. A charity-society approach, in which government did what it could on an ad hoc basis. Eleanor Roosevelt, for instance, implored her husband to do more, more, always more. This approach assumed that the hidden hand did not work and that any decent society must do something to help.
3. A more Keynesian approach wherein there was an attempt to solve the problem by restructuring, for instance, through resettlement. This school of thought argued that "we cannot think of solving the problem by

admitting refugees, there are too many of them; resettlement is the only structural solution." The Zionist goal of a Palestinian homeland offered the only effective solution of this kind.

Wasserstein contended that it was unreasonable to expect leaders of sovereign states to intervene on behalf of someone else's citizens. Poland did not even regard its three million Jewish citizens as its own problem. He again raised the "free rider" issue. The charity approach, he emphasized, only mitigated the problem, which always grew worse. For this reason, only the postwar solution of a homeland in Palestine, an Israel, offered any hope. Even in this context, FDR fell short.

He cited FDR's exchange with Governor-General Nogues, the resident general of French Morocco, at the end of the Casablanca Conference in 1943, in which FDR accepted the logic of laws in North Africa restricting Jewish dominance, suggesting the same would have to hold true in Germany for Jews after the war. Quotas, according to FDR, would be needed for Jews in business and the professions after the war. Was this conversation simply another example of FDR agreeing with whomever he last talked to, or was it the real Roosevelt?[16]

Still, Wasserstein emphasized, the Jews were not FDR's responsibility. The United States was not the world's problem solver. The administration's view was that the United States should be part of the restructuring—both in terms of a postwar Jewish state and international structures to deal with refugees.

In terms of FDR's view of searching for long-term, structural solutions, **William vanden Heuvel** pointed out that after Yalta, FDR went to Cairo to discuss a postwar Jewish state with King Ibn Saud. Saud, recalled vanden Heuvel, responded to Roosevelt that room should be found in Europe to resettle Jews—and that since the Germans were responsible for the Holocaust, German land should be made available for a Jewish state. Why should the Arabs, the king insisted, be asked to give up their lands? After all, they had not caused the Holocaust. FDR had undertaken the trip to Cairo despite his fatigue and ill health, already worsened by the Yalta trip, to seek help for the Jews in Palestine.

Bernard Bellush apologized for ranging back to the 1930s, but noted his own activities on behalf of the anti-Nazi boycott and efforts for refugees. The experience convinced him that it is possible to be dedicated to humanitarian change, even if it conflicts with the big picture. The big picture should never overwhelm vital day-to-day activities. The United States should have done more. It was a revelation to him at the time of the abortive Wagner-Rogers Bill just how negative and anti-Semitic the opposition was. Yet no cabinet member spoke for the bill. No national Democratic Party spokesman testified. FDR made no public comment. The impact would not have been great; only twenty thousand children were involved. When FDR was governor of New York he at least had the state librarian write letters to editors around the state. He might have catalyzed those who needed inspiration to fight on. The silence was deafening. He could have maneuvered more, just as he did on other issues in which he did not want to appear too conspicuous.

Karen Greenberg endorsed Wasserstein's suggestions to think in terms of categories of foreign-policy dynamics. She noted that even though Americans like to think of themselves as motivated by humanitarian impulses, in fact the humanitarian arguments for major foreign-policy initiatives were not very compelling. Even when a major initiative was taken, as with the Fort Ontario experiment,[17] the administration very consciously avoided justifying the required funds on humanitarian grounds. And on that point, Harold Ickes, secretary of the interior, assessed the experiment a failure if judged on humanitarian terms.

When Varian Fry[18] went to France for the purpose of bringing back talented artists and thus expanded his visa list, he was recalled. The cold rationale of what was in the national interest seemed more important. By succumbing to humanitarian impulse, Fry was recalled for violating instructions. After 1938 the argument for admission took on a more humanitarian urgency. The early professionals and scholars, however, were not brought in for humanitarian reasons. The private groups who sponsored the early scholars backed off this line of argument, and eventually they stopped supporting exiles when they became refugees.

Henry Feingold suggested there are other chronological divisions—for instance, how governments responded before and after the Bermuda Conference.[19] Similarly, there were greater possibilities after Stalingrad. In talking about the possible bombing of Auschwitz, he noted that Americans have an exaggerated notion of the successes that can be achieved through bombing; it is almost as if it is regarded as a magic bullet. At the same time, he said he believes that had the United States announced retaliatory bombing of German cities in retribution for extermination of the Jews, it would have drawn greater world attention to the atrocities. So we must ask why were these things not done? Feingold concludes it was a failure of the mind. He acknowledged that Fort Ontario was a breakthrough, that laws were bent that in 1940 had seemed unbreakable because the argument was made that this was in the national interest.

But whether America's collective attitude was that of a charity society or one disposed toward Keynesian restructuring, a statesman like FDR must be judged on how he handled the critical problem of his time. When we judge FDR in his last years, preoccupied with winning the war, possibly sick, we can conclude that he did not understand that his world was going up in smoke at

Auschwitz. He knew of the Holocaust in a sense, but in another sense he "didn't get it." Why could he not believe in the extent of the atrocities? Perhaps because of the World War I propaganda that greatly exaggerated atrocities.

Bernard Wasserstein responded by pointing out that the British war cabinet rejected retaliatory bombing for very logical reasons. In the first place, if the Germans had made any promises on their treatment of the Jews, the Allies might have been compelled not only to cease retaliatory bombing, but also to cease bombing even against military targets. Wasserstein also noted that David Engel's 1987 book on Poland and the Jews[20] shows that the Polish exile government also advocated retaliatory bombing, but to achieve other purposes, not on behalf of the Jews. He also suggested that bombing German cities in retaliation for the murder of Jews might make cities like Hamburg even more anti-Semitic. At least these were among the arguments made in the British decision.

Richard Breitman expressed his agreement with Bellush that FDR could and should have done more on the Wagner-Rogers Bill even if he could not win on the issue. FDR did quietly manipulate at the margins in combining quotas in 1938-1939. Only when he could lead quietly did he do so. What he refused to do was take a strong public stand. This may have been the wrong decision. A number of advisers urged him not to be distracted from the priority of getting ready to combat Nazi Germany. Advisers like Messersmith urged Roosevelt to get as many supporters on board as possible and not to alienate others. Roosevelt could not have stopped the Holocaust, but he might have saved a larger fraction. The satellite nations (Romania, Hungary, and the like) were weaker and incapable of influence. Switzerland could have taken more refugees, even if only temporarily. The same with Sweden. All of these steps would have been small in scope, to be sure, but still they would have mattered.

Bombing Auschwitz would have been a symbolic act. But for this very reason it would have been important to do. Yet bombing Auschwitz is not a good example to use in pointing to Roosevelt's failure. The proposal was much too divisive. The World Jewish Congress opposed bombing Auschwitz. And bombing Auschwitz would not have dealt with the larger issues. To illustrate this point Breitman told of an interview he did after the war with Gerhart Riegner, representative of the World Jewish Congress in Switzerland, in his Geneva office. On the wall was a picture of FDR. Riegner was asked what he thought of Roosevelt nearly 50 years later. Breitman remembered Riegner's response: "Yes, I think it is right to have a photograph of FDR on the wall. We needed inspiration; FDR's image served that purpose—even if it was a disappointment to learn later that FDR was also another politician. Still, I will give him credit; he had a strategy to win the war."

Verne Newton picked up on Feingold's observation that FDR "didn't get it." He noted that many who should have really understood the "Final Solution" did not, among them German Jews, David Ben-Gurion, and Chaim Weizmann. Riegner could not understand from Geneva how uncomprehending everyone, particularly American Jews, were about what was happening in Europe. Riegner described how American Jews were sending packages to people long since deported to addresses that no longer existed. "We [in Geneva]," Riegner later recalled, "had the impression that they no longer understood what was happening. . . . [F]or us this was simply incomprehensible."[21]

Newton also quoted from an article by Henry Feingold, who wrote: "[T]he most certain means of rescue required a basic redirecting of the war strategy to save the Jews. . . . [M]ilitary strategists never would have accepted such a redirection." He asked Henry Feingold what he meant by "redirecting the war strategy."[22] He also asked what change in military strategy Feingold had in mind that would have saved the Jews—a cross-channel landing in 1942 or 1943?

Charles Maier argued that the decision not to bomb Auschwitz was not cynically made. We understand that bureaucracies only reluctantly do what they are not programmed to do. Bombing Auschwitz would have put the Germans on notice that the United States thought it was important. He also suggested that Wasserstein's "restructuring" approach could have been used as an excuse not to give away a few pennies. For FDR, the structural answer was to win the war. The Zionist emphasis on Palestine had the appeal of a "structural"—that is, long-term—solution, but it could also be viewed as an alibi for not dealing with the immediate problem of annihilation.

Bernard Bellush reiterated the importance of chronology in knowing and understanding the magnitude of the problem.

Michael Marrus suggested less distinction between humanitarian and structural policies. The United States, in effect, was going from one to the other. You draw upon humanitarian idealism to justify the structural changes necessary. One builds upon the other. Marrus also said that a recent article on bombing Auschwitz is persuasive in its argument that bombing would not have been an easy success.[23] He cited a Chaim Weizmann interview with Anthony Eden in which bombing Auschwitz was seventh on a list of priorities. It would have had a symbolic effect only. Regarding David Engel's book on Poland, Marrus said it shows that Poland was concerned with Polish national interests. This means the Poles were obsessed with the Soviets. The Polish government did find that the Jewish interests could be connected to Polish national interests and thus used them accordingly. Can we say the same for FDR?

Bernard Wasserstein responded to the point about Poland's definition of its national interest. This definition is crucial. The Polish government in exile did not define Poland's three million Jews as part of its constituency. This raises a fundamental question: To what extent does a sovereign state have responsibility for citizens of another country? The issue is caring. How much did Americans care about the Jews? Is this a naive question? Research indicates that Churchill spent more time and energy thinking and caring about the Jews than did FDR, yet Britain's record is worse than America's record. Both leaders were constrained by *structures* that precluded *care* from becoming policy. Wasserstein's basic point: You needed your own government or homeland to care. You needed a Zion.

Doris Kearns Goodwin reiterated the distinction between knowing and understanding. There is no doubt FDR read Riegner's report,[24] but did he grasp it? Jan Karski, Polish exile, saw FDR in the summer of 1943. Goodwin, who interviewed Karski while researching for her book *No Ordinary Time* (1994), says that "He is not anti-FDR. He does not blame FDR. He won the war. That was his (FDR'S) main interest." She also interviewed John Pehle of the War Refugee Board, who said he wished the board could have been established earlier, perhaps as early as 1940. Had it been, Kearns insisted, it would have been an important structure. As it was, the War Refugee Board became a catalyst. Goodwin said she thought the bombing of Auschwitz would have been worthwhile if it had saved only one Jew. FDR somehow missed seeing how big an issue it was. Bombing Auschwitz never got past Assistant Secretary of War John J. McCloy. It stayed in the bureaucracy at the third level because evidently FDR wanted it that way.

Henry Feingold cited Ben-Gurion's commitment to the proposition that Palestine was necessary to resettle the remnants of the Holocaust, even as those remnants disappeared. Feingold asked whether Auschwitz got lost among all the other atrocities—Katyn, Bataan, Lidice, and the like. FDR did misunderstand what Auschwitz meant. Real rescue would have required a much different war strategy. The government could not mobilize the American people to make war to rescue the Jews. This said, Feingold still argued that more was possible at the margins. The Holocaust did not come up for discussion at the summits. Poland ignored its own citizens. Juxtapose this vis-à-vis FDR. What, he asked again, can we reasonably expect the U.S. government to do? We are asking that it help people beyond its own citizenry. We were not giving some of our own citizens fair treatment. Limits were clearly present. Yet Henry Morgenthau, Jr., in a way, served to redeem secular American Jews. He was the only one of FDR's circle to act, though belatedly. His behavior tells us whether secular Jews could be mobilized. Morgenthau becomes more and more important to American Jewish history every year.

Robert Dallek suggested that FDR *was* interested in the Wagner-Rogers Bill and did care about the twenty thousand children. Yet we must understand the day-to-day context. This was the same time that FDR was revising the Neutrality Act to permit the sale of arms and munitions on a cash-and-carry basis. A fight on the Wagner-Rogers Bill would have crippled his main objective. The opposition would have doubled. Whether he was morally on the side of the angels or morally inadequate is not relevant. Of course FDR did not "get" the Holocaust in the sense we understand it today.

Michael Marrus repeated that there was a great disinclination to make any rescue attempt appear as a pro-Jewish effort, even to the point of discouraging overt Jewish participation.

John Blum underscored this point by recalling how his father urged him to keep out of sight.

William Korey responded to the issue of whether FDR "got it" or "grasped" the meaning of Auschwitz. In the film *Schindler's List*, women in slave labor camps, on hearing the rumors of gas chambers, totally rejected that it could happen to them because they were, after all, helping the German war effort. Denial and disbelief in the death camps were rampant, naturally. FDR knew about the massacre, but it did not register. A crucial point is that even if we regard FDR as engaging in some balancing of initiatives—even within his own set of priorities—very little has penetrated at the popular level about the positive acts of his administration, including the War Refugee Board (WRB) and Morgenthau's intervention. No one relates the War Refugee Board to the well-known efforts of Raoul Wallenberg, even though he was working for the WRB. A more balanced public image about FDR and his administration would appear to be appropriate.

Richard Breitman stated that as for Auschwitz, the bombing should have been attempted, even if its importance has been exaggerated. Bombing would have sent a message. Breitman said he believed that the United States had essentially given up on large-scale rescue by late 1944 and was reluctant to do more.

Verne Newton also responded again to the point that FDR was somehow singular in his failure to comprehend the meaning of Auschwitz or the Holocaust. He pointed out that at times Weizmann and Ben-Gurion became impatient with American Zionists for failing to understand the magnitude of the disaster in Europe. At one time Weizmann pleaded with Zionists that if something weren't done to rescue the Jews of Europe, there would be no one to live in Israel.

Doris Kearns Goodwin pointed out that in November 1942 a War Powers Bill was introduced with a clause to make it easier for Allied personnel to enter and move about the United States. The bill lost because it was deemed a ruse for easing refugee entrance. *Newsweek*[24] cited the anti-Semitic motive of opposition. Goodwin pointed out that this episode coincided with the Riegner cable.[25]

AFTERNOON SESSION: 1:45–3:00 P.M.

Richard Breitman started this session by considering both existing scholarship and, more importantly, what areas need further historical investigation—that is, where do we go from here? We have had scholarly studies of immigration laws and how they have changed over time, and of how government action and inaction influenced the influx of refugees. But except for Henry Feingold's writings, America's resettlement policies have not been fully explored. Much of the writing on America's response to the Holocaust has been covered in broad strokes; balance and nuance still have to contend with emotion. A major study of the War Refugee Board would be a significant contribution to the body of scholarship.

Another area needing further study is the connection between U.S. policies and those of other state actors, including Germany. How did one country's policy influence another's? This is crucial to any understanding of the evolution of Nazi policies and options. Additionally, the Schacht-Rublee negotiations need further research and analysis. Breitman expressed skepticism that the Nazis would have followed through on the ransom plans, but further digging must be done to try to determine how seriously the idea was taken.

Similarly, very little has been done in the way of research on Congress and America's refugee policy. With U.S. intelligence files opened only in recent years, scholarly research on what we knew and when we knew it is still ahead of us. British intelligence files on the Holocaust are still closed. Important individual stories remain to be told, for instance, Jan Karski's; and one of Avra Warren, who oversaw U.S. consular activities in Europe in 1939-1940, is needed. Raymond Geist, consul-general in Berlin and an early Cassandra in predicting the Holocaust, deserves a biography. His warning to Messersmith in the spring of 1939 eerily anticipated evolving German plans to deal with Jews in Germany. Finding Warren's and Geist's papers in other collections, archives, and the like will make them targets for larger research efforts. Two books on Sumner Welles, not yet scheduled for publication, are being written by Irwin Gellman and Benjamin Welles. According to Gellman, Welles was FDR's "man for Jewish affairs" in 1942-1943. **Trude Lash** noted he was the one State Department official who was most sympathetic. He may be the key to what was considered, and why it was rejected, during these years.

More research needs to be done, even with all of the emotional concerns, about the activities of Jewish organizations and leaders. The Holocaust Museum in Washington, D.C., intends to become the repository for microfilmed archival materials from Europe, including the former East Germany and the former Soviet Union.

Breitman also raised the question of comparison, noting the differences and similarities between the Holocaust and Bosnia, Somalia, and other trouble spots. Knowing that the U.S. government has done virtually nothing to stop the killing in Bosnia since 1992 may help to assess U.S. behavior in the 1940s, or at least to appreciate the constraints FDR faced. The irony is that today America is the strongest power and has the capacity to do something, but, in fact, it has done little. This points out perhaps that too many critics have assumed that America could have done so much more in the Holocaust. Take away anti-Semitism and fire Breckinridge Long, and the American response to the Holocaust would still have been meager.

Breitman suggested that there was a deeper conflict between humanitarian concerns and national interests. Is this a real distinction? Politically, a distinction has been accepted. But is this not a narrow definition of national interest? Humanitarianism should have a foothold.

Trude Lash, who had been involved in refugee work and the International Student Service, recalled her days in the White House during the debate over the Wagner-Rogers Bill. She emphasized the frequency with which Rabbi Stephen Wise's daughter, Justine Wise Polier, came to the White House and, in this instance, worked on a draft of the bill with Eleanor Roosevelt's help. It was known around the White House and through Ms. Wise that FDR favored the bill. He told his friends but issued no public statement. Franklin Roosevelt was not uncaring. The White House door was always open for Rabbi Wise. Wise could always see ER; he sat in on discussions. It is true that winning the war was Roosevelt's top priority. "Nothing else matters," FDR would say.

Bernard Wasserstein responded to Breitman's juxtaposing the issue of Bosnia today with the extermination of the Jews during World War II. Bosnia is on our minds, he noted. Rwanda, however, is not. Genocide is going on in both places. Yet we won't intervene. Caring takes place at two levels: human caring and institutional caring. We can ask questions. Six million Jews died during World War II. As many as twenty million Chinese died. Why did Americans not weep at the Rape of Nanking? Wasserstein was not offering palliatives. But he argued that we cannot expect our government to intervene in such matters. As such, those against whom such policies are aimed must "face the music."

Charles Maier raised again Evian and the "free rider" problem. The issue was finding a solution so that when genocide occurs it requires action by all states. Yet weren't such international conferences as Evian passing the buck, providing an alibi, rather than creating real structures? But even if intervention is undertaken, there is also the question of how to intervene without causing more harm. We have international structures such as the North Atlantic Treaty Organization (NATO) and the Helsinki Accords, but they do not serve as remedies for Bosnia or Rwanda. Sometimes international structures are fig leaves.

William vanden Heuvel, in searching for the degree and the time period when German extermination programs were grasped by the rest of the world, pointed toward a series of actions in 1943. For instance, Rabbi Wise and others were particularly vocal in confirming the news of the Final Solution and, at about the same time, playwright Moss Hart launched his "We Shall Never Die" effort. Also, in March 1943 Congress condemned Nazi policies. Similarly, there was a clamor in Britain and pressure in Parliament to act. Do these not point to a mind-shift of recognition in early 1943?

Bernard Wasserstein pointed out that the United Nations Declaration on War Crimes in December 1942 had far more impact in Britain than in the United States. As for the structure that arose from the Evian meeting, the Intergovernmental Committee on Political Refugees, he said he had never read such brilliant memoranda or seen such ineffectual policy. The British in the 1940s resisted pressure to solve the refugee problem via open immigration to Palestine. Britain held on to the notion of reintegrating the Jews within Europe, even those Jews "temporarily" seeking refuge in Britain.

John Blum saw the War Refugee Board as dealing with a political and bureaucratic problem, not a humanitarian one. It was the one substantial effort, and it was instigated mainly by Christians, Randolph Paul and John Pehle, pushing through Morgenthau. They were just fed up with State Department obstruction.

Michael Marrus argued that Evian did provoke a sincere effort on FDR's part. Roosevelt regarded changing the quotas as only a slight palliative. Influenced by Raymond Geist's reports from Berlin, Roosevelt was inclined to approve the ransom schemes, and he urged Jewish leaders to get moving, save lives, get them out while you can. This was the good FDR. He was no public campaigner here, only a manipulator behind the scenes. When the war began in Europe in September 1939, he shifted to a "win the war" attitude. We'll deal with the big picture after the war, he seemed to say. Trying to sort out Roosevelt's policies, his attitudes, and his thinking is complicated by the Fifth Column issue and the response of the government bureaucracy. All in all, no one emerged as a saint. Yet FDR was not wholly insensitive either.

Karen Greenberg picked up on FDR's encouragement of private Jews. She suggested that these are among the unwritten stories in the 1930s. More needs to be done on the relations between the private groups, especially the nonsectarian Anti-Nazi League, and the Roosevelt administration. Because the private groups did so much, it took pressure off the government. Private agencies, Jewish and nonsectarian, for instance, backed the economic boycott. Because these groups were organized nationally, their records give a more complete sense of public opinion than that measured by the polls. In terms of further research, some papers are at Columbia University, others are at the Holocaust Museum.

In terms of Bosnia, Greenberg said what is happening there and the response of Western governments affected some of her views on events in the 1930s. In her work to develop an academic exchange program between the United States and Eastern Europe, she has dealt with Eastern Europeans who want to use Western resources to rebuild their countries. But too often this suggests "humanitarian patching"—that is, such an approach does not provide much hope for the long term unless it also includes fundamental restructuring.

Michael Marrus asserted that Bosnia is on the moral agenda precisely because of the Holocaust. He had recently participated in a conference in Paris at which the French kept bringing up the precedent of the Holocaust with regard to Bosnia. But what we must remember is that those in the 1930s and 1940s did not have the precedent of the Holocaust to inform them. Similarly, we know of the massacre in Armenia largely because of Holocaust comparisons.

William Korey commented further on the relationship between national interests and humanitarian interests. He argued that there is no contradiction, although policymakers frequently contend that there is such a distinction and act on these supposed distinctions. Human rights are broader than humanitarian goals and should be an ingredient of the national interest. General George C. Marshall said it best in 1946, that a nation's lack of internal human rights serves as the motor force for that nation engaging in external aggression. John F. Kennedy made the same point in his American University speech of 1963: Peace, in the last analysis, is a matter of human rights. The United Nations Genocide Treaty, which was only recently endorsed by the United States, should have sensitized us. Human rights are part of national security. For that reason Korey expressed dismay when in the autumn of 1993 U.S. Secretary of State Warren Christopher said that Bosnia was not a matter that involved America's national security. Institutional structures are vital whatever their motives. They help move solutions along. The War Refugee Board showed what could be done. Wallenberg saved thousands in Hungary. The argument that a war-crimes trial on Bosnia would be a waste is not compelling. It would crystallize world opinion. What is lacking is the will to use the structures. The public needs to know more about the success of the War Refugee Board, however limited it was.

Carl Schorske noted that a unanimity seemed to have formed among the participants—namely, a shared and intense will to historicize the Roosevelt administration's efforts toward the Holocaust. We all see the important connection between the past and present, and we try to explain past events, though our perceptual grids filter differently. Genocide and large-scale killing are very different from the issue of how to help and how to receive refugees. Can we connect the Holocaust to solving contemporary problems? Were there precedents for the 1940s—or, as Michael Marrus had suggested, did the policymakers of those times have no "Holocaust" to draw on? The Red Cross, Schorske observed, was established in the nineteenth century to help civilians and prisoners of war (POWs) in wartime. It was a story of private organizations penetrating sovereign states, forming networks across national lines, and setting precedents for new behavior. He cited the Helsinki Watch and Amnesty International as modern analogues. He suggested that if one looks at the world's efforts and responses in these areas, it suggests a very slow shift in the world's consciousness, achieved only through great pain and suffering. He worried that Holocaust history has been pursued too ethnocentrically. We should be more comparative, even though discourse has focused on the fate of the Jews alone. Other losses need similar reckoning. All share the fate of victims. Thinking internationally is a terribly fitful process.

Michael Marrus saw public sensibility outstripping scholarly sensibility. The public does draw wider comparative conclusions. As for the Red Cross analogy, he noted that the institution could not deal adequately with civilians and non-POWs in the 1930s and 1940s. There is a greater *national* interest in soldiers than in stateless refugees.

Verne Newton said that one of the great challenges for the FDR Library and the Franklin and Eleanor Roosevelt Institute is how to teach the Holocaust. There is great student interest in the subject, but that is stimulated in part because it fits in with various conspiracy theories of past American history. Young students constantly confront us with the assertion that "FDR knew" that the Japanese were going to attack at Pearl Harbor or that Japanese internment proves we were no better than the Germans or the Japanese during World War II. It is the mind-set that made Oliver Stone's movie *JFK* so popular with young moviegoers. Newton asked the group for any advice they may care to give. The subject was discussed over lunch.

AFTERNOON SESSION: 3:15–4:30 P.M.

Henry Feingold commented on the ethnic focus of Holocaust studies. Even though victimization is not a subject to celebrate, Jews cannot escape a special interest in the Holocaust when one in three Jews perished. He said he did not wish to trivialize or vulgarize it, but the Jewish interest in the Holocaust is a particular one. He noted again FDR's response to the Schacht-Rublee negotiations in urging the Jews to accept. This conjured up the irony of the Jews becoming their own stereotype. Feingold said he regards the ransom proposal as an illusion, not a real opportunity.

In terms of the success of the War Refugee Board, Feingold agreed that not enough has been made of it. He asked again why it was possible to evade the law in setting up the Fort Ontario experiment in 1944. Just what had changed? Feingold also commented on the unfair judgments condemning Rabbi Wise as a "betrayer." He thought it unlucky that Wise had run politically afoul of FDR as governor of New York and did not get back into the inner circle until 1936. More might have been accomplished earlier. Notwithstanding his "Dear Boss" obsequiousness and his "slowness" to pick up on some things, Wise deserves condemnation the least.

John Blum complimented Feingold for his "passion bound by concern for historical context."

Doris Kearns Goodwin commented that the public needs to have this balanced understanding, too. She said that she sees real anger about FDR and the Holocaust as she lectures to audiences and that she tries to explain that these failures do not undo his presidency. The public needs to understand the context as well.

Bernard Bellush told of a phone call from a friend telling him of the difficulty of raising money for a renovation of the Roosevelt house, partly because of the perception of FDR's moral failure regarding the Holocaust. Bellush agreed that the War Refugee Board needs more publicity as a "brighter" success story. It was belated, but still a success; it gave hope to refugees. Pehle bought fifty thousand lives. Bellush recalled a conversation with his mother 30 years ago. She told him: "I think FDR made serious errors, particularly about the Jews, and I cannot forgive him for that." Bellush said he tried to explain the context to her, but the argument became too heated for him to do it effectively. Today he would ask her forgiveness. "I suppose, Mom, you were right, and so was I."

Bernard Wasserstein said we have a twofold problem: how to assess intentions and results. We split the two categories. Results do not necessarily follow from intentions. He did not assess such positive results from the War Refugee Board and said he thinks that fifty thousand rescued is too high a number. Nor did he see Fort Ontario as all that important; the 907 refugees were already safe in liberated Italy. To illustrate the difference between results and intentions, he cited that unlikely humanitarian, Joseph Stalin, who deported thousands of Jews from the Baltic region—along with other ethnic groups—to Siberia; this was not humanitarian in intention but because Stalin regarded these people as suspicious elements. They nonetheless survived, inadvertently. Wasserstein also spoke of *Les Dossiers Du Kremlin*—that is, archival openings in Russia and Eastern Europe. The Russians, it turns out, captured larger German archives than did the United States. Vast records will require revising history as did the published Allied intercepts of German and Japanese communications. We will be able to see even more details, although this will not necessarily make interpretation any easier.

John Blum mentioned that one of the objectives of this conference was to further identify new archival sources. We have now learned about the most important ones.

Richard Breitman noted that the Holocaust Museum will have many European archival sources on microfilm.

Bernard Wasserstein commented that only a small percentage are available on microfilm, as evidenced by his own visit to Ukrainian archives this past summer.

Michael Marrus added a nonecumenical note. As a Canadian citizen, he said, he is a bit uneasy about the Holocaust Museum in Washington, D.C., becoming the normative center for our understanding of the Holocaust. He noted the danger of a canonical role and said he feared a close-minded approach to issues that beg for debate. Having visited Auschwitz, he noted what appears to the Polish authorities as Washington's imperial reach.

Charles Maier reiterated that the problems discussed today are not archive driven. The smoking guns are not in the Kremlin dossiers. The problem of judgment is conceptual. The historical message is complex. There is no historian pope either.

Arthur Schlesinger, Jr., expressed gratitude for the conference, especially the respectful way in which everyone interacted. He quoted Peter Geyl's definition of history as "argument without end." History retains its vitality through controversy. Archives won't solve all questions, but materials accumulate and historians interpret and judge. If we are haunted by Bosnia and references to the Holocaust, we remember Croce's comment that "all history is contemporary history." Will there be a conference on Bosnia 25 years from now in which we ask similar questions on what could and should have been done? He thanked all participants for the restraint, comity, and civility in judging the past.

John Blum also thanked everyone for the civility of the conference. He said Carl Schorske had put his finger on it in noting agreement on the importance each participant placed on making historical complexity understandable. This is particularly important now. He said he was disturbed by President Clinton's reference, at the dedication of the Holocaust Museum in April 1993, to U.S. "complicity" in the Holocaust. A better word is Hilberg's designation of "bystander." As memory of the Holocaust disappears, as survivors pass away, history must supplant memory. And history will re-create complexity more effectively than memory. If there is currently an absence of foreign policy toward Bosnia or Somalia, we can evoke the problems of rescuing refugees 50 years earlier.

Henry Feingold read, as a fitting epilogue, the last paragraphs from *The Politics of Rescue*.[26]

—J. Garry Clifford, rapporteur

Notes

1. Michael Marrus's works include *The Unwanted: European Refugees in the Twentieth Century* (New York: Oxford University Press, 1985); with Robert Paxton, *Vichy France and the Jews* (New York: Basic Books, 1981); and *The Holocaust in History* (Hanover, N.H.: University Press of New England/Brandeis University Press, 1987).

2. John Hope Simpson was vice president of the British Refugee Settlement Commission in Athens, Greece, in the period 1926-1930. He was sent on a special mission to Palestine for the British government in 1930 and was director-general of the Flood Relief Commission in China in the period 1931-1933. An acknowledged expert on refugee issues, he published works on Palestine in 1930 and major studies of the refugee crisis in general in 1938-1939.

3. Richard Breitman and Alan Kraut, *American Refugee Policy and European Jewry, 1933-1945* (Bloomington: Indiana University Press, 1987).

4. Raul Hilberg, *Perpetrators, Victims, Bystanders: The Jewish Catastrophe, 1933-1945* (New York: Asher Books, 1992).

5. Lucy Dawidowicz, "Could the United States Have Rescued the European Jews from Hitler?" *This World* (fall 1985), 15-30.

6. The Charles Lindberg Des Moines, Iowa, speech appears in the *New York Times*, 12 September 1941.

7. George Mosse, Bascom Professor of History at the University of Wisconsin, Madison, is the author of *Crisis of German Ideology* (New York: Grosset, 1964); *Nazi Culture* (New York: Grosset, 1966); *Germans and Jews* (New York: Grosset, 1971); and *Toward the Final Solution* (New York: Harper's, 1979).

8. "Public charge" clause: In response to massive domestic unemployment in 1930, President Hoover ordered State Department consular officials to be stringent in enforcing the "public charge" clause of the 1924 Immigration Act and thereby restricted the immigration of persons "likely to become a public charge" in the United States.

9. Charles Wyzanski was the solicitor for the U.S. Department of Labor. Breitman and Kraut recount the battle between the State Department and the Labor Department over the "public charge" clause in *American Refugee Policy*, 11-27.

10. A worldwide forum called in July 1938 at Roosevelt's suggestion, the Evian (France) Conference failed almost totally in its major task: finding countries that would accept Jewish refugees. Henry Feingold devotes a chapter to it in *The Politics of Rescue: Administration and the Holocaust 1938-1945* (New Brunswick, N.J.: Rutgers University Press, 1970) 22-44. See also S. Adler-Rudel, "The Evian Conference on the Refugee Question," *Leo Baeck Institute Yearbook* 13 (1968), 253-273.

11. Hjalmar Schacht, spokesman for the moderates within the Nazi Party and head of the Reichsbank, met with George Rublee—an American, a classmate of FDR at Groton, and the director of the Intergovernmental Committee on Political Refugees—in London in December 1938 and in Berlin in January 1939 to formulate a workable plan for the emigration of German Jews. The centerpiece of Schacht's original proposal was the creation of a giant trust fund financed by "international Jewry." Roosevelt referred to the plan as "ransom" and "barter in human misery," and it received little support from the democracies. Although Adolf Hitler did endorse Schacht's plan, negotiations broke down on 20 January 1939 following Schacht's dismissal from his post in the Reichsbank and as intermediary with the Intergovernmental Committee (IGC). Schacht's reversal of fortune stemmed from his refusal to inflate the German currency. See Joseph Tenenbaum, "The Crucial Year, 1938," *Yad Vashem Studies* 2 (1958), 49-79.

12. Dorothy Thompson, "Refugees: A World Problem," *Foreign Affairs* 16 (April 1938), 375-387.

13. John Cooper Wiley was a career diplomat who served as a foreign-service officer and minister to Russia (1934-1935), Belgium (1935-1937), Austria (1937-1938), and Estonia and Latvia (1938-1940). The Wiley Papers, National Union Catalog of Manuscript Collections (NUCMC) 75-587, are among the archival holding of the Franklin D. Roosevelt Library, Hyde Park, N.Y.

14. Freda Kirchway, "The State Department versus Political Refugees," *Nation* 156 (28 December 1940), 648-649.

15. Henry Feingold, "Roosevelt and the Resettlement Question," in *Rescue Attempts during the Holocaust: Proceedings of the Second Yad Vashem International Historical Conference* (Jerusalem, 8-11 April 1974), ed. Yisrael Gutman and Efraim Zuroff (New York: KTAV, 1978), 123-181.

16. A transcript of FDR's conversation with Governor-General Nogues appears in *Foreign Relations of the United States (FRUS): Conference at Casablanca, 1943* (Washington, D.C.: Government Printing Office, 1968), 606-608.

17. On 4 August 1944, Harold Ickes, the secretary of the Interior, welcomed approximately one thousand carefully selected refugees to an 80 acre former army post at Fort Ontario, in Oswego, N.Y.

18. Varian Fry was the European director of the Emergency Rescue Committee. His writings include "The Massacre of the Jews," *New Republic* 107(21 December 1942); and "Our Consuls at Work," *Nation* 154 (2 May 1942).

19. The United States and Great Britain held bilateral meetings in Hamilton, Bermuda, in April 1943 to discuss the rescue and relocation plans. The Bermuda Conference accomplished nothing in this regard, however. Both nations maintained that the defeat of the Axis powers was the key to rescuing European Jewry. See Monty N. Penkower, "The Bermuda Conference and Its Aftermath: An Allied Quest for 'Refuge' during the Holocaust," *Prologue* 13 (fall 1981), 145-173.

20. David Engel, *In The Shadow of Auschwitz: The Polish Government-in-Exile and the Jews, 1939-1942* (Chapel Hill: University of North Carolina Press, 1987).

21. The Riegner report is cited in Walter Laqueur, "Jewish Denial and the Holocaust," *Commentary* 68 (n.6 1979), 55.

22. Henry Feingold, "Who Shall Bear Guilt for the Holocaust: The Human Dilemma," *American Jewish History* 68 (March 1979), 261-282.

23. James H. Kitchens III, "The Bombing of Auschwitz Reexamined," *Journal of Military History* 58 (April 1994), 233-266.

24. *Newsweek*, 30 November 1942, 11.

25. In July 1942, Gerhart Riegner of the World Jewish Congress received a report from a German industrialist stating that Adolf Hitler was considering a plan to exterminate from 3.5 to four million Jews beginning that autumn. A condensed 20-page version of the Riegner report entitled "Blueprint for Extermination" is attached to information about the 8 December 1942 meeting between Roosevelt, Rabbi Stephen Wise, and other leaders of the American Jewish community in Official File 76C (Church Matters-Jewish), Franklin D. Roosevelt Library, Hyde Park, N.Y. There is no indication in the files at the FDR Library that President Roosevelt actually read the Riegner report.

For a description of the 8 December 1942 meeting and the Riegner report, see also Doris Kearns Goodwin, *No Ordinary Time* (New York: Simon and Schuster, 1994), 396-397; David S. Wyman, *The Abandonment of the Jews: America and the Holocaust, 1941-1945* (New York: Pantheon Books, 1984), 71-73; Breitman and Kraut, *American Refugee Policy,* 146-166; and the Adolph Held (Jewish Labor Committee) notes of the 8 December 1942 meeting, which are located in the Jewish Labor Committee Archives, New York, N.Y.

26. Henry Feingold, *The Politics of Rescue,* p. 307:

These then were some of the reasons why the Roosevelt Administration responded only halfheartedly to the challenge of saving Jewish lives. But even if the problems that prevented rescue had been solved—if Breckinridge Long had been converted to the rescue cause; if the divisions within European Jewry had been magically healed; if the immigration laws had been circumvented earlier; if Alaska had been made available for resettlement; if Whitehall had abandoned its inhumanely political attitude towards Jewish immigration into Palestine; if the Pope had spoken out; if the ICRC [International Committee for the Red Cross] had been more courageous; in short, if there had been a will to save lives—we still have no assurance that mass rescue could have been realized, although many thousands more might have been saved. Something like such a miracle occurred in Hungary in 1944. Yet within full view of the world and when the Nazi authorities could no longer doubt that they had lost the war, the cattle cars rolled to Auschwitz as if they had a momentum of their own. Over half of Hungary's Jews went up in smoke.

Appalling as it may sound, the saving of lives was a far more formidable task than the practice of genocide. Even a passionate will to save lives could prove insufficient, given Nazi determination to liquidate the Jews of Europe. Something more was required, something to soften the hearts of those in Berlin who were in physical control of the slaughter. Such a miracle was never in the power of the Washington policymakers. It belongs to a higher kingdom whose strange indifference has become an overriding concern of the theologians.

2

The Burden of Being Human:
An Essay on Selected Scholarship
of the Holocaust

Karen J. Greenberg

For nearly five decades now, historians of the Holocaust have confronted a formidable task. They have endeavored to explain the unexplainable. As Charles Maier has put it, it is an attempt to master the "unmasterable." Beginning in 1961, with the first edition of Raul Hilberg's monumental *The Destruction of the European Jews*[1] and extending to Michael Berenbaum's catalog for the U.S. Holocaust Memorial Museum, historians have wondered how the extermination of millions of Jews could have happened as the world looked on. In searching for answers, scholars have looked to find the villains, the perpetrators, the guilty. Despite the admitted futility of coming to terms with this particular piece of the past, they nevertheless persevere. What they have left us, amidst a medley of stories and probing analyses, is an ever-expanding network of complicitors. Accordingly, much of the impetus for arguments at the heart of Holocaust historiography lies in questions about who exactly is guilty, and, conversely, who escapes condemnation.

Now this past has been brought to the public at large. The opening of the U.S. Holocaust Memorial Museum, in April 1993, signifies America's permanent representation of the events surrounding the extermination of the Jews of Europe. Henceforth, public knowledge of those years will appear to many as it appears there. As the public lines up to confront the issue of blame and guilt it seems an appropriate moment to reflect upon the trends in the historiography of the Holocaust.

The accusatory impetus that has characterized the field of Holocaust studies has had both subtle and direct manifestations. On the simplest level, the crime of genocide is attributed to individuals, beginning with Adolf Hitler. But for Hitler, many argue, there would have been no Holocaust. In his most recent contribution to the field, *Perpetrators, Victims, Bystanders: The Jewish Catastrophe, 1935-1945,*[2] an overview intended for a general audience, Hilberg argues, as many before him have, that the supreme architect of the Jewish catastrophe was Hitler. By 1941 he had transformed the liquid ideas of 1940 into a hard reality. Often, chief architects of the Final Solution or functionaries are presented alongside Hitler as the agents of destruction. Richard Breitman's study of Heinrich Himmler,[3] like the many biographies of Hitler, tries to unite personal characteristics with the social and political environment. Christopher Browning's masterful study, *Police Battalion 101: Ordinary Men,*[4] does so for the rank-and-file perpetrators. The guilt of these individuals is not at issue. Rather, historians are concerned with the set of circumstances that enabled these men to implement the extermination of the Jews. In establishing explanations for the willingness of these individuals to commit genocide, scholars portray a Germany rife with the frustrations and disappointments of economic insecurity and bureaucratic anonymity, a Germany prone toward a hatred of Jews and plagued by the rapid social transformations of the postwar era.

Looking to establish context, historians point more generically to Germany and the Germans. William Sheridan Allen demonstrates in *The Nazi Seizure of Power: The Experience of a Single German Town, 1930-1935*[5] that small-town bourgeois life in Germany established pressures of conformity and a network of values that fed well the middle-class German's desire for economic stability, even if the cost amounted to the loss of civil freedoms and decency. In looking specifically at Germany, historians have asked: Was the Holocaust an aberration in German history or the logical outcome of decades, even centuries, of history? In *The Twisted Road to Auschwitz: Nazi Policy Toward German Jews, 1933-1939,* Karl Schleunes has demonstrated that the road to the Holocaust was neither straight nor fated. Yehuda Bauer's *The Holocaust in Historical Perspective* takes Schleunes's conclusion one step further, arguing that the Holocaust cannot be attributed to an inexplicable fate or a supernatural intervention, but rather is one logical outcome of European history. Further, historians on either side of a famed *historikerstreit* (historical debate) wonder whether the Holocaust is an event capable of comparison—or a singularity that appropriately must stand by itself.

The most compelling portrayals of the Holocaust as a local outcome of historical context have appeared in works that extend the idea of responsibility beyond Germany, to Europe, and in particular to Europe's pervasive and virulent history of anti-Semitism. With poignancy, Martin Gilbert begins his study of the Holocaust with a quotation from Martin Luther. Drawing an invisible but unbroken line from the Reformation to the twentieth century, Gilbert quotes: "First, their synagogues should be covered or spread over with dirt . . . Jewish homes should be 'broken down or destroyed,'" and perhaps Jews should be "driven out of the country 'for all time.'"[6] Lucy Dawidowicz has nodded assent to this reading of history. "A line of anti-Semitic descent from Martin Luther to Adolf Hitler is easy to draw,"[7] she writes. Historians have readily demonstrated that anti-Semitism enabled the Nazis to enlist the help of forces in Poland, Hungary, and France. They note, by contrast, the fact that where anti-Semitism was less pronounced, the fate of the Jews was less disastrous, as in the case of Italy, and obstructable, as in the case of Denmark, where the Jews were moved discreetly to Sweden so as to evade the Nazis. Gerald Fleming[8] has documented Hitler's strong and consistent commitment to the annihilation of the Jews and has demonstrated that he created a web of secrecy and deception around that goal. "Functionalist" historians, including Hans Mommsen,[9] disagree and see an evolutionary path to the Final Solution. Either way, by 1941, as Richard Breitman has argued, the Nazi leadership had made the decision to use technological means to exterminate the Jews in their territory.[10]

The issue of guilt is not, however, limited to the perpetrators or their culture. Instead, those whom scholars have termed bystanders played a crucial, if often passive, role in the events of the Holocaust. One group of bystanders to which scholars have paid much attention is that of the governments outside of Germany. The chronicle of these bystanders appears primarily in numerous firsthand accounts of the Nazi years and, in a scholarly vein, in works about refugees and rescue. During the 1930s, the issue of refugees was understood by the countries outside of Germany as one of primary importance. Throughout the 1930s, Hitler encouraged emigration of the Jews as a means of ridding Germany and its annexed territories of their evil influence. Most of the European countries, England, and the United States tightened their policies in response to the growing masses of refugees that came with the onset of Germany's expansion and then war. Spain, Italy, France, and Switzerland found themselves reconsidering their immigration policies in light of the onset of the Jewish migration from Germany, but only Denmark and Finland actually worked to liberalize those policies. Britain remained stalwart against the admission of refugees from Nazi Europe and adhered to the 1939 White Paper in regard to Palestine. The White Paper held that, at the most, seventy-five thousand Jewish immigrants would be allowed into Palestine in the subsequent five-year period and that after that, there would be no further Jewish immigration to Palestine. The countries of the Western world voted consistently; they did not want to add Jews to their numbers. Perhaps unfairly, historians have equated long-standing anti-Semitism with complicity in the Holocaust.

The bystander that has received the lion's share of the attention is the United States. In 1967, Arthur Morse published *While Six Million Died: A Chronicle of American Apathy,*[11] launching an attack upon the policies of the U.S. government. Over the years, historians have provided the details of personality and policy that led not only to unfilled quotas throughout the prewar years but also to a callous indifference to perils faced by the Jews in Europe. In *The Politics of Rescue: The Roosevelt Administration and the Holocaust, 1938-1945,*[12] Henry Feingold laments the "politics of gesture" that characterized the government's response to refugees before the war and to rescue after the outbreak of the war. Feingold condemns the implications of the State Department's inactivity, labeling the stinginess in the matter of visas, the "paper walls" described by David Wyman,[13] as an adjunct to Berlin's murderous plan for the Jews. Feingold's work, though it recognizes the inactivity of the United States, soft-pedals the assignment of blame. He contends that even had all of the forces in support of rescue combined with one another, the fate of the Jews remaining in the hands of the Nazis might not have been significantly altered. Appallingly, Feingold observes, saving lives proved a far more formidable task than the practice of genocide. David Wyman refuses to let the government off so easily. He makes the Roosevelt administration active complicitors in the Holocaust. In *The Abandonment of the Jews: America and the Holocaust, 1941-1945,* he insists that "it was not a lack of workable plans that stood in the way of saving many thousands more European Jews. . . . The real obstacle was the absence of a strong desire to rescue Jews"[14] on the part of Roosevelt and his advisers. When the net of blame is extended to the U.S. government it tends to focus, albeit often indirectly, upon the person of Franklin Roosevelt himself. Richard Breitman and Alan Kraut have suggested that Roosevelt was hindered in making any response to the refugee crisis by bureaucracy and his own brand of politics in which political expediency took precedence over other issues or concerns.[15] Many historians, notably John Morton Blum in *V Was for Victory: Politics and American Culture during World War II,*[16] point out that it was Roosevelt's decision to make the "win the war" strategy not only of paramount importance but of sole importance.

Central to the work of the students of failed rescue is the study of what information people had and when they first obtained it. Walter Laqueur has documented well the fact that the Riegner cable, announcing in July 1942 the German decision to liquidate Jewry through the use of poison gas, was met primarily with disbelief.[17] From that point on, there was a clear availability of facts about the destruction of the Jews. Yet incredulity and resistance to those facts were difficult to overcome. As Deborah Lipstadt has pointed out, knowledge and belief were two different states of mind. In *Beyond Belief: The American Press and the Coming of the Holocaust, 1933-1945*[18] she demonstrates that although much information was available even in the 1930s about Nazi atrocities, it was difficult for people to assimilate the facts they were fed. The American press only exacerbated this disbelief by attributing stories of genocide to Jewish sources; by burying stories, as repeatedly happened in the pages of the *Christian Science Monitor;* by castigating the Jews for their whining and for jeopardizing postwar circumstances; and by failing to see the problem as a pointedly Jewish problem. By contrast, the British press proved more condemnatory and explicit about Nazi atrocities.

Risking the perils of impassioned controversy, some scholars have placed blame on the victims themselves, the Jews. Hannah Arendt and Raul Hilberg initially suggested the idea that the Jewish leaders in Europe bear some responsibility for the fate of the Jews. Those leaders collaborated with the Nazis ostensibly to make life better for the Jews.[19] In fact, these historians contend, they quelled the possibilities for active resistance. Lucy Dawidowicz addressed her volume to this accusation and instead portrayed the Jews as resistant particularly in their insistence upon retaining their humanity in the face of orderly and total dehumanization within the camps. Others have joined Dawidowicz in defending the victims, a group it is considered highly distasteful to include among the guilty. In the ghetto, we are reminded, noncompliance meant either suicide or outright refusal to obey on the part of the Judenräte[20] official. Such refusal, in turn, inevitably resulted in being shot on the spot or immediately deported. Jewish tradition forbade this suicide. Yehuda Bauer sees active resistance in numerous places, insisting that the Jews were not passive victims.[21] They tried to survive, to escape, to run. And even without weapons they tried to fight for their existence. Michael Marrus has pointed out in his bibliographical review, *The Holocaust in History,*[22] that few Jews realized, before the massive deportations to the east in the summer of 1942, that their very survival was at stake. For this reason, Jewish resistance generally lacked the suicidal desperation of underground activities. Once again, historians have sifted through the ashes of facts to find skeletal remains of guilt and complicity in acts of omission as well as those of active villainy.

Foreign Jews have received rebuke as well. The American Jewish community, at a safe distance from the murderous elements in Europe, is often condemned for not exerting enough influence in Washington. Its members are chastised for their divisiveness and for not wanting to alienate, in Breitman and

Kraut's portrayal, FDR as the only man who stood between the Jews and American anti-Semitism.[23] Rabbi Stephen Wise is condemned for the blind trust he placed in Roosevelt. Bauer is lenient here as elsewhere. His study of the Jewish Joint Distribution Committee, which oversaw rescue and relief during the Nazi period and the war years, is a work of admiration for the committee's efforts, however ultimately futile.

This matter of blaming the Jews seems to me a sign that the history of the Holocaust has come full cycle, from an historical event in which the world failed to understand the virulence of anti-Semitism to historical interpretations in which scholars chastise the Jews for their behavior, largely forgetting the circumstances of the Jew in 1930s America. The most recent and disturbing work in this respect is Arno Mayer's *Why Did the Heavens Not Darken?: The "Final Solution" in History.*[24] Mayer argues, contrary to most if not all of the historians considered in this chapter, that the study of the Holocaust is too Judeocentric. The Holocaust must be understood not as an all-out attack upon Jews per se, but as a total breakdown of civilization in which the Jews suffered from a time out of control. The transition from incapacitating restrictions in Germany to genocide beyond its borders, Mayer believes, must be seen as correlated with the compulsions and vicissitudes of unrestrained war. In describing the fate of the Jews during the invasion of Russia, Mayer also sees a difference in the immediate virulent attack on Soviet Russia and the assault on the Jews. Mayer's conclusions could be comforting, but he stands alone among a chorus of voices that demonstrate clearly and with little room for doubt the centrality of the Jew to the Nazi's destructive enterprise.

A more persistent question underlying the entire field of study is: Could anything have stopped Hitler? For all of their moral preoccupation, historians desperately want to answer, "No." Answering in the negative would exonerate all but the Germans. As Martin Gilbert has pointed out in *Auschwitz and the Allies,* by 1942 when their armies had conquered Europe and North Africa, the Germans were able, under a cloak of secrecy and deception, to carry out a war of total destruction against millions of captive civilians. They were also confident that even if the secret became known, the Allies would be unable to take any effective military action to liberate the captives or to reverse the tide of war. In assessing American decisionmaking to put victory ahead of saving lives, Richard Breitman and Alan Kraut conclude that while bombing Auschwitz should have been done for humanitarian reasons, it was no panacea. Elsewhere, Breitman asserts that by 1941 Hitler and Himmler had set in motion the machinery for the effective implementation of the Holocaust.[25] Rabbi Haskel Lookstein insists that moral behavior was mandated even in futile circumstances.[26] Even if American Jewry could not have stopped the Final Solution, he observes, it should have been unbearable for them. And it wasn't. Others, notably Yehuda Bauer,[27] take umbrage in the notion that, as Jewish tradition specifies, he who saves one soul is likened to one who has saved the whole world. The construction of what-if history has had particular resonance in the examination of Hungary. The deportations of the Jews of Hungary did not begin until March 1944 when the pro-German Sztójay government was installed. By war's end, 70 percent of the Jews of Greater Hungary had perished. Here was an instance when the fate of the Jews was known, when explicit forms of rescue and salvation were put forth, and even carried out in the instances of Raoul Wallenberg and Joel Brand. But knowledge did not forestall the deaths. Neither did the defiance of the admiral regent of Hungary, Miklos Horthy, and the ex-prime minister of Hungary, Miklos Kallay, who resisted German demands for control of Hungary. Randolph Braham[28] concludes that the Hungarian defiance of the Nazis brought down increased wrath and punishment against Hungary and, by extension, upon the Jews of Hungary. Further participants in the debate have extended Braham's conclusion, asserting, as Istvan Deak[29] has, that a correlation exists between survival of the Jews in a country and that country's loyalty to the Jews.

The final conclusions of many of these works find humans as a species guilty. As Henry Feingold points out, the indictment of the witnesses is based on the old assumption that there exists such a spirit of civilization.[30] To his mind, these witnesses failed to mobilize a spirit that did not exist. To some extent, the evolution of Holocaust historiography might be seen as constituting a misreading of Hannah Arendt's[31] concept of the banality of evil. Arendt identifies the way in which the execution of the Final Solution rested upon the shoulders of the regular soul, the functionary, the bureaucrat. But Arendt did not mean to say that all were guilty by virtue of being human. In condemning everyone, a focus on the active perpetrators is indeed diluted, even lost. Moreover, further questions are somehow submerged, among them the issues of the reincorporation of Germany into the powerful Western powers and the failure of the war-crimes tribunal to prevent subsequent atrocities against groups of people as in the instance of the Bosnians today.

The most recent contribution to the historiography of the Holocaust lies in the U.S. Holocaust Memorial Museum, in its haunting brick fronts designed to recall the gas chambers and ghetto walls, in its glass passageways etched with the names of lost persons and buried communities. The museum fulfills that which Lawrence Langer deems the backbone of the field: It tells the story of heroes and villains. Yet in many ways the exhibits sidestep the question of guilt and thereby stand in contradistinction to the history of blame. The museum devotes much space to extolling the rescuers, as in its opening exhibit on Varian Fry and the Emergency Rescue Committee, and to mourning the victims, as in the piles of hair and the mountains of shoes. Here is testimony to the commitment to hope that Dawidowicz detected in the Jews in the camps. The museum searches for few answers either in Jewish tradition or in the annals of European anti-Semitism or German history. Instead, it bears witness. That is its central mission. And in bearing witness, it performs its most powerful deed: It refuses to cast blame in any specific or directed way. The atmosphere created there is best summed up in an encounter I witnessed between two American historians who visited the museum. On finding themselves face to face with the wall of ten thousand names of those who came to the aid of the Jews, one commented, "I can't believe there were so many." Her companion retorted, "I can't believe there were so few." If there is blame, it seems to say, it is up to the individual to assign it. By assigning blame, one accepts the responsibility of judging human behavior as if to take the oath, "Should it happen again, I won't be to blame." This, it seems, is an apt and constructive outcome for historians whose lives have been given to re-creating the story of the Holocaust. But it is also a dodge. In its refusal to judge, the museum sidesteps some of the most disturbing aspects of inquiry in the field.

There is more than meets the eye in the juxtaposition of an appeal to the individual conscience and a general condemnation of humankind. For this is not all of mankind but European civilization broadly conceived. For those of us whose researches and fields of inquiry focus on Western arts and letters, the chilling conclusion that indeed the Holocaust was not an aberration in European history but the eradication of yet another minority is at least among the possible interpretations. Istvan Deak has considered this trajectory from the time of the French Revolution to the current struggles in Eastern Europe. Americanists might add the European attacks upon native populations throughout the New World. The *historikerstreit* in which historians divide themselves among those who see the Holocaust as worthy of comparative histories and those who don't, seems almost moot when compared to the larger reality of European history. Perhaps even Arno Mayer's analysis might find a home in this conceptual context.

In a speech delivered at the opening of the Central European University in Budapest, Eric Hobsbawm made a distinction between the history written for scholars and that which is disseminated to the public at large. Consistent with his career as a champion of the working classes, Hobsbawm made an appeal for the latter form of history, that which reaches a wider public. The past that is known to the people at large, Hobsbawm continued, is a fundamental building block in the creation of civic decency and a humanitarian public spirit. The U.S. Holocaust Memorial Museum is aimed at the public (and, essentially, at the non-Jewish population, for whom the most basic rituals of Jewish life need to be explained and the horrors of the Holocaust replayed). Abroad, the public is even more ignorant. In Hungary, the Czech Republic, and Slovakia, for example, major works on the Holocaust have yet to be translated. In Israel many of these texts, including Hilberg's monumental work,[32] have not appeared. If Hobsbawn is right, if the significance of the historian's task is to raise popular consciousness, then surely the task before historians is clear: The discourse about the Holocaust must be extended to included the full range of nations associated with the annihilation of the Jews. Then and only then, one might argue, can the issues be confronted clearly and can the issue of shared guilt be transcended.

Yet even before the conversation is stabilized, a number of writers are calling for a reconsideration of the accumulation of details about the evils and explanations of the Holocaust. The literature on memory and the Holocaust, once focused on the questions of whether it was possible to translate the experience of the camps and the ghettoes into art and aesthetics, has now yielded to more structured analyses of the role of memory in influencing the present and the future. Once regarded as positive, even cathartic, memory, argue Langer, Tony Judt, and others, may have its disabling side. Echoing Yehuda Elkana, Amos Elon has brought the issue to a head: ". . . [W]here there is so much traumatic memory, so much pain, so much memory innocently or deliberately mobilized for political purposes, a little forgetfulness might finally be in order."[33]

Whether or not historians temper their inquiries with the goals of forgiveness and public awareness, the history of the Holocaust carries to the future a satchel of interpretations laden with the weight of moral questions. Before the "unmasterable" yields to the forgotten, it may be wise to note that in casting wide the net of blame, the goal of understanding has underlain the search for evildoers. Perhaps the goal of constructing a more positive future through the device of forgetfulness will prove less elusive.

Notes

1. Raul Hilberg, *The Destruction of the European Jews* (New York: Harper and Row, 1961).
2. Raul Hilberg, *Perpetrators, Victims, Bystanders: The Jewish Catastrophe, 1933-1945* (New York: Asher Books, 1992).
3. Richard Breitman, *The Architect of Genocide: Himmler and the Final Solution* (New York: Bodley Head, 1991).
4. Christopher Browning, *Police Battalion 101: Ordinary Men* (New York: Harper Perennial, 1992).

5. William Sheridan Allen, *The Nazi Seizure of Power: The Experience of a Single German Town, 1930-1935* (Chicago: Quadrangle Books, 1965).

6. Martin Gilbert, *The Holocaust: A History of the Jews of Europe during the Second World War* (New York: Henry Holt, 1985), 25.

7. Lucy Dawidowicz, *The War against the Jews, 1933-1945* (New York: Holt, Rinehart, and Winston, 1975), 23.

8. Gerald Flemming, *Hitler and the Final Solution* (Berkeley: University of California Press, 1984).

9. Hans Mommsen, "The Realization of the Unthinkable: The Final Solution of the Jewish Question in the Third Reich," *From Weimar to Auschwitz* (Princeton, N.J.: Princeton University Press, 1991).

10. Richard Breitman, *The Architect of Genocide.*

11. Arthur Morse, *While Six Million Died: A Chronicle of American Apathy* (New York: Random House, 1967).

12. Henry Feingold, *The Politics of Rescue: The Roosevelt Administration and the Holocaust, 1938-1945* (New Brunswick, N.J.: Rutgers University Press, 1970).

13. David Wyman, *Paper Walls: America and the Refugee Crisis, 1938-1941* (Boston: University of Massachusets Press, 1968).

14. David Wyman, *The Abandonment of the Jews: America and the Holocaust, 1941-1945* (New York: Pantheon Books, 1984), 399.

15. Richard Breitman and Alan Kraut, *American Refugee Policy and European Jewry, 1933-1945* (Indianapolis: Indiana University Press, 1987).

16. John Morton Blum, *V Was for Victory: Politics and American Culture during World War II* (San Diego, C.A.: Harcourt, Brace, Jovanovich, 1976).

17. Walter Laqueur and Richard Breitman, *Breaking the Silence* (New York: Simon and Schuster, 1986), 143-164.

18. Deborah Lipstadt, *Beyond Belief: The American Press and the Coming of the Holocaust, 1933-1945* (New York: Free Press, 1986).

19. Hannah Arendt, *Eichman in Jerusalem: A Report on the Banality of Evil* (New York: Viking, 1965). Raul Hilberg, *Destruction of the European Jews.*

20. The creation of the Jewish council of elders, Judenräte, was first propsed in 1933. The Judenräte was established in each Jewish community to carry out the instructions of the Einstatzgruppen.

21. Yehuda Bauer, *A History of the Holocaust* (New York: Franklin Watts, 1982), 245-277.

22. Michael Marrus, *The Holocaust in History* (New York: New American Library, 1987).

23. Richard Breitman and Alan Kraut, *American Refugee Policy and European Jewry.*

24. Arno Mayer, *Why Did the Heavens Not Darken?: The "Final Solution" in History* (New York: Pantheon Books, 1990).

25. Martin Gilbert, *Auschwitz and the Allies* (New York: Holt, Rinehart and Winston, 1981), 339-341. Richard Breitman, *The Architect of Genocide.*

26. Haskel Lookstein, *Were We Our Brothers Keepers: The Public Response of American Jews to the Holocaust, 1938-1944* (New York: Hartmore House, 1985).

27. Yehuda Bauer, *American Jewry and the Holocaust: The American Jewish Joint Distribution Committee, 1939-1945 (Detroit: Wayne State University Press, 1981).*

28. Randolph Brahman, *The Destruction of Hungarian Jewry: A Documentary Account* (New York: World Federation of Hungarian Jews, 1962), and *The Politics of Genocide in Hungary* (New York: Columbia University Press, 1980).

29. Istvan Deak is a professor of modern European history at Columbia University and former director of the Institute of East Central Europe. He is an authority and author of numerous works on modern Hungary.

30. Henry Feingold, "Who Shall Bear Guilt for the Holocaust: The Human Dilemma," *American Jewish History* 68 (March 1979), 261-282.

31. Hannah Arendt, *Eichman in Jerusalem.*

32. Raul Hilberg, *Destruction of the European Jews.*

33. Amos Elon, "The Politics of Memory," *New York Review of Books* 40 (7 October 1993), 3-5.

3

Roosevelt as Foreign Policy Leader

Robert Dallek

At the Hyde Park Conference, Robert Dallek consistently attempted to place the "hot button" issues of the Wagner-Rogers Bill, U.S. immigration laws, and the role of Breckinridge Long in the context of Roosevelt's overall priorities and problems.

Henry Feingold challenged whether—even given the broader picture— Roosevelt did enough. At the same time, Feingold has written extensively on a theme he also struck at Hyde Park: the degree to which American Jewry's efforts to save the Jews of Europe should be judged "insufficient."

This chapter by Dallek and the subsequent one by Feingold expand on their arguments. (Italicized headnotes for this and other chapters are written by the editor.)

In the years since 1945, Franklin Roosevelt has come under sharp attack for his handling of foreign affairs. To be sure, historians generally agree that he was an architect of victory in World War II, but they find little to compliment beyond that: His response to the London Economic Conference of 1933; his neutrality and peace plans of the 1930s; his pre-Pearl Harbor dealings with Japan; and his wartime approach to China, France, and Russia have evoked complaints of superficiality and naivete. His cautious reactions to the Italian conquest of Ethiopia; the demise of the Spanish Republic; Japanese expansion in China; Nazi victories from 1938 to 1941, the destruction of Europe's Jews; and apparent wartime opportunities for cementing ties with Russia, transform-

ing China, ending colonialism, and establishing a truly effective world body
have saddled him with a reputation for excessive timidity about world affairs.
His indirection and guarded dealings with the public before Pearl Harbor and
his secret wartime agreements have provoked charges of arbitrary leadership
destructive to American democracy.

These complaints certainly have some merit. Roosevelt made his share of
errors in response to foreign affairs. His acceptance of Britain's lead in dealing
with the Spanish Civil War, his sanction of wiretaps and mail openings, his
wartime internment of the Japanese, and his cautious response to appeals for
help to Jewish victims of Nazi persecution were unnecessary and destructive
compromises of legal and moral principles. Beyond these matters, however, I
believe that too much has been made of Roosevelt's shortcomings and too little
of the constraints under which he had to work in foreign affairs.

During the 1930s, when public and congressional opinion fixed its
attention on national affairs and opposed any risk of involvement in "foreign
wars," Roosevelt felt compelled to rely on symbols to answer challenges and
threats from abroad. His handling of the London Economic Conference, for
example, was less the expression of confusion or overblown visions of curing
the Depression from outside the United States than of an abortive effort to
restore a measure of faith in international cooperation. Likewise, his suggestions
for preserving peace during the 1930s were less the product of an idealized view
of world affairs than of a continuing desire to encourage leaders and peoples
everywhere to work against war and, specifically, to signal aggressor nations that
the United States was not indifferent to their plans.

Similarly, his acceptance of the neutrality laws of the 1930s was less an
act of conviction than of realistic calculation about what he could achieve at
home and abroad. Since winning congressional approval for domestic programs
essential to national economic and political stability ruled out bold initiatives
in foreign affairs, Roosevelt acquiesced in the widespread preference for a passive
foreign policy. Instead, he aimed to meet worldwide attacks on democracy by
preserving it in the United States. "You have made yourself the trustee for those
in every country who seek to mend the evils of our condition by reasoned
experiment within the framework of the existing social system," John Maynard
Keynes, the noted economist, publicly told him in December 1933.[1] "If you
fail, rational change will be gravely prejudiced throughout the world, leaving
orthodoxy and revolution to fight it out." Between 1935 and 1938, his
reluctance openly to oppose aggression in Ethiopia, Spain, China, Austria, or
Czechoslovakia rested not on an isolationist impulse or a desire to appease
aggressors but chiefly on a determination to retain his ability to influence crucial
developments at home. Roosevelt turned this influence to good account abroad.

Under his leadership, a Montevideo newspaper commented, the United States had again become "the victorious emblem around which may rally the multitudes thirsting for social justice and human fraternity." "His moral authority, the degree of confidence which he inspired outside his own country," the historian Isaiah Berlin later said, "... has no parallel.... Mr. Roosevelt's example strengthened democracy everywhere."[2]

Yet Roosevelt's contribution to the survival of international democracy came not through symbolic gestures in the 1930s but through substantive actions during World War II. His appreciation that effective action abroad required a reliable consensus at home and his use of dramatic events overseas to win national backing from a divided country for a series of pro-Allied steps were among the great presidential achievements of this century. In the years 1939-1941 Roosevelt had to balance the country's desire to stay out of war against its contradictory impulse to assure the defeat of Nazi power. Roosevelt's solution was not to intensify the conflict by choosing one goal over the other but rather to weave the two together: The surest road to peace, he repeatedly urged the nation to believe throughout this difficult period, was material aid to the Allies. And even when he concluded that the country would eventually have to join the fighting, as I believe he did in the spring of 1941, he refused to force an unpalatable choice upon the nation by announcing for war.

Roosevelt's dissembling created an unfortunate precedent for arbitrary action in foreign affairs, which subsequent presidents have been quick to use. This consequence, however, needs to be evaluated alongside two other considerations: first, that Roosevelt's indirection forestalled a head-on clash with the Congress and majority opinion that would have weakened his ability to lead before and after Pearl Harbor; and, second, that for all his willingness to deceive the public in the interest of persuading it to go to war, he never lost sight of the fact that a national commitment to fight required events beyond his control to arrange. Indeed, what seems most striking in this period was not Roosevelt's arbitrariness in pushing the country toward war but rather his caution and restraint. For all of his talk at Argentia of needing an "incident," and for all of his efforts even to manufacture one in the case of the Greer, he refused to ask for a declaration of war until a genuine provocation from abroad made the nation ready to fight.

Did Roosevelt, then, maneuver or, at the very least, permit the country to become involved in a war with Japan as a back door to the European fighting? "Had FDR been determined to avoid war with the Japanese if at all possible," George Kennan has argued, "he would have conducted American policy quite differently ... than he actually did. He would not, for example, have made an issue over Japanese policy in China, where the Japanese were preparing, anyway, to undertake a partial withdrawal . . . and where this sort of American pressure was not really essential. He would not have tried to starve the Japanese navy of oil. And he would have settled down to some hard and realistic dealings with the Japanese."³ This picture of Roosevelt's options leaves out the domestic context in which he had to operate. The struggle against fascism, in American minds, was indelibly linked with China's fight against Japan. Though mindful of the advantage of concentrating American power against Berlin, Roosevelt also appreciated that opposition to Japan was an essential part of the moral imperative Americans saw for fighting. To have acquiesced in Japan's domination of China and allowed oil and other vital supplies to fuel Japan's war machine would have provoked an outcry in the United States against cynical power politics and weakened the national resolve to confront fascist power outside of the Western Hemisphere. In short, to gain a national consensus for fighting fascism overseas, Roosevelt could not discriminate between Germany and Japan; both had to be opposed at the same time.

None of this is meant to suggest that Roosevelt foresaw and accepted the surprise attack at Pearl Harbor as a necessary means of bringing a unified nation into the war. Seeing the fleet in Hawaii as a deterrent rather than a target, lulled by the belief that the Japanese lacked the capability to strike at Pearl Harbor and by the information or "noise," as Roberta Wohlstetter calls it, indicating that an attack might come at any one of a number of points, Roosevelt, like the rest of the nation, failed to anticipate the Pearl Harbor attack. Later contentions to the contrary had less to do with the actuality of Roosevelt's actions than with isolationist efforts to justify the idea that the country had never, in fact, been vulnerable to attack.⁴

Historians generally give Roosevelt high marks for his direction of wartime strategy. As this and other recent studies conclude, Roosevelt was the principal architect of the basic strategic decisions that contributed so heavily to the early defeat of Germany and Japan. Commentators immediately after 1945, however, thought otherwise. Generalizing from the actualities in the last stages of the war, they described Roosevelt's thinking on wartime strategy as almost entirely a reflection of decisions reached by the Joint Chiefs. Undoubtedly for reasons of wartime unity, Roosevelt encouraged this idea, saying that he never overruled his staff and that they had no basic differences or even minor disagreements. But the record of the years 1938-1943 shows otherwise. Until the first Quebec Conference in August 1943, military historian William Emerson has written, "it is no exaggeration to say that . . . the basic decisions that molded strategy were made by the Commander-in-Chief himself, against the advice of his own chiefs and in concert with Churchill and the British chiefs." Indeed, "whenever the military advice of his chiefs clearly diverged from his own notions," Emerson also says, "Roosevelt did not hesitate to ignore or override them." In 1940, for example, when a U.S. Air Force planner presented detailed figures showing that aid to Britain was undermining American air rearmament, "the President cut him off with a breezy 'Don't let me see that again!'" Roosevelt was rarely so blunt. With few exceptions, he masked differences with his Chiefs by having the British carry the burden of the argument. As in so many other things, this allowed him to have his way without acrimonious exchanges that could undermine his ability to lead.[5]

In his handling of major foreign-policy questions as well, Roosevelt was usually his own decisionmaker. Distrustful of the State Department, which he saw as conservative and rigid, he divided responsibility for foreign affairs among a variety of agencies and men. "You should go through the experience of trying to get any changes in the thinking, policy, and action of the career diplomats and then you'd know what a real problem was," he once told Marriner Eccles of the Federal Reserve Board. By pitting Sumner Welles, undersecretary of state (1937-1943), against Cordell Hull, secretary of state (1933-1944); political envoys against career diplomats; the Treasury Department against the State Department; Henry Stimson, secretary of war (1940-45), against Henry Morgenthau, Jr., secretary of the Treasury (1934-1945); and a host of other official and personal representatives against each other for influence over foreign policy, he became a court of last resort on major issues and kept control in his own hands. In 1943, for example, when George Kennan, then in charge of the American mission in Portugal, objected to Washington's method of gaining military facilities in the Azores as likely to antagonize the Portuguese government and possibly push Spain into the war on Germany's side, the State Department called him back to Washington. After a meeting with Stimson, Frank Knox, secretary of the navy (1940-44), Edward Stettinius, Jr., undersecretary of state (1943-1944), and the Joint Chiefs in which he made no headway, Kennan gained access to the president, who endorsed his solution to the problem. But what about the people in the Pentagon, who seemed intent on a different course, Kennan inquired. "Oh, don't worry," said the president with a debonair wave of his cigarette holder, "about all those *people* over there."[6]

Outwardly, Roosevelt's diplomatic appointments also suggest an ad hoc, disorganized approach to foreign affairs. Career diplomats, wealthy supporters of his campaign, academics, military men, journalists, and old friends made up the varied list of heads of mission abroad. But, as with major decisions on foreign policy, there was more method and purpose behind Roosevelt's selection of diplomats than meets the eye. William E. Dodd, the Jeffersonian Democrat in Berlin, signaled the president's antipathy for Nazi views and plans. Openly sympathetic to the Soviets, ambassadors William Bullitt and Joseph Davies had been sent to Moscow to improve relations between Russia and the United States. Nelson T. Johnson in China and Joseph C. Grew in Japan, both holdovers from the previous administration, reflected Roosevelt's desire for a continuation of the Hoover-Stimson Far Eastern policy. Joseph Kennedy, who went to London in 1938, seemed likely to keep his distance from the British government and provide critical estimates of the appeasement policy. His failure to do so disappointed and annoyed FDR. John G. Winant, a former Republican governor of New Hampshire who succeeded Kennedy in London in 1941, reflected the president's commitment to Britain's triumph over Berlin. Ambassadors William H. Standley and Averell Harriman, both skeptics in differing degrees about Soviet intentions, had been sent to Moscow partly to provide a contrary perspective to the wartime euphoria about Russia. All of these men were instruments of presidential purpose, expressions of Roosevelt's designs in foreign affairs.

No part of Roosevelt's foreign policy has been less clearly understood than his wartime diplomacy. The portrait of him as utterly naive or unrealistic about the Russians, for example, has been much overdrawn. Recognizing that postwar stability would require a Soviet-American accord and that Soviet power would then extend into East-Central Europe and parts of East Asia, Roosevelt openly accepted these emerging realities in his dealings with Joseph Stalin. The suggestion that Roosevelt could have restrained this Soviet expansion through greater realism or a tougher approach to Stalin is unpersuasive. As an aftermath of World War II, George Kennan has written, no one could deny Stalin "a wide military and political *glacis* on his Western frontier . . . except at the cost of another war, which was unthinkable." Since the West could not defeat Adolf Hitler without Stalin's aid, which "placed him automatically in command of half of Europe," and since public questions about postwar Soviet intentions would have shattered wartime unity at home and with the Russians, Roosevelt endorsed the new dimensions of Soviet power, in the hope that such an action would encourage future friendship with the West. As his conversation with Niels Bohr, prominent nuclear physicist, in 1944 indicated, Roosevelt also left open the question of whether he would share control of atomic power with the Russians.[7]

At the same time, however, he acted to limit the expansion of Russian power in 1945 by refusing to share the secret of the atomic bomb, agreeing to station American troops in southern Germany, endorsing Winston Churchill's arrangements for the Balkans, working for the acquisition of American air and naval bases in the Pacific and the Atlantic, and encouraging the illusion of China as a "great power" with an eye to using it as a political counterweight to the USSR. Mindful that any emphasis on this kind of realpolitik might weaken American public resolve to play an enduring role in world affairs, Roosevelt made these actions the hidden side of his diplomacy. Yet however much he kept these actions in the background, they were a significant part of his wartime Soviet policy. Hence, in the closing days of his life, when he spoke to Niels Bohr of becoming "'tougher' [with Russia] than has heretofore appeared advantageous to the war effort," he was not suddenly departing from his conciliatory policy but rather giving emphasis to what had been there all along. Moreover, had he lived, Roosevelt would probably have moved more quickly than President Truman did to confront the Russians. His greater prestige and reputation as an advocate of Soviet-American friendship would have made it easier for him than for Truman to muster public support for a hard line.[8]

Did Roosevelt's equivocal wartime approach to Russia poison postwar Soviet-American relations? Many forces played a part in bringing on the Cold War, James MacGregor Burns contends, "but perhaps the most determining single factor was the gap between promise and reality that widened steadily during 1942 and 1943." Roosevelt's failure to give full rein to the policy of common goals and sacrifices by delaying a second front in France until 1944, Burns believes, aroused Soviet anger and cynicism and contributed "far more than any other factor" to the "postwar disillusionment and disunity" we call the Cold War.[9] But could Roosevelt have arranged an earlier cross-channel attack? British opposition and want of military means, particularly landing craft, made a pre-1944 assault difficult to undertake and unlikely to succeed. Such a campaign would not only have cost more American lives, it would also have played havoc with the president's entire war strategy, undermining the nation's ability to break German and Japanese power as quickly and as inexpensively as it did.

More to the point, would an earlier, less successful, or unsuccessful European attack have quieted Soviet suspicions of the West? Failure would certainly have brought forth a new round of Soviet complaints, and even a successful cross-channel attack in 1942 or 1943 would have been no hedge against the Cold War. The Soviets, according to Adam B. Ulam, were not easily dissuaded from "their suspicions about the intentions of the Western Powers. Not the most intensive credits, not even the turning over to the Russians of sample atomic bombs could have appeased them or basically affected their policies. Suspicion was built into the Soviet system."[10] On other major postwar questions as well, Roosevelt was more perceptive than commonly believed. His desire for a new world league with peacekeeping powers rested less on a faith in the effectiveness of Wilsonian collective security than on the belief that it was a necessary vehicle for permanently involving the United States in world affairs. Though convinced that postwar affairs would operate under a system of "great power" control, with each of the powers holding special responsibility in its geographical sphere, Roosevelt felt compelled to obscure this idea through a

United Nations organization that would satisfy widespread demand in the
United States for new idealistic or universalist arrangements for assuring the
peace.

His commitment to a trusteeship system for former colonies and man-
dates is another good example of how he used an idealistic idea to mask a
concern with power. Believing that American internationalists would object to
the acquisition of postwar air and naval bases for keeping the peace, Roosevelt
disguised this plan by proposing that dependent territories come under the
control of three or four countries designated by the United Nations. The
"trustees" were to assume civil and military responsibilities for the dependent
peoples until they were ready for self-rule. In this way, the United States would
both secure strategic bases and assure self-determination for emerging nations
around the globe.

This idea strongly influenced Roosevelt's wartime policy toward France.
He opposed Charles de Gaulle's plans for taking control in France and resur-
recting the French Empire as dangerous to postwar stability in Europe and
around the world. De Gaulle's assumption of power seemed likely to provoke
civil strife in France, feed revolutionary movements in French African and Asian
colonies longing to be free, and inhibit American or "great power" control over
areas that were strategic for keeping postwar peace. Roosevelt preferred a
malleable French government ready to accept the reality of reduced French
power and ultimate independence for former colonies temporarily under
United Nations civil and military control.

Roosevelt's broad conception of what it would take to assure the postwar
peace was fundamentally sound: a greatly expanded American role abroad, a
Soviet-American accord or "peaceful coexistence," a place for a "great power"
China, and an end to colonial empires have all become fixtures on the postwar
world scene. But these developments emerged neither in the way nor to the
extent Roosevelt had wished. His plans for a United States with substantial, but
nevertheless limited, commitments abroad; an accommodation with the USSR;
a stable, cooperative China; a passive France; and a smooth transition for
dependent peoples from colonial to independent rule could not withstand the
historical and contemporary forces ranged against them. Roosevelt was mindful
of the fact that uncontrollable conditions—Soviet suspicion of the West and
internal divisions in China, for example—might play havoc with his postwar
plans. His decision to hold back the secret of the atomic bomb from Stalin and
his preparation to meet a political storm over Chiang Kai-Shek's collapse testify
to these concerns. But his vision of what the world would need to revive and
remain at peace after the war moved him to seek these ends nevertheless. That
he fell short of his aims had less to do with his naivete or idealism than with the

fact that even a thoroughgoing commitment to realpolitik or an exclusive reliance on power would not have significantly altered developments in Europe and Asia after the war. Russian expansion, Chinese strife, and colonial revolutions were beyond Roosevelt's power to prevent.

By contrast with these developments, external events played a central part in helping Roosevelt bring the country through the war in a mood to take a major role in overseas affairs. Much of Roosevelt's public diplomacy during the war was directed toward this goal: The portraits of an effective postwar peacekeeping body, of a friendly Soviet Union, and of a peaceful China had as much to do with creating an internationalist consensus at home as with establishing a fully effective peace system abroad. Principally influenced by Pearl Harbor, which destroyed isolationist contentions about American invulnerability to attack, and by the country's emergence as the world's foremost power, the nation ended the war ready to shoulder substantial responsibilities in foreign affairs.

One may assume that postwar developments would not have surprised or greatly disappointed FDR. As he once told someone impatient for presidential action, Abraham Lincoln "was a sad man because he couldn't get it all at once. And nobody can. . . . You cannot, just by shouting from the housetops, get what you want all the time."[11] No doubt American willingness to play a large part in postwar international affairs would have impressed him as a major advance, while postwar world tensions would surely have stimulated him to new efforts for world peace. And no doubt, as so often during his presidency, a mixture of realism and idealism, of practical short-term goals tied to visions of long-term gains, would have become the hallmark of his renewed struggle to make the world a better place in which to live.

Notes

1. William C. Leuchtenburg, *FDR and the New Deal* (New York: Harper & Row, 1963), 337.

2. Nicholas Halasz, *Roosevelt through Foreign Eyes* (Princeton: Princeton University Press, 1961), 318-319.

3. Kennan's remarks are from a symposium titled "World War II: 30 Years After," published in *Survey* 21 (winter-spring 1975), 30.

4. Roberta Wohlstetter, *Pearl Harbor: Warning and Decision* (Stanford, C.A.: Stanford University Press, 1962).

5. William Emerson, "Franklin Roosevelt as Commander-in-Chief in World War II," *Military Affairs* 22 (winter 1958-1959), 181-207.

6. For the Eccles and Kennan exchanges, see James M. Burns, *Roosevelt: Soldier of Freedom* (New York: Harcourt, Brace, Jovanovich, 1970), 352-353.

7. Kennan's observation is in the *Survey* symposium, 35-36; see also Hugh Seton-Watson's comments, 37-42.

8. Charles Bohlen also believed that Roosevelt would have moved more quickly against the Russians than Truman did. See his *Witness to History, 1929-1969* (New York: Norton, 1973), 211.

9. Burns, *Roosevelt: Soldier of Freedom*, 373-374.

10. Adam B. Ulam, *Expansion and Coexistence: Soviet Foreign Policy, 1917-1973* (New York: Praeger, 1974), 399.

11. Arthur Schlesinger, Jr., *Coming of the New Deal,* (Boston: Houghton Mifflin, 1958), 529-530.

4

"Courage First and Intelligence Second": The American Jewish Secular Elite, Roosevelt, and the Failure to Rescue

Henry L. Feingold

Excerpt from phone conversation on 13 January 1944 between Samuel Rosenman, President Roosevelt's speechwriter and adviser, and Henry Morgenthau, Jr., the secretary of the Treasury. Morgenthau is inviting Rosenman to a meeting on 15 January, the day before he plans to deliver to Roosevelt a report entitled "Report to the Secretary on the Acquiescence of This Government in the Murder of the Jews":

> Morgenthau: Well, look, if the only thing you are worrying about is publicity. I can guarantee you there will be no publicity.
>
> Rosenman: All right. Well then certainly it doesn't make much difference who is there. If it is—if there were to be publicity, I think the choice of the three people is terrible. [i.e., Rosenman, Morgenthau, and Ben Cohen, three Jews.]
>
> Morgenthau: Don't worry about the publicity. What I want is intelligence and courage—courage first and intelligence second.
>
> Rosenman: All right. I can't get there at 9:30 because I am over in the bedroom, [FDR's] but I will come over as soon as I leave the bedroom.[1]

The precariousness of the Jewish community's position in the world has lent a special urgency to the American Jewish political agenda. Its leaders customarily assume an advocacy role before the American seat of power. During the Roosevelt era, how effective it was in playing that role became literally a matter of life and death for millions of European Jews. In recent years a bitter debate has taken shape on the question of whether American Jewry did enough, whether it used the power available to it effectively. A reasoned resolution of that debate depends on making an accurate and fair judgment on the extent and nature of the power Jews exercised. That is no easy task. In American society, determining the flow of power, who exercises it in relation to what interest, is problematic because power both public and private is diffused and concealed. Sometimes its play in human affairs is altogether denied. Conventional wisdom has it that there was a considerable enhancement of Jewish power during the New Deal. Yet the Jewish community's business, made more urgent than ever before by the developments in Germany, did not go particularly well. Its power could not match the responsibility that kinship assigned to it. It failed to project coherent demands on power holders. It discovered that it was not a community bound by a common interest but rather a subgroup composed of numerous contending factions. Yet it assigned a task to itself that it did not possess the power to accomplish and a humanitarian mission to the Roosevelt administration that was seemingly more fitting for a government of saints. That unwillingness to deal with the reality of politics and power, and the attempt to deal only with what politics and power should be, is characteristic of American Jewish political culture. This idealism complicated the situation at the time and is behind the current indictment. How did a fragmented, disunited subculture, unaccustomed to even thinking of itself as a coherent political entity, assume such an awesome responsibility? How did it use its supposedly enhanced power? What conduits to the Oval Office were available to its leaders? How attuned was the occupant of that office to understand the special need for action? These questions serve as the focus of this chapter.

American Jewish political culture—the assumptions, style, and habits it brought into the political arena—had a great affinity with the New Deal, especially the aspect of the welfare state.[2] But at the same time its heavy ideological freight made it ill-suited for the practice of practical politics. It never managed to deliver to Roosevelt a simple direct request, by one recognizable constituency, willing to reinforce its bargain through a "normal" political transaction. Roosevelt heard instead, when he bothered to listen, a cacophony of sound from a subgroup whose interior political life was so raucous as to be uncivil.

Yet despite deep internal dissension, Jews probably projected influence slightly above that of a minority constituting only 3.69 percent of the population.[3] This group came reluctantly to the political arena and often found itself unwelcome, but once there it displayed an intense activism coupled with a high voting volume and formidable mastery of issues, and a willingness to make its passionately held opinions known.[4] The activist period begins in earnest during the third period of American Jewish history, which was dominated by the values and style of the immigrants from Eastern Europe.

After World War I the Jewish vote, whose existence was denied by "uptown" stewards, had twice veered off to third parties. The community favored Eugene Debs, of the American Socialist Party, with 24 percent of its vote in 1920 and Robert La Follette, of the Progressive Party, with 17 percent in 1924.[5] Its maverick character was reinforced by a strange nonparochial ethnicity. The Jewish vote did not seem to cohere ethnically. Rather than backing a candidate of flesh and blood, and incidental rewards, Jewish voters supported a "constellation of values."[6] When those values were joined with the feeling of kinship, as they were in the case of anti-Jewish depredations in Russia and Romania, the galvanization of Jewish energies and resources became an important factor in the local political arena. The Jewish political club did belatedly make its debut in the 1920s but again ideology was as important as ethnic loyalty. Nevertheless, the advent of a second and third generation of American-born Jews, descendants from Eastern European immigrants during the 1920s and 1930s, marks the historical juncture when American Jewry was fully prepared to practice grass-roots American politics, albeit of its own distinctive variety.

Jewish voters switched to the Democratic Party, and remain to this day its most loyal ethnic constituency. Al Smith's "Brown Derby" campaign drew their enthusiastic support. Probably the preference for Smith was based more on the belief that the presidency ought to be accessible to all groups regardless of religious affiliation than to the fact that Belle Moskowitz and Joseph Proskauer, as well as Judge Samuel Rosenman, all well known among Jewish voters, were prominent in the Smith entourage. It was that newly developed preference for the Democratic Party on the national level that was transferred to Franklin Roosevelt in 1932.[7] This was, however, not a totally new relationship. In the "solemn referendum" election (1920) they had preferred him as vice president, not only because the concept of a League of Nations was close to the heart of the Jewish voter but also because Warren Harding had opposed the appointment of Louis Brandeis to the Supreme Court. In the New York State gubernatorial election of 1928 Roosevelt received the first evidence of the peculiar attraction he had for Jewish voters. They voted for him in greater numbers than they did for his Republican Jewish opponent, Albert Ottinger, who paradoxically was compelled to spend much energy in defending himself against the charge that he was a "bad" Jew. By 1930 the switch to the

Democratic Party was complete. Six of the eight Jews elected to Congress were Democrats, a complete reversal of the election of 1920 when ten of the eleven Jews elected to Congress were Republican.[8]

The most prominent characteristic of the American Jewish political persona is its concern for the welfare of Jewish communities abroad, which can be traced back to colonial times. Its tilt outward, as if to hear the cry of its brethren, precedes the establishment of the Zionist consensus in the late 1930s. Since the Damascus Blood Libel (1840) American Jews had been requesting statements of intercession from the federal government. These had been routinely formulated when anti-Jewish depredations occurred in the Swiss Cantons, in Romania, and in Russia. Extraordinary incidents such as the Dreyfus Affair (1894) in France and the Kishinev pogrom (1903) in Russia triggered strident demands for action from the Jewish masses in America.[9] It was discovered that they could be assuaged by philo-Semitic diplomatic dispatches, which were publicized in Jewish population centers. Yet the effect such diplomatic gestures had in ameliorating the conditions of Jews abroad, especially if they were communities within nations that were immune to moral suasion, was not significant. There developed well before the Roosevelt era a kind of ritual that saw Jewish leaders requesting a supporting gesture, which was granted by the administration in power because it entailed no political price while it earned political points. In developing a "politics of gestures," Franklin Roosevelt was adhering to a well-established precedent.[10] It was the nature of the crisis faced by Jewry during World War II that makes gestures such as the calling of the refugee conference at Evian, France (1938), and the conference in inaccessible Bermuda (1943) seem cruelly inappropriate.

The concern for the security and welfare of Jewish communities abroad is part of a constellation of interests that gave Jews a special concern for foreign relations. In the 1930s that interest was reflected in a consistently interventionist posture that distinguished Jews from other hyphenate groups. It was undoubtedly more true of the Jewish rank and file than its opinion-leader intellectuals, many of whom had their confidence in the system shaken to the core by the Depression and were inclined to pacifism in the international arena. Generally, however, they were earlier than other groups to perceive Adolf Hitler as a dire threat to world peace. Jews opposed the Ludlow Amendment and the neutrality laws; they favored aiding the Spanish loyalists; they considered the appeasement at Munich a grave miscalculation; they favored the Destroyer-Bases deal (September 1940) with London; they favored the concept of Lend Lease (February 1941) and convoying the leased war equipment.[11] The strong interventionist posture was undoubtedly related to the special ordeal experienced by German Jewry, but it transcended this as well. It was strongly linked to a preexisting penchant for universalist and humanitarian doctrines that abhorred tyrannies such as the kind developed in Germany and the Soviet Union.[12]

Yet it is easy to make too much of the defining interventionist stance of American Jewry. Every one of the issues of the "great debate" drew a sizable Jewish minority that favored the isolationist position.[13] In 1937 a slim majority of Jews actually opposed the admission of refugees.[14] It is, in fact, difficult to draw a clear-cut conclusion from the available poll data of the 1930s because of the small size of the Jewish sample and because repeatedly the Jewish position on any issue is attained by the thinnest of margins.[15] Jewish interventionism, such as it was, may have been far more a passion among Jewish spokesmen than a reality among the Jewish rank and file. Then, as today, it was possible, in the absence of hierarchy in the Jewish community, for self-appointed spokesmen to preempt the Jewish voice.

If Jews were distinguishable in the urban ethnic coalition of which they had become part, it was for their unerring support of the welfare-state concept. This concept bore some remote resemblance to their social democratic proclivities. Some of its programs in social security, cheap housing, and the rights of organized labor were previewed by the Jewish labor movement. The American Labor Party, founded and funded by David Dubinsky of the International Ladies Garment Workers Union (ILGWU), viewed itself as "the permanent New Deal party of our country."[16] Paradoxically, while Jews were loyal to Roosevelt because of his domestic program, it would be in the area of foreign policy that they most required some evidence of concern. The conspicuous absence of evidence of concern did not seriously interrupt the developing Jewish "love affair" with Roosevelt. He had received approximately 80 percent of the Jewish vote when he ran for governor in 1928. It rose to 83 percent in the presidential election of 1932. After 1936, when the ardor of the hyphenate vote began to wane, Jewish support reached new plateaus.[17] At least one explanation for such loyalty is that at the outset Jews shared with other Americans a preoccupation with the domestic crisis, which they abandoned only reluctantly for the menacing events in Europe and the Far East. Another is that before 1939 American Jewry, in fact, "grossly underestimated" the length to which anti-Semitism would be carried by the Nazis.[18] American Jews were faced with their own credibility problem after 1939 as well. It proved difficult to fathom the difference between "normal" anti-Semitism and the murderous biological anti-Semitism behind the Final Solution. Roosevelt was fully informed during the election of 1940 of the increased solidity of Jewish support and was grateful for it.[19] But from a political point of view, that loyalty, the certain knowledge that the Jewish vote was his, diminished the leverage of Jewish leaders, who could not threaten removal of the Jewish vote. He did not have to transact business with the Jews. The Jewish "love affair" with Roosevelt was from the outset fated to be unrequited. But we shall learn presently that all who unstintingly loved Roosevelt suffered a similar fate.

Yet the thought that there was something special in the American Jewish relationship with Roosevelt, which ironically fed both the anti-Semitic and the Jewish imagination, had some basis in fact. For Roosevelt, Jewish loyalty may have been heartening, but it also entailed liabilities, since Jews were not winning medals for popularity during the 1930s while at the same time Nazi machinations created a need to take measures requiring tampering with the sacrosanct immigration laws during the Depression. Yet if Roosevelt would usually not assume the political risk involved, Washington did become a welcome place for the formally educated generation of Jews that made its debut in the 1920s. The "Jew Deal" label that haunted the Roosevelt administration was based partly on the appearance of these Jews in the upper echelons of the federal civil service, where they combined with elite groups of Jews who emerged at the top of other power centers—the law, the university, organized labor, journalism, and politics—and also found their way to the Capitol. For some it might have seemed as if Jews were inundating the Roosevelt administration. Adlai Stevenson, then a young lawyer in Washington and one day destined to be idealized by Jewish voters in a manner reminiscent of Roosevelt, vented his resentment: "There is a little feeling that the Jews are getting too prominent and many of them are autocratic," he informed a friend.[20]

Of these bridging elites the law was, in fact, the most conspicuous. Frozen out of prestigious law firms to which merit as reflected in law school class rank entitled them, Jewish lawyers found employment in the new regulatory agencies. From these citadels they were often called upon to do battle with their counterparts in the prestigious law firms of the private sector—counterparts whose religious and class rank qualifications were found more suitable. By the spring of 1936, much to the chagrin of Felix Frankfurter, the eight Jewish editors of the Harvard Law Review could not find positions in private law firms. The New Deal thus became an arena for a silent struggle between outsiders and insiders that contributed fuel to the burning resentment of the Roosevelt haters.[21]

A second link to the Roosevelt administration was anchored in the community of scientists and technocrats, whose ranks had been penetrated by Jews in the 1920s and then supplemented in the 1930s by refugee scientists, many of whom were Jewish.[22] Within American Jewry, evidence that the prestige of scientists had begun to overshadow that of orator-rabbis was manifest in the enthusiastic reception given to Chaim Weizmann and Albert Einstein during their whirlwind tour in April 1921. For the Jewish community the refugee scientists, armed with a firsthand knowledge of the dangers of National Socialism, were able to serve as a balance against the powerful influence of the peace movement among Jewish intellectuals. For the Roosevelt administration their power stemmed from their expertise especially in theoretical physics, which would soon become a cardinal factor in American security. Their role in the Manhattan Project was acknowledged in the Smyth report in 1976.[23]

Social work, which had become a favorite profession chosen by committed young Jews and upper-class Protestants alike, formed yet another link to the administration. Social workers possessed access to the Oval Office through fellow professionals like Eleanor Roosevelt, Harry Hopkins, and Frances Perkins and formed, in effect, a group with administrative skills with a direct link to the Jewish "masses and classes."[24] Similarly, the self-conscious, largely Jewish, New York intellectual community was a Jewish power source. This was not because its members pressed for Jewish causes; they were, in fact, mostly unable to recognize a Jewish interest apart from that of humanity at large. But they did have power as opinion leaders, and those opinions were resonated first through the Jewish community, which took ideas very seriously. The ideational support of the New Deal, the explanation of the welfare state, and the finding of a rationale for Roosevelt's often inconsistent countercyclical measures emanated in some measure from the New York intellectual community.[25]

Yet despite the presence of Jewish lawyers in government and the influence of Jewish opinion leaders, it is difficult to find evidence of actual enhancement of Jewish power. The Jews who made their way to Washington or other power centers usually had little relationship to the Jewish enterprise. Their success was a tribute to private drive and talent. They did not view themselves as advocates of specifically Jewish causes, and many undoubtedly would have been embarrassed to do so. Moreover, the influence of these "bridging elites," such as it was, was projected outside the political process to which Roosevelt was attuned.

The appearance of a special consonance between American Jewry and Roosevelt may stem from the fact that Jews strongly favored what the Roosevelt administration wanted for "relief, recovery, and reform." Undoubtedly, many believed automatically that the reverse was true as well, that the administration supported special Jewish needs. But in the case of the admission of Jewish refugees such support was not forthcoming. Roosevelt refused to publicly endorse the Wagner-Rogers Bill, which would have admitted twenty thousand refugee children in 1939 and 1940, outside the quota system. Public opinion polls showed that 61 percent of Americans were opposed to such an exemption.[26] Administration support entailed a political price Roosevelt was unwilling to pay. He would tolerate his wife favoring the measure, but the only administration person who spoke in favor at the congressional hearings was Katherine Lenroot, chief of the Labor Department's Children's Bureau. The bill was amended to death in committee.[27] The incident is important because it was one of the few examples we possess that shows concretely what Roosevelt actually was willing to do for refugees. It also serves as a paradigm of the role of Jewish leadership and organizations. They were divided, uncertain, and fearful of domestic anti-Semitism. The brunt of support for the measure was borne by non-Jewish agencies.[28] The elaborate apparatus created by Louis Howe that monitored and sometimes deeply intruded into the politics of the ethnic constituencies was designed to garner votes, not to allay suffering.

Priding himself on the number of advisers of his faith near the seat of power, the average Jewish voter knew little of the complexities of ethnic politics. He assumed automatically that such a presence meant an enhancement of Jewish influence. He was unaware that the price of such political attainment was often surrender of ethnic and religious identity. That trade-off was marked in all of the Jews in Roosevelt's entourage. Judge Samuel Rosenman, a politically astute legal expert with a talent for the spoken word, whom Roosevelt picked up from Al Smith's circle, viewed his Jewishness primarily in denominational terms. Like many such Jews he associated himself with the American Jewish Committee (AJC), in which he sometimes played a leading role.[29] His interest in fighting anti-Semitism led him to arrange for a special chair in human relations to be endowed at Newark University. The occupant would monitor anti-immigration sentiment in textbooks and keep a watchful eye on German exchange students and professors.[30] His view, like those of the leaders of the American Jewish Committee, was that long-range changes in consciousness through education offered the best strategy for the Jewish community. But in the short-range crisis, the admission of refugees, the furnishing of resettlement havens elsewhere, and virtually every other rescue measure advocated by Jewish leaders was opposed by Rosenman. By his own account he never broached directly to Roosevelt any matters pertaining to Judaism or the Jewish situation and observed that the president himself evinced little interest in Jewish matters.[31]

Most resembling Rosenman in background and career was Joseph Proskauer, who became head of the American Jewish Committee in 1943 and thereby a leader of the Jewish community, if not a prominent Jew near Roosevelt. Like Rosenman he began his political career as a supporter of Al Smith but could not manage the transition to Roosevelt. Born in Mobile, Alabama, in 1877, Proskauer bore his religion as a "persistent torment." His biography speaks of a profound sense of alienation he experienced as a youth in the almost total Christian environment of Mobile.[32] Smith appointed him to the New York State Supreme Court, and Proskauer retained his political loyalty to his mentor, sharing fully his estrangement from the Roosevelt administration. So pronounced did that animus become that Proskauer was one of the rare prominent Jews to join the Liberty League. Undoubtedly, he would have become solicitor general had Smith become president; as it was he became president of the AJC in 1943. A key Jewish leader thus never had access to the Oval Office and confined his government contacts to the State Department, which was sensed by Jews at large, and within the government, to be anti-Semitic. But Proskauer, who insisted that he was more American than Jewish and who required the approval of non-Jews, found suitable the role of mediator between the State Department and the organized Jewish community. His assumption of a leading post in the Jewish community seems in retrospect to be a strange misalliance of a man and the times. Proskauer had early involved himself in Jewish philanthropy and social work among the Jewish immigrant poor, but there was little early evidence that a leadership position in the Jewish community would interest him. He occupied seats on various local Jewish agency directorships, but his was to be a public career. He was a member of the remnant of "uptown" Jews who continued to be associated with the AJC. He was staunchly anti-Zionist, when Zionism had become the binding consensus of American Jewry, and anti–New Deal when most Jews were passionate advocates of the welfare-state concept. Even had access to the Oval Office been available to him it is likely that Proskauer would have advocated policies totally out of touch with the deepest concerns of the committed Jewish community. For him, activist rabbis such as Stephen Wise and Abba Hillel Silver, who were far closer to the heart of American Jewry, seemed inappropriate.[33] He worried about the international Zionist conspiracy and the question of dual loyalty when Louis Brandeis had solved these vexing problems for most Jews in the 1920s. His inability to see beyond his own affluence and social position made the world of the descendants of the Eastern European immigrants, despite his early work in settlement houses, *terra incognita* for him. He never really fully fathomed the Jewish plight during the Holocaust.[34] Had he done so he might have thought much more about leading the AJC out of the American Jewish Conference in October 1943. There was, of course, ample cause for doing so, and some will maintain that the organizational integrity of the agency demanded it. But that step, perhaps more than most others, forever foiled the possibility of a unified coherent community emerging during the crisis.

In his mind-set and background, Proskauer resembled much more those Jews who earned a place near Roosevelt for renown earned in the law, the university, the labor movement, journalism, finance, or business. Felix Frankfurter, who made his debut in Washington in 1906 and whose reputation was made as a professor of law at Harvard University, was among the most prominent of these power holders. On the surface his early recruitment into the American Zionist movement by Louis Brandeis, his mentor, gave him some credentials as a committed Jew. At the Versailles negotiations he played a crucial role in moving the Zionist program forward.[35] Yet so bifurcated was his life that Zionism, for most Jews the most contemporary expression of Jewish identity, did not interfere with enthusiastic assimilationism. Zionism, he observed, helped him get "a fresh psychological relationship to other Jews and Gentiles."[36] Yet it was never more than a part-time interest. His main energies and talents were freely and enthusiastically expended in matching talent, especially talent in the law, with those who held power. In the Roosevelt administration law would become a crucially important area of politics.

But to serve as an agent for the Jews to Roosevelt, or as Roosevelt's Jew, was too confining a role, especially for someone who felt himself more than merely ethnic. Frankfurter was more circumspect than Brandeis in using his influence for purely Jewish causes. It might be that philosophically his conservative notion of the limits of government interest caused him to reject the idea that the Roosevelt administration should preoccupy itself with a Jewish community in Germany whose members were not American citizens and not its legal responsibility. Withal, had rescue advocates succeeded in mobilizing Frankfurter's energy and influence in the rescue cause, more might have been achieved. As in the case of the appointment of Brandeis to the Supreme Court in 1916, what was celebrated as a great Jewish victory in fact deprived Jews of a potential influence wielder since, even more than Brandeis, Frankfurter believed that maintaining a direct link to the Jewish community would be impolitic. He probably recalled that the maintenance of an even behind-the-scenes leadership by Brandeis of the Zionist movement led to bitter charges of impropriety by both Judah Magnes, the president of Hebrew University, and the *New York Times*. It literally drove Brandeis out of direct Jewish political activity.[37] Predictably, no such apprehensions are in evidence when it came to playing his nonethnic role in relation to the president. After his appointment he continued to offer advice, solicited and unsolicited, to help with speechwriting, and to point out the fine points of the law.[38]

For Frankfurter it must have been something of an irony that his far-flung influence made him a target for anti-Semitic barbs. Their persistence during the Roosevelt era may have been caused by the mystery regarding the source of his influence since he did not, until his appointment to the Court, have an official position. William Randolph Hearst called him "the Iago of the Administration," and Hugh Johnson's image of a behind-the-scenes operator with octopus-like tentacles was uncomfortably close to a classic anti-Semitic portrait dating back to the Populists.[39] Similarly, *Fortune* singled him out as "the most influential single individual in the United States." He was likened to Rasputin. Calvert Magruder detected "oriental guile," while Raymond Moley saw a "Patriarchal sorcerer."[40]

For all of the suggestions of anti-Semitism, Frankfurter's influence did not stem from Jewish sources. Arthur Hayes Sulzberger, in fact, opposed his appointment to the Court, fearing it would stimulate anti-Semitism. His influence came from an entirely new source. Frankfurter, who had an unerring instinct for recognizing talent, became its merchandiser and broker. Legal skills, power to communicate, and knowledge of the intricacy of government administration had become crucial in the management of the public business. Frankfurter, using the bright young men of the Harvard Law School, became an enabler through this access to a rare pool of high talent. Over a period of years he built up a network of bright young lawyers, Frankfurter's "happy hot dogs," in many of the agencies of the administration. This network further enhanced his influence, which was, in fact, considerable simply by virtue of the number of people he knew in high places. Two of his "hot dogs," Tom Corcoran and Ben Cohen, became influential power wielders in their own right. In the spring of 1935 both had become permanent features in the White House.

To the team of Frankfurter, Cohen, and Corcoran are attributed the legislative mechanics of the Social Security Act of 1935, the Public Utility Holding Company Act, and several revenue measures. Frankfurter was not only strategically placed to bring such talent and skills to the Roosevelt administration; he was himself such a talent, one with sufficient insight to perceive how important it had become.

One of the Harvard boys of high station whom Frankfurter had known since 1914 was Franklin Roosevelt. Always on the lookout for "comers," Frankfurter befriended the tall young assistant secretary of the Navy, who carried the famous Roosevelt name, when both served in the Wilson administration. The strands were picked up again after Roosevelt's impressive victory in the 1928 gubernatorial race in New York State. That renewal of a mere acquaintanceship became the basis of one of those leader-adviser relationships that dot the pages of American history.[41] For Roosevelt it meant contact with one of the keenest, most engaged minds in the America of the 1930s, and for Frankfurter it filled some special need to be near power.

Yet Frankfurter's was never an exclusive access to the president. His influence was at times hotly contended by the Columbia University–based "brain trust."[42] Its members distrusted him for personal reasons, because he represented Harvard University and, in the case of his former student Adolph Berle, Jr., Frankfurter was convinced, for the fact that he was Jewish.[43] Frankfurter did join talent and brains to power, but that was hardly a Jewish enterprise. The few Jews for whom he attained positions were good lawyers who happened to be Jewish. Moreover, as his fallout with Corcoran indicates, Frankfurter could not hope to enlist his network of "hot dogs" in all causes of his choosing, much less Jewish ones. What he did do was to serve as a conduit to bring newly found talent to power holders.

From the Jewish vantage, Frankfurter's influence and access to the Oval Office made little difference. Even when it involved personal matters, Frankfurter rarely used that influence to further a Jewish interest. When he received news that his aged uncle, who held a high position with the national library in Vienna, had been incarcerated, Frankfurter turned, not to Roosevelt, but to Lady Nancy Astor for help.[44] The Zionist cause was, of course, a special interest, but even here Frankfurter spoke to the president in very general terms. He rarely accompanied Zionist delegations to the Oval Office even while he may have laid the groundwork for the visit. That occurred in June 1942 when he forwarded a memorandum from David Ben-Gurion, head of the Jewish Agency, to the president with a cover letter that characterized Ben-Gurion as a person "in whom Isaiah (Brandeis) had the greatest confidence."[45] Yet the note, which acknowledged the "smallness" of the Palestine problem and spoke of its symbolic importance, was self-effacing.[46] The request was denied by a busy and somewhat exasperated Roosevelt. Later Frankfurter was informed by Roosevelt of the growing opposition to Zionism in the State Department and the military, and Frankfurter meekly requested permission to pass this news on to Ben-Gurion and Weizmann. Roosevelt wanted to freeze the Palestine question until after the war.[47] "He also asked me to tell you," states the prefacing note from Grace Tully, FDR's secretary, "that quite frankly in the present situation in Egypt, Palestine, Syria, and Arabia he feels that the less said by everybody of all creeds, the better."[48] On matters of Jewish concern, Frankfurter learned, it was better to tread softly and approach the president indirectly. As early as October 1933 his memorandum describing the deterioration of conditions in Germany, which proposed that Roosevelt broadcast directly to the German people, observed that "the significance of Hitlerism far transcends ferocious anti-Semitism and fanatical racism."[49] The flow of letters designed to keep Roosevelt apprised of the deterioration of civility mentioned the depredations against the Jews within the general context of the Nazi threat. Frankfurter forwarded a list prepared for the American Jewish Committee that carefully cataloged precedents for American diplomatic intercession in relation to anti-Semitism.[50] In turn, the White House staff passed on to him such random information on anti-Semitic activity in America as came to the Oval Office. Sometimes the exchange assumed a lighter tone. When Frankfurter informed Roosevelt that a refugee who had found a haven in Palestine had named his child Franklin

Delano, the president requested that it be put in writing since it was "the greatest compliment I ever got."[51] It was the sort of light banter that the president preferred.

Frankfurter's approach to power was less confrontational than that of his mentor, Brandeis, who supported Frankfurter's enterprise with a monthly subsidy because he understood that his disciple's far-flung contacts yielded a greater influence in party politics.[52] Moreover, Frankfurter had a zest for public life, which the almost reclusive Brandeis did not share. It was Frankfurter who linked Brandeis to Roosevelt in 1928, forming a relationship that lasted until the justice's death. Frankfurter revered Brandeis as a "moral preceptor" but insisted to Raymond Moley that he was not the voice of Brandeis in politics. It was the justice's austere morality he admired.[53] The difference in approach surfaced during the ill-starred court-packing scheme. To Roosevelt's chagrin, Brandeis made his opposition public while the more politic Frankfurter kept his position private.[54] His very connectedness made a clear-cut stand impossible. Tom Corcoran was one of the conceivers of the court-packing scheme and later was involved in a tampering designed to bring Frankfurter to the Court by encouraging the retirement of "Isaiah." While the bond between Brandeis and Frankfurter was originally forged by a common concern for Zionism, during the Roosevelt era their transactions were overwhelmingly concerned with legislation and policies pertaining to American society and government. There was very little of specific Jewish concern in it.

The notion of a coherent Jewish interest in the minds of those Jews close to Roosevelt, the kind of Jewish conspiracy so central to the anti-Semitic imagination, is belied by Frankfurter's troubled relation to another Jew close to Roosevelt, Henry Morgenthau, Jr. There was a mutual feeling of antipathy between the two men. Frankfurter was sensitive to the fact that in terms of class, a certain mercantile patricianism, and even neighborhood proximity, Morgenthau was naturally preferable to Roosevelt. The president had known Morgenthau's father, who had carried out certain delicate diplomatic missions for Wilson. In fact, Frankfurter never forgot the desperate mission he and Chaim Weizmann undertook in 1917 to dissuade the fame-seeking Morgenthau, Sr., from trying to detach Turkey from the Central Powers so that a separate peace with the Allies could be achieved.[55] For the Zionists the possible success of Morgenthau's mission would have spelled disaster since the establishment of a Jewish homeland in Palestine, a promise embodied in the Balfour Declaration, required the demise of the "sick man of Europe."

Perhaps Frankfurter was transferring to the son an animus first directed at the father. But beneath it all it was this sense that Morgenthau's position was unearned by merit that most nettled. Frankfurter thought the secretary of the

Treasury was a "stupid bootlick" who was ashamed of his Jewishness and who above all did not want to be associated with "liberal" Jews.[56] He was unimpressed with the caliber of assistants with which Morgenthau surrounded himself after ousting Dean Acheson and Tom Corcoran, two of the Harvard men Frankfurter had placed in the Treasury. He was also well aware that Morgenthau had pushed for the appointment of James Landis for the vacant seat on the Supreme Court left by Benjamin Cardozo's death. Above all Frankfurter could not forgive Morgenthau's apparently easy glide to high position through an inside connection.[57] That same snobbishness limited Frankfurter's usefulness to the Jewish community. Rabbi Stephen Wise was occasionally able to use Frankfurter to gain access to Roosevelt, but Jews of lesser stature were unceremoniously dismissed. Frankfurter preferred "elevated messengers." Except for Morris Cohen, who was his roommate at Harvard, he retained few contacts with other talented sons of Central and Eastern European immigrants whose background and culture he once shared but now preferred to forget.[58] In that, too, he differed sharply from Brandeis, who devoted much energy to familiarizing himself with a religious culture he regretfully never knew.

As with other Jews near Roosevelt, the heart of the dilemma concerning Frankfurter pertains to his Jewishness. Was there a possibility of fully enlisting Frankfurter and other Jews in high position in the urgent rescue work required to save European Jewry? Could they recognize and support a purely Jewish cause? Frankfurter never denied the fact of his Jewishness, but despite an affiliation with Zionism his link to Judaism had over the years become tenuous.[59] He was far more interested in the legislative program of the New Deal than he was in the refugee problem and the rising tide of anti-Semitism.

The months before his appointment to the Supreme Court brought the problem of his Jewishness to the fore. If Frankfurter was disappointed when Roosevelt informed him privately that he could not appoint another Jew to the Court, he did not openly show it. But to Roosevelt's chagrin, Frankfurter's supposed indifference was belied by the fact that he did not signal his supporters, especially Corcoran, to stop their relentless pressure in favor of his appointment.[60] For Frankfurter the denial of a long sought-after seat on the Supreme Court was especially painful not only because it flew in the face of merit he possessed and service he had given to the nation, but also because it was a rejection based on a Jewishness with which he was not connected and which had not shaped his professional life. He never associated himself as directly with the Zionist movement as Brandeis did, and his link to it apparently did not help alert him to the special dangers National Socialism posed for the Jews as it did Stephen Wise.[61] He did not see the danger only in terms of the Jews, and by the time, in 1942, he was made fully aware of Hitler's genocidal intent he found it difficult to give the "Jewish question" the kind of central focus it was receiving in Berlin. That may explain the strange response made to a courier from the Polish underground who, as a firsthand witness, was able to explain to Frankfurter the actual implementation of the Final Solution in the most gruesome detail. He told Jan Karski, the courier, that he didn't believe what he was being told. What he undoubtedly meant was that he could not conceive that an actual mass-murder operation had been implemented by the Reich.[62]

Involved in the intricacies of monetary policy, Henry Morgenthau, Jr.'s, relation to the early stages of the anti-Jewish depredations in Germany was remote. He rejected a White House invitation to head the quasi-official President's Advisory Commission on Political Refugees (PACPR). Not until the final months of 1943, when he became aware of the State Department's concerted effort to block the entrance of refugees and to suppress news of the actual implementation of the Final Solution, did Morgenthau fully involve himself. Yet after the "scramble and bits and pieces" of news had become an agonized picture of wholesale slaughter planned at the highest level, Morgenthau's path of action was radically different from Frankfurter's.[63] One could read much of his subsequent political career, including the conception of his "plan" for the treatment of postwar Germany, as a response to that news.

As Dutchess County, New York, neighbors, the Morgenthau family was enlisted in Roosevelt's revived political career in the mid-1920s. Eleanor Roosevelt's relationship with the father and son can be traced back to her settlement-house days. The Morgenthaus actively supported the Henry Street settlement house in New York City. Roosevelt, as assistant secretary of the Navy, undoubtedly knew of Morgenthau, Sr.'s, activities, but it was with the son that he knitted a close relationship. Ultimately Morgenthau, Jr., became, according to Eleanor, "Franklin's conscience."[64] But that concerned general political matters, not the Jews.

In relation to Roosevelt, Henry Morgenthau, Jr., became a kind of admiring younger member of a social set. "They often differed and were annoyed with each other and probably said things neither of them meant on occasion," relates Eleanor Roosevelt, "but there was an underlying deep devotion and trust which never really wavered."[65] Roosevelt was as aware of Morgenthau's unflinching loyalty as he was of his migraine headaches. He was grateful that Morgenthau was "not a rival or a sycophant or a scold."[66] Yet Morgenthau learned that he could expect to have little of his devotion reciprocated. His earnestness, and a certain lack of the mental agility that Roosevelt possessed in good measure, made Morgenthau a natural foil for the president's penchant for good-natured bullying and merciless teasing. That peculiar relationship sometimes brought Morgenthau's latent insecurities regarding his qualifications for high office to the surface. There were others like Frankfurter to remind him of his unearned place. It was probably his dislike and fear of Frankfurter's influence that led to the dismissal of Acheson and Corcoran.[67]

Morgenthau's Jewishness held true to the "uptown" pattern noted in Rosenman and Proskauer. It was viewed primarily in denominational terms, had a philanthropic component, and typically had an implacable hostility to political Zionism. Roosevelt understood the tensions concerning Zionism within the Jewish community. He thought it hilarious when an anti-Semitic journal reported that Morgenthau had accepted the title "Leader in Zion." He took time out to inform Frankfurter that he and Eleanor "are telegraphing him . . . that we will not receive him unless he arrives with a long black beard. Incidentally also, he will be disowned by his old man."[68] It was Roosevelt's way of showing how much he knew of the inner workings of Jewish politics. But "Leader in Zion" had somehow gotten confused in his mind with Zionism or perhaps "Elders of Zion."

Roosevelt understood that the Morgenthaus were not sympathetic to Zionism, and since the Treasury secretary was also aware that the possibility of lifting the immigration barriers faced by the refugees was slim, the idea of resettlement elsewhere had a natural attraction. Jewish pioneering of a new nation in an unsettled part of the world, the way the Puritans had done in New England and the Mormons in Utah, required no commitment from the administration, circumvented the sticky Palestine problem, and yet allowed Roosevelt to maintain a principled position.[69] Morgenthau introduced Isaiah Bowman, the nation's best-known geographer and the president of Johns Hopkins University, to the president. Although Bowman could muster little confidence in pioneering resettlement in the twentieth century, the administration nevertheless enlisted his aid together with that of several other resettlement experts.[70] The president was particularly drawn to large-scale ventures that, by capturing the imagination of the world, might also attract financing, especially from the many wealthy Jews he knew of.[71] That was probably what was behind his request to Morgenthau to bring him a list of the thousand richest Jews in America. He would tell each how much he should contribute. Morgenthau brought Roosevelt down to earth by reminding him that "before you talk about money you have to have a plan."[72] Yet such visions of wealthy Jews waiting in the wings to invest their fortunes in the resettlement of their fellow Jews were after all not so far removed from those projected by Henry Ford's *Dearborn Independent* in the 1920s or, for that matter, from those images then popular in Germany.

Sometimes Morgenthau was the visionary and Roosevelt the practical man. When, as a substitute for free immigration to Palestine, the British government offered British Guiana for resettlement of refugees, Morgenthau welcomed the offer. It would be acceptable as partial payment of the outstanding British debt and thereby contribute to the solution of the vexing debt-reparations dispute that had complicated international monetary relations since the Treaty of Versailles. It would also help by contributing to a solution of the chaotic refugee problem caused by Berlin's extrusion policy. Roosevelt reminded his Treasury secretary that it "would take Jews five to fifty years to overcome the fever."[73]

It is difficult to see how from such indifferent beginnings Morgenthau would develop the interest and courage to take political risks in the cause of rescue. The change was apparent in Morgenthau's response to an offer by Romania to release seventy thousand Jews if outsiders would cover the expenses of moving them. Morgenthau granted a license for transferring $170,000 to the Joint Distribution Committee and overcame the foot-dragging of the State Department and the opposition of the British Foreign Office.[74] Soon thereafter he granted a license for $25,000 for the support of Jewish children in the Italian-occupied part of France. By the end of 1943 he had become fully involved in the rescue cause. When he received the now-famous "Report to the Secretary on the Acquiescence of This Government in the Murder of the Jews," he was ready to act. After deleting some details and changing the title to the less dramatic "A Personal Report to the President," he delivered it personally to Roosevelt on 16 January 1944. The report led directly to the establishment of the War Refugee Board (WRB), the apogee of the American effort to rescue European Jewry.[75] Yet even here no mention of the word Jew could be made. The term "political refugee" found in all American reports dealing with Jews was preferred by the president.

In some measure it was the rarely discussed Jewish question that triggered Morgenthau's split with the State Department and eventually with the Truman administration. It played a role in the secretary's conception of a "hard" policy for the treatment of postwar Germany. Morgenthau preferred to believe that it was his overriding concern for a peaceful world order that motivated the Morgenthau plan for the "pastoralization" of Germany. He did not think peace was possible as long as Germany was able to dominate Europe, and he recalled the strutting of German officers in Turkey during World War I when his father was ambassador to Turkey.[76] He found the very idea of anti-Semitism incredible. He was nonplussed when Father Charles Coughlin called silver a Gentile metal and condemned him for upholding the gold standard.[77]

But once aware of the unfairness and murderous intent of anti-Semitism, Morgenthau was more outspoken in using his position to fight openly against it. While Frankfurter patiently and almost apologetically explained to Lady

Astor why her latest canard concerning Jewish control of the press was inaccurate, Morgenthau confronted Breckinridge Long, an assistant secretary of state whose anti-Semitism had become well known, directly. He explained why he opposed the State Department's energetic policy of keeping Jewish refugees from landing on American shores. The United States had served as a refuge "starting with Plymouth," he explained to Long, "and as secretary of the Treasury of 135 million people I am carrying this out as secretary of the Treasury, not as a Jew."[78] It was a forthright position marred only by the fact that the secretary seemed uninformed that the notion of America acting as a haven for those in need had been largely undone by the restrictionist immigration laws of the 1920s, to which the administration was compelled to adhere.

As the news of the extent of the Nazi depredations began to filter out of occupied Europe, Morgenthau's anti-Nazi animus became more substantial. In May 1945, after Germany had surrendered, he confided to Georges Bidault, the French foreign minister, that the contemplated War Crimes Commission would take too long to do justice and that Justice Robert H. Jackson, the American representative for the trial of major Nazi war criminals, was too legalistic. Meanwhile, the SS and the Gestapo would go underground. "My motives," he explained, "are not revenge but one hundred years of peace in Europe.[79]

He had published a ringing defense for his "hard" policy for Germany, but already there were policymakers in Washington and London who were convinced that the locus of the postwar problem would not be Berlin but Moscow.[80] A "pastoralized" Germany could not serve as a bulwark against the Soviet Union, now conceived to be expansionist. Why was the secretary of the Treasury intruding into the realm of foreign policy, and was he not more interested in revenge than the national interest? Morgenthau seemed to confirm these fears by his emotional response when asked about the fate of millions of German workers in the Ruhr should his plan be implemented:

> Just strip it. I don't care what happens to the population. . . . I would take every mine, every mill and factory and wreck it . . . steel, coal, everything. Just close it down. . . . I am for destroying it first and we will worry about the population second. . . . But certainly if the area [the Ruhr] is stripped of its machinery, the mines flooded, dynamited—wrecked—it would make them impotent to wage future wars. . . . I am not going to budge an inch. . . . [S]ure it's a terrific problem. Let the Germans solve it. Why the hell should I worry about what happens to their people? . . . It seems a terrific task, it seems inhuman, it seems cruel. We didn't ask for this war, we didn't put millions through gas chambers, we didn't do any of these things. They have asked for it."[81]

Clearly the Holocaust had a profound impact on the secretary. He believed that some type of response was required. Morgenthau's conviction also suggests that one key to a stronger response within the Roosevelt administration was the activation of those power holders of Jewish background who, like Morgenthau, had found a place in Roosevelt's official family. The response of men like Frankfurter, Rosenman, Cohen, and others indicates that it was by no means an easy task. But the activation of Morgenthau suggests that it was not an impossible one.

Stephen Wise, who bears much of the calumny heaped on American Jewry for its ostensible failure to act energetically during the crisis, was a Jewish leader rather than a prominent government official who incidentally, and usually remotely, happened to be Jewish.[82] He seemed ideally suited to play such a role because he sat astride the vague consensus of American Jewry during the New Deal period. He was a Reform rabbi who nevertheless had broad support among the descendants of the Eastern Jewish immigrants.[83] He was a founder of the American Zionist movement, which by 1938 was clearly becoming the binding ideology of American Jewry. He was a leader of the reconstituted American Jewish Congress, which began by advocating democracy in Jewish life. In 1934 he helped found the World Jewish Congress, a Zionist-oriented umbrella organization whose goal was to bring some coherence on the Jewish presence in the international arena. Since 1900, when he assumed his first pulpit in Portland, Oregon, he had played a dual role by involving himself in secular as well as Jewish politics. He was one in a series of rabbis who gained sufficient stature to act as Jewish representative to the Gentile world. The key to that role may have been his remarkable ability as an orator. Before the days of radio, when an enthusiasm for scriptures prevailed, the turning of a neat biblical aphorism and a keen sense of political theater was sufficient to earn renown. By the time Roosevelt gained the presidency no Jewish leader was better located at the juncture where Jewish and national politics intersected. Yet Jewish politics in the 1930s was not sufficiently coherent to permit one spokesman to power. Stephen Wise, who might have become such a spokesman, never became "the pope of the Jews" Roosevelt sometimes might have desired the Jews to have.[84]

In the critical years between 1933 and 1936 Wise had no access to Roosevelt. These were the crucial years of the refugee phase when a more generous policy on their admission might have deferred temporarily or permanently the decision for a solution through mass murder.[85] Wise's outspoken liberalism was not easily harnessed to practical politics. Much of the political capital he had earned by supporting the Cox-Roosevelt ticket in the election of 1920 was dissipated by his later outspoken opposition to Jimmy Walker's corrupt administration in New York City. He had supported Al Smith's gubernatorial campaign in 1918 and again in 1926, and after the lost Presidential campaign of 1928 he lingered on in the Smith camp. In 1929 he supported Norman Thomas, the Socialist candidate, against Jimmy Walker for the New York City mayoralty. Rabbi Wise's daughter Justine joined him in denouncing the corruption and criminal ties of the Walker administration. For Roosevelt, who required Tammany support, it was all very embarrassing. The governor's hand would not be forced until the Seabury investigation in 1931, which led to Walker's resignation. In the meantime Wise was given an hour lecture on practical politics by Roosevelt. It confirmed Wise's impression that Roosevelt was superficial and untrustworthy.[86] He became unwelcome in the Roosevelt camp and remained so until the death of FDR's closest political adviser, Louis Howe. Only in 1936 did Frankfurter succeed in paving his way back into Roosevelt's good graces.[87] Encumbered by a heavy ideological cargo, Wise was far slower than Frankfurter in gauging the political wind. He was late in sensing that Roosevelt was being groomed for the presidency.

Yet once he realized what was afoot Wise made a complete about-face, one of several in his public life. Barely five years later he became completely entranced by Roosevelt, for whom he campaigned in 1936. The four years it took to get into striking position may have taught Wise a lesson about the Jewish relation to power. The president did not have to address the Jewish community through him. He could do so through anyone he chose. Later Wise would learn that, given the overwhelming enthusiasm for Roosevelt among Jewish voters, the president did not have to transact business with Jews at all. Roosevelt could keep Jewish loyalty through small gestures. Wise himself was especially pleased when Roosevelt employed a phrase in his second inaugural, "Nor will the American democracy ever hold any faithful and law-abiding group within its borders to be superfluous."[88]

Within his heavy reformist rhetoric Wise was not totally devoid of political acumen. He had, after all, built a career in the rough-and-tumble world of American Jewish politics. Yet there was little in his prior experience to teach him how to transmit to the Oval Office the urgent Jewish need for succor. He was more perceptive and far ahead of other Jewish leaders in recognizing the threat posed by Hitler. He had spoken out against the threat in the 1920s and shortly before Hitler came to power he had called for a meeting with the leaders of the American Jewish Committee and B'nai B'rith to plan a course of action should the National Socialists come to power. But it proved nigh impossible to transmit his sense of urgency to other Jewish leaders.[89]

Hitler's actual coming to power in January 1933 galvanized Wise into action. His American Jewish Congress helped organize a boycott against German goods. By 1934 it had become an international movement.[90] "A handful of us," he told an audience, "who have not wholly lost faith in the triumph of decency in the world have felt it our duty to unite in a boycott against Nazi goods and services, a boycott being a moral revolt against wrong, making use of economic instruments."[91] It was typical Wise rhetoric, highly charged with moral mission. But even at this early stage his oratory proved insufficient to unite the community behind such an effort. Even members of his own Congress were reluctant to use the boycott, and the American Jewish Committee was convinced that it furnished grist for anti-Semitism and a pretext for retaliation against Jewish businesses in Germany as well as America. Wise's speaking out, his refusal to be what he called a "sh . . . sh Jew," earned him no plaudits from the leaders of the "uptown" remnant that had remained in the Jewish fold. It was the first evidence that the so-called Jewish community would not be able to act communally in the face of the crisis. Jews showed more disapproval of Wise's activist tactics at times than of the State Department.[92] In April 1933 an old friend dismayed Wise by writing: "Dr. Wise will kill the Jews of Germany."[93] He was anathema not only in Nazi Germany, where Joseph Goebbels wrote disparagingly of him in his diary, and similarly to Breckinridge Long, who frantically opposed his every move, but also to many of his fellow Jewish leaders who similarly found him too radical and outspoken.[94] It is this fact that makes the emerging indictment of him for not having done enough so bitterly ironic.

Wise was no newcomer to the strife that characterized American Jewish political life. He may even have contributed his fair share to it. He had built alternate Jewish organizations, which some thought were monuments to his own ego and created disunity. He had been deeply involved in the strife within the American Zionist movement. He was 66 years old in 1940 and had had several nervous breakdowns, probably caused in part by an inability to rein in his many activities. In the 1930s he had taken on even more responsibilities. His minute books, written in a bold hand with green ink, show day after day crowded with speaking engagements and appointments in his two separate worlds. He was probably tired, yet he clung stubbornly to every position and fought attempts to relieve him of leadership responsibility.[95]

The Wise who faced the crisis in 1940 had spread his waning energies rather thinly and tried to give leadership to a deeply divided community while his access to Roosevelt was intermittent and rarely exclusive. He faced challenges from the Right. Both Rabbi Abba Hillel Silver and Peter Bergson (Hillel Kook) sensed that Wise had become so tuned in to the administration that he was reflecting its low priority to the refugee-rescue cause. In 1934 Wise had complained of that low priority, but now the headiness of the atmosphere in Washington, the excitement of watching the New Deal at work, and the imminence of war seemed to place the special danger faced by Jews in a larger perspective. The entire world seemed intent on plunging over an abyss. Not only the Jews were in danger. Wise found it difficult to speak exclusively of the plight faced by European Jewry in the face of such a dire emergency. Thus when Roosevelt and George Messersmith, an assistant secretary of state, impressed on him the need to tone down the fiery rhetoric emanating from his election to the World Jewish Congress, he complied. To be sure he did not check every move with the State Department, as did Morris Waldman, executive secretary of the American Jewish Committee, and Joseph Proskauer. But almost imperceptibly he caught Washington's priority on the Jewish question and, in face of the larger crisis of the war, withheld pushing his own with vigor. "I find a good part of my work," he explained to Frankfurter, "to explain to my fellow Jews why our government cannot do all the things asked or expected of it."[96] He had become an insider aware of the limitations of Jewish power and influence.

His lifelong penchant for universalism tended to conceal even from his own consciousness the special crucible of the Jews during the first years of the crisis. "The greatest crime against the Jewish victims of Hitler," he stated in 1940, "would be to treat the crimes against the Jews differently from the treatment of crimes against French, Czechs, or Poles or Greeks."[97] Even while he was aware of the anti-Jewish depredations there is no clue in his thinking that the fate the National Socialist regime had planned for the Jews would, in fact, be qualitatively different from that for any other people under its heel. There would be no historical precedent for this kind of mass murder. By 1942, when news of the Final Solution was confirmed, he had to change his mental set and face the difficult task of convincing Roosevelt, now himself involved as a leader in a war for survival whose outcome was by no means certain.

Full details of the fate of European Jewry were contained in the Riegner cable (which reported that the Germans had formulated the Final Solution). It confirmed Wise's worst fears, but he understood that the mood of the country and within the administration would dismiss the incredible story as atrocity mongering. World War I had witnessed a similar cadaver story that told of the German army processing dead corpses taken from the battlefield for soap and fertilizer. Moreover, revisionist historians had drawn a picture of a gullible American public opinion manipulated into entering World War I by skillful British atrocity mongering.[98] Wise gave the cable to Sumner Welles, undersecretary of state, for confirmation. There could be no fear of suppression of the story since a duplicate cable had been received by the agent of the World Jewish Congress in London. The three-month delay in confirmation by State has been one of the sources of the calumny heaped on Wise's leadership during the crisis, but the circumstances of how the news was received make his course of action seem reasonable in retrospect. More difficult to understand is Wise's despair at his inability to change the course of the administration's action, which was based on the notion that the safest way to save the Jews was to win the war as quickly as possible. He knew that the Jews of Europe would be in ashes at that point. "The truth is," he observed about his inability to break through to Roosevelt, "in the midst of war, it is very difficult to make anyone see that we [Jews] are most particularly hurt. These wounds are deeper and sorer than any other wounds inflicted."[99] Wise, who had spoken about the need for struggle for his entire adult life, somehow was overwhelmed by the news. It was a human reaction for, even from a contemporary vantage, the gulf between available Jewish power and what had to be done was awesome. In 1943 Wise lived with the knowledge that Hitler would be allowed to destroy the Jews and nothing would be done.

It made him despair but it did not radicalize him as it did Rabbi Silver, who almost single-handedly pushed through the Biltmore Program in May 1942 (which called for the reopening of Palestine to Jewish immigration, and the creation there of a Jewish commonwealth). For Wise there was no place else to go but to continue to support Roosevelt. His position was in some way similar to that of Weizmann in relation to Britain. He distrusted Weizmann, but by 1940 he saw the necessity of making peace with him and his faction in the Zionist movement. But no sooner had Weizmann been granted an honorary degree from Wise's Jewish Institute of Religion (JIR) when the much desired united front came apart. The plea made by Zionist leader Zev Jabotinsky at Manhattan Center in 1940 for a Jewish army could not be implemented in America, but what of a Jewish contingent? Wise believed that the mainline Zionists had allowed the revisionists to steal their thunder. He was in 1940 willing to follow a more conciliatory policy if the Bergson group would agree to adhere to the line laid down by the mainline organizations. But that was precisely what they believed they could not do. The bitter acrimony between the two groups, which broke out in the press, could not be resolved.[100] By 1943 the hope that there could be Jewish unity had vanished. The American Jewish Committee left the American Jewish Conference. Lessing Rosenwald established the American Council for Judaism, and on the other extreme the Biltmore Resolution had been passed. The gaps dividing American Jewry were too wide for one man to bridge.

The huge rallies at Madison Square Garden, beginning in 1933 and culminating in the massive rallies of July 1942 and March 1943, which gave Wise a platform to deliver the most stirring speeches of his life, were really examples of the political theatrics to which Wise was drawn. They gave more the illusion of unity than the reality. The rhetoric was stirring but the method had grown arcane. To stir the public one had to speak to millions, as Roosevelt did in his "fireside chats." Wise spoke only to thousands of concerned Jews who needed no reminder of what had to be done.[101]

The model here drawn indicates that the most effective representation of the Jewish interest depended ultimately on the activation of those nominal Jews who made up part of Roosevelt's entourage. That is what happened when Henry Morgenthau, Jr., was finally activated in the cause of rescue. But that neat model omits the enigmatic figure of Franklin Roosevelt, who is at the very heart of the problem. Ultimately, Jewish-rescue advocates had to involve the highest political office in the nation for an enlistment of the full energies and resources of the government. The president had to understand the meaning of the liquidation of European Jewry not in terms of the Jewish interest, but the American. Only an understanding of rescue that went beyond sympathy for Jews to link it to the national interest would have given the potential proddings of men like Frankfurter and Morgenthau some chance for success. We have seen that Roosevelt did well by his Jewish constituency, but that benevolence fell short of extending help to the Jews of Europe, who were not legally the responsibility of the United States. The answer that is gradually emerging regarding Roosevelt and the Jews is that as a result of the natural constraints of the office of the presidency which he could not overcome; the critical nature of his time in history, a time marked first by the Great Depression and then war; and his emotional disposition he was incapable of fully fathoming the meaning of the death camps and implementing a rescue policy.

Contemporary portraits describe Roosevelt as buoyant, a patrician type, exuding self-confidence.[102] It may not be a wholly accurate picture. He was not, much to his regret, Eleanor informs us, very popular at Reverend Peabody's Groton or at Harvard.[103] His mother seems to have been omnipresent, especially after the death of his father. He was considered a bright, but never a first-rate, student. He was a startlingly handsome, somewhat overprotected, almost effete young man. The family was not poor but hardly comparable to the "new" wealth of the Rockefellers or even the Seligmans. Yet somehow the inner confidence sometimes associated with a regulated and secure life, relatively free of adversity, transmitted itself not only to millions of radio listeners but to many of those who knew him personally. If Roosevelt was occasionally depressed, especially after his illness, he did not show it. He preferred to generate a spirit of "boisterous good humor."[104] For rescue advocates it may have been that cheeriness that made it seem inappropriate to bring up the question of the camps. There were those who detected behind the gaiety and good cheer a steadfast, if conventional, religious faith that sustained him during his crucible. He served as a trustee of St. James Church in Hyde Park throughout his adult life. The youthful superficiality that some have noted as late as his appointment as assistant secretary of the Navy, in 1913, was ostensibly dissipated by the attack of polio in August 1921. The illness and handicap supposedly added a new dimension to the future president's character, greater depth and compassion and contact with a strata of the population, the handicapped, that he would not ordinarily have had.[105] Yet the deepening of character was not observed by Alice Roosevelt Longworth, who dismissed the notion as an "absurd idea." "He was what he always would be!" Longworth observed, "He took polio in his stride."[106]

If anyone was "deepened" by the illness, it was Eleanor, who returned to a marriage that had all but failed and patiently nursed her husband, keeping from him the pessimistic prognosis that he would never really walk again without some outside aid.[107] The other was Louis Howe, his longtime political manager, who throughout the worst stages of the illness maintained a skillful selected correspondence to generate the image that Roosevelt remained a viable potential political leader.[108]

Indeed, Roosevelt maintained that confidence, a seeming personal "freedom from fear," throughout his adult life. "The same self-assurance," one historian observes, "insulated Roosevelt from intimate involvement with people. . . . He loved the adoration and attention of people, even when elementary privacy was violated. With consummate art, he played for his audience and won their plaudits. Some grew to love him and projected onto him their hopes and joys and deepest longings. They invested so much in the relationship, he invested so little and invested so broadly."[109] It was an observation meant to apply to his personal relationships, but in a peculiar way it holds even more true for the relationship with American Jewry, which by 1936 had all of the earmarks of unrequited love.

Roosevelt never really distinguished between what was happening in the death camps, about which he was fully informed, and the dozens of other problems of the war that pressed in on him. The Final Solution became a not too important atrocity problem of the war. "Insulated from fear, Roosevelt was also free of doubt," observes Paul Conkin. "It gave his mind and spirit the cast of broadness but never depth. There was little capacity for sustained thought, no ability to make careful distinctions, or to perceive crucial issues."[110] Often pictured as a bright, quick study, Roosevelt was almost totally unencumbered and unenriched by conceptual thought. The larger meaning of Auschwitz thus totally eluded him. He was attuned to people rather than ideas, to the operational rather than the ideological, to the concrete rather than the abstract, and to the political rather than the personal. He felt certain of his ability to achieve his ends by a certain mode of behavior, by charm and manipulation. Perhaps that posture had been developed at Harvard, where he felt a desperate need to be popular especially after invitations to the clubs of his choice eluded him.[111] He tended to mute or join otherwise obfuscatory issues that did not directly enhance his popularity or were simply distasteful or entailed a price.[112]

How that manipulation worked in practice is illustrated by the experience of a Jewish delegation that visited him on 8 December 1942, after the news of the systematic mass murder of the Jews had been confirmed by the administration. The delegation wanted not only some form of intercession, a warning to Berlin regarding the atrocities, but also reassurance of concern. But little occurred at the meeting; Roosevelt overwhelmed them with his banter. According to the diary of one of the participants, "the entire conversation lasted only a minute or two. As a matter of fact of the twenty-nine minutes spent with the President, he addressed the delegation for twenty-three minutes." No one dared interrupt the president to get to the business at hand. There was barely sufficient time to present their plan of action. At the final moment they were given authority to quote from the administration's earlier statement on war crimes.[113] Roosevelt could not be put on the spot with a direct demand. He skillfully used his office and high position to shield himself from such unpleasant confrontations.

There is a sense of a historical disjuncture, for what may today be developing into a major issue was, during the Roosevelt era, a minor one. The refugee crisis of the 1930s became eventually a minor aspect of the "great debate" between isolationists and interventionists. Its disposition was partly decided on the basis of national security. The notion that Berlin was using the refugee stream to filter spies into the country had become a veritable security psychosis. On the level of administrating the immigration law it became increasingly difficult to gain access to the American haven. The later rescue issue was similarly subsumed beneath the larger issue of winning the war quickly. To say that rescue had a low priority is to misstate the case. It had no independent priority at all.[114] Until 1944 it was simply not considered. The creation of the War Refugee Board (WRB) in January 1944 is remarkable because it gave the notion of rescue an independent priority and an independent agency to administer it. But one should note that the turnabout in policy that the establishment of the WRB signified occurred only when it was fairly certain that the major priority, winning the war, was on its way to being achieved. Three months later it also became possible to conceive of a plan to circumvent the immigration law by offering a handful of refugees a temporary haven at Fort Ontario in Oswego, New York.[115] Two years before, the immigration laws were still considered immutable.

The idea that Jews could be kept in line and politically loyal by gestures should be attributable not only to Roosevelt's talents as a manipulator. Such statements of concern had been used to placate Jewish leaders since the Damascus Blood Libel (1840).[116] On the administration's part the motivation in making them was expressed by Pierepont Moffat, an assistant secretary of state, who was concerned with how the administration should react after the unexpected mounting outcry triggered by Kristallnacht, the "night of the broken glass," 9-10 November 1938: "The difficulty was to find ways and means of making a gesture that would not either inherently hurt us or provoke counter retaliation that would hurt us."[117] The gesture settled upon was to bring Ambassador Hugh Wilson home "for consultation."

Any assessment of Roosevelt's relationship to American Jewry should note that we are dealing with a 17-year period of continuous evolvement in Roosevelt and American Jewry. The Roosevelt of the first "Hundred Days" was, in terms of political power and aura, different from the Roosevelt of the second New Deal, with its renewed Depression and politically disastrous scheme to "pack" the Supreme Court. The Roosevelt of the war years, preoccupied and in failing health, departed considerably from both. The Jewish need became urgent at the least-opportune moment to press a special case. The renewed Depression in 1937, during which unemployment again reached 11 million, profits fell by 82 percent, and industrial production declined to the 1929 level, was a vote of "no confidence" on the countercyclical measures the New Deal had implemented to fight the Depression.[118] It was at this juncture that Roosevelt seems to have lost his political touch and ventured into the ill-starred court-packing scheme. That debacle placed a new stress on the political coalition that buttressed his administration. It demonstrated Roosevelt's fallibility. Meanwhile, events in Europe and the Far East suggested that the time for domestic reform would soon draw to a close.

American Jewry turned to Roosevelt for succor when his aura as a leader and his personal power base had been somewhat diminished and when the priorities created by the war in Europe left little space for the special needs of the Jews. Moreover, it was a request for action that entailed considerable political risks requested by an unpopular minority, one whose support was in any case assured.[119] The notion that more might have been achieved had Jewish leaders had better access to the Oval Office and had a concerned public outcry developed, both unlikely to happen, is based on an oversimplified model of how the agendas of minorities are translated into public policy.[120] We have noted here that even the extra advantage of a conduit to Roosevelt furnished by prominent Jews in his entourage was uncertain and ultimately inadequate for the task at hand. There was the fact that, by emotional disposition, Roosevelt's currency was people and politics, not pain.

Given these conditions, the nature of the times, and one circumstance barely touched upon—the virulent anti-Semitism of the 1930s—the notion that Roosevelt could muster a sustained interest in an unpleasant and remote problem for which he was not responsible—the rescue of the Jews—is a highly dubious one. He was unwilling and probably incapable of engineering the necessary rearrangement of wartime priorities required to rescue European Jewry. For rescue advocates the bitterest pill may not even have been Roosevelt's inurement but the realization that the contenders for his high office, Wendell Wilkie in 1940 and Thomas Dewey in 1944, held out even less hope for action.

In one sense the developing indictment of American Jewry's posture during the Holocaust is a manifestation of a habit deeply embedded in Jewish political culture. Traditionally, history combined with a strong sense of kinship assigned an awesome responsibility to American Jewry. It was compelled to request things from the political process that virtually preordained failure. That process, designed originally to govern as minimally as possible, resisted the mission Jews would assign it. American Jewish leaders were hard pressed to wring any action from an administration preoccupied first with the Depression and then with the war. They never possessed sufficient political power to adequately discharge the responsibility American Jewry had assumed as a matter of course since the colonial period, the support of their brethren abroad. In retrospect, most of the painful "might have beens"—if American Jews had been more unified, if they could have gotten the story believed and mobilized public opinion, if they could have raised their own army, if the camps could have been bombed—vanish back into the unreality from which they came. Often they are merely forms of self-flagellation by a people torn by such heavy losses. But a nagging doubt remains about one such possibility: mobilizing the new Jewish secular elite, whose leaders had found position in Roosevelt's entourage, for rescue. This chapter has probed that possibility and discovered that it was a real one. That is the meaning of the activation of Henry Morgenthau, Jr., in 1943.[121] Yet for the most part the members of the new elite gained personal power and influence that they did not use for the enhancement of Jewish corporate power. The very process of secularization that triggered their rise prevented them from recognizing and acting upon a matter of specific Jewish interest. Something had changed since the 1920s, when men like Jewish philanthropists Jacob Schiff and Louis Marshall were the intermediaries between Jewry and power holders. By the Roosevelt period a group-leadership function formally exercised by a single cohort had become bifurcated. It now required that leaders such as Rabbi Stephen Wise, whose influence stemmed directly from his position in the Jewish community, act through men such as Frankfurter, Rosenman, Morgenthau, and others, who were power holders who only incidentally happened to be Jewish. It was the failure to mobilize this new group that may in retrospect mark the most conspicuous failure of American Jewry during the Holocaust.[122]

Notes

1. 13 January 1944, 11:35 A.M., H. Morgenthau, Jr., Diaries, Book 693, 205-208. Franklin D. Roosevelt Library (FDRL), Hyde Park, N.Y.
2. Lawrence H. Fuchs, *The Political Behavior of American Jews* (Glencoe: Free Press, 1958), 99-107, 177-187.
3. That percentage (3.69) is taken from the government census of religious bodies conducted during 1936-1937. It counted 4,641,000 Jews concentrated in the larger cities of the eastern seaboard. See H. S. Linfield, "Jewish Communities in the United States," *American Jewish Yearbook (AJYB)* 42 (1940), 216, 220.
4. For Jewish political activism see Alfred O. Hero Jr., *American Religious Groups View Foreign Policy: Trends in Rank and File Opinion, 1937-1969* (Durham: Duke University Press, 1973), 21, 39. See also Stephen Isaacs, *Jews and American Politics* (Garden City: Doubleday, 1974); and Charles Kadushin, *The American Intellectual Elite*, (Boston: Little, Brown, 1968), 319-320.
5. Fuchs, *Political Behavior*, 151-169; Albert J. Menendez, *Religion at the Polls* (Philadelphia: Westminster Press, 1977), 24-35, 115, 221-223 (tables 16-19).
6. Deborah D. Moore, *At Home in America: Second Generation New York Jews* (New York: Columbia University Press, 1981), 210-211. Raymond E. Wolfinger, "The Development and Persistence of Ethnic Voting," *American Political Science Review* 59 (December 1965), 896-897.
7. Samuel Lubell, *The Future of American Politics* (New York: Doubleday, 1956), 36-37; Fuchs, *Political Behavior*, 66.
8. James M. Burns: *Roosevelt: The Lion and the Fox* (New York: Harcourt, Brace & Co., 1956), 104; Mark R. Levy and Michael S. Kramer, *The Ethnic Factor: How American Minorities Decide Elections* (New York: Simon and Schuster, 1972), 103. The eleventh was a Socialist.
9. Cyrus Adler and Aaron Margalith, *With Firmness in the Right: American Diplomatic Action affecting Jews, 1840-1945* (New York: Arno Press, 1977); Egal Feldman, *The Dreyfus Affair and the American Conscience, 1845-1906* (Detroit: Wayne State University Press, 1981); Naomi Cohen, *Not Free to Desist: The American Jewish Committee, 1906-1966* (Philadelphia: Jewish Publishing Society of America, 1972); Louis L. Gerson, *The Hyphenate in Recent American Politics and Diplomacy* (Law-

rence: University of Kansas, 1964); Henry L. Feingold, "American Power and Jewish Interest in Foreign Affairs," in *A Midrash on American Jewish History* (Albany: SUNY Press, 1982); Gary D. Best, *American Jewish Leaders and the Jewish Problem in Eastern Europe, 1890-1914* (New York: Greenwood Press, 1982). Best generally overestimates the role of Jewish power holders.

10. The phrase is used first in Feingold's *The Politics of Rescue: The Roosevelt Administration and the Holocaust, 1938-1945* (New Brunswick: Rutgers University Press, 1980), 22-44. Similarly, Senator Tydings of Maryland introduced on 8 January 1934 a resolution calling for the Senate and the president to express "surprise and pain" at German treatment of Jews and to urge the German government to restore Jews' civil rights. See *Congressional Record*, 73rd Cong., 2nd sess., 68, pt. 1, 176. The State Department opposed the resolution, and it was never reported out of the Senate Foreign Relations Committee. For a full examination of executive manipulation of private pressure groups, see Robert C. Hildebrand, *Power and People: Executive Management of Public Opinion in Foreign Affairs, 1897-1921* (Chapel Hill: University of North Carolina Press, 1981).

11. Hero, *American Religious Groups*, see polls of the American Institute of Public Opinion (AIPO), 26, 145-146, 279-284. They were, however, clearly the strongest constituency to favor welfare-state measures, 144, 466.

12. Fuchs, *Political Behavior*, 171-177.

13. Hero, *American Religious Groups*, 279-284. The majority that favored the Spanish Loyalists was a narrow one. After the fall of France in June 1940, 32 percent of the Jews questioned thought it was more important to stay out of the war than to help Britain. (AIPO, 30 September 1940, 283). After the initial defeat of the Soviet army, 46 percent of Jews questioned disapproved convoying ships to Britain (AIPO, 9 September 1941, 284).

14. See David Brody, "American Jewry, the Refugees, and Immigration Restriction, 1932-1942," *Publication of the American Jewish Historical Society (PAJHS)* 45 (June 1956), 219-247.

15. Hero, *American Religious Groups*, 26, 279-284.

16. Moore, *At Home*, 23.

17. Menendez, *Religion at the Polls*, 215; Werner Cohn, "The Politics of American Jews," in *The Jews: Social Patterns of an American Group*, ed. Marshall Sklare (New York: Free Press, 1958), 614-626; Lawrence Fuchs, "American Jews and the Presidential Vote," *American Political Science Review* 49 (June 1955), 385-401; Burns, *The Lion and the Fox*, 104.

18. Hero, *American Religious Groups*, 202.

19. Burns, *The Lion and the Fox*, 453-455.

20. Quoted in Jerold S. Auerbach, *Unequal Justice: Lawyers and Social Change in Modern America* (New York: Oxford University Press, 1976), 188. Under

Harding, Coolidge, and Hoover, for example, only 8 of the 207 federal judges appointed were Jewish. The figure rose considerably under Roosevelt and even more under Truman, but Catholics, not Jews, received the lion's share of federal judicial appointments. See Lubell, *Future,* 83-84.

21. Michael F. Parrish, *Felix Frankfurter and His Time: The Reform Years* (New York: Free Press, 1982), 229 ("the New Deal was a 'lawyers deal'"); Auerbach, *Unequal Justice,* 159, 184-189. See also John W. Johnson, *American Legal Culture, 1908-1940* (Westport: Greenwood Press, 1981), xi, 185, for the triumph of the socially conscious Brandeis-style brief; also Peter H. Irons, *New Deal Lawyers* (Princeton: Princeton University Press, 1982).

22. Daniel J. Kevles, *The Physicists: The History of Scientific Community in Modern America* (New York: Random House, 1979), 212-221, 278-279, 288; Donald Fleming and Bernard Baylin, eds., *The Intellectual Migration: Europe and America, 1930-1960* (Cambridge: Harvard University Press, 1969); Laura Fermi, *Illustrious Immigrants: The Intellectual Migration from Europe, 1930-1941* (Chicago: University of Chicago Press, 1968); Stephen Duggan and Betty Drury, *The Rescue of Science and Learning: The Story of the Emergency Committee in Aid of Displaced Foreign Scholars* (New York: Macmillan, 1948); Abraham Flexner, *I Remember* (New York: Simon and Schuster, 1940).

23. Henry DeWolf Smyth, *Atomic Energy for Peaceful Purposes* (Princeton: Princeton University Press, 1976).

24. Roy Lubove, *The Professional Altruist: The Emergence of Social Work as a Career* (Cambridge: Harvard University Press, 1969); Jacob Fisher, *The Response of Social Work to the Depression* (Boston: G. K. Hall & Co., 1980).

25. They are best described in Irving Howe's *Decline of the New Deal* (New York: Harcourt, 1970) and *World of Our Fathers* (New York: Harcourt, 1976), 598-603; Lewis S. Feuer, "The Stages in the Social History of Jewish Professors in American Colleges and Universities," *American Jewish History* 71 (June 1982); Seymour M. Lipset and Everett C. Ladd, Jr., "Jewish Academics in the United States: Their Achievement, Culture, and Politics," *AJYB* 72 (1971), 89-128; Seymour M. Lipset and Richard B. Dobson, "The Intellectual as Critic and Rebel with Special Reference to the United States and the Soviet Union," *Daedalus* 101 (summer 1972), 137-198; Stephen Steinberg, *The Academic Melting Pot: Catholics and Jews in American Higher Education* (New York: McGraw, 1974); Charles Kadushin, *The American Intellectual Elite* (Boston: Little Brown, 1968); Stephen J. Whitfield, "The Imagination of Disaster: The Response of American Jewish Intellectuals to Totalitarianism," *Jewish Social Studies* 42 (winter 1980), 1-20.

26. Charles H. Stember et al., *Jews in the Mind of America* (New York: Basic Books, 1966), 149.

27. *Congressional Record,* 76th Cong., 1st sess., 85, 1457-1458, 2338-2341; David
    Wyman, *Paper Walls: America and the Refugee Crisis, 1938-1941* (Amherst:
    University of Massachusets, 1968), 78, 96-97, 244; Feingold, *Politics of Rescue,*
    149-153.

28. With the exception of two major components of the Jewish Labor Committee,
    the International Ladies Garment Workers Union (ILGWU) and the Amalga-
    mated Clothing Workers of America (ACWA), Jewish agencies preferred to let
    sectarian agencies take the lead. See *New York Times,* 10 November 1939; the
    rank and file donated a day's pay to the refugee cause, and the bill itself was
    endorsed by the Executive Council of the American Federation of Labor (AF of
    L) and the Congress of Industrial Organization (CIO), *New York Times,* 9
    February 1939.

29. Samuel Rosenman, *Working with Roosevelt* (New York: Harper & Row, 1952);
    Samuel B. Hand, *Counsel and Advise: A Political Biography of Samuel I. Rosenman*
    (New York: Garland, 1979); see also oral history interviews, Wiener Library
    (N.Y.C.), American Jewish Committee.

30. Cohen, *Not Free,* 198.

31. Although Rosenman eventually contributed to the establishment of the War
    Refugee Board he continued to be reluctant to broach the refugee and rescue
    issue to Roosevelt directly. See transcription of telephone conversation, Mor-
    genthau and Rosenman, 13 January 1944, 11:35 A.M., H. Morgenthau, Jr.,
    Diaries, Book 693, FDRL; Henry Morgenthau, Jr., "The Refugee Run Around,"
    Colliers, 1 November 1947, 65. See also FDRL/President's Personal File (PPF)
    4, Rosenman memorandum to FDR, 5 December 1938, on his pessimism
    regarding mass resettlement of Jews in Latin America and elsewhere; FDRL/Of-
    ficial File (OF) 318, Rosenman to Myron Taylor, 23 November 1938, on his
    opposition to the relaxation of the quota system. See also Feingold, *Politics of
    Rescue,* 102-103.

32. Joseph Proskauer, *A Segment of My Time* (New York: Straus, 1950), 12-13; Louis
    M. Hacker and Mark D. Hirsch, *Joseph M. Proskauer: His Life and Time* (Mobile:
    University of Alabama Press, 1978).

33. Jerold S. Auerbach, "Joseph M. Proskauer: American Court Jew," *American
    Jewish History* 69 (September 1979), 103-114, 115.

34. Ibid.

35. Parrish, *Frankfurter,* 129-149; Bruce A. Murphy, *The Brandeis-Frankfurter
    Connection: The Secret Political Activities of the Two Supreme Court Justices* (New
    York: Oxford University Press, 1982); H. N. Hirsch, *The Enigma of Felix
    Frankfurter* (New York: Basic Books, 1981); Joseph P. Lash, ed., *From the Diaries
    of Felix Frankfurter* (New York: Norton, 1975); Harlan B. Phillips, ed., *Felix
    Frankfurter Reminiscences* (New York: Secker and Warburg, 1960).

36. Parrish, *Frankfurter*, 132.

37. J. L. Magnes to Brandeis, 25 July 1916, in Arthur A. Goren, ed., *Dissenter in Zion: From the Writings of Judah L. Magnes* (Cambridge: Harvard University Press, 1982), 22, 154-155, document no. 24. See also Yonatan Shapiro, *Leadership of the American Zionist Organization, 1887-1930* (Urbana: University of Illinois Press, 1971), 94-96; Parrish, *Frankfurter*, 131-132, 242. In 1938 Hugh Johnson again brought up the impropriety charge against Brandeis. Frankfurter insisted upon and received a written apology. Max Freedman, ed., *Roosevelt and Frankfurter: Their Correspondence, 1928-1945* (Boston: Little, 1967), 482.

38. Rosenman, *Working with Roosevelt*, 173.

39. Freedman, *Roosevelt and Frankfurter*, 310.

40. Ibid., 303; Parrish, *Frankfurter*, 220-221. See Lash, *Diaries of Felix Frankfurter*, 64, for Sulzberger's opposition to court appointment.

41. Parrish, *Frankfurter*, 20. The comparison made is with Roger Taney and Andrew Jackson, Will Herndon and Abraham Lincoln, and Woodrow Wilson and Colonel House. The difference is that Frankfurter never had, nor was given by Roosevelt, that sense of exclusivity and mutual trust.

42. Raymond Moley, *After Seven Years* (New York: Harper & Row, 1939); Parrish, *Frankfurter*, 204-205, 218; on the workings of the "brain trust," see Eliot A. Rosen Hoover, *Roosevelt and the Brain Trust* (New York: Columbia University Press, 1977).

43. Parrish, *Frankfurter*, 206; James E. Sargent, *Roosevelt and the Hundred Days: Struggle for the Early New Deal* (New York: Garland, 1981).

44. Freedman, *Roosevelt and Frankfurter*, 474-475. A didactic response, detached and civil, was written to Lady Nancy Astor, who accused Jews of controlling American advertising. (Frankfurter to Astor, 2 June 1938.)

45. Frankfurter to Roosevelt, 6 June 1942, in Freedman, *Roosevelt and Frankfurter*, 451, 611.

46. Ibid.

47. Freedman, *Roosevelt and Frankfurter*, 661.

48. Tully to Frankfurter, 17 July 1942, Ibid., 667.

49. Frankfurter to Roosevelt, 17 October 1933, Ibid., 164.

50. Max J. Kohler, *The United States and German-Jewish Persecution: Precedents for Popular and Government Action;* and *The Jews in Nazi Germany: The Factual Record of Their Persecution by the National Socialists.* Both reports prepared for the American Jewish Committee. See Frankfurter cable to Roosevelt, 20 February 1934, regarding Nazi depredations in Austria, in Freedman, *Roosevelt and Frankfurter*, 194.

51. Roosevelt to Frankfurter, 31 October 1942, in Freedman, *Roosevelt and Frankfurter*, 678.

84   HENRY L. FEINGOLD

52. Between 1916 and 1938 Brandeis gave Frankfurter ca. $50,000 to cover incidental expenses. Murphy, *Brandeis-Frankfurter,* Parrish, *Frankfurter,* 6, 224, 248. On the differences in economic approach to the New Deal, see Nelson L. Dawson, *Louis D. Brandeis, Felix Frankfurter, and the New Deal* (Hamden: Shoe String Press, 1980).

53. Parrish, *Frankfurter,* 210; Paul A. Freund, "Justice Brandeis: A Law Clerk's Remembrance," *American Jewish History* 68 (September 1978), 716-717; Frankfurter to Roosevelt, 21 November 1928, and Roosevelt to Frankfurter, 11 June 1934, in Freedman, *Roosevelt and Frankfurter,* 25, 39, 222. It was Frankfurter who was instrumental in bringing Roosevelt and Brandeis together in 1928 and convincing Roosevelt that "old Isaiah" was a "great soul."

54. Parrish, *Frankfurter,* 267-274.

55. Phillips, *Felix Frankfurter Reminiscences,* 145 ff.

56. Parrish, *Frankfurter,* 142, 224, 248.

57. Ibid., 142. Of Morgenthau, Sr., Frankfurter observed, "Take base metal, stamp on it the seal of government, call it an ambassador and you can never drive it out of circulation."

58. Ibid., 131-132.

59. Ibid., 242. The plight of Jewish refugee children in France and the Low Countries, which was the background of the Wagner-Rogers Bill, apparently did not greatly move the Frankfurters. They did adopt two British children in 1940 who found refuge from the blitz in America.

60. James Farley, *Jim Farley's Story: The Roosevelt Years* (New York: Whittlesey, 1948), 161-162; Parrish, *Frankfurter,* 275.

61. Brandeis did directly intrude himself on the refugee crisis and the Zionist issue in a meeting with secretary of state Cordell Hull. (See Freund, "Brandeis", 716-17). But there was in most members of the Brandeis group a curiously thin, almost part-time quality to their new-found Jewishness and their investment in Zionist activities. See Ben Halpern, "The Americanization of Zionism," *American Jewish History* 69 (September 1979), 32-33. See also Thomas Karfunkel and Thomas W. Ryley, *The Jewish Seat: Anti-Semitism and the Appointment of Jews to the Supreme Court* (Hicksville: Exposition Press, 1978), 87-97.

62. Jan Karski, "Reaction of Frankfurter, Wise, and Goldmann to First Reports of Warsaw Ghetto Uprising and Belzen Death Camp," in "The Impact of the Holocaust on Judaism in America" (colloquium, American University, Washington, D.C., 23 March 1980), 34 (unpublished).

63. John M. Blum, *Roosevelt and Morgenthau: A Revision and Condensation of From the Morgenthau Diaries* (Boston: Houghton Mifflin, 1970), 520.

64. Ibid., xvi.

65. Ibid.

66. Ibid., 25.

67. Ibid., 257-258.
68. Roosevelt to Frankfurter, 31 October 1942, in Freedman, *Roosevelt and Frankfurter*, 678.
69. Henry L. Feingold, "Roosevelt and the Resettlement Question," in *Rescue Attempts during the Holocaust: Proceedings of the Second Yad Vashem International Historical Conference.* Jerusalem, April 11, 1974. Ed. Yisrael Gutman and Efraim Zuroff (New York: Ktav, 1978). 123-181.
70. See Isaiah Bowman, *Limits of Land Settlement: A Report on Present-Day Possibilities* (New York: Council on Foreign Relations, 1937); Blum, *Morgenthau*, 519.
71. Feingold, *Politics of Rescue*, 91, 113-117.
72. Blum, *Morgenthau*, 519.
73. Ibid.
74. Ibid., 522-524; Feingold, *Politics of Rescue*, 182-183, 239-240; Yehuda Bauer, *American Jewry and the Holocaust: The American Jewish Joint Distribution Committee, 1939-1945* (Detroit: Wayne State University Press, 1981), 346-347. The offer was not authentic.
75. Feingold, *Politics of Rescue*, 239-244.
76. Cordell Hull, *The Memoirs of Cordell Hull*, vol. 2 (New York: Macmillan, 1948), 471.
77. *New York Times*, 9 April 1934. See also Blum, *Morgenthau*, 92.
78. Blum, *Morgenthau*, 529.
79. Ibid., 639.
80. Henry Morgenthau, Jr., *Germany Is Our Problem* (New York: Harper, 1945).
81. Blum, *Morgenthau*, 582-583.
82. See Saul S. Friedman, *No Haven for the Oppressed: United States Policy toward Jewish Refugees, 1938-1945* (Detroit: Wayne State University Press, 1973); and Yitshaq Ben Ami, *Years of Wrath, Days of Glory: Memoirs from the Irgun* (New York: Speller and Sons, 1982).
83. The best sources for details of Wise's public life are his autobiography, *Challenging Years: The Autobiography of Stephen Wise* (New York: Putnam, 1949); Melvin L. Urofsky, *A Voice That Spoke for Justice: The Life and Times of Stephen S. Wise* (Albany: SUNY Press, 1982); Carl Hermann Voss, *Rabbi and Minister: The Friendship of Stephen S. Wise and John Haynes Holmes* (Cleveland: World Publishers, 1964).
84. Selig Adler, "Franklin D. Roosevelt and Zionism: The Wartime Record," *Judaism* 21, (summer 1972), 265-276.
85. That has been suggested by several researchers, including Karl A. Schleunes, *The Twisted Road to Auschwitz: Nazi Policy Toward German Jews, 1933-1939* (Urbana: University of Illinois Press, 1970) 2, 169-213, 255-262.
86. Urofsky, *Wise*, 240, 247.

87. Ibid., 256.
88. Ibid., 258.
89. Ibid., 260, 263, 264. See also Cohen, *Not Free,* 159.
90. Moshe Gottlieb, "In the Shadow of War: The American Anti-Nazi Boycott Movement in 1939-1941," *American Jewish Historical Quarterly* 62 (December 1972), 146-161.
91. Stephen S. Wise, *As I See It,* (New York: Jewish Opinion Publishing Corporation, 1944), 101.
92. Joint Statement by the American Jewish Committee and B'nai B'rith, April 1933, in American Jewish Committee, *27th Annual Report* 42.
93. Wise to Rabbi Rosenau, 10, 19 April 1933, quoted in Carl H. Voss, "Let Stephen Wise Speak for Himself," *Dimensions in American Judaism* 3 (fall 1968), 37.
94. Fred L. Israel, ed., *The War Diary of Breckinridge Long* (Lincoln: Burns and MacEachery, 1966), 4 September 1941, 216-217; 17 April 1943, 332.
95. See Doreen Bierbrier, "The American Zionist Emergency Council: An Analysis of a Pressure Group," *American Jewish Historical Quarterly* 60 (September 1970), 84-85.
96. Voss, *Rabbi,* 39; Friedman, *No Haven,* 145.
97. Wise, *As I See It,* 123-124.
98. Shimon Rubinstein, "Did the Germans Set up Corpse Utilization Establishments during World War I?" (Jerusalem: 1977); Walter Laqueur, *The Terrible Secret: Suppression of the Truth about Hitler's Final Solution* (Boston: Weidfield and Nicholson, 1980), 8-9; H. C. Peterson, *Propaganda for War: The Campaign against American Neutrality, 1914-1917* (Norman: University of Oklahoma Press, 1939).
99. Urofsky, *Wise,* 327.
100. Feingold, *Politics of Rescue,* 237-239; Aaron Berman, "American Zionism and the Rescue of European Jewry: An Ideological Perspective," *American Jewish History* 70 (March 1981), 310-330; Monty N. Penkower, "In Dramatic Dissent: The Bergson Boys," *American Jewish History,* 70 (March 1981), 281-309.
101. Henry L. Feingold, "Stephen Wise and the Holocaust," *Midstream* 29 (January 1983), 45-48. A similar analysis is also given by Louis Lipsky, *Memoirs in Profile* (Philadelphia: Jewish Publication Society of America, 1975), 192-200.
102. For recent examples, see James A. Farley, "FDR the Man," in David E. Kyvig, ed., *FDR's America* (Arlington Heights, IL: Forum Press II, 1976), 23; Joseph Alsop, "Roosevelt Remembered," *Smithsonian* 12 (January 1982), 39-48.
103. Joseph P. Lash, *Eleanor and Franklin* (New York: New American Library, 1973), 150-157; Burns, *The Lion and the Fox,* 10-11.
104. Farley, "FDR the Man," 23.
105. That is the view propounded by a rehabilitation psychologist, Richard T. Goldberg, *The Making of Franklin D. Roosevelt: Triumph over Disability* (Cambridge: Abt, 1982).

106. Ibid., 1, 36. Goldberg also presents some evidence of a well-developed sense of entitlement that prevented Roosevelt, during the rehabilitation process, from accepting the full reality of his illness and his subsequent handicap.
107. Lash, *Eleanor and Franklin*, 359-373; Goldberg, *Roosevelt*, 39.
108. Goldberg, *Roosevelt*, 35.
109. Paul K. Conkin, *The New Deal* (New York: Crowell, 1967), 5.
110. *Ibid.*, 6-7, 11.
111. Alsop, "Roosevelt Remembered," 39-48. See also interview with Thomas Beale, a classmate at Harvard. Quoted by Goldberg, *Roosevelt*, 12.
112. Conkin, *The New Deal*, 10-11, 14-15.
113. Eliyho Matzozky, "An Episode: Roosevelt and the Mass Killing," *Midstream* 26 (August-September 1980), 17-19.
114. Henry L. Feingold, "The Importance of Wartime Priorities in the Failure to Rescue Jews," in Alex Grobman and Daniel Landes, eds., *Critical Issues of the Holocaust* (Los Angeles: Simon Wiesenthal Center, 1983), 300-307.
115. Sharon Lowenstein, "A New Deal for Refugees: The Promise and Reality of Oswego," *American Jewish History* 71 (March 1982), 325-341.
116. See note 8 above.
117. Journal entry, 14 November 1938, in Nancy H. Hooker, ed., *The Moffat Papers, 1919-1943*, (Cambridge: Harvard University Press, 1956), 221-222.
118. Conkin, *The New Deal*, 96.
119. Stember et al., *Mind of America*, 88-135.
120. The contention that greater public pressure would have gotten the Roosevelt administration to act earlier and "far more decisively" is made by Professor David Wyman, "American Jews and the Holocaust," *New York Times Magazine* 8 May 1982, 94.
121. How far Morgenthau had developed in contrast to Rosenman is illustrated by Rosenman's resistance to being involved before Morgenthau delivered the "Acquiescence" report to the president. Rosenman demurred first on the ground of timing, then on the fear that three prominent Jews were involved (Morgenthau, Ben Cohen, and himself), and finally that leaks would cause unwelcome publicity. "Don't worry about the publicity," replied Morgenthau. "What I want is intelligence and courage—courage first and intelligence second." Transcription of telephone conversation, Morgenthau and Rosenman, 13 January 1944, 11:35 A.M., H. Morgenthau, Jr., Diaries, Book 693, 205-208. FDRL.
122. For a probing of this dilemma, see Peter Lowenberg, "Walter Rathenau and Henry Kissinger: The Jew as a Modern Statesman in Two Political Cultures," *Leo Baeck Memorial Lecture No. 24*, (Jerusalem: Leo Baeck Institute, 1980).

5

Was There Communal Failure?
Some Thoughts on the American
Jewish Response to the Holocaust

Henry L. Feingold

The American Jewish response to the Holocaust has become a central question in the group's historiography and has produced a plethora of books and articles that question not only the effectiveness of that response but the character of the leaders who organized it.[1] Before I began research for *A Time for Searching* (Johns Hopkins Press: 1992), I suspected that there was much more to the story than merely noting that the second and third generations had become uncaring Jews.[2] American Jewry's prior record of reaction to overseas crises was, after all, a good one. Calls for help from abroad had elicited a generous Jewish response during the Damascus Blood Libel case (1840), the Mortara kidnapping (1858), the Dreyfus Affair (1894), the Beilis Blood Libel case (1903-1907), and the Kishinev pogrom (1903). Including the familiar mass-protest ritual and the quest for government diplomatic intercession, the community response to these crises was neither notably different from what Jews were doing in the 1930s and 1940s nor more effective. Were the researchers who found American Jewry indifferent to the fate of their European brethren imagining a Jewry that they wanted to exist rather than contending with the one that did? I suspected that the best clues to explain the behavior of American Jewry during the Holocaust were hidden in its experiences during the interwar years. Specifically, the roots of the Jewish response could be found in the individual and group identity changes of the post-immigrant generations, which made them at once freer of communal constraints and less able to identify with a worldwide Jewish interest.

There was also a qualitative difference between these former crises and the one that began in 1933. The crisis faced by Jewish communities everywhere as a result of the advent of National Socialism threatened the survival of Judaism as a distinct religious civilization. It threatened the Jewish collectivity as well as hundreds of Jewish communities. There had been, during former crises, no modern nation state that had made anti-Semitism an intrinsic part of its public policy. Other conditions were also different during the 1930s. There was a worldwide Depression that heightened extremism at both ends of the political spectrum. While the impending disaster threatened to be of unprecedented scale and ferocity, few were able to foresee a movement to annihilate the Jewish people. Clearly, the inability of the modern imagination to envision the world of Auschwitz affected the early Jewish response to the Holocaust. But these factors cannot account for the loss of communal cohesiveness that became discernible as the crisis unfolded. During the Roosevelt era American Jews were more politically active than ever before, and they had achieved a place in the Roosevelt administration; but throughout the crisis they remained a divided community wracked by bitter internecine strife. What could account for this? Had the bonds between them become so weak that they could not hold in a crisis?

The picture of American Jewry that emerges in *A Time for Searching,* the fourth volume in *The Jewish People in America,* is complex and yields no easy answers. Ultimately, the historian is compelled to question whether a Jewish community in the accepted sense—a group bound by common culture, language, experience, and religion—was still functioning during the interwar years. The reader learns how historical forces associated with modernization and acculturation, which American Jewry experienced simultaneously and which were superimposed on a reenergized anti-Semitic movement, reshaped the consciousness of American Jewry. This is not the place to reexamine the entire interwar experience of American Jewry, about which the reader may want to read more in *A Time for Searching.* I have confined my observations to the impact of anti-Semitism superimposed on a people caught in transition and to how a people insecure and afraid that "it might happen here" responded to the deepest crisis in postemancipation Jewish history, perhaps in all Jewish history.

Anyone examining this period in the American Jewish experience cannot escape the impression that anti-Semitism was the most constant source of concern for Jews. But to note simply that there was anti-Semitism in the 1920s and 1930s, even of a particularly virulent variety, is like observing that there was a cycle of seasons. Anti-Semitism can, after all, be found in every epoch of postexilic Jewish history. Even those who observe that it was particularly virulent during the interwar years must also note that the series of incidents and practices that composed it were not cut from the same cloth and that their impact on Jewish well-being varied considerably. The rantings of Henry Ford's *Dearborn Independent* or Father Charles Coughlin's post-1938 radio addresses may have seared the collective Jewish spirit, but they hardly affected the conditions of daily Jewish life. Second- and third- generation Jews did not spend every waking moment worrying about anti-Semitism. Members of the aging immigrant generation may, in fact, have found the American brand of anti-Semitism mild compared to what they had experienced in Europe. Indeed, for the growing number of Jews who were in the process of severing their links to the community, anti-Semitism probably meant little and may, in some cases, have hastened that separation. Curtailment of employment or housing opportunities, which impacted directly on the material conditions of life, were usually far more telling. The rantings of such anti-Semitic publicists as Burton J. Hendricks or the Reverend George Simons fed the deep underlying wellsprings of anti-Semitism. Their poisonous effects on public morality were cumulative, but they did not directly affect access to the American dream, which had such an impact on the way Jews shaped their lives. But the minor blood libel that took place in September 1928 in Massena, a small town in New York State, placed these Jews directly in danger's path. Local authorities, including the mayor, held Jews for questioning; the threat was here and now, palpable and frightening. Similarly, the 1922 Harvard enrollment-limitations case affected only a handful of Jewish students but impinged on the interests of Jewish elites in formation. Leaders such as Louis Marshall, who played an active role in the campaign to undo the limitations policy, understood that access to the highest positions in the country was involved because Harvard established the conventions of the American university culture. For practical and historical reasons Jews placed enormous value on higher education. If Harvard's quotas stood, Jewish goals would be limited; if they fell, young Jews could aspire to almost any position. The case itself may have baffled less-acculturated Jews who could not understand why anyone would want to be in a place where they were not wanted.

In the most serious case of public anti-Semitism during the 1920s, the restrictionist immigration laws of 1921 and 1924, we encounter difficulty in determining where a specific anti-Jewish animus begins and general "Nordicism" ends. The immigration laws had the greatest potential impact on American Jewry, for if they had been aimed exclusively at Jewish immigrants, the result would have been a case of political anti-Semitism such as existed in nineteenth-

century Tsarist Russia or the Germany of the 1930s. With the exception of
General Order Number II (1862) in which General U.S. Grant called for the
expulsion of Jews from his army department, such political anti-Semitism was
virtually unknown in the American Jewish experience. In the case of the
restrictionist immigration laws of 1921 and 1924 there is no question that
lawmakers were especially concerned about a "flood" of Jewish immigrants from
eastern Europe, which they imagined was poised to burst forth on America. But
there is also evidence that the arrival of masses of penniless Jews was not the
only fear of restrictionists. Potential Jewish immigrants shared the status of
"undesirable" with immigrants from southern and eastern Europe, whose
quotas were accordingly limited on the basis of national origin. If there was an
exclusive desire to keep out Jews, it was difficult to prove. Emanuel Celler, who
represented an almost all-Jewish district in Brooklyn, New York, noted that
there was contempt for all "new" immigrants. He realized, finally, that "they
simply didn't want any more 'wops, dagoes, Hebrews, hunkies, bulls. . . .'" As
one U.S. House Immigration Committee member put it—in response to an
accusation made by Gedaliah Bublick, editor of the Orthodox *Tageblatt,* that
the law was anti-Semitic in intent—there would have been no restriction had
the Jews taken care to have been born in Scotland.[3]

Paradoxically, these laws, whose anti-Semitic intent was embedded in a
general distaste for the people of Eastern and Southern Europe, would have a
formidable impact on retaining in the United States a distinctive ethnic culture
based on Yiddish. They meant that the infusion of cultural and religious energy
from abroad, on which American Jewish communal and religious life was in
some measure dependent, would be throttled. Only approximately seventy-one
thousand Jews were able to enter the United States between 1921 and 1929, a
far cry from the hundreds of thousands who entered in the first decade of the
century. Deprived of a steady stream of consumers, the Yiddish press and theater
as well as numerous institutions for cultural transmission declined markedly
during the 1920s. Of course, there were those such as Cyrus Adler, who insisted
that "if three and a half million Jews in America cannot maintain Judaism
without a constant stream of immigration then they are unworthy of Judaism."[4]

That the laws would be the source of loss of Jewish life would not be
understood until a decade later. During the 1920s few were prescient enough
to realize that, by permitting no distinction between refugees in dire need of
haven and ordinary immigrants, the quota laws would become lethal during the
refugee crisis of the 1930s, when Adolf Hitler sought to make the Reich
judenrein (free of Jews) by forcing German Jews, and later the Jews of Austria
and Czechoslovakia, to emigrate. The strict implementation of the laws by the
Hoover administration, especially the LPC (likely to become a public charge)

provision, made it virtually impossible to gain access to America. Only in the year 1939 were the relevant quotas fully used. If one had a taste for historical symmetry one could note that the ideology of "Nordic supremacy" behind the quota system was the same as Hitler's notions of racial purity embodied in the mystique of Aryanism. During the interwar years America would not welcome Jews for much the same reason that Berlin wanted to get rid of them.

As raucous as the anti-Semitic rhetoric of the 1920s often was, as troublesome as it could be for Jewish job seekers, as limiting as the immigration laws would prove to be for the continuance of Jewish culture, anti-Semitism hardly put a crimp in the second generation's drive to achieve middle-class status. More than anything else, it was this aspiration that marked Jewish life during the decade of the 1920s. More energy and concern were expended on the private drive to achieve than on any public endeavor in Jewish American life. American Jews were an extraordinarily ambitious, some might say driven, group. It was as if the freedom of America had caused the release of a steel coil pent up for millennia behind confining ghetto walls. Their campaign to open government civil service to merit furnished more and better employment, especially in teaching, but it also incurred the wrath of the Irish, who had grown to think of municipal civil service as their own fief. There were complaints in the *Brooklyn Eagle* that few Irish names could be found on the new civil-service lists. But Jews were delighted with the merit system. Their children did well in school and on such tests, which above all required good reading comprehension. The *American Hebrew* boasted that the list of regent scholarship winners in New York State "reads like a confirmation roster at a temple."[5] Indeed, the second generation reached the ivy-covered halls of academe fully one generation before other groups in the post-1890 immigration.

That Jews shared fully in the prosperity of the 1920s is demonstrated by the continued growth of the Jewish ethnic economy. By 1937 two-thirds of the thirty-four thousand factories and one hundred four thousand wholesale and retail establishments in New York City were owned by Jews. A similar pattern was discernible in other large cities.[6] The 1920s were also a period of self-improvement and professionalization of the Jewish work force. A finisher in the garment industry might strive to become a cutter, a bookkeeper an accountant, a teacher a principal. Jews were prone to using their limited capital to invest in the human capital of themselves. The entire family often shared the expense of sending a son to college and then for professional training. Medical and law schools were flooded with Jewish applicants, who seemed to redouble their efforts when blocks were placed in their path. When housing in desirable neighborhoods was restricted, Jewish developers built their own. They did the same when Jews were rejected for membership in country clubs. Anti-Semitism was real, but it could be fought, as in the Ford and Harvard cases of the 1920s. If that seemed too remote a goal for impatient Jews at the grass roots, it could be circumvented as in the case of the young Jewish job applicant who obtained a note from the local minister testifying to the fact that she was not Jewish so that she might get a position with the telephone company. "Would going around jobless and having to come to her father or mother for a dollar be better?" queried the chagrined mother.[7] Name changes and other subterfuges to conceal Jewish origins were sometimes resorted to by those who refused to suffer for a faith whose tenets they no longer observed.

Such strategies might gain one employment, but they could not shield one from the more virulent anti-Semitism of the 1930s that attacked Jews collectively. Ford's rantings, the Rosenbluth trial, the Harvard quota case, and the dozens of other anti-Semitic incidents of the 1920s were part of the nativist xenophobic atmosphere of that decade, which also produced the reenergized Ku Klux Klan and the dozens of patriotic societies that agitated for immigration restriction. This atmosphere was more indigenous and less target-centered on Jews, who shared the antiforeign animus with other ethnics of the "new" immigration. But after the advent of National Socialism in Germany in 1933 there was a steady infusion of financial and ideological support from Berlin and Rome to specific anti-Semitic organizations. Like the National Socialists, the Fascist Party of Italy sought to bring Italian Americans closer to the regime. "Italian consuls do nearly everything but administer the Fascist oath to Italo-Americans," wrote one observer.[8] Berlin viewed anti-Semitism as a heightened form of political consciousness and spared no effort to energize the existing anti-Semitic organizations with money and propaganda. That infusion gave indigenous anti-Semitism a new stature and virulence. It was now part of a worldwide movement that everywhere produced cadres of professional anti-Semites. More than 120 professional anti-Semitic organizations were active during the 1930s, producing anti-Semitic literature, organizing rallies and boycotts of Jewish businesses, and offering a full social life based almost entirely on a distaste for Jews.

Such right-wing organizations as Fritz Kuhn's German-American Bund, William Dudley Pelley's Silver Shirts, and ultimately Father Charles Coughlin's Social Justice movement seemed to possess the potential for becoming popular mass movements, as had already happened in Germany. That possibility haunted American Jewry, which watched in disbelief as the highly integrated Jews of Germany were restricted in the professions and finally lost their civil and political rights as a result of the Nuremberg Laws (1935). The physical attack on Jewish persons and property known as Kristallnacht, which occurred on 9 November 1938, may have shocked American Jews more than their

German compatriots since they were totally unprepared to believe that the rights of citizenship associated with emancipation could be withdrawn. Small wonder that *Fortune* magazine began its special issue on American Jewry in 1936 with the observation that there was a need to quiet "Jewish apprehensiveness," which had reached pathological dimensions.[9] Particularly worrisome for Jews was the possibility that the right wing of the isolationist movement represented by the America First Committee might gain the upper hand in the political arena. It was the members of the movement who often openly echoed Berlin's Judeophobia. When the popular folk hero Charles Lindbergh warned in his Des Moines, Iowa, address (September 1941) that Jews should not push the nation to war because they would be the first victims, it sent shivers down the American Jewish spine. The speech echoed the warning Hitler had made in an address before the Reichstag in April 1939. Though the public did not take well to Lindbergh's speech, Jews feared that the wall between isolationism and anti-Semitism was being breached. Just nine months later, on 21 June 1942, the House Un-American Activities Committee secretly questioned a professional anti-Semite who, according to Congressman Martin Dies, stated that he favored "not the persecution, but execution of the Jews."[10]

Small wonder that as the war approached, American Jewry's sense of security seemed badly shaken. The cumulative effects of the indigenous anti-Semitism of the 1920s had been heightened during the Depression by the virulent brand that had made its debut in Europe. In the beleaguered perception of the second and third generations it seemed that the next step would be the appearance of a "Jewish question" on the American political agenda, in the form of how much power and wealth Jews should be allowed to have. Private anti-Semitism would be transformed into a far more dangerous political anti-Semitism. The result was fear in the Jewish population and paralysis among its leaders. No understanding of the American Jewish response to the crisis in Europe is possible without knowing the context in which that response had to be organized. A shaken, insecure American Jewry had become more uncertain than ever of its place in America.

For the players on the historical stage, perception and reality are indivisible, but with hindsight there can be a gap between the two. Did American Jewry overreact to the anti-Semitism of the 1930s? That there was a heightened anti-Semitism in the 1930s and 1940s few will dispute. As late as 1944, 65 percent of Americans believed that Jews had too much power. But survey research is not particularly reliable in measuring the depth of anti-Semitism and often yielded contradictory results. Some polls indicated that only 12 percent of Americans were actually classifiable as anti-Semitic during the 1930s. After Kristallnacht a strong "spectator sympathy" for Jews developed. Ninety-four percent of Americans disapproved of Nazi anti-Semitic depredations, which became a cause for concern in Berlin.[11] At the height of isolationism there was probably little danger of a Jewish question becoming part of the political dialogue, and in 1944, the year when anti-Semitism reached its zenith, Americans were far more concerned with winning the war than with worrying about whether it was a war to save the Jews. The nation, after all, waged war against an opponent that placed anti-Semitism at the center of its ideology. Such anti-Semitic demagogues as Fritz Kuhn, Gerald L. K. Smith, William Dudley Pelley, Gerald Winrod, and Robert Edmondson were not a particularly impressive lot who might fit comfortably into the mainstream of American politics. Moreover, the general influence in politics of such ethnics as German and Italian Americans, groups in which an imported anti-Semitism might have been planted, had declined considerably as they acculturated. Just as in the case of the Yiddish press, there was a parallel decline in the readership of these American ethnic groups' press and in membership in their fraternal organizations. Anti-Semitism remained an isolated, largely inchoate force. Most important, America's entrance into the war against Germany in December 1941 militated against a racist worldview held by the Axis powers.

Clearly, the Jewish perception of danger went beyond the reality. America was not Germany, and the ability of organized anti-Semitism to insert itself into the political process was limited by its aberrance and its alienation from the American mainstream; yet the Jewish perception of the imminence of such a thing happening is understandable. This perception was built on the experience of anti-Semitism during the 1920s and its increased virulence during the 1930s, which witnessed a fallout of interethnic hostility stemming from the Depression.

The Jewish perception of anti-Semitism, or, perhaps better, the misperception of it, serves as background noise in the environment in which the American Jewish response to the Holocaust was fashioned. The factors directly affecting the quality of that response were the subtle alteration of the mind-set and self-image of second- and third-generation American Jews. These changes gradually deprived them of traditional cohesiveness and self-understanding. In the free atmosphere of America the divisions that everywhere characterized postemancipation Jewish communities were exacerbated. It was not that secularizing Jews felt less Jewish but that they no longer felt exclusively so. The American Jewish identity was multileveled. The Jewish citizen functioned in a professional and in a private identity, he responded to crisis both as a Jew and an American. The freer secularized communal structure made unified action more difficult to achieve since there was no one to order Jews to their Judaism or even to mute their ideological differences in order that they might act together. The four efforts between 1938 and 1944 to create an institutional mechanism for unified action to rescue European Jewry came to nought. The only recorded instance of successful coordination came in the important area of fund-raising when, pressured by the newly established Council of Jewish Federations and Welfare Funds (October 1932), the United Jewish Appeal (UJA) attained a fragile unity in 1939. It raised $124 million between 1939 and 1945, insufficient for the need at hand but a remarkable feat when compared to organized fund-raising in other areas of American society. During the Depression, a period of heightened political activism for Jews, their talents and energy continued to flow in traditional fund-raising philanthropic channels. It was only after the war that Jews qua Jews became fully involved in the political process.

By the 1930s total communal unity was probably no longer achievable even in the face of the murderous threat emanating from Berlin. On the one hand, the traditional sources of unity—religion, a common language and culture, and a common interest and worldview—had grown weaker. On the other, ideological and political diversity had grown stronger so that one generation could barely recognize, much less find something in common with, its successor. Listen to one writer ruefully describing the distinctions between first-generation Jews who settled on the East Side of Manhattan and their successors who had moved to the new neighborhoods in the Bronx and Brooklyn:

> It's the second generation Jew with all the outward characteristics minus beard and mustache, playing baseball, great fight fans, commercial travelers, clean-shirted, white-collared, derby-hatted, creased-trousered. The woman are stylish and stout, social workers, actresses, stump-speakers, jazz dancers with none of the color and virtues of the erstwhile bewigged parents, and a few vices of their own acquisition. But they bathe frequently.[12]

Something was lost in the passage from the first generation to the "clean-shirted, creased-trousered" second that went beyond appearance. The "bewigged" first generation continued to generate a fairly strong sense of Jewish identity. It was strong enough so that even while "uptown" German Jews may have looked down upon their brethren from Eastern Europe they nevertheless supported a liberal immigration law and dozens of programs and institutions to ameliorate their condition. But in the second generation the weakening of the religious and ethnic bonds that bound all Jews together had become more noticeable. By the 1930s it was the bewigged Jews who would appear to be aberrant. To be sure, synagogue building and membership in congregations actually rose during the 1920s, and the Yiddish theater flourished until 1927.

But the traditional sources of strength and unity, rooted in the family and the Yiddish-based secular culture, were weakening. The acculturating second generation was establishing new behavioral norms that were often in conflict with traditional ones. For example, the matchmaker *(shadkin)* who helped negotiate the path to marriage in the older generation was being replaced by new courting patterns based on the notion of romantic love, which, in turn, was based on a more liberated position of women. Going to a matchmaker, complained one young woman, was "like going on the slave market . . . to be weighed and measured like a cow at a fair."[13] The laws of family purity that guided the behavior of religious Jews were especially difficult to adhere to in the hedonistic culture of the 1920s. The result was generational conflict, which sometimes became the subject of Yiddish plays and *romanen* (pieces of fiction) published in the Yiddish press.

But only a few contemporaries such as Mordecai Kaplan, who in 1921 founded the Reconstructionist movement, perceived what was happening as a massive crisis that needed to be resolved if American Judaism was to survive. This crisis was manifested in the weakening of corporate group identity. Inherent in the secularization process was a strong drive for individuation and autonomy, which led ultimately to detribalization. That process was an inevitable product of living in a free secular society. Matters of religious law such as *kashrut* (traditional Jewish dietary laws), which formerly could be enforced by rabbinic or community sanction, no longer could be in a complex and free urban environment. To the extent that traditional behavioral norms still applied concerning relations between the sexes or in business, they were adhered to voluntarily. Compliance with religious practices came to depend on the individual Jew finding a balance between the new life goals, which placed a high value on self-realization and becoming American, and the ethnic and religious tenets of the Jewish tradition. Many modified such practices, and some abandoned them altogether. The second-generation American Jew remained recognizably Jewish, but he was now also influenced by behavioral norms and goals that prevailed in the majority culture. The generation that reached maturity in the 1920s possessed less knowledge of the traditional religious culture from which such values stemmed; the generations that followed would know even less. A ramshackle, ineffective Jewish education system and a family preoccupied with achieving material success or simply making a living meant that the traditional agencies for transmitting Jewish knowledge and values had lost influence. At the same time widespread use of the public school system meant that familiarity with secular American culture increased at the juncture where knowledge of the traditional culture waned. The second-generation Jews no longer learned *yiddishkeit* (the warm spirit of Jewish culture) or the religious culture with their mother's milk. A special effort and new institutions were required to teach the culture. People were increasingly free to shape their own relationship to the community, which could be expressed through philanthropy or culinary habits or simply by insisting that Judaism was something heartfelt. The strong individuation inherent in the culture of self-realization would be reflected in a more diverse and weakened community structure. It was this internally weakened community that was called upon to respond to the impending catastrophe facing European Jewry.

Thousands of Jews retained their linkage to the community through voluntary organization and fraternal orders. During the interwar years the 4,228,000 Jews of America developed the richest organizational infrastructure of any American ethnic group. It consisted of 17,500 organizations of 49 different categories ranging from community-service agencies such as the Hebrew Immigrant Aid Society (HIAS) to multicountry agencies such as the American Jewish Joint Distribution Committee (JDC). Eighteen percent of these organizations were associated with religious concerns, the bulk of which were a growing number of congregations that were establishing themselves in areas of second settlement. Defense organizations, service organizations, and fraternal orders provided their memberships with medical insurance, cemetery plots, and even vacation resorts at reasonable prices. There were dozens of Zionist organizations, each representing a different ideological stripe, and a growing number of federations whose goal it was to bring order into the chaotic fund-raising activity. But programming for Judaism, which these organizations did, proved no substitute for living it. Hadassah or the dozens of other organizations to which a second-generation Jew might belong could generate great acts of devotion, but they did not create communities of faith.

During the 1920s, philanthropy became an important way for secularizing Jews to continue their community connections. It also added a new dynamic factor to Jewish communal life, especially after growing Jewish affluence dramatically increased the sums raised. Now the millions of dollars collected yearly represented real "spoils" whose allocation would be bitterly contested by the various political factions. The conflict over the allocations formula between Zionists and non-Zionists during the interwar period warrants a separate book. It became particularly bitter during the Crimean resettlement venture undertaken by the JDC after 1924. Zionists thought that such funds should go to build up the Yishuv (prewar Jewish settlement in Palestine), whereas the JDC argued that resettling Jews where they were was cheaper and more practicable. The Arab riots of 1929 reinforced that argument, which predictably also won the support of the Communist element in the community. The alliance between the wealthy Jewish "philanthropoids" and the Kremlin is one of the strangest episodes in American Jewish history.

The proliferation of Jewish organizations should not be confused with the existence of a strongly bonded community, for the reverse proved to be the case. The innumerable political and ideological divisions actually caused the organizations to multiply. Each ideology, even a shading of any ideology, tended to produce its own organizational expression. Lack of flexibility, which ideological commitment tended to bring in its wake, created dividing walls between the various factions of the community during the years of the Holocaust, making it almost impossible to find a middle ground. The huge sums of money involved compounded the problem. Except for the federations, which tried to play a bridging role, as in the case of the reformation of the UJA in 1939, there was little to hold the Jewish community together.

By the late 1930s the reenergized American Zionist movement might have played such a binding role. Its failure to do so warrants special comment. After the divisive 1921 Cleveland convention of the Zionist Organization of America (ZOA) led American Zionists Louis Brandeis and Judge Julius Mack to give up their leadership to Chaim Weizmann, leader of the European Zionists, the movement entered a period of decline. That was reflected in the difficulties of the United Palestine Appeal, the fund-raising arm of the Zionist movement, in achieving its goals and a decline in membership. By 1931 its principal umbrella organization, the ZOA, had about eight thousand shekel payers, a shekel being the requisite token payment for membership. When the Nazis took power in January 1933 the American Zionist movement was in the humiliating position of advocating grandiose goals of nation building while having neither the finances nor the organizational coherence to realize them. It seemed as if the American Zionist movement was moribund.

Yet, eight years later, this sad picture of decline and disarray was completely reversed. ZOA's membership rose to fifty-five thousand in 1939, and membership in the world Zionist organization rose to almost two hundred fifty thousand. Zionists also finally penetrated the American Jewish fund-raising apparatus. What had happened? American Jews had begun to view the crisis of German Jewry in Zionist terms. They came to Zionism not through the esoteric ideology of Zionist thinkers who spoke of the "renaissance of the Jewish people" but through the refugee crisis. Few nations welcomed the Jewish refugees being forcibly extruded from the Reich in order to make itself *judenrein* (free of Jews). They understood in simple terms that what Jews required was a refuge, a piece of land, where they could find a haven should it become necessary.

But the American Zionist movement was ill-prepared to receive the human bounty cast out by the events in Germany. Ironically, although some leading Zionist thinkers had warned about the untenability of Jewish life in the Diaspora, the Zionist movement generally was late in evaluating the crisis befalling European Jewry and, therefore, was slow in making a transition from a group of loosely held together organizations devoted to philanthropy to the political agent of American Jewry. Its leadership was old and driven by personal ambition, and the movement was divided into factions that reflected the riven state of the world Zionist movement. The thin line of settlements in Palestine, which had become the pride of all committed Jews, concealed an economy that was developing painfully slowly and would not be prepared for years to absorb all of the Jews who needed to find a home.

Most important, the solutions the Zionist leadership sought in the face of the crisis either ran counter to the effort of Jews to mobilize themselves or were too narrowly conceived to be effective for the primary task of rescuing Jews. During the 1920s the movement's efforts were hampered by a low ebb of organizational energy. It never fully recovered from the bitter internal conflict between the Americanists, led by Louis Brandeis, and the Palestinianists, headed by Louis Lipsky. The victory of the latter meant that the bridge to the "uptown" philanthropists, whom Brandeis sought to link to the development of Palestine on a project-by-project investment basis, was weakened. Rabbi Stephen Wise, the Zionist leader who was president of the American Jewish Congress, might give vent to his frustration regarding the power of these philanthropists by declaring that one Haim Bialik, the beloved Jewish writer and poet, was worth more than 100 Felix Warburgs, the leading Jewish philanthropist of the interwar period.[14] But the reality was that the major portion of funds required to manage community affairs was still raised by such "philanthropoids." In the years between 1921 and 1925 the Zionist organizations launched 4 "appeals" but raised only $6 million, a paltry sum when compared to the $20.8 million raised by the JDC in the same period. The JDC's sponsorship of Jewish resettlement in the Crimea demonstrated that in the Jewish community the monied piper still played the tune. The expansion of the Jewish Agency to include American philanthropists in 1929 did not resolve the problem.

As in the world Zionist movement of which it was part, the American Zionist leadership was forced by the crisis to make terrible choices between its own development and the crying need to rescue European Jewry. The choice did not, of course, appear that way to Zionists who were convinced that the best way to rescue European Jews was to allow them to settle in Palestine, whose economy would thereby be strengthened. During the 1930s, the Zionist movement placed the development of Palestine's economy above the boycott of German goods. There was relative prosperity in Palestine during the depressed 1930s because Hjalmar Schacht, the president of the Reichsbank, had reached an agreement with

the Bank of Palestine whereby a portion of blocked German Jewish assets could
be transferred in the form of capital goods. But by participating in the transfer
agreements, the Zionist movement inevitably faced a bitter confrontation with
the militant Jews who had organized a boycott of German goods, the first Jewish
communal effort to hit back against their tormentors.[15] Similarly, after the 1939
British White Paper limited the number of refugees allowed to enter and the
amount of land that could be purchased in Palestine, the Zionist movement, led
by David Ben-Gurion (who then headed the Jewish Agency), mounted a campaign to change British policy. Ben-Gurion was convinced that sufficient pressure
could be brought to bear to do so. But the contest between the British government
and the Zionist movement was from the outset an uneven one and grew more so
as the war progressed. The energy and resources spent on trying to mobilize public
opinion against the White Paper were of no avail. All attempts to change British
policy failed. At the same time the Zionist leaders were unwilling to expend
precious resources to settle European Jews elsewhere. Thousands of Jews who
would have settled anywhere for the moment in order to save their lives were
instead transported eastward for Berlin's version of resettlement, which usually
meant death. Zionists could neither easily transfer their skills in resettling Jews
nor expend the necessary resources to develop such areas as British Guiana or
Mindanao without short-changing their own enterprise. There were not sufficient
resources to do both, and the prospects for developing the more than six hundred
areas searched out by the Roosevelt administration were not good. The hapless
refugees fell between two chairs.

   Might things have happened differently had the world Zionist movement,
and especially its American wing, focused exclusively on getting Jews out of
Europe? After decades of resistance American Jews seemed ready to follow
Zionist leadership during the Holocaust. But they discovered that the movement was badly split and that its rescue strategy was focused on safeguarding
the development of the Yishuv, and only through it on rescuing the millions.
Disunity was nothing new in the world Zionist movement, but the crisis, rather
than healing old conflicts, exacerbated them. The conflict with the revisionists,
which began in 1926 when the followers of Vladimir (Zeb) Jabotinsky left the
movement, exploded with a vengeance in the United States after a small group
of Irgunists led by Hillel Kook (Peter Bergson) capitalized on the compelling
idea of organizing a Jewish army to fight the Nazis. For a victimized people the
notion of having its own army to fight its enemies proved to be irresistible. This
idea catapulted the Bergson group into prominence, and their skillful use of
public relations kept them there.

   Throughout the conflict the Irgunists remained a thorn in the side of the
mainline Zionist organizations, refusing all offers to bring them into the fold.

In some measure the popularity of the "Bergson boys," which belied their small number, was related to the fact that American Jewry, especially its now-weighty Zionist component, was radicalized by events in Europe. That radicalization led the Zionist convention meeting in the Biltmore Hotel in New York in May 1942 to accept the idea of establishing a Jewish Commonwealth, a euphemism for a sovereign Jewish state in Palestine. The Biltmore Program became in itself a new source of disunity. Tamar de Sola Pool and others on the left end of the political spectrum did not agree with Ben-Gurion, who had counseled the delegates of the Biltmore convention that "Palestine would be as Jewish as the Jews will make it."[16] They argued that the resolution brought rescue no closer while it needlessly antagonized the Arab world. In 1943, when the American Jewish Conference approved the Commonwealth Resolution, which caused the American Jewish Committee and the Jewish Labor Committee to leave the Conference, Judah Magnes, rector of the Hebrew University and leader of a group who favored a binational state in Palestine, warned that the Commonwealth Resolution was "a declaration of war by Jews on the Arabs."[17] More disturbing for rescue advocates was the fact that the Commonwealth Resolution did not directly confront the issue of rescue since few European Jews could get to Palestine. A new division between maximalists and conciliators was now superimposed on the myriad preexisting divisions of the Zionist movement, which remained hopelessly divided throughout the crisis.

Ironically, the American Zionist movement had achieved a new high point in political effectiveness by the time the divisions within the community had become unbridgeable. Mobilized by the reorganized AZEC (American Zionist Emergency Committee), which became the political arm of the American Zionist movement, its 400 local emergency committees would soon be able to flood the Oval Office or Congress with 10,000 telegrams within hours of the announcement of a need to do so. But despite such prowess the Zionist movement proved too weak to change Roosevelt's Middle East policy, which was not inclined to challenge British dominance in Palestine during the war. Despite strong support in Congress, the Wright-Compton Resolution (H.R. 418) and the identical Wagner-Taft Resolution (S.R. 247), in which the Commonwealth Resolution and the anti–White Paper policy were embedded, were easily defeated by the Roosevelt administration by the simple strategy of questioning the propriety of passing such resolutions during wartime. The blame for that failure does not belong exclusively to the Zionist movement. American Jewry simply did not possess the power to change foreign-policy priorities during hostilities.

A divided American Zionist movement thus failed to unify American Jewry; but even had it been able to do so it could not have broken Roosevelt's hold on the Jewish voter. In the election of 1944 Jews continued their love affair with Roosevelt despite his weak rescue policy and his failure to support the Jewish homeland idea. Roosevelt, after all, was the leader who led America into a war against the archenemy of the Jewish people. Jewish leaders could not hope to threaten the administration by removing the Jewish vote. They did not have that kind of control of the maverick, heavily ideological Jewish voters who viewed themselves as patriotic American citizens rather than victimized Jews. There is a lesson in the election of 1944 for those who see an all-powerful Jewry ready to serve a Jewish cause exclusively and able to dictate public policy. They need only observe its ignominious failure to unify itself and project influence on the Roosevelt administration during that crucial year.

America's entrance into the war, a war first to defeat National Socialism, rekindled Jewish confidence and a sense of solidarity with the nation. Earlier than most Americans, Jews were convinced that Hitlerism posed a threat to civilized world order, not only to Jews. American Jews were by 1941 virtually unanimous in their support for America's entry into the war, which they viewed as a just one. The Roosevelt administration's argument that a quick victory was the best way to save the Jews was not directly challenged by American Jewry. Given the patriotic fervor of American Jewry and fear of the accusation that Jews were fighting for an ethnic rather than a national interest, it was difficult for Jewish leaders to oppose the administration's argument. For most American Jews, winning the war—not the rescue of their brethren—received priority. The two objectives did not seem in conflict because few understood until 1944 that by the time victory came European Jewry would be in ashes. The ferocity of the assault on European Jewry eluded them. The warning that nothing must be allowed to interfere with the war effort sent the Wright-Compton Resolution for a Jewish Commonwealth in Palestine down to defeat, and it also cast suspicion on Henry Morgenthau, Jr.'s, "hard" plan for the postwar treatment of Germany.

During the war American Jews were also preoccupied with their own security. Even as they mobilized all communal resources to help achieve victory, the fear persisted that the still-powerful anti-Semitic elements would single Jews out as draft dodgers and war profiteers. With the anti-Semitic allegations made during World War I still etched sharply in their memories, Jewish leaders would be prepared this time. Jewish defense organizations planned to wage a separate battle to deflect the expected attacks, which did, in fact, materialize. In October 1941 the Jewish Welfare Board established a Bureau of War Records to assure that the Jewish contributions to the war effort were made known to the American public. Eventually, the bureau informed the nation that five hundred fifty thousand Jewish men and women served in the U.S. armed forces, 8 percent above their proportion of the population. Every person who won a medal for valor and every casualty was duly registered and publicized by the bureau.

What the historian observes in the interwar years is that the elements on which traditional Jewish communalism was based had become weaker, with the result that it becomes increasingly difficult to speak of a single American Jewish community. Only the anti-Semite, whose organizations proliferated during the 1930s, could imagine that American Jewry was a unified, conspiratorial tribe. The erosion of the religious tradition and the loosening of ethnic ties, both traditional pillars of cohesiveness, left American Jewry a divided confederation. American Jewry had to find a new base for unity in the face of crisis. In the mid-1930s the strongest hope that such unity might still be achieved lay within the growing dominance of the American Zionist movement. But that movement, too, was beset by strife, and its rescue strategy was limited by what its leaders imagined to be the needs of the Yishuv. Its aspiration to compel Britain to open the gates of Palestine was far beyond what it could achieve. For ideological and financial reasons it could not wholeheartedly support the temporary resettlement of European Jews elsewhere. Only with the movement to establish the Jewish state was a new foundation for unity set in place.

The task faced by American Jewry between 1933 and 1945 was forbidding. It first required Jews to persuade the American people to liberalize their restrictionist immigration policy in the midst of a severe Depression and then to convince the Roosevelt administration to change wartime priorities to allow for the rescue of European Jews. The kind of political influence required to change such basic public policy was simply not available to American Jewish leaders, whose position, despite the rantings of anti-Semites regarding the "Jew Deal," was, in fact, only marginally enhanced during the Roosevelt era.

Nevertheless, Jews probably overestimated the danger posed by organized anti-Semitism during the 1930s. They knew there was a financial and informational link between the reenergized anti-Semitic organizations and Berlin. The huge rallies staged by Fritz Kuhn's German-American Bund had a suspicious "made in Germany" look. When they shared the "hit list" with other minority groups, American Jews showed that they understood this was not the Ku Klux Klan of the 1920s. The Klan had, in fact, lost most of its steam by the 1930s, but many concluded that what had happened in Germany might very well happen here. Insecure and fearful, the second and third generations reacted with enormous apprehension. Until America entered the war they felt they were alone in facing a powerful foe bent on destroying all Jewish civilization.

American Jewry also faced the Holocaust as a riven people. Caught between a demanding acculturation and secularization process, which called for alteration of the group's ethnic and religious identity but left its members uncertain that making such changes would yield complete access to the promise of America, Jews were unable to determine where history had positioned them. The Depression radicalized much of American Jewry's younger generation, who believed that the way to save the Jews was to join in the fight against fascism. Recruitment for the Lincoln Brigade, organized to fight "the scourge of fascism" in Spain, was disproportionately Jewish. But in 1940 there would be little enthusiasm when the call went out for the formation of a Jewish army. During the war it was difficult for secular, Americanized Jews to perceive a specific Jewish interest apart from an Allied victory.

Some people indict American Jewry for what it was becoming, as if it had the power to halt the historical forces that were transforming it. There are, however, few instances in history when a people have been able to reverse such processes in order to meet better the needs of the moment. Had Jews by some divine intervention suddenly possessed the power to transform themselves, they probably would have rejected the opportunity to reclaim their Judaism, especially if they believed that it would mean abandoning their success in the private realm. They had no assurance that such an abandonment would have meant a greater achievement in the public realm, where rescue policy was made.

It develops that those who are convinced that the second and third generations of American Jewry, who determined the shape of Jewish life during the interwar years, performed the way they did during the Holocaust because they were indifferent Jews see only the tip of the iceberg. It was, after all, the same Jewry that a few years later generously nurtured, and was able to move mountains to win diplomatic recognition for, the newly established Jewish state. The war and the Holocaust accelerated the process of reshaping American Jewry. It became an organized, effective community finally able to carry fully the mantle of leadership formerly held by European Jewry. The historian must take great care not to read this new coherence and effectiveness back into the interwar period. That is not what American Jewry was during those fateful years.

Notes

1. The latest example is Rafael Medoff, *The Deafening Silence: American Jewish Leaders and the Holocaust* (New York: Shapolsky, 1987). There are others as well. Haskell Lookstein, *Were We Our Brothers' Keepers? The Public Response of American Jews to the Holocaust, 1933-1945* (New York: Hartmore House, 1986); Seymour M. Finger, ed., *America Jewry during the Holocaust* (New York: Homes and Meier, 1984); Saul S. Friedman, *No Haven for the Oppressed: United States*

Policy toward Jewish Refugees, 1933-1945 (Detroit: Wayne State University Press, 1973).

2. See, for example, Henry L. Feingold, "'Courage First and Intelligence Second': The American Jewish Secular Elite, Roosevelt, and the Failure to Rescue," *American Jewish History* 72 (June 1983), 459; and Feingold, "Rescue and the Secular Perception: American Jewry and the Holocaust," in *Organizing Rescue: Jewish National Solidarity in the Modern Period,* ed. Selwyn I. Troen and Benjamin Pinkus (London: Frank Cass, 1992,) 154-166.

3. Emanuel Celler, *You Never Leave Brooklyn: The Autobiography of Emanuel Celler* (New York: Day, 1953), 81; U.S. House Committee on Immigration and Naturalization, *Restriction of Immigration,* H.R. 5, 105, 561, *Congressional Record* 68th Cong., 1st sess., 3 January 1924, 388-389.

4. *American Hebrew,* 26 September 1924.

5. *American Hebrew,* 13 October 1922; see also Paul E. Anderson, "Are Jewish Children Brighter?" *American Hebrew,* 17 May 1926.

6. Nathan Reich, "The Role of the Jews in the American Economy," *Yivo Annual of Jewish Social Science* 5 (1950), 198-202; Jacob Letchinsky, "The Position of Jews in the Economic Life of America," in *Jews in a Gentile World,* ed. I. Graeber and S. H. Britt (New York: Macmillan, 1942), 406-415.

7. Issac Metzker, *A Bintel Brief: 60 Years of Letters from the Lower East Side to the "Jewish Daily Forward"* (New York: Doubleday, 1971), 160-161.

8. Quoted in "The War of Nerves: Hitler's Helper," *Fortune* 22 (November 1940), 85-86, 108-110.

9. "Jews in America," *Fortune* 13 (February 1936), 79-85.

10. *Jewish Telegraphic Agency Community News Report* 32 (2) (10 January 1992), 2.

11. Henry L. Feingold, *The Politics of Rescue: The Roosevelt Administration and the Holocaust, 1938-1945* (New York: Holocaust Press, 1980), 41-42; Deborah Lipstadt, *Beyond Belief: The American Press and the Coming of the Holocaust, 1933-1945,* (New York: Free Press, 1986), 98-104.

12. Konrad Bercovici, "The Greatest Jewish City in the World," *Nation* 117 (12 September 1923), 261.

13. Metzger, *Bintel Brief,* 150-151.

14. Charles Reznikoff, *Louis Marshall, Champion of Liberty: Selected Papers and Addresses,* vol. 2 (Philadelphia: Jewish Publication Society, 1957), 786-789.

15. Moshe R. Gottlieb, *American Anti-Nazi Resistance, 1933-1945* (New York: Ktav, 1982), 45-75. A highly partisan examination of the transfer agreements is presented by Edwin Black, *The Transfer Agreement: The Untold Story of the Secret Pact between the Third Reich and Jewish Palestine* (New York: Macmillan, 1984).

16. David Shapiro, "From Philanthropy to Activism: The Political Transformation of American Zionism in the Holocaust Years" (Ph.D. diss., Hebrew University

of Jerusalem, n.d.), 147; Dann Kurtzman, *Ben-Gurion: Prophet of Fire* (New York: Simon and Schuster, 1983), 235-237.

17. Arthur A. Goren, *Dissenter in Zion* (Cambridge: Harvard University Press, 1982), 46-47.

6

Roosevelt and the Holocaust

Richard Breitman

The synthesis of Dallek and Feingold's approaches can be found in Richard Breitman's chapter on Roosevelt and the Holocaust. He stresses the need to trace Roosevelt's behavior rather than speculate on his attitude. Roosevelt emerges in a somewhat sympathetic light.

To write about Franklin Roosevelt's reaction to the Nazi murder of approximately six million Jews is to engage in speculation. As far as is known, he said very little about it and wrote virtually nothing. It does not follow, however, that FDR was unconcerned or indifferent to Nazi mass murders of Jews.[1] Some of his comments and his actions during the late 1930s seem to indicate the contrary; he wanted to get Jews out of Germany before the murderers gained full sway.[2]

This complex master of the art of politics was at once loquacious and terse. He was outwardly gregarious but kept much to himself and often left associates and subordinates with sharply different impressions about his attitudes. Who else could keep both Assistant Secretary of State Breckinridge Long and Rabbi Stephen Wise pacified at the same time? His calculated ambiguity may be proof of necessary political skills, but it makes life very difficult for historians of the Roosevelt presidency, whose problems are compounded by the absence of cabinet minutes (expressly prohibited by the president).

To judge Franklin Roosevelt's reaction to the Final Solution, we must first review his prior views on refugee policy, then calculate when he received information about the overall Nazi plan, and finally gauge any immediate or subsequent changes in his behavior. We must keep in mind that outside forces may have limited his ability to react in certain ways. Even a powerful president was not a free agent. But in the end we can assess FDR's attitudes only through his behavior.

In 1940 FDR reversed his previous view that the full German-Austrian quota (27,370) should be available for the many victims of Nazi persecution. Roosevelt did not simply turn visa policy over to the bureaucrats in the State Department. The evidence indicates that he gave the signal to tighten immigration regulations partly out of real concern for national security, partly out of recognition of political realities.

As early as 6 September 1939, he had requested that the attorney general instruct the Federal Bureau of Investigation (FBI) to take charge of all investigative work regarding espionage, sabotage, and violation of neutrality laws. Representatives of the FBI later held a series of conferences with local law enforcement agents throughout the country, stressing the seriousness of the danger and formulating detailed plans to cope with it. At one conference held in Washington, D.C., on 5-6 August 1940, Attorney General Robert Jackson read a presidential statement about the danger of espionage, sabotage, and Fifth Column activity to representatives of 42 state governments. The president condemned efforts during World War I in this field as inadequate and called for FBI direction of activity this time. Attorney General Jackson added that the Axis powers were now trying to weaken the United States as they had already weakened France before war had broken out in Europe.[3]

FDR's worries had been magnified in the spring of 1940. Already embarked upon an anti-Axis course in foreign policy, FDR had learned that an American code clerk named Tyler Kent, serving in the American Embassy in London, had turned over to fascist sympathizers in London secret American— British diplomatic correspondence from 1938 on, including the exchanges between FDR and British Prime Minister Winston Churchill. The material quickly found its way to Rome and Berlin. Another by-product of the leak was that the Germans were able to crack the American codes, which then had to be changed. This was a psychological blow that struck the president hard. From this point on, FDR could hardly overemphasize the Fifth Column danger.[4]

Another high-ranking official who shared this view of an endangered national security was former Assistant Secretary of State George Messersmith, who had become ambassador to Cuba. Messersmith told Undersecretary of State Sumner Welles that the German conquest of France had gone so smoothly because French morale had already been undermined, not only by aliens but also by French citizens opposed to the government. Messersmith urged the president to take preventive measures against similar happenings in the United States and claimed that the American public would overwhelmingly support a temporary sacrifice of civil liberties. Again, to presidential adviser Felix Frankfurter, Messersmith argued that the failure to restrict an insignificant minority had led to the breakdown of more than one European country. He advocated immediate controls over aliens and over certain native-born and naturalized Americans, whom he considered potentially even more dangerous.[5] With the administration's backing, Congress passed the Smith Act in June 1940, requiring all aliens to be registered and fingerprinted. Those who were presently or previously members of Communist or Fascist organizations could be deported. The Smith Act also made it a crime to advocate the violent overthrow of the government.[6]

Concern for security meant that the president was no longer willing to take many chances with foreign refugees. When a reporter asked the president how the American public's suspicions about aliens, particularly refugees, could be allayed, FDR in effect referred that task to private immigration organizations. But he defended the need to check refugees, because there were spies—voluntary and involuntary—among them. He specifically cited the German government's alleged threat to shoot the relatives of German Jewish refugees unless the latter agreed to work as spies for Germany.[7]

Precisely where the president obtained this information is uncertain. One possibility was Colonel William Donovan, who was receiving briefings and information from the British during the summer of 1940. British officials made no secret of their fears of a Fifth Column.[8] But FDR's source was more likely to have been Ambassador William Bullitt in France. In August 1940, having returned to the United States, Bullitt gave a major foreign-policy address backing the sale or lease of U.S. destroyers to Great Britain. In the course of this speech, given to the American Philosophical Society in Philadelphia, Bullitt stated that war was coming to the United States and that the agents of the dictators were already preparing the way. He went on to describe how hundreds of Communist and Nazi agents in France had transmitted the movements of the French army by shortwave radio to Germany. Bullitt then blamed the French for being even more hospitable to refugees from Germany than the United States was; allegedly, more than one-half of the spies captured in France were refugees from Germany. What is of particular interest about this diatribe is that both Undersecretary Welles and the president read Bullitt's speech beforehand. Welles went so far as to say that he approved every word of it. Two days after the speech, the *New York Times* editorialized: "Our own history in the next few years will be happier if our people act now, in the spirit of Mr. Bullitt's warning."[9] Bullitt was an anti-Semite whose testimony on the issue of "refugee" agents might be doubted. But Roosevelt, Messersmith, Welles, and the *New York Times* were all reacting to the same fears. In fact, some of those most committed to an anti-Axis foreign policy, including the president, seemed most concerned about the danger of spies among the refugees.

The State Department could hardly show leniency to visa applicants in this atmosphere, nor did Breckinridge Long wish to. Circular telegrams went out in June, July, and September 1940 urging consuls to reject or at least suspend any visa application about which there was any doubt. One consul in Stockholm replied: "Very difficult, sometimes impossible [for] refugees here [to] satisfy us completely [regarding] past and potential future activities, criminal record, etc. . . . Result has naturally been delay and drastic reduction [in the] issuance [of visas] as envisaged [in] Department's telegraphic instructions [of] June 29."[10]

Even the privileged lists of intellectuals and labor leaders compiled by the President's Advisory Commission on Political Refugees (PACPR) and other American organizations came under close scrutiny, which set off a prolonged political battle in Washington. Breckinridge Long told FDR that the emergency visa arrangements were being abused. Some of the applicants were not in entire accord with U.S. policy (that is, too far to the Left, in Long's view), and consular officers considered others not to be "of the desirable element." Moreover, the PACPR was submitting too many names. Long wanted to change the procedure by adding an additional check to weed out German agents and other undesirables and to cut down the number of names added in the future.

Roosevelt heard both sides, and, faced with conflicting testimony, he brought in Sumner Welles and Justice Department officials to help resolve the dispute. But Long eventually got what he really wanted: an interdepartmental visa review board in Washington that would scrutinize visa applications and weed out security problems. The restrictionists were bolstered further in June 1941 when Congress passed a law enabling consuls to deny any kind of visa to anyone who would endanger public safety. After jurisdictional disputes broke out again in July between the State Department and the Justice Department, Secretary of State Cordell Hull consulted FDR, who decided that the basic responsibility on visas should remain with the State Department.[11]

Long's victory over the head of the PACPR, James G. McDonald, was not accidental. The president believed that security came before all else. When McDonald complained again to Eleanor Roosevelt, she spoke to her husband and brought back a message. FDR wanted the PACPR and the Intergovernmental Committee on Political Refugees to continue because of the future (not the present). The PACPR should not be discouraged even if its nominees were not given visas, because sometimes investigations turned up information that made it necessary to refuse admission, and investigations had to be made.[12] This was, in effect, an endorsement of much of Long's position and a renunciation of the short-term changes in the immigration program that the president had advocated as late as October 1939.

Not all bureaucrats took the same view as Long. Taking advantage of a loophole in the immigration law for the Virgin Islands, Henry Hart of the Justice Department and Nathan Margold of the Interior Department devised a plan in late 1940 to have the governor and the legislature of the Virgin Islands admit refugees without visitors' visas. But Long and the State Department raised objections. Although Secretary of the Interior Harold Ickes backed the proposal, FDR came down on the other side:

> I yield to no person in any department in my deep-seated desire to help the hundreds of thousands of foreign refugees in the present world situation. The Virgin Islands, however, present to this Government a very serious social and economic problem not yet solved. If the Interior Department could find some unoccupied place . . . where we could set up a refugee camp without involving a small but highly difficult population problem now underway as in the case of the Virgin Islands, that would be treated with sympathy by the State Department and by me.[13]

When Margold persisted, the attorney general ultimately ruled the Virgin Islands plan illegal.[14]

Although Long was the administration's point man on the refugee issue, one must really speak of a State Department stance. Undersecretary Welles was free of Long's prejudices. But Welles, too, harbored deep suspicions about German government motives. In December 1940, he wrote to FDR that recent deportations of German Jews to unoccupied France indicated that the Germans were trying to "force our hand on the refugee problem:"

> Were we to yield to this pressure all the evidence indicates that in the wake of the ten thousand Jews recently forced into France the Germans would drive on the French the remaining Jews from Germany and the occupied territories, hundreds of thousands of persons, in the expectation that the French in turn would persuade this country and the other American republics to receive them. Information reaching us is conclusive that if we or the other American Republics yield to these blackmailing totalitarian tactics the Germans will inaugurate something approaching a "reign of terror" against the Jewish people. . . .[15]

The undersecretary believed that German persecution and deportation of Jews were primarily instruments to weaken the opponents of Nazi Germany.

This, indeed, had been one aspect of German policy during 1938-1939, but Welles and others now failed to perceive that Nazi policy had entered a new and more deadly phase. Assistant Secretary of State Adolf Berle, who had favored a formal American protest against German deportations of Jews to Poland in early 1940, found it "unhappy" but "necessary" in early 1941 to tighten the visa machinery, because the Russians and the Germans were forcing some refugees to act as spies.[16] Lower-level State Department officials as well as foreign-service officers abroad were hardly less diligent in protecting national security and eschewing risky humanitarian undertakings.

After December 1941, the idea of protecting national security remained a prime concern for FDR. The president approved the War Department's plan to intern the Japanese Americans on the West Coast, and he urged Attorney General Francis Biddle to press criminal charges against his antiwar critics. He even wanted to get rid of alien waiters from Washington, D.C., restaurants, where customers exchanged all too much confidential information about the war. As other scholars have noted, the war eroded the president's respect for due process and civil liberties.[17] In this context, it is easier to understand why FDR approved of the State Department's tighter visa regulations. Fairness to visa applicants was not even a remote presidential concern then.

Some in Congress were much more extreme. Senator Robert Reynolds (D, North Carolina) announced in June 1941 that, if he had his way, he would, without the slightest hesitation, "build a wall about the United States so high and so secure that no single alien or foreign refugee from any country upon the face of the earth could possibly scale or ascend it."[18] Reynolds was more outspoken than most congressmen, but he was hardly alone on this issue. FDR certainly harbored no fondness for the isolationist Reynolds, but he had to work with an often-refractory Congress. A bill to extend the length of military service to 18 months passed the House by only one vote in August 1941. The president did not want immigration to add to his foreign policy disputes with the Hill.

Obstructed for years by a strong isolationist faction in Congress, pilloried by right-wing extremists as "President Rosenfeld," depicted as being surrounded by Jews, well aware of a significant anti-Semitic current among the American public, and seeing the war as the greatest crisis in Western history, FDR reacted as most realistic politicians would. He limited his visibility on Jewish issues partly in self-defense, partly in the hope that the public and Congress would be less likely to object to his defense and foreign policies.

As Roosevelt scholar Robert Dallek has observed, FDR wanted more than the support of a bare majority in Congress and among the public. If the United States entered the European war, it would need a broad, stable consensus, which was why the president waited for the other side to strike the first blow.[19]

Conveniently, after the Japanese attack at Pearl Harbor, the German government came to the aid of its ally and declared war against the United States first. Hitler's foolhardy action eliminated the need for FDR to go to Congress and explain why the United States should work for the defeat of Germany, too. That did not stop former Ambassador William Bullitt from telling people that the Roosevelt administration's emphasis on the European war as opposed to the Asian one was the result of Jewish influence.[20]

In actuality, considerations of strategy and propaganda during the war led Roosevelt to temper inclinations to do anything publicly on "Jewish" causes. In October 1942, knowing that political conditions in the Middle East and North Africa were sensitive and that the area was crucial to Allied military success, FDR thought it would be a good idea to have someone do a firsthand analysis on resettlement of refugees, which resulted in a tour of three and one half months for an American lieutenant colonel, Harold Hoskins, and an accompanying British officer. Among Hoskins's findings, reported back to the president in May 1943, were growing tensions between Arabs and Jews in Palestine and in the Middle East and North Africa generally:

> There is an ever-present Arab fear of American support for political Zionism with its proposed Jewish State and Jewish Army in Palestine. . . . *The experiences of British troops during their retreat in Burma are a grave and recent warning of the serious effects that a hostile, rather than friendly, native population can have on our military operations* [Hoskins's italics].[21]

The primacy of the war effort dictated FDR's reaction. The president hastened to reassure King Saud of Saudi Arabia that no decision would be reached altering the basic situation in Palestine without full consultation of both Arabs and Jews.[22] He sent this message in spite of the fact that privately, to Treasury Secretary Henry Morgenthau, Jr., FDR had talked about moving Arabs from Palestine to some other part of the Middle East to make room for additional Jews and an independent Jewish state.[23] This pro-Zionist solution was hardly an idea one could even raise publicly in the midst of an all-out war.

FDR also seemed quite sensitive to anti-Semitic currents in Spain and Latin America. When Gerardo Murillo, alias Dr. Atl, came out with the first booklet of a planned three-volume series entitled *Judios Sobre America* (Jews over America), FBI Director J. Edgar Hoover sent a translated copy to the White House. The author claimed to demonstrate that FDR himself was of Jewish ancestry and that he had surrounded himself with Jewish advisers and cabinet members. Pictures even allegedly showed a physical resemblance between FDR, his family members, and various Jews. The president expressed the hope that the State Department and the Mexican government would be able to prevent publication abroad. The White House asked the attorney general to prevent publication and distribution in the United States.[24]

When the president addressed the issue of war crimes, he avoided emphasizing the Nazi crimes against Jews. American Jewish organizations arranging a Madison Square Garden rally in July 1942 asked for a presidential statement to be read to the audience. FDR's response was: "The American people not only sympathize with all victims of Nazi crime but will hold the perpetrators of these crimes to strict accountability in a day of reckoning which will surely come." Another presidential statement issued in August 1942 simply denounced barbaric crimes against civilian populations in Axis-occupied countries, particularly on the continent of Europe. FDR mentioned crimes carried out in many of the European countries, as well as in Japanese-controlled China and Southeast Asia. Those involved in such behavior would eventually be brought to justice, he promised. According to presidential confidant Adolf Berle, Dutch government pressure as well as Berle's own feeling that the statement might deter crimes led to the presidential statement. Another presidential declaration was issued in October. Noting that the Axis crimes continued unabated, the president warned that the United States and other nations would bring the perpetrators before courts of law and that all war criminals would have to be surrendered at the end of the war.[25]

There is little question that the President was aware of the Final Solution by November 1942, if not earlier. Given Roosevelt's unwillingness to stir up additional trouble over European Jewry with Congress, certain lobbies, and Middle Eastern nations, he likely resisted believing the early reports of Jews being killed en masse in death factories. If Felix Frankfurter, a Jew, could not force himself to believe them,[26] why should FDR have been different? But the reports kept coming in. It strains credulity to think that Undersecretary Welles would have confirmed the information in Riegner's cable of August 1942 and given Rabbi Wise leeway to make the information public without notifying the president of the situation.[27] And there were signs of minor shifts in policy, quite possibly as the result of the accumulated information. In the fall of 1942, the president did not hesitate to approve the admission, as a special case, of five thousand Jewish children from France—no chance of spies there. But Sumner Welles, who had taken charge of the matter, took pains to avoid adverse publicity.[28]

A second indicator was Roosevelt's request to Congress in the Third War Powers Act for the power to suspend immigration laws in the interest of the war effort. The bill was introduced in November 1942, and Roosevelt lobbied personally with House Speaker Sam Rayburn for the immigration provision only two days after Rabbi Wise's press conferences on the Final Solution.[29] To be sure, the president's emissaries expressly denied, under hostile congressional questioning, that he intended to bring civilian refugees into the United States, but one cannot rule out this possibility. What is clearer is that hostile congressional reaction and suspicion about the entrance of refugees, and the deletion of the provision from the bill, could only have strengthened FDR's inclination not to do battle publicly on behalf of European Jews.

Stephen Wise then asked the president to receive a delegation of Jewish leaders at the White House in early December as part of an international day of mourning (2 December) for European Jews. The Jewish leaders wished to give FDR specific information about the Final Solution. FDR did not wish to see the group and tried to avoid the meeting. He suggested that the delegation go to the State Department instead. Wise persisted, and, with the assistance of presidential adviser David Niles, he obtained an appointment for a small group of Jewish leaders with the president on Tuesday, 8 December, at noon.[30]

The president announced to the group that he had just appointed Herbert Lehman to head the new Office of Foreign Relief and Rehabilitation Operations. It gave him "sadistic satisfaction" to appoint a Jew to this post; "Junkers" (young German noblemen) would eventually have to go to Lehman on their knees and ask for bread. After Wise read the delegation's declaration and presented a detailed memorandum about the Final Solution, he appealed to FDR to bring the extermination program to the world's attention and "to make an effort to stop it." The president said that the government was familiar with most of the facts, but it was hard to find a suitable course of action. The Allies could not make it appear that the entire German people were murderers or agreed with Hitler's actions. He agreed to release another statement denouncing Nazi mass killings. When the delegation wanted some statement that it could release immediately, FDR authorized the rerelease of his statement to July's Madison Square Garden rally, which, he said, had to be quoted exactly. That meant no specific emphasis of Nazi crimes against Jews. The delegation press release exceeded the president's instructions and quoted FDR as saying that he was shocked to learn that two million Jews had, in one way or another, already perished as a result of Nazi rule and crimes.[31]

In his thank-you note to Niles afterward, Wise wrote that the "Chief" could not have been more "friendly and helpful," that he was "cordiality itself." Wise continued:

> The word he gave us will carry through the country and perhaps serve in some degree as warning to the beasts. . . . Thank God for Roosevelt. We ought to

distribute cards throughout the country bearing just four letters, TGFR, and as the Psalmist would have said, thank Him every day and every hour.[32]

It is hard to escape the conclusion that Wise was more impressed by FDR's cordiality, his anti-Nazism, and his strong war leadership than any specific service to European Jewry. The president had not promised retribution against Germany or changes in refugee policy. And the 17 December 1942 United Nations Declaration on War Crimes, which condemned the Nazis' "bestial policy of cold-blooded extermination," resulted more from pressure from the Polish government in exile and Winston Churchill's interest than anything the U.S. government did.

In early 1943, partly because of growing public pressure, the United States and Great Britain agreed to hold the Bermuda Conference to consider refugee assistance. But the early indications were that both governments would hold to their strict line that nothing could be done that might detract from the war effort. Moreover, the layers of visa committees in Washington had slowed visa approvals to a trickle. When a delegation of seven Jewish congressmen sought an appointment with the president to press their complaints on visas and related issues, again FDR tried to divert them to the State Department. Congressman Emanuel Celler refused to accept that and promised an "off the record" session. They got their meeting at the White House on April 1.

White House Secretary Edwin Watson subsequently informed Breckinridge Long that the members of the delegation had criticized the voting of the military officials on the visa committees and had urged a simplification of the visa process. They also apparently pointed out the sharp decrease in the number of visas approved, and the president responded that perhaps visitors' visas would again be issued. In a follow-up meeting with Sumner Welles, Judge Joseph Proskauer of the American Jewish Committee, now also representing the Joint Emergency Committee on European Jewish Affairs, pressed for a Jewish delegation to attend the Bermuda Conference. That request was denied, and the Joint Emergency Committee itself was unable to obtain an audience with FDR before the conference, despite an urgent request.[33]

When Secretary of State Cordell Hull reported the results of the Bermuda Conference to the president, he posed a number of questions of "high policy" that needed presidential decisions. FDR agreed to the idea of moving a specific number of refugees from vulnerable locations to designated temporary havens, the costs to be shared by the United States and Great Britain. He rejected the idea of trying to bring refugees into the United States without compliance with the immigration laws or in excess of quota limitations. He advised against sending large numbers of Jews to North Africa and agreed that anything that would set off prolonged congressional debate should be avoided. FDR shared Hull's view that refugees should not be admitted to the United States as temporary visitors, because that would be seen as an evasion of the quota laws.[34] This did not leave a great deal of room for action.

From 1940 until the middle of 1943, Franklin Roosevelt's behavior with regard to European Jewry showed general consistency. He undoubtedly regretted reported Nazi killings of Jews in Europe, but they did not affect him deeply enough to override his basic instinct: For domestic and foreign-policy reasons, he could not allow the United States to be seen as giving Jews special leniency or assistance. Many millions of Europeans were suffering under Nazi rule, and Allied troops had their hands full with the Germans. It was not advisable—it was strongly inadvisable politically—to make a public issue of the Holocaust. It is significant that the two moves to relax tight immigration restrictions in the fall of 1942 were both supposed to go through quietly and that, when the immigration provision of Third War Powers Act became controversial, the president backed down.

If there was a deeper, more personal reason for presidential inaction, it may well lie in Roosevelt's upbringing and milieu. The president's mother was anti-Semitic, his half brother even more so. The young Franklin Roosevelt absorbed some of this sentiment and only gradually grew out of it. By the time he reached the governorship of New York, he appreciated men and women of talent, whatever their background and descent. Steven Early, his friend and presidential press secretary, apparently did not. Some of FDR's best friends were anti-Semites.[35] If there was anyone aware of the influence of anti-Semitism in the United States, it was Franklin Roosevelt. He may have been overly sensitive to the danger of anti-Semitic reaction to American policies.

By the summer of 1943, three factors began to alter the president's attitude. The first was the improvement of the war situation. The invasion of Italy gave the Americans and the British a toehold on the Continent; the war on the eastern front was going better for the Allies. The war was far from over, but one could now confidently predict the outcome. The president began to take an interest in matters such as shipping food to suffering populations, but he ran into British resistance. He told Francis Pickett of the American Friends Service Committee that the worst conditions were in Poland and that he felt frustrated by the problem.[36] This was not yet a specific concern for the fate of European Jewry, but it was evidence of humanitarian concern.

The second influence, whose weight is difficult to measure, was a personal presentation of the horrors of the Final Solution. On 28 July 1943, at 10:30 A.M., the Polish ambassador, Jan Ciechanowski, and Jan Karski, a lieutenant in the Polish underground army, went upstairs in the White House to the president's study. Serving as a courier from the Polish underground, Karski had arrived in London with messages for the Polish government in exile, the Allied governments, and Polish Jewish leaders. One of his most important messages concerned the Final Solution:

> The unprecedented destruction of the entire Jewish population is not motivated by Germany's *military* requirements. Hitler and his subordinates aim at the total destruction of the Jews *before* the war ends and *regardless* of its outcome. The Allied governments cannot disregard this reality. The Jews in Poland are helpless. . . . Only the powerful Allied governments can help effectively.[37]

Roosevelt began to question Karski about German methods of political terrorism. Karski described mass arrests and concentration camps in Poland, some where mass murders were carried out daily. He went on to talk of his own clandestine visit in 1942 to the Belzec extermination camp, which he entered disguised in the uniform of an Estonian guard. He saw hundreds of dead Jews packed into railway cars, which then were closed and moved outside the camp. When the doors were opened, the corpses were removed and the bodies taken out and burned. He did not actually get to see the gas chambers themselves, which were enclosed and under tight security. Karski emphasized that there was no exaggeration in the accounts of how the Nazis were handling the Jewish question. Polish underground sources estimated the number of Polish Jews killed by November 1942 (when Karski left Poland) at 1.8 million, and the underground was convinced that the Nazis were out to exterminate the entire Jewish population. The president asked many other questions about various underground activities and, after an hour, said good-bye to Karski with a noncommittal comment. "Tell your nation we shall win the war."[38]

Five days before the Roosevelt-Karski meeting, Roosevelt had told Stephen Wise to "go ahead" with his plan for the relief and evacuation of Jewish refugees in Romania and France. That was not quite evidence of presidential backing, although Wise certainly got the impression that FDR approved. Wise followed up his meeting with a letter to the president, who then took the initiative of inquiring with the Treasury Department (not the State Department) on the status of the proposal.[39] That inquiry led to the battle between the Treasury Department and the State Department, which resulted, ultimately, in the formation of the War Refugee Board.[40] The sequence of events suggests that Karski's presentation may have had an impact on the president's action and on initial approval of the rescue plan.

By far the most important factor inducing the president to take action was a changing public and congressional climate. One day after Congressman

Will Rogers, Jr., Joseph Baldwin, and Senator Guy Gillette of Iowa introduced House and Senate resolutions calling upon the president to create a rescue commission to save the surviving European Jews from extinction, Undersecretary of State Edward Stettinius, Jr., who had replaced Sumner Welles, reported to high State Department officials that the president was convinced that not enough was being done on the Jewish refugee problem. FDR suggested establishing small offices in Algiers, Naples, Portugal, Madrid, and Ankara to assist Jews. There might also be another refugee camp and a small amount of money available for the purpose. But European Division Chief Ray Atherton told Stettinius that the United States should avoid unilateral sponsorship of this type of activity, or it would be paying all the bills. Stettinius decided to refer the matter to Breckinridge Long, who was to consult Secretary of State Hull.[41] Whatever impetus FDR generated was quickly dissipated.

Growing criticism of Long and the State Department in Congress and in the media made FDR aware of a political problem, in addition to a humanitarian one. Even then, it took the decisive intervention of Josiah DuBois relayed by Treasury Secretary Morgenthau to make FDR aware, in January 1944, that he had to take the refugee problem away from Long and the State Department or he would face a nasty political scandal. He took what action the Treasury Department contingent wanted but installed Secretary of War Henry Stimson on the War Refugee Board to curb possible impetuousness by Morgenthau and his subordinates.

It is extremely difficult to calculate whether a more active American refugee policy gained significant public support beyond the American Jewish community and liberal circles. There were still plenty of diehard opponents of immigration as well as of any diversion of effort on behalf of non-Americans. The most that one can say is that by 1944 there was less public and congressional resistance to the idea of a special government agency to look after the interests of victims of Nazi persecution.

FDR's willingness to support most of the proposals put forward by the War Refugee Board during 1944, including stern public warnings to the Hungarian government not to turn over its Jews to Germany, represented a significant reversal of earlier wartime policy. The most likely explanation for the turnabout is not that the president saw a chance to score political points during a presidential election year (since the political risks at least equaled the benefits), but that he was now confident about the outcome of the war and was willing to take some risks on behalf of a cause that he had neglected for some time. Still, there were limits to what the president would approve. The idea of bringing Jewish refugees into the United States outside the quota system and the usual immigration regulations obviously raised political as well as legal concerns, which troubled him. The stringent limitations on the refugee camp at Oswego, New York, demonstrate how sensitive the president was about giving European Jews a special status to enter the United States.

It is true that President Roosevelt might have ordered the bombing of the gas chambers at Auschwitz-Birkenau. Even if he had wished to do so (for which there is no evidence), he must have been aware of the political risks. To send American pilots on a long and dangerous mission for the benefit of European Jews threatened with extinction might be justified morally. But would the American people understand it and approve of it? To override the stance of the War Department and to substitute his own moral impulse for official policy would carry grave risks for the president. If the requests for the bombing of Auschwitz reached him through General John J. McCloy, which is likely,[42] FDR shunned the potentially damaging political repercussions of a risky humanitarian strike. Only in retrospect does the efficacy of bombing Auschwitz and the moral imperative outweigh all else. It is instructive, however, to note that Winston Churchill, against the views of the Foreign Office and the military, favored bombing Auschwitz but was unable to prevail.[43] When dealing with large bureaucracies, even chief executives are not all-powerful.

A comparison of Roosevelt's and Churchill's behavior makes it clear that the British prime minister was far more concerned and motivated to make public statements on behalf of European Jewry. The same comparison, however, should make one beware of making the president the archvillain of American refugee policy. For despite Churchill and despite less unfavorable public opinion in Great Britain, British refugee policy toward European Jewry during the war was even less humanitarian than American refugee policy.

Although FDR was adept at manipulating government agencies and bureaucrats, he was to some degree the prisoner of bureaucratic government. A president could set general lines of policy in many areas and try to resolve conflicts and priorities. He could not continually supervise implementation of policy in more than one or two spheres, no matter how great his interest. Refugee policy during the Depression, the era of Nazi expansion, and the World War could not command much of the president's time. Roosevelt had to depend upon the State Department and the War Department to carry out his foreign policy and military action against the Axis powers. He could force some officials to compete with each other. He could insert some of his own appointees into these agencies, New Dealers who understood his own goals and methods better than traditional civil servants and military officers. He could use his chief adviser Harry Hopkins and others as troubleshooters. But he could not carry out a radical purge of the bureaucracy, particularly not in time of war, without serious impairment of administrative efficiency and adverse political repercussions in

Congress as well. All of this meant that the president had to operate in the bureaucratic world around him, however much he disliked it.

That world was stamped by certain traditions and nationalist values. Before 1933 the United States was far more the aloof isolationist seeking to insulate itself from the world's troubles than it was the defender of universal "human rights." Most American civil servants and military officers had received their training and experience in this pre-1933 world; they were not about to revolutionize their attitudes overnight. The institutional climate in the State and War departments, as well as in newer agencies such as the Office of War Information, was strongly opposed to active American assistance to European Jews. Proposed measures on behalf of European Jews frequently seemed to interfere with the normal functions of these agencies, and thereby with the success of the war effort. The fact that relatively few American officials could comprehend the extent and horror of the Final Solution only made it easier for them to pass on to other matters. Europe would always have its problems; the important thing now was to win the war.

The fluctuations in American refugee policy during the Roosevelt administration were determined in part by presidential initiatives but in part also by bureaucratic politics. The Labor Department's initiatives to loosen immigration regulations in 1933-1934 contributed to the State Department's increased willingness to recognize affidavits from American citizens and residents pledging financial support for their European relatives. The transfer of the Immigration and Naturalization Service from the Labor Department to the Justice Department in 1940 weakened the Labor Department's influence over refugee policy and facilitated the State Department's tightening of immigration regulations. The creation of the War Refugee Board in 1944 gave advocates of humanitarian measures a new foothold within the government and thus made possible a variety of lifesaving measures in Europe.

The evidence presented in this chapter indicates that the president was quietly more liberal on the admission of Jewish refugees to the United States than the bureaucracy was during the 1930s and approximately as restrictionist as the bureaucratic consensus during the 1940s. But, even when FDR chose to intervene personally in refugee policy, as he did in 1938-1939, he needed help to carry out his ideas. The history of American refugee policy between 1939 and 1945 indicates that most government agencies and officials were more efficient restrictionists than humanitarians.

The U.S. government did not match Adolf Hitler's single-minded frenzy to wipe out the Jewish "race" with corresponding determination to save those Jews who could be saved during the Holocaust. FDR's reluctance to engage himself directly in the cause of European Jewish refugees resulted, first, from his almost exclusive focus on the war itself; second, from his perception of adverse political realities in the United States and in the West generally; and, third, from his dependence upon a bureaucracy largely unaccustomed to humanitarian initiatives.

There are always questions about how far a politician can be ahead of his own time and his own society and remain a successful politician. American refugee policy was one area where Franklin Roosevelt, so venturesome in other spheres, did not feel free to take on much additional risk.

Notes

1. David S. Wyman, *Abandonment of the Jews: America and the Holocaust, 1941-1945* (New York: Pantheon Books, 1984), 2-113, admits the problem posed by lack of clear evidence of Roosevelt's views. This does not prevent him from labeling FDR as insensitive and indifferent. See also ibid., xi, 103.

2. Ibid., 19-41.

3. Copy in memo to Attorney General Jackson to Secretary of War, 1 August 1940, Record Group (RG) 107, Fifth Column Correspondence, National Archives (NA). See also Department of State, Division of Current Information, Radio Bulletin No. 185, 5 August 1940, copy in RG 107, Records of the Office of the Secretary of War, NA.

4. Breckinridge Long Diary, 22 May and 22 June 1940, Library of Congress (LC), cited and discussed in Joseph Lash, *Roosevelt and Churchill, 1939-1941: The Partnership that Saved the West* (New York: Norton, 1976), 137.

5. Messersmith to Welles, 22 May 1940, Messersmith Papers, Folder 1360, University of Delaware; and Messersmith to Frankfurter, May 1940, Frankfurter Papers, Messersmith Folder, LC.

6. Wyman, *Abandonment of the Jews*, 79-103.

7. Presidential Press Conference, 5 June 1940, in *Presidential Press Conferences*, vol. 13-14 (New York: Da Capo Press, 1972). See Wyman, *Abandonment of the Jews*, 79-103.

8. Richard Dunlop, *Behind Japanese Lines* (Chicago: Rand McNally, 1979), 210-11; and Bernard Wasserstein, *Britain and the Jews of Europe, 1939-1945* (New York: Oxford University Press, 1979), 84-102.

9. Bullitt's speech is reprinted in the *New York Times*, 19 August 1940. Information about Welles and Roosevelt is in Bullitt's memorandum, 12 August 1940, reprinted in *For the President, Personal and Secret: Correspondence between Franklin D. Roosevelt and William C. Bullitt*, ed. Orville H. Bullitt (Boston:

Houghton Mifflin, 1972), 499. Bullitt had earlier, well before the fall of France, written FDR much the same thing—that large numbers of Jewish refugees in France were spying for Germany. See Ted Morgan, *FDR* (New York: Grafton Books, 1986), 498-499.

10. Circular telegram, 19 September 1940, RG 59, 811.111 Refugees/260, NA; Johnson to Secretary of State, 28 September 1940, RG 59, 811.111 Refugees/376, NA.

11. Secretary of State's memo, 26 July 1941, RG 59, 811.111 War Regulations/366A, NA.

12. Eleanor Roosevelt to McDonald, 2 March 1941, Eleanor Roosevelt Papers, Franklin D. Roosevelt Library (FDRL), Hyde Park, N.Y.

13. FDR Memorandum for the Secretary of the Interior, 18 December 1940, Official File (OF) 86, FDRL.

14. Henry Feingold, *Politics of Rescue: The Roosevelt Administration and the Holocaust, 1938-1945.* (New York: Rutgers University Press, 1980), 155-156.

15. Welles to Mr. President, 21 December 1940, RG 59, Central Decimal File (CDF) 840.48 Refugees/23 52, NA.

16. Feingold, *Politics of Rescue,* 142; Berle Diary, 5 March 1941, Berle Papers, FDRL.

17. Robert Dallek, *Franklin D. Roosevelt and American Foreign Policy, 1932-1945* (New York: Oxford University Press, 1979), 334-335.

18. *Congressional Record,* 5 June 1941.

19. Dallek, *Franklin D. Roosevelt,* 277, 285, 267.

20. Frankfurter telephone conversation with Secretary of War Stimson, 16 June 1943, transcript in Stimson Papers, Roll 127, LC.

21. Hull to FDR, 7 May 1943; undated summary of Colonel Hoskins's report on the Near East; Welles to the President, 14 June 1943, President's Secretary's File: Confidential File, State Department 1943, FDRL.

22. Roosevelt to King Saud, 15 June 1943, President's Secretary's File: Confidential File, State Department 1943, FDRL.

23. Morgenthau Presidential Diaries, 3 December 1942, FDRL.

24. J. Edgar Hoover memo to Watson and President, 2 December 1942; Early to Welles, 4 December 1942; Welles to Early, 12 December 1942, President's Secretary's File: Confidential File, State Department, FDRL.

25. The comment of July 1942 is quoted in Jewish Delegation press release, 8 December 1942, RG 1, EXO-29, Waldman Papers, Germany/Nazism/American Jewish Congress, American Jewish Committee Archives, New York, N.Y. For the other statements, see OF 5152; White House press release, 7 October 1942; and Berle Diary, 18 August 1942, and attached Statement of the President of the United States, FDRL.

26. Walter Laqueur, *The Terrible Secret: Suppression of the Truth about Hitler's "Final Solution"* (Boston: Little, Brown, 1980), 3, 237.

27. Ibid. 157-195.

28. Ibid.

29. Ibid.

30. Watson memorandum, 30 November 1942; Watson comment about FDR's reaction, 1 December 1942; Wise to Dear Boss, 2 December 1942, OF 76-C, FDRL; Wise to Niles, 2 December 1942, Wise Papers, American Jewish Historical Society (AJHS); and Welles to Watson, 4 December 1942, OF 76-C, FDRL.

31. President of the Jewish Labor Committee Adolph Held's account of meeting, pt. 3, sec. 1, no. 15, Jewish Labor Committee Archives, quoted by Monty Noam Penkower, *The Jews Were Expendable* (Illinois: University of Illinois Press, 1983), 85-86; and Jewish Delegation Press Release, 8 December 1942, copy in RG 1, EXO-29, Waldman Papers, Germany/Nazism/American Jewish Congress, American Jewish Committee Archives.

32. Wise to Niles, 9 December 1942, Wise Papers, AJHS.

33. Watson to Long, 1 April 1943, and attached documents, OF 86, FDRL, copy also in RG 59, 811.111 Refugees/4-143, NA. See also Celler's report in Meeting of the Joint Emergency Committee on European Jewish Affairs, 10 April 1943, American Jewish Committee Archives.

34. *Foreign Relations of the United States (FRUS)*, 1943, vol. 1, 177-179.

35. Morgan, *FDR*, esp. 23, 37, 47, 275, 445.

36. Pickett Journal, 12 April and 15 June 1943, American Friends Services Committee (AFSC).

37. Jan Ciechanowski, *Defeat in Victory* (Garden City: Doubleday, 1947), 179-180. Nowak's message is reprinted in Laqueur, *The Terrible Secret*, 232.

38. Ciechanowski, *Defeat in Victory*, 182; and Laqueur, *The Terrible Secret*, 231, 236.

39. Wise to the President, 23 July 1943, and handwritten comment on Meltzer memorandum, "Proposed Arrangement for Relief and Evacuation of Refugees in Rumania and France," 30 July 1943, RG 59, CDF 862.4016/2286 and 840.48 Refugees/4211, NA. On 10 August 1943, Wise reported confidentially and off the record about the evacuation plan to the Joint Emergency Committee for Jewish Affairs, stating that the government had approved the plan. RG 1, EXO-29, Waldman File, Joint Emergency Committee, American Jewish Committee Archives.

40. Laqueur, *The Terrible Secret*, 229-238.

41. Meeting of the undersecretary with the assistant secretaries, political advisers, and geographic division heads, 11 November 1943; Stettinius to Long, 11

November 1943, Stettinius Papers, 215, Meeting with Assistant Secretaries, October 1943 and Long Folders, respectively, University of Virginia.

42. Laqueur, *The Terrible Secret,* 229-238.

43. Martin S. Gilbert, *Auschwitz and the Allies* (New York: Holt, Rinehart and Winston, 1981), esp. 267-76.

7

The Failure to Provide a Safe
Haven for European Jewry

Richard Breitman

Writing several years later, however, Breitman seems to render a harsher judgment in this chapter on "The Failure to Provide a Safe Haven for European Jews." However, he also admonishes historians who are critical of the Roosevelt administration that they must "present evidence that alternative policies were logistically and politically possible."

During the Hyde Park Conference, Breitman also reminded participants that historians eager to issue moral judgments about policymakers of the 1930s and 1940s must remember there was no conception then of a Holocaust. Yet Breitman also demonstrates how difficult it is to view the past without imposing the knowledge of the present. He argues the West "should have conducted refugee negotiations with Germany in 1938-1939 more aggressively, if only because there was some chance of saving substantial numbers of lives." But of course at the time, no one had any notion that substantial numbers of lives were at risk.

Virtually all of the specialists on American reaction to the Holocaust agree that America collectively paid little attention to Nazi persecution of the Jews and failed to offer refuge to most of those Jews who might have escaped a Nazi-dominated continent. These conclusions have both moral and political dimensions: Government policies that saved lives would have served U.S.

national interest as well. (I will concentrate in this chapter on government policies, and on the works primarily about government policies, rather than on the role of Jewish organizations.) Yet the handling of the moral dimension poses problems for the historian, for moral sensibilities often differ.[1]

Perhaps the most moralistic of the previous studies of American policies during the Holocaust is David S. Wyman's well-researched *The Abandonment of the Jews: America and the Holocaust, 1941-1945.*[2] Wyman lashes out against a wide range of targets: The American government (in passing, also the British government), the press, Christian and some Jewish organizations, and the American public all willingly ignored or discounted the tragedy of European Jewry. The sweeping nature of his criticism, however, makes it hard for Wyman to weigh the importance and interaction of each political factor. Could the State Department and the White House have adopted a radically different course in light of anti-Semitic and anti-immigrant attitudes entrenched in Congress and the public, as well as reluctance and resistance in other executive agencies? Wyman merely notes that strong currents of nativism and anti-Semitism diminished the possibilities of sympathetic response.[3]

Conversely, could a more generous Congress and public opinion, stimulated perhaps by more active and unified Jewish organizations and/or a more attentive and interested press, have put sufficient pressure upon a reluctant executive branch? Or were congressional and public attitudes so far removed from sympathy to refugees that this scenario was out of the question?[4] If the latter is true, was Franklin Roosevelt's attitude toward Jewish refugees and the Holocaust abnormally insensitive, as Wyman maintains without direct evidence? Where was the primary obstacle to rescue measures, and how much would have had to change before the United States could have attempted rescue and relief on a significant scale?

Broader studies of American society can provide some assistance in weighing the obstacles. In *One Nation Divisible: Class, Race, and Ethnicity in the United States since 1938,* Richard Polenberg describes an American society strongly divided by, and concerned with, class, color, and ethnicity. Pragmatic New Deal officials including FDR "seemed" insensitive to racial injustice because minorities were politically powerless and Southern voters and congressmen had great political leverage.[5]

Polenberg's picture of the president and the administration on these moral issues is far from flattering; on one occasion FDR's silence is "deafening." But whatever his own sympathies, Polenberg admits that the administration had other important objectives—for example, in foreign policy—some of which could have been impaired by liberal racial or ethnic stands. The result is certainly not to justify Roosevelt's behavior, but not to overlook or discount his political difficulties either. The greatest obstacle to more progressive and humane measures here was the American public—or at least major segments of it.

Polling data support Polenberg's emphasis on ethnic divisiveness and anti-Semitism. A *Fortune* magazine survey in July 1938 showed 4.9 percent willing to raise immigration quotas to accommodate refugees and 18.2 percent willing to allow immigration within existing quotas, while 87.4 percent wanted to limit immigration further. Immediately after Kristallnacht in November 1938, 94 percent of a sample in a poll (by the National Opinion Research Center in Chicago) disapproved of Nazi treatment of Jews, but 72 percent were also opposed to admitting a large number of German Jews into the United States, and 52 percent were opposed to providing assistance to resettle Jews elsewhere. Polls consistently showed that most Americans thought Jews had too much power, with 58 percent holding that view in June 1945.[6]

If public sentiment against increased immigration and particularly immigration of Jewish refugees was roughly consistent during the Depression, the recovery years, and the war, however, government policy was not. In spite of public opinion, sometimes quietly and within certain limits, the government could and did undertake initiatives. The first step is to discover when and how they occurred.

Most previous studies have begun with Jews seeking escape from Germany in 1938 and carried it through the end of the war.[7] In actuality, Jews sought to emigrate from Germany in substantial numbers from 1933 on, but they were initially blocked by existing barriers to immigration into the United States. The biggest immediate problem was not the limit of the annual German quota, a relatively generous 25,957, little of which was being used. The main obstacle was that the State Department, in 1930, had instructed consular officials abroad to adopt a new interpretation of a regulation barring prospective immigrants likely to become a public charge. Instead of forcing a judgment on the individual's capacity to do useful work in the United States, this regulation now was used to curtail immigration because of perceived labor conditions in the United States.[8] Any prospective immigrant who needed to work to support himself or herself was suddenly considered likely to become a public charge.

An early 1933 debate over the possibility of accommodating "political and religious refugees" embroiled the State Department and the Labor Department and was discussed in cabinet. Ultimately, Attorney General Homer Cummings and his assistant Alexander Holtzhoff decided that the Labor Department could legally accept a bond from an outside party to guarantee support for a prospective immigrant, precluding a consul from declaring him or her financially ineligible for a visa.[9]

This early controversy, most of which was kept out of the press, typified later developments in a number of respects. First, the issue was not changing immigration laws, but using regulations to adjust the flow of refugee immigrants, either restricting it or easing it. Second, there was disagreement over whether the State Department and consular officials abroad should have exclusive jurisdiction over immigration/refugee matters. Third, there was a degree of presidential involvement in the dispute between two departments.[10] Finally, neither the refugee advocates within the administration nor American Jewish organizations lobbying from outside wanted to take the cause of Jewish refugees to Congress or the public, a fact that their opponents inside and outside of government recognized and exploited. The Labor Department, worried by anti-Communist and anti-alien hysteria, in the end backed away from use of "public charge" bonds in 1934.

The State Department won the battle over jurisdiction in part with a concession. By lessening the stringency of its regulations, it raised the level of immigration from Germany. The level of immigration from Germany rose from 1,300 in fiscal 1933 to more than 4,000 in fiscal 1934, with Commissioner of Immigration Daniel MacCormack boasting that the Labor Department's pressure on the State Department was primarily responsible for this increase. The State Department and the Labor Department, meanwhile, both informed Congress that there was no need to reduce the quotas through legislation.[11]

In late 1936 came a second adjustment of the "public charge" regulation, this one stimulated partly by slightly more progressive elements within the State Department and partly by the new political climate after the 1936 presidential election. Now consuls were told—and specifically because of the quality of German Jewish applicants and the willingness of American relatives to provide support—to make a judgment whether an applicant would "probably" become a public charge, not whether he or she could possibly become one. This time, the number of immigration visas granted nearly doubled within a year, from less than 7,000 in fiscal 1936 to about 12,500 in fiscal 1937.[12] Affidavits of support from relatives (how much money was required and how close the relatives had to be were still under dispute) were used to lessen the danger of immigrants burdening the American taxpayer.

After the Anschluss in March 1938, President Roosevelt himself suggested further liberalizing immigration procedures (as well as combining the German and Austrian quotas, giving Austrian Jews a better shot at immigration visas), a message that quickly was translated into use of the full German quota. After Kristallnacht and after prompting by Secretary of Labor Frances Perkins, FDR also announced in mid-November that he was extending the visitors' visas of twelve thousand to fifteen thousand German Jews already in the United States by at least six months.[13]

In three steps and through administrative measures, the government raised the flow of German Jewish refugees from fewer than two thousand in

1933 to more than thirty thousand in fiscal 1939. In spite of a consultative role given in 1938 to a President's Advisory Commission on Political Refugees, however, the State Department ended up retaining exclusive jurisdiction over immigration policy. If administrative changes had occurred earlier, or if outside restraints had been imposed upon State Department control of immigration policy, tens of thousands more Germans Jews would have been able to enter the United States, and regulations might not have been so easily abused from 1940 to 1944.

What the State Department and its consuls reluctantly granted in the way of easing, they could remove under new political circumstances. Security concerns—among the public and government officials—about Communists, Fascists, and even unwilling refugee spies coerced by threats against their relatives still in Germany resulted in a significant reduction of visa approvals to Jews in Germany during 1940,[14] partly through an instruction to consuls in mid-1940 not to admit applicants if there was any doubt about them whatsoever. In June 1941, Congress passed the Bloom-Van Nuys Bill authorizing consuls to withhold any type of visa if they knew or had reason to believe that the applicant might endanger public safety. New and more extensive application and screening procedures added delays and provided opportunities for further denials. For the rest of the war, only a small fraction of the German quota and some other European quotas were used, although Jewish refugees in some neutral countries applied for visas under the quotas of the countries where they had been citizens.

There is, therefore, a degree of irrationality in concentrating criticism on the immigration quota system, when the full German quota was used to allow Jews from Germany and Austria to leave only during the period from mid-1938 to late 1939. The quota system was a big obstacle to immigration for Polish, Czech, Hungarian, or Romanian Jews, the quotas for these countries being tiny compared with their large Jewish populations. But German Jews seemed to be in greatest peril in 1938-1939, and scholars have concentrated on what might have been done for them. If the West had only acted promptly, some historians argue, Germany would have been more than willing to give over its Jews.[15]

More than 300,000 Germans, perhaps 90 percent of them Jews, had applied for immigration visas to the United States by early 1939.[16] The Roosevelt administration had only two avenues to bring about a greater exodus of Jews from Germany: legislation in Congress and international diplomacy. In early 1939, Senator Robert F. Wagner (D, New York) pushed a bill to admit 20,000 German Jewish children to the United States outside the regular quota. The political possibilities of bringing in children were far greater than the odds of winning the admission of adults beyond the quota limit, and the substantial impact of Kristallnacht was still fresh in the minds of Americans. Yet two-thirds of the American public, according to a poll, rejected the Wagner-Rogers Bill. Not surprisingly, a private poll of the Senate in March indicated that the bill would likely fail. The Senate Immigration Committee subsequently amended the bill to give the 20,000 children preference within the German quota, but to count them as part of the annual limit (by then) of 27,370. A majority in the Senate then registered approval in another (July) private poll, but the House Immigration Committee never reported the bill out. It is certainly possible that a vigorous endorsement by the White House might have brought passage of the Wagner-Rogers Bill in some form. But the president gave instructions not to take action. In August, facing an obstreperous Congress, FDR made it known that he would not ask for government funds to resettle refugees *abroad* unless he had an even chance on the Hill.[17]

Given the fate of the Wagner-Rogers Bill and the evidence of congressional attitudes, it is hard to imagine any other liberal immigration initiative in Congress at any other time from 1933 to 1945 being successful. Neither the administration nor Jewish leaders can be blamed much for this result; perhaps they can be blamed for not trying hard enough in the face of long political odds. They can be blamed for a moral lapse, not for the fact that the path of immigration legislation could not have substantially reduced the toll of the Nazi Final Solution.

Mindful of the political difficulties at home, in the spring of 1938 FDR called for an international conference on the refugee problem and pressed for a new international organization. Meanwhile, the president considered the possibility of settling refugees on a broad scale in sparsely settled territories throughout the world.[18] Settlement abroad, of course, posed fewer political problems than immigration at home; if private Jewish money were used, the problem of Jewish refugees was largely removed from the purview of the congressional committee on Immigration and Naturalization. But the Evian (France) Conference and then the Intergovernmental Committee on Political Refugees accomplished little.

For refugee diplomacy to work, other countries or colonies had to accept more Jewish refugees. While more and more German Jewish refugees were entering the United States during 1938, it was a fact that the immigration quota for Germany had not changed. In this sense, the United States set a poor example. (Its use of regulations to smooth the path for refugees here came back to haunt the Roosevelt administration.) The president might have reversed the impression that the United States was willing to do little itself if he had sought and won congressional approval for funding of refugee resettlement. Meanwhile, the State Department, perhaps more concerned about American relations with other countries than with the refugee problem, did not pressure other countries to change their existing immigration laws.[19]

The Intergovernmental Committee on Political Refugees had to manage the additional Sisyphean task of negotiating with Germany for the orderly emigration of Jews. The situation in Berlin was cloudy, and, even in retrospect, it is hard to determine whether Nazi Germany in fact wanted a negotiated settlement of its "Jewish problem." Hjalmar Schacht and Hermann Göring certainly were interested in an arrangement to allow some German Jews to leave for places of settlement abroad in return for economic benefits to Germany: seizure of Jewish property in Germany, "world Jewry's" financing of resettlement, stimulation of German exports. But Joseph Goebbels, Joachim Ribbentrop, Richard Heydrich, and Heinrich Himmler were opposed to negotiations with the Intergovernmental Committee on Political Refugees as well as any regulated Jewish emigration.[20] No one could fathom where Adolf Hitler stood, and Hitler's approval was essential for any bargain. Based on what we now know of the nature of the Nazi regime, all of these differences were not artificial poses—part of a calculated "good-cop–bad-cop" strategy—but rather typical of the factionalism and ideological variations within the Nazi elite.

George Rublee of the Intergovernmental Committee on Political Refugees and Helmut Wohlthat of the Economics Ministry did exchange memoranda of understanding in February 1939 that gave Germany economic benefits from refugee resettlement to be financed by Jewish money from outside Germany. None of the parties, including Western Jewish representatives, took steps to carry the agreement out, a situation that President Roosevelt himself criticized in a May 1939 meeting with American Jewish leaders and some State Department officials.[21] All in all, the West could have and should have conducted refugee negotiations with Germany in 1938-1939 more aggressively, if only because there was some chance of saving substantial numbers of lives.

Even if it had been successful, however, the Rublee-Wohlthat arrangement could not have prevented the Holocaust. Hundreds of thousands of Jews, even under this arrangement, would have remained in Germany. There is new evidence that the SS had plans even before the war to kill those Jews left in the country.[22] Then there were the millions of Jews within Eastern Europe soon to fall under the jackboot of the Nazis. Hitler was fixated not just with German Jews, but with "world Jewry." Theories about avoiding the Holocaust through resettling Jews rest on a lack of knowledge of Nazi ideology and military objectives and lack of consideration of how many millions of Jews needed to be removed from Nazi reach.

From 1939 to 1942, the war submerged the issue of Jewish refugees in more than one respect. First, there were now hundreds of thousands of non-Jewish refugees (as well as additional Jewish refugees) in flight from Poland, Finland, France, Belgium, the Netherlands, and (for different reasons) Spain. Some fled from the fighting or the destruction of cities and towns; others sought to escape the hardship and/or political danger of hostile foreign occupation. For Western nations to single out Jews as particularly vulnerable and deserving of immediate assistance would have been to defy pressure from the various governments in exile for help for their people—inconceivable unless there was clear Western realization that the Nazis were slaughtering Jews en masse, simply because they were Jews. In spite of some available information about Nazi killings, there were many psychological and political obstacles to consciousness and acceptance of the existence of a Final Solution.[23] Moreover, the military situation was so critical for the Allies during most of this time that there was no disposition to provide aid or outside assistance to civilians in enemy territories anywhere.

As most of the specialists have argued, reliable information of an overall Nazi plan to exterminate the Jews of Europe first came to the West through Switzerland in August 1942. It took several months before Undersecretary of State Sumner Welles was willing to concede to Rabbi Stephen Wise that the State Department had gathered enough information from other sources to confirm the original report; other State Department officials were not so forthcoming.[24] An inter-Allied declaration of 17 December 1942 denouncing Nazi implementation of Hitler's oft-repeated intention to exterminate the Jews of Europe represents a major turning point in the level of official Allied recognition of the Final Solution, but this declaration only threatened retribution against war criminals and avoided all mention of rescue.[25]

American and British government policies toward the rescue and relief of Jews did not change substantially, and much of what was done between December 1942 and December 1943—especially the Bermuda Conference of April 1943—was largely for show. British public opinion was aroused, and American Jewish organizations and some congressmen were pressing for action, so there was a virtue in seeming to consider rescue and relief. But neither Britain nor the United States wanted to give support to Nazi propaganda that the Allies were fighting on behalf of the Jews.[26]

Within this framework, however, there are some significant differences of interpretations among historians. Henry L. Feingold argues that Allied "silence" encouraged Nazi officials to continue with the extermination of the Jews, whereas more open criticism might have forced the cancellation of the Final Solution. He also maintains that an effort to arouse the German public against the Nazi leaders on this issue might have succeeded.[27] The thrust of most research in recent years on the Final Solution does nothing to support these claims, and only a few courageous Germans gave the fate of Jews a high priority. Feingold and Wyman both present relatively optimistic pictures of what releases of Jews might have been arranged in 1943 through negotiations either with Germany or such Axis satellites as Romania and Bulgaria. So far, the studies of the German side about the prospects for such negotiations are not encouraging. Hitler seemed to be willing to permit small releases of Jews only in exchange for major political and economic benefits for Germany, and Germany frequently blocked its satellites from releasing Jews.[28]

The steps that led to the creation of the War Refugee Board involved a major and dramatic behind-the-scenes battle during the last four months of 1943 between the Treasury Department and the State Department and considerable pressure by the Treasury Department—especially by Josiah DuBois—on the White House. All of the major studies here agree on the basic chronology and dynamics, differing only on points of detail.[29] Most of the authors give the War Refugee Board credit for belatedly ending the American government's passivity about the Nazi slaughter of Jews, but there are mixed reviews of the board's effectiveness.[30]

Scholars and the public alike have paid great attention to the Allied unwillingness to bomb Auschwitz-Birkenau as a means of halting the "extermination" of Jews there, especially since the publication of an article on the subject by David Wyman.[31] In some ways, this missed opportunity has come to symbolize, in the popular mind, all of the failures of American and British refugee policy since 1938.

The War Department took a resolute stand in January 1944 against involvement in rescue operations for civilians that were unrelated to military operations. So the requests from Jewish organizations and eventually from the War Refugee Board itself, from June until November 1944, for the bombing either of the rail lines to Auschwitz or of the gas chambers at Birkenau were never seriously considered—in spite of the fact that the I. G. Farben complex at nearby Monowitz was bombed and aerial reconnaissance photographs of Birkenau were available.[32]

I, too, believe that Auschwitz-Birkenau could have and should have been bombed because, if the gas chambers had been destroyed, it would have slowed down the killing of tens of thousands. Wyman's conclusion that the Nazis would also have been forced to reassess the extermination program in light of the need to commit new manpower to it seems stretched,[33] however, given the fact that Nazi officials continued to kill Jews in various ways even after Auschwitz was evacuated in January 1945.

The Nazi mass murder of some six million Jews, as well as smaller numbers of Gypsies, Poles, Soviets, POWs, civilians, and assorted other groups is the most horrifying and traumatic episode in Western history. It is natural for anyone re-creating the events to want to find ways to have brought about a different result, as well as to use the historical memory of this catastrophe to help prevent future holocausts. The historian certainly may criticize the inadequacies of government policies and government efforts, but he or she also needs to present evidence that alternative policies were logistically and politically possible, as well as likely to achieve desired results. Governments and politicians do not lightly undertake humanitarian initiatives outside their own countries— even when they do recognize a great moral crisis of Western civilization. They have to be convinced that the initiatives will work and that their constituents are willing to pay the price. If scholars' moral outrage interferes with accurate presentation and careful analysis of events here, neither the historical community nor the public will be served.[34]

Perhaps the more that the politicians, the press, and the pulpits denounce what the United States did and did not do during the Holocaust, the less it is likely that the United States will make the same mistakes in the event of genocide elsewhere. But the effects of historical-moral condemnation do not seem to have resonated very far into the U.S. government in the cases of Cambodia and Bosnia. And Breckinridge Long, John J. McCloy, and Franklin Roosevelt cannot be blamed for insensitivity there.

Notes

1. My coauthor Alan Kraut and I, in our study of American refugee policy, for example, have been charged with providing "mitigating circumstances" for the Roosevelt administration. The term "mitigating circumstances" indicates that our judgment about politicians, officials, and events was less unfavorable than the received view; it also implies that we offered some justification of immoral behavior. Richard Breitman and Alan M. Kraut, *American Refugee Policy and European Jewry, 1933-1945* (Bloomington: Indiana University Press, 1987), reviewed by Henry L. Feingold in *Moment* 17 (April 1992), 61. Another reviewer complained that we had deliberately omitted moral considerations and failed to treat the Holocaust as the great moral crisis in modern Western civilization. Melvin I. Urovsky, "The Law's Delay," *Midstream* 35 (February-March 1989), 62. Having written two additional books on the Holocaust, I trust that most observers will grant that I regard the subject as important.

2. David S. Wyman, *The Abandonment of the Jews: America and the Holocaust 1941-1945* (New York: Pantheon Books, 1984).

3. Ibid., 327.
4. Detailed investigation of congressional attitudes is lacking in all of the studies of American refugee policy, including mine. There is some useful material on Congress in Roland Young, *Congressional Politics in the Second World War* (New York: Columbia University Press, 1956). Leonard Dinnerstein has done very good work on Congress in the period following World War II. See "Anti-Semitism in the 80th Congress: The Displaced Persons Act of 1948," in Leonard Dinnerstein, *Uneasy at Home: Anti-Semitism and the American Experience* (New York: Columbia University Press, 1987), 197-217, and, more generally, Dinnerstein, *America and the Survivors of the Holocaust* (New York: Columbia University Press, 1982). Saul S. Friedman, *No Haven for the Oppressed: United States Policy toward Jewish Refugees, 1938-1945* (Detroit: Wayne State University Press, 1973); Monty N. Penkower, *The Jews Were Expendable: Free World Diplomacy and the Holocaust* (Illinois: University of Illinois Press, 1983); Haskel Lookstein, *Were We Our Brothers' Keepers? The Public Response of American Jews to the Holocaust, 1938-1944* (New York: Hartmore House, 1986); and Aaron Berman, *Nazism, the Jews, and American Zionism, 1933-1948* (Detroit: Wayne State University Press, 1990) all deal with government policy to some extent but focus on the activities (and failures) of American Jewry in the struggle for rescue and relief, without persuasively demonstrating that more Jewish pressure could have budged the government. Of considerably lower quality is Rafael Medoff, *The Deafening Silence* (New York: Shapisky Publishers, 1987).
5. Richard Polenberg, *One Nation Divisible: Class, Race, and Ethnicity in the United States since 1938* (New York: Penguin Books, 1980), 31-45. FDR quietly lobbied the governor of Alabama to commute the sentences of the African American Scottsboro youths unjustly convicted of raping two white women, but did not speak out. Similarly, the president watched a filibuster send an antilynching bill to defeat in the Senate without taking a stand. Ethnic divisions contributed to the public hysteria regarding the Fifth Column threat in 1940-1941. The government took measures to curb aliens (and reduce immigration) but also did a good deal to check the hysteria and reassure the public, according to Polenberg.
6. *Fortune* 18 (July 1938), 80, cited by Judith Tydor Baumel, "The Jewish Refugee Children from Europe in the Eyes of the American Press and Public Opinion 1934-1945," *Holocaust and Genocide Studies* 5 (fall 1990), 296-297. Daniel Yankelovich, "Re-creation of the American Public's Perception of the Events from 1933-1945" (paper presented at "The Holocaust and the Media," Harvard Divinity School–WCBV-TV Conference, 19 May 1988); Dinnerstein, *Uneasy at Home,* 179. Generally on polls, see Charles Stember, ed., *Jews in the Mind of America* (New York: Basic Books, 1966).

7. Typical here is David S. Wyman, *Paper Walls: America and the Refugee Crisis, 1938-1941* (Amherst: University of Massachusets Press, 1968), vii: "If in the crucial years from 1938 to 1941, the world had opened its doors to the victims of persecution, the history of Europe's Jews from 1942 to 1945 would have been significantly different." See also Arthur D. Morse, *While Six Million Died: A Chronicle of American Apathy* (New York: Random House, 1967); Henry L. Feingold, *The Politics of Rescue: The Roosevelt Administration and the Holocaust, 1938-1945* (New Brunswick, N. J.: Rutgers University Press, 1970 and New York: Rutgers University Press, 1980); and the works cited in note 2 and note 4 above.

Some more recent literature has emphasized the continuities in Jewish efforts to escape Germany from 1933 on. See Herbert A. Strauss, "Jewish Emigration from Germany: Nazi Policies and Jewish Responses" (I) and (II), in *Leo Baeck Institute Yearbook* 25 and 26 (1980 and 1981), 313-361 and 343-409, respectively; Irving Abella and Harold Troper, *None Is Too Many: Canada and the Jews of Europe, 1933-1948* (New York: Random House, 1983); Michael Blakeney, *Australia and the Jewish Refugees, 1933-1948* (Sydney: Pergamon Press, 1985); and Judith Tydor Baumel, *Unfulfilled Promise: Rescue and Resettlement of Jewish Refugee Children in the United States, 1934-1945* (Juneau: Denali Press, 1990). On a related subject, see Deborah E. Lipstadt, *Beyond Belief: The American Press and the Coming of the Holocaust, 1933-1945* (New York: Free Press, 1986). Also noteworthy in its "early" start is an older work by A. J. Sherman, *Island Refuge: Britain and Refugees from the Third Reich* (Berkeley: University of California Press, 1973).

8. According to one well-informed observer, the consuls in Germany had been told in 1930 to limit immigration visas to a maximum of 10 percent of the national quota. Breitman and Kraut, *American Refugee Policy*, 15.

9. See a more detailed account in Breitman and Kraut, *American Refugee Policy*, 15-28.

10. There are several signs of FDR's involvement in this dispute. See Breitman and Kraut, *American Refugee Policy*, 18, 21, 254n33.

11. Ibid., 22-25.

12. Ibid., 48-50.

13. Wyman, *Paper Walls*, 43-73; Feingold, *Politics of Rescue*, 22-44; Breitman and Kraut, *American Refugee Policy*, 52-63.

14. Although almost all of the German quota was used during the calendar year 1940, most of the visas were given to German Jews already outside Nazi control—some in the Western Hemisphere. It was difficult for German Jews still in Germany to assemble the documentation they needed to emigrate, as well as to obtain transportation, though some thousands still managed to do so in

early 1940. But by, mid-1940, American security concerns sharply cut the number whose visa applications were accepted in Germany.

15. Feingold, *Politics of Rescue,* 58, 66-74.
16. Breitman and Kraut, *American Refugee Policy,* 66.
17. Wyman, *Paper Walls,* 75-87. Friedman, *No Haven,* 91-104. Breitman and Kraut, *American Refugee Policy,* 73, 75.
18. In October 1939, the president went so far as to estimate the number of potential refugees—people who were unwanted where they were and who would prefer to start new lives elsewhere—at ten million to twenty million. Breitman and Kraut, *American Refugee Policy,* 76.
19. George S. Messersmith's attitude and role were not constructive here. In addition to Breitman and Kraut, *American Refugee Policy,* 60-61, see Jesse H. Stiller, *George S. Messersmith: Diplomat of Democracy* (Chapel Hill: University of North Carolina Press, 1987), 123-124, 131-132.
20. Richard Breitman, *The Architect of Genocide: Himmler and the Final Solution* (Hanover, N.H.: Bodley Head, 1992), 59-62.
21. Breitman and Kraut, *American Refugee Policy,* 69.
22. The American consul-general in Berlin, Raymond H. Geist, warned in December 1938 that the Jews in Germany were being condemned to death and urged measures to rescue them. On 28 February 1939, representatives of the German Interior Ministry, the High Command of the Armed Services (OKW), the Security Police, the Order Police, and the concentration camp system discussed the imprisonment of all Jews in concentration camps, under the authority of the brutal anti-Semite Theodor Eicke, and the selection of those capable of hard labor by physicians. Geist followed in April 1939 with a more specific forecast: Nazi Germany would soon place all able-bodied Jews in work camps, confiscate the wealth of the entire Jewish population, isolate the Jews from the German population, and get rid of as many as possible by force. Geist got at least some of his information directly from Karl Hasselbacher, the Sicherheitsdienst (Security Service) official in charge of the department dealing with Jews and Free Masons. On 4 May 1939, at a meeting with American Jewish leaders and some refugee specialists, President Roosevelt warned them that he was convinced that the warnings received from the American Embassy in Berlin were sound and not exaggerated. What was at stake was not money but actual lives. Geist to Messersmith, 5 December 1938, George S. Messersmith Papers, Item 1087, University of Delaware. Best's Vermerk, 1 March 1939, Zentrale Staatsarchiv, AST Berlin. Konrad Kwiet graciously supplied me with a copy of this document. Geist to Messersmith, 4 April 1939, Messersmith Papers, Item 1139, University of Delaware. Breitman, *Architect of Genocide,* 64.

23. On the increase in refugees, see a survey in Michael R. Marrus, *The Unwanted: European Refugees in the Twentieth Century* (New York: Oxford University Press, 1985), 189-203. On the inability to recognize the Final Solution, see Walter Laqueur, *The Terrible Secret: Suppression of the Truth about Hitler's "Final Solution"* (Boston: Little, Brown, 1980).

24. Breitman and Kraut, *American Refugee Policy*, 148-160, 281n47. Wyman, *Abandonment of the Jews*, 65.

25. John Fox, "The Jewish Factor in British War Crimes Policy in 1942," *English Historical Review* 92 (January 1977), 82-106; David Engel, *In the Shadow of Auschwitz: The Polish Government in Exile and the Jews*, 1939-1942 (Chapel Hill: University of North Carolina, 1987), 191-202; Tony Kushner, "Rules of the Game: Britain, America, and the Holocaust in 1944," *Holocaust and Genocide Studies* 5 (winter 1990), 384.

26. Richard Breitman, "The Allied War Effort and the Jews, 1942-1943," *Journal of Contemporary History* 20 (January 1985), 135-157.

27. Feingold, *Politics of Rescue*, 196, 257, 305.

28. Ibid., 181-182; Wyman, *Abandonment of the Jews*, 86-87, 93, 98-99, 331. In contrast, see Breitman and Kraut, *American Refugee Policy*, 179, 281n14. An often-overlooked fact is that during early 1943 the Swedish government offered to accept all Norwegian Jews and a number of Jews from the Netherlands. Germany turned down both offers, according to Swedish Foreign Office Secretary-General Erik Boheman.

Nonetheless, after prodding from the World Jewish Congress, the Swedish government offered, in April 1943, to accept twenty thousand Jewish children from the Low Countries. Cabinet approval was made dependent upon British and American payment of the costs of maintaining twenty thousand children in Sweden, an increase in food imports to Sweden for the children, and a promise to remove the children at the end of the war. But even after the Allies stalled, Sweden went ahead and initiated discussions with Germany. The German government claimed transportation was not available. Johnson to Secretary of State, 13 April 1943, Record Group (RG) 59 Central Decimal File (CDF) 840.48 Refugees/3748 Confidential File, National Archives (NA); Johnson to Secretary of State, 17 April 1943, RG 59, CDF 840.48 Refugees/3755 Confidential File, NA. Steven Koblik, *The Stones Cry Out: Sweden's Response to the Persecution of the Jews, 1933-1945* (New York: Holocaust Library, 1988), 62-63.

For later ransom schemes, see Richard Breitman and Shlomo Aronson, "The End of the Final Solution? Nazi Efforts to Ransom Jews in 1944," *Central European History* 1993 (forthcoming). Yehuda Bauer is said to have a major manuscript on Jewish negotiations with the Nazis for ransoming Jews.

29. Arguing largely from the sequence of events, Breitman and Kraut, *American Refugee Policy*, 245-246, suggest that Jan Karski's private discussion with President Roosevelt may have pushed the president to move along with the Treasury Department a World Jewish Congress plan for relief of Jews in Romania and France. State Department (and British) opposition to that plan started the battle that ended with the creation of the War Refugee Board (WRB). Since then John Pehle, director of the War Refugee Board, has credited Karski's mission as playing a major role in the establishment of the WRB. See "The Mission That Failed: An Interview with Jan Karski by Maciej Kozlowski," *Dissent* 31 (summer 1987), 326, cited by Frank W. Brecher, "America's Response to the Holocaust," *Holocaust and Genocide Studies* 5, (1990); 444n59.

    Wyman, *Abandonment of the Jews*, 193-204, gives the Emergency Committee to Rescue the Jews of Europe, led by Peter Bergson, major credit for the establishment of the WRB; Feingold, *Politics of Rescue*, 233, and Breitman and Kraut, *American Refugee Policy*, 190, are more restrained.

30. Feingold, *Politics of Rescue*, 280, 282, is the most negative. Wyman, *Abandonment of the Jews*, 209-307, and Breitman and Kraut, *American Refugee Policy*, 184-221, emphasize the lack of cooperation of other government agencies with the WRB.

31. David S. Wyman, "Why Auschwitz Was Never Bombed," *Commentary* 5 (October 1980), 39-44. This subject consistently raises public interest at lectures, conferences, and in the form of letters to the editor in newspapers and magazines. The National Air and Space Museum held a conference on this topic on 30 April 1993.

32. Wyman, *Abandonment of the Jews*, 291-304; Martin Gilbert, *Auschwitz and the Allies* (New York: Holt, Rinehart and Winston, 1981), 299-336. Dino A. Brugioni and Robert C. Poirier, *The Holocaust Revisited: A Retrospective Analysis of the Auschwitz-Birkenau Extermination Complex* (Washington, D.C.: United States Printing Office, 1979). Kai Bird, *The Chairman: John J. McCloy, the Making of the American Establishment* (New York: Simon and Schuster, 1992), 212-222, has McCloy choosing not to believe in the authenticity of eyewitness reports of extermination at Auschwitz-Birkenau and chary of getting the military involved in bombing missions for rescue. Nonetheless, Bird does not regard McCloy as anti-Semitic.

33. Wyman, *Abandonment of the Jews*, 304.

34. Frank W. Brecher, "David Wyman and the Historiography of America's Response to the Holocaust," *Holocaust and Genocide Studies* 5 (winter 1990), 423-446, presents an even sharper critique of Wyman's moralism as well as his emphasis on the achievements of Bergson's organizations.

8

Review of David Wyman's
The Abandonment of the Jews: America and the Holocaust, 1941–1945

Henry L. Feingold

Though David Wyman was not at the Hyde Park Conference, his book has set the tone for much of the debate over America and the Holocaust. Those familiar with Henry L. Feingold's work might have expected him to be enthusiastic about Wyman's approach. But in this review, Professor Feingold spells out what he sees as the shortcomings of Wyman's work and his often puzzling conclusions.

Michael R. Marrus reviews Wyman's book and Monty Penkower's in the following chapter. He concludes both fail "to appreciate how difficult it was to grasp the full horror of the Holocaust."

How strange it must seem for those who recall the eerie silence at the time of the slaughter of European Jewry to observe the current noisy media events and the proliferation of research on that catastrophe. If only there was such public concern at the time. In the case of the failing role of the American government alone we now have innumerable books and articles, several documentary films, and there is more research in the pipeline. The latest of these is David Wyman's prize-winning *The Abandonment of the Jews: America and the Holocaust, 1941-1945*. It is such a tour de force that it cannot fail to have an impact on the uninformed reader. For the historian, however, it raises more questions than it answers.

Composing the history of an event as accurately and fully as possible, which this work achieves so admirably, is merely one aspect of writing good history. History is also shaped by the historian's cherished assumptions, which determine what questions are asked, what data collected, how they are ordered, and, finally, how the narrative is chiseled into final form. Wyman is a committed Christian who is convinced that government should want to help people in distress, even when they are citizens of another country or stateless. He believes that Christian love should govern the behavior of nations and that there is an obligation for a Christian witness to suffering. Those are the assumptions that underlie this impressive book, which documents more fully than ever before how remote these aspirations were of realization during the war.

It is a bitter story made more so by first presenting a highly detailed account of a particular event that usually contains evidence of government indifference or outright sabotage. That is followed by the author's projection of what it might have been possible to do had there only been a will to do so. Yet, so consistent is the failure, so unrelenting the callousness toward life, that one begins to sense something awry. Clearly, the assumptions Wyman assigns to government were not shared by those who actually governed at the time. Were they all un-Christian or anti-Semitic? Or is this cataloging of failures and "might have dones" part of a historical morality tale? It is difficult to recognize it because we are unaccustomed to reading history that contains at once superb historical craftsmanship and a lucid uncluttered prose that are skillfully placed in the service of an outraged Christian conscience.

One might have expected something different at this stage in the development of Holocaust historiography, especially the witness role of the Roosevelt administration, which has been exhaustively researched. Customarily, the writing of history is accretional, with each new generation of historians standing on the shoulders of the prior generation. At the same time, however, the story undergoes change to suit a new sensibility, which poses new questions, and to accommodate new data that have become available. Wyman makes good use of new data, provided in some cases by the Freedom of Information Act, but then plunges us back to the moral fulminations that characterized the earliest work on this topic, Arthur Morse's *While Six Million Died: A Chronicle of American Apathy* (1966). It may well be that the indifference of the Roosevelt administration, which in other areas gave so much evidence of being motivated by humanitarian concern, makes it unusually difficult to overcome one's natural sense of moral outrage. It serves to give Wyman's narrative a quiet passion. In an age of situational ethics most readers will find Wyman's certainty about where culpability lies and who the "bad guys" were refreshing. Yet, that is insufficient for the historian, who seeks to go beyond the failures, missed opportunities, lying, sabotage, inurement, and incompetence, to discover the reasons behind the choices made.

Withal, this book does make an impact even on those who know the contours of this story well. Wyman picks up the reader at the "paper wall" (the title of his first book), which was built to assure that even those refugees who might have found a haven in the United States under the quota system would not. Only in the year 1939 were the relevant quotas filled. Not only did that cost Jewish lives directly, but the restrictionist policy also played a crucial role in Berlin's decision to solve its "Jewish problem" by more radical means. The Final Solution not only meant the finality of death, but it also meant that this was the final step after it no longer seemed possible to make the expanded Reich *judenrein* (free of Jews) by means of forced emigration. He shows how top U.S. officials resisted recognizing that a policy of processed murder had been implemented and only belatedly warned Berlin that German officials would be held to account. Part of that concealment was achieved by the use of a special camouflage terminology so that the term "Jew," which the National Socialists used obsessively, rarely could be found in American diplomatic correspondence or pronouncements by political leaders. The military establishment was unwilling to implement retributive bombing, which was suggested by the Polish government in exile in late 1942. This bombing would have made sense of the savage bombing of German cities in 1943 and opened up the question of what was happening to the Jews being deported to the East. That rejection by the military serves as the context for the later unwillingness to bomb the death camps and the rail lines leading to them. There is a telling depiction of the War Department's refusal, as a matter of policy, to become involved in the rescue of Jews, even when such rescue was eminently possible. Moreover, that policy was maintained even after the War Refugee Board (WRB) directive mandated rescue activity in such cases. The same kind of resistance to rescue occurred in the OSS (Office of Strategic Service) and the OWI (Office of War Information). Several instances of outright lying by government spokesmen are documented. Especially tragic in its consequences was the oft-repeated rationale that no Jews could be brought out of Europe because of the shortage of shipping. The truth was that ships actually returned with virtually empty holds. Had they been filled with refugees many more lives might have been saved by simply establishing a flow through neutral countries like Spain. More important, it would have been a signal to other countries that Washington was concerned about saving lives and was willing to take the lead in doing so.

What is inexplicable is that the government bureaucracy's natural reluctance to take initiatives could have been overcome if only those institutions that embody such humanitarian consciousness—the churches, the universities, the press, the intellectuals, the student community—had raised their voices; yet they, too, were strangely silent for the most part. Government indifference reflected the overwhelming lack of concern of American society generally. It was a classic case of democracy at work, the very democracy that Wyman and all of us hold in such high regard.

It is possible to conceive that Wyman's expectation of America and Americans is unrealistic. It was not really until mid-1943, several months after the Battle of Stalingrad, that one could predict with some certainty that victory would go to the Allies. Even then it would not be achieved without a heavy price in lives. Some might well argue that America's willingness to pay that price should be considered in calculating its record on the Holocaust. Those few officials who did act—Chief Counsel for Treasury's Foreign Funds Control Division Josiah Du Bois, Treasury Secretary Henry Morgenthau, Jr., Interior Secretary Harold Ickes, and others—were so exceptional that they appear almost eccentric. They serve in a small way to redeem our good opinion of mankind, but they stand out precisely because they were not typical.

During the war most government officials and people in policymaking positions simply gave no priority to the rescue of Jews. They thought very little about it. Were they alive today few would recognize the world described by Wyman, especially not his preoccupation with the fate of the Jews. They did not separate the notion of rescue from the major goal of winning the war as quickly as possible. Their perception of what should and should not be done, therefore, differed radically from Wyman's. One can, in fact, seriously wonder if Wyman has done what historians are supposed to do: penetrate the reality of the actors so that we might understand why they acted as they did. Why did they not see and feel what Wyman does 40 years later?

That difference in perception between the historian and the actors in the historical drama is also widely different in the few brief sections of Wyman's book dealing with the role of American Jewry and its leaders. The perception of the Peter Bergson group on rescue possibilities was not shared by most Jewish leaders at the time. One needs to be very careful before one concludes that a small group of Palestinians, comparatively unfamiliar with the American political and social scene, understood better what was in the realm of the possible than those who had spent their entire lives in this arena. One may argue, as Bergson did in 1943, that leaders like Rabbi Stephen Wise were blind and "locked in" and needed the prodding and the fresh vision of possibilities that his group proffered. Still, the historical verdict is not in yet. It will have to take into account whether the intensification of conflict triggered by the entree of this strange group onto an already crowded and strife-ridden stage so compromised the possibility of Jewish leaders playing their advocacy role in relation to the Roosevelt administration that, despite the attention the Bergson group successfully focused on the need for rescue, their net effect was negative. In that historical judgment the massive evidence of government indifference and sabotage of the rescue effort compiled by Wyman is more easily deployed to prove that the more pessimistic judgment of mainline leaders like Stephen Wise was, in fact, far closer to reality. Until late 1943 the Roosevelt administration was unwilling to move on the rescue question, and, even after the creation of the WRB, it moved reluctantly and sluggishly.

A similar disparity exists in Wyman's evaluation of the role of organized American Jewry. Even if one agrees with his judgment of what it might have been possible for Jewish leaders to do, the picture that emerges is somehow awry. The Jews consistently played their advocacy role more effectively in the twentieth century than the German Americans, who could not stop President Woodrow Wilson from declaring war on the fatherland in April 1917 or the Irish Americans, who could not prevent the Anglo American rapprochement after 1895, or the Polish Americans, who could not prevent the "crime of Crimea." In the context of ethnic history Wyman's standard for the Jews seems much too high. That is especially apparent when one realizes that the influence of ethnic groups on policy is circumscribed not only by their internal dissonances but also by the American political process.

The nub of the problem is whether Wyman's reading of the American political scene before and during the war is realistic or aspirational. Clearly, he believes that there exists a spirit of concern in the world, housed in part in the Oval Office, that simply needs to be mobilized to prevent "abandonment" of groups like the Jews. The "abandonment" of the Jews during the Holocaust, however, is not a startling new datum from the perspective of Jewish history, just as the "abandonment" of Israel would not come as a surprise to many Jews today. Is there any better evidence than the millennial history of the Jews needed to teach the historian that the rules that govern the relations between the powerful and the powerless are governed by something other than Christian love? It was, after all, the Zionist ideology, which today serves as a major binding force of Jews everywhere, that was based on the notion that a viable Jewish life could no longer be maintained in the Diaspora.

From a historical perspective this then is a strangely disturbing book. Its research is meticulous, and, within the author's frame of reference, its judgments are fair and balanced. Yet it is a strangely flat chronicle of insufficiency and failure. Wyman is content to delve deeply into the surface of things when the things we need to know about the Holocaust witness may lie just beneath.

9

Bystanders to the Holocaust (Review
of Monty Penkower's *The Jews
Were Expendable: Free World Diplomacy
and the Holocaust* and David Wyman's
*The Abandonment of the Jews: America
and the Holocaust, 1941–1945*)

Michael R. Marrus

We have now a growing shelf of books and a burgeoning file of articles on bystanders to the Nazi Holocaust, focusing particularly on the response of the Anglo-American world to the persecution and massacre of European Jews. Among the best known are the volumes on Britain by Joshua Sherman and Bernard Wasserstein; on Canada by Irving Abella and Harold Troper; and on the United States by Arthur Morse, David Wyman, Saul Friedman, Henry Feingold, Yehuda Bauer, and Leonard Dinnerstein. The news, as we all know, is not good: Research has uncovered a persistent unwillingness to assist the Jews in their hour of need and a remarkable failure to grasp the nature of the Jewish catastrophe. The drift of scholarly opinion is summed up in the titles of the two solid investigations under review, important additions to the foregoing list: *The Abandonment of the Jews: America and the Holocaust, 1941-1945* by David Wyman and *The Jews Were Expendable: Free World Diplomacy and the Holocaust* by Monty Penkower.[1]

Now that the genre has become established, and with still more works on the way, it may be worthwhile to reflect upon the serious problems associated with this line of investigation. In the first place, it should be appreciated that many of these analyses center upon what did *not* happen: Jews were not admitted, Jewish communities failed to unite. Allied governments spurned rescue suggestions, rail access to Auschwitz was not bombed, and Nazi ransom hints were not pursued with any deliberation. Lay readers may not always appreciate the difficulty scholars have in writing what is, in essence, a negative report—the history of inaction, indifference, and insensitivity. The obvious temptation in this kind of exposition is to assess bystanders, not from the standpoint of their own culture, priorities, and preoccupations, but from what we assume *ought* to have been their beliefs and actions. This line of thinking imposes upon historical actors our own values, our own judgment, and our own appreciation of the events of the Holocaust. The thrust of such work can then become a lamenting of the fact that the people written about failed to live up to our standards. This temptation is the historian's form of hubris: To yield fully to it is to denounce the characters we write about for not being like ourselves.

Second, it should by now be apparent that the professional task of Holocaust historians, 50 years after the event, must increasingly turn to explanation rather than condemnation. Admittedly, each of us has his own interpretive starting point and his own philosophic and moral commitment to the scholarly exercise. But I venture to suggest that we shall not go much further in the attempt to comprehend the past without a remorseless, painstaking effort to suspend anger, to try to understand how the people we describe perceived the world and why they acted as they did. When writing about bystanders, such effort is particularly necessary in view of some harsh accusations recently made from a strongly defined political or ideological vantage point. Of course, it is incumbent upon all historians to probe the seamy underside of Allied and Jewish policy, to search the records sometimes deliberately hidden from public view and to examine every aspect of public activity during the Holocaust—whether or not it casts credit upon the contemporary actors. But I want to urge responsibility in this exercise: We should avoid the tendency to castigate outsiders without fully understanding them. The words of contemporaries are usually far more eloquent than our own denunciations so many years later. Let us listen carefully to what they said to each other, estimate as carefully as possible what they said to themselves, and strive to put all of this in a context that is not our own.

The authors of the two books discussed here struggled with these kinds of problems, emerging with books quite different in tone, though with similar conclusions. Monty Penkower presents nine separate essays examining aspects of Allied diplomacy and the Holocaust, incorporating several previously published articles. He surveys the campaign for a Jewish fighting force, the transmission of news about the Final Solution, Allied responses to refugees and rescue possibilities, some Jewish reactions, and the origins of the War Refugee Board (WRB). Unfortunately, his chapters do not relate well to each other and frequently overlap. Extraordinarily detailed, his exposition at times becomes a tangled skein of diplomatic exchange, difficult to unravel and follow through time. His research is wide-ranging, including Hebrew-language material and dozens of interviews with surviving personalities—almost all of them Jews. He has visited not only the principal archival holdings in New York, Washington, London, and Jerusalem but has used a remarkable array of private papers, institutional collections, and other manuscript sources. Wyman's work, while more narrowly focused on American policy, is more comprehensive in its survey of the war period and more direct in its analysis. Unlike Penkower, whose anguish about his subject charges his prose and prompts obscure allusions, Wyman never leaves the reader in doubt about where he stands. While his research is equally extensive, tending more to government material, he resists the temptation to load his book with unnecessary detail. His account is clear, strongly argued, and unadorned. The result is a more forceful indictment, a book that will likely become the standard work on its theme.

Wyman begins by emphasizing anti-Semitism in the United States, which he suggests was pervasive throughout the 1930s and the war period. Between one-third and one-half of the American people, according to a variety of polls, were animated by some degree of anti-Jewish feeling. A good deal flowed from that. Anti-immigration sentiment was particularly strong when it came to Jews, with the result that they were practically barred from an American refuge during the Holocaust. Only twenty-one thousand gained entry during the war years, a mere 10 percent of those who could have been legally admitted under existing immigration quotas. In barring Jews and in the failure to respond to virtually all Jewish concerns, the State Department was particularly active. But Congress, the War Department, the Office of War Information, and other agencies also turned their backs on the Jews at important moments. The major exception, energizing late in the war, was the Treasury Department under Henry Morgenthau, Jr., which prodded the president early in 1944 to establish the WRB. By then, however, it was too late for most of Adolf Hitler's victims. Even at this late date, moreover, the president took little interest in the board's work: Its funding came largely from Jewish sources, and the State Department hampered its activities. In perhaps the most original part of his book, Wyman offers a thorough evaluation of the achievements of the WRB, based on its extensive records at the Franklin D. Roosevelt Library in Hyde Park, New York. Largely accepting the board's assessment of its own activity, he concludes that it saved approximately two hundred thousand Jews and twenty thousand non-Jews.

Both authors believe that far more could have been done—and much beyond the admission of additional refugees. Wyman takes seriously the various suggestions that the Germans were prepared to release their victims and argues that these hints should have been explored. He agrees with former WRB officials that the agency could have saved many more if it had been formed a year or even a few months earlier. Axis satellites and neutrals should have been pressured to assist in various ways. Outside havens should have been secured. Shipping space—readily available when needed for other nonmilitary projects, according to Wyman's convincing demonstration—should have been made available. Money, supplies and information should have been mobilized on behalf of the trapped Jews of Europe. The Auschwitz death factory could easily have been bombed, when targets were constantly being hit in its vicinity in 1944. Both writers tend, in my view, to underestimate the commitment and the ability of the Nazis to destroy Jews no matter what the Allies did—a point to which I shall return shortly. In his discussion of the campaign for a Jewish army, Penkower laments that because of Allied failures, "Europe became a Jewish graveyard rather than a battlefield commensurate with the honor of the Jewish people" (p. 29). Unfortunately, the alternative he presents simply did not exist. Wyman is more careful in exploring the contemporaneously proposed "might have beens," often demonstrating the low cost of such efforts and the unlikelihood that various suggestions would have interfered with the war effort.

What accounts for this inaction? Penkower is rather short on explanation, blending references to obvious strategic interests, such as the British concern over Palestine, together with the failure to grasp the nature of the Nazi program of mass murder. Oddly, in a volume that concentrates on the Jewish victims, there is little evaluation of the role of anti-Semitism. Penkower's closely meshed description of events leaves little space for reflection on the various political and intellectual forces that shaped events. In the end, after his litany of callousness, cruelty, and indifference, he falls back upon a global judgement—"Western civilization's gradual loss of the sense of solidarity," a "decay of conscience," and a "loss of a sense of certain decencies" (p. 301). Yet he demonstrates no reasons for this apparent moral collapse and offers no demonstration that the milk of human kindness flowed more freely in earlier periods of history. He closes with a powerful moral appeal but leaves the main historical question unanswered.

Wyman identifies several causes for the American failure to act. Key individuals obviously played a role. An important source of State Department obstruction was Assistant Secretary Breckinridge Long (whose name is persistently misspelled in Penkower's book), an extreme nativist in charge of refugee matters. With Long and with several other highly placed officials, anti-Jewish feeling was clearly at work. Yet although he hardly depreciates the role of anti-Semitism in Congress and the country, Wyman does not think it decisive in government itself. Notably, he claims that "direct proof of anti-Semitism in the [State] [D]epartment is limited," and his research uncovered "only two documented examples" (p. 190).

Much more important was the indifference of Franklin D. Roosevelt to the Jewish tragedy, a lapse that the author calls "the worst failure of his Presidency" (p. xi). Although periodically informed about mass killings, FDR was prepared to run no risks for the Jews, thought that action on their behalf meant trouble politically, and seems to have kept the issue out of his mind. We have no indication that he was ever preoccupied with the fate of European Jewry and no knowledge of his inner thoughts on the matter. Revered and idealized by American Jews, the president had only a superficial grasp of Jewish issues and trimmed his policies to the winds of political expediency. And in his insouciance, the politically astute FDR reflected the indifference of the wider American public. Indeed, throughout the Holocaust the massacre of European Jews was not even important news. Wyman attempts a systematic evaluation of news coverage, concluding that "most of the mass media, whether from disbelief or fear of accusation of sensationalism or for some other reason, played down information about the Jewish tragedy" (p. 327). This media inattention, in his view, may well have prevented a full grasp of the catastrophe.

In what will undoubtedly be his most controversial theme, Wyman attributes an important degree of responsibility to the American Jewish leadership for failing to unite and mount a sustained rescue campaign. Such action, he feels sure, would have produced results. Zionism, of course, was the principal basis for disagreement. While Jewish organizations stood together on the need to end the British White Paper restrictions on Jewish immigration to Palestine, they divided on the priority to be given to rescue and the campaign for a postwar Jewish state. Distracted by communal squabbling, and sometimes failing to see their way out of a situation judged hopeless, the Jewish organizations were dominated by Stephen Wise, an aging Reform rabbi who shared his coreligionists' awe and trust in the president. Dynamism and imagination came from the fringes of the American Jewish world. Wyman paints a largely positive picture of the Palestinian Irgun organizer Peter Bergson and his group of young pro-rescue activists, who burst on the scene in early 1943. Bergson's Emergency Committee to Save the Jewish People of Europe sent out shock waves of protest, contributing vitally, in Wyman's view, to the creation of the WRB. Yet, while the emergency committee proved strong enough to shake the established Jewish leadership and provoke bitter divisions over rescue priorities, it was too weak to move the Roosevelt administration wholeheartedly toward saving Jews. So long as American Jewry did not join this campaign, Wyman implies, an American-backed rescue potential could not fully be realized.

Critics of this viewpoint dispute the likelihood of the Nazis permitting significant numbers of Jews to escape their clutches at any time after America entered the war. Neither Wyman nor Penkower challenges the Nazis' obsessive determination to solve the "Jewish question" by any means necessary or their utter conviction that "world Jewry" was to be destroyed. Penkower certainly goes too far in stating that Jews "would fall victim to the democracies' procrastination and unsurpassed callousness *as well as* to the Nazis' prussic acid" (p. 97, emphasis mine)—as if the gassings were on the same order of criminality as Allied wrongdoing. His implication, if I read him right, is that Allied indifference helped cause mass murder on a spectacular scale—a serious charge for which he presents no evidence whatsoever.

Critics may also question whether American Jewry, which amounted to only 3.6 percent of an indifferent public, among which anti-Semitism was widespread, could ever have exercised important political leverage in Washington—united or not united. The Jews, as many of them realized, faced a near hopeless situation, accounting for much of the demoralization that analysts now have the luxury to condemn. What, as they scanned the political horizon, was their alternative? The Republican Party offered no plausible appeal to rescue advocates, and in any event the prospect of prying loose masses of Jews from Roosevelt's New Deal was virtually nonexistent. Attempting a media campaign, as Wyman's work suggests, was futile. (One particularly forlorn exercise stands out in my mind as emblematic of Jewish powerlessness: In December 1942, in New York City, half a million Jewish workers stopped work for ten minutes to protest the Nazis' murder of Jews. Labor leaders had considered striking for an hour but abandoned the idea lest they be accused of hampering war production. On the following day, the Jews made up the ten minutes of lost working time.) However much it may be disparaged now, the argument that real rescue could come only with an Allied victory was compelling and persuasive. This was the position that Eleanor Roosevelt, presumably one of the staunchest friends of the Jews, maintained throughout. Breaking with this line seemed a sure way of increasing anti-Jewish feeling and injuring the Jews' postwar prospects for a national home.

Wyman's answer to these arguments would be that attempts should at least have been made. Of course, no one can say that more Jews might not have been snatched from the Nazi inferno if the bystanders had not seen more clearly, made greater efforts, and undertaken serious sacrifices. Yet, such charges can be made about virtually any man-made disaster one can imagine. More could always have been done, and in a personal as well as a collective sense there is little point in endless recrimination over missed opportunities and mistaken perceptions. More useful, and more consonant with the historical method, is to reconstruct the frame of mind that prevailed at the time. Both authors make real efforts to do this, yet both are distracted—Penkower by moral outrage, and Wyman by his concern with rescue projects that might have been.

Both fail, in my view, to appreciate how difficult it was to grasp the full horror of the Holocaust, and how the imagination often collapsed under the staggering burden of reports from the Nazi slaughterhouse. Wyman presents a lengthy discussion of the message sent from Geneva in August 1942 by Gerhart Riegner, the World Jewish Congress representative who cabled Washington and London about extermination rumors. Coming together with other reports, notably in the *Jewish Labor Bund* the previous May, this was indeed a shocking revelation. But Wyman errs in considering this telegram as a clear confirmation of the existence of a plan for systematic mass murder. Riegner carefully hedged his message with qualifications as to its exactitude, and in any event the report turned out to be wrong in most of its details. Had Wyman quoted the original cable, as does Penkower, this would have been clear. Seen in this way, the incredulity of the State Department analysts becomes more understandable. Moreover, even when the news was presented with greater clarity, it was often rejected as too fantastic, too bizarre, too macabre to be believed. People wavered in their acceptance of the awful truth. Sometimes they seemed fully to grasp it, and sometimes they ignored the messages before them. Even in the Palestinian Yishuv, as new research suggests, indications about mass murder were often pushed aside until November 1942, when several dozen refugees arrived with eyewitness reports from Poland and the rest of Europe.

While full understanding of the nature of the Holocaust often eluded bystanders, other concerns pressed in upon them, further preventing a grasp of the dreadful Jewish reality. Above all, the fate of the Jews was submerged in the titanic global contest, the outcome of which appeared strongly in doubt until mid-1943. Remarkably, neither author mentions Japan when assessing American indifference to the appeals of the Jews. Yet it is worth remembering that, for most of the war, ordinary Americans considered the Japanese the main enemy they faced and believed that war priorities should be ordered accordingly. (Roosevelt, of course, swam strongly against this tide.) Wartime atrocities, it was certainly felt, were largely Japanese in origin. To take another case, it is clear that the Jews were not the only group to meet frustration when calling for Allied help to counter the massacre of civilians. Polish leader Wladyslaw Sikorski proposed precisely this in mid-1942, in his plea for retaliatory bombing of the Reich for crimes against non-Jewish Poles. It would be well to probe this and other such episodes, to see the extent to which an outlook having nothing to do with Jews conditioned responses to Jewish appeals. At certain times, other peoples, too, were expendable.

On the Jewish side, Wyman ignores the intense love affair the community had with Roosevelt, who gave the Jews dignity and self-respect as did no one before in American history. Grateful for what they correctly thought was an entirely new attitude toward them in government, Jews working for the president conspicuously played down specifically Jewish concerns. (It has recently been pointed out, for example, that Jews in the New Deal contributed significantly to reforms in Native American affairs, while doing little for Jewish civil rights.) One can, of course, simply deplore this as an instance of "false consciousness." As with Stalinist historiography, however, such denunciations are no substitute for understanding and, in this case, cut short an effort to explain why Jews acted as they did.

Research on the bystanders to the Holocaust should be undertaken with the same scrupulous care to reconstruct thought and action as is taken with other historical subjects. We are at an early stage in this process, and it is perhaps understandable that emotion and an urge to expose villainy still dominate much writing on the subject. But it is time to go on. At their best, the books discussed here point the way to further study by their painstaking research and careful assessment of complex channels of communication. Wyman's distinguished work deserves particular praise for its comprehensive research, analysis, and the clarity of his argument. But both studies also, in my view, show tendencies that can divert us from satisfactory explanations: an unwillingness to place the bystanders' negligence fully into historical perspective and a disposition to be drawn into "might have beens," to wrestle with the phantoms of men who have gone before.

Notes

1. David S. Wyman, *The Abandonment of the Jews: America and the Holocaust 1941-1945* (New York: Pantheon Books, 1984); Monty N. Penkower, *The Jews Were Expendable: Free World Diplomacy and the Holocaust* (Chicago: University of Illinois Press, 1983).

10

Did FDR Betray the Jews?
Or Did He Do More Than
Anyone Else to Save Them?

Arthur Schlesinger, Jr.

In response to the appearance, in April 1994, of the Public Broadcasting System (PBS) film "America and the Holocaust: Deceit and Indifference," Arthur Schlesinger, Jr., expressed wonder at how attitudes toward FDR have changed so drastically in the past decades. This in spite of the fact that very little has been offered to change the historical record from the time Roosevelt was considered a champion of the Jews and a hero for rallying the nation to defeat Adolf Hitler.

There has been a strange turn in the attitude of American Jews toward Franklin D. Roosevelt. For a long time he was a hero. No president had appointed so many Jews to public office. No president had surrounded himself with so many Jewish advisers. No president had condemned anti-Semitism with such eloquence and persistence. Jews were mostly liberals in those faraway days, and a vast majority voted four times for FDR.

In recent years this has changed. Historians have unearthed evidence of prewar official resistance to the admission of Jewish refugees. Questions are raised about the failure to bomb Nazi death camps. Some Jews today see FDR not as a hero, but as the president who might have saved millions of Jews from Hitler and instead abandoned them to a terrible fate. PBS has now put on a television program indicting the Roosevelt administration for "deceit and indifference."

The attack on FDR shows a striking disregard of historical context. Alone among world leaders, Roosevelt stood in opposition to Hitler from the beginning. In a succession of speeches he explained to an isolationist nation that Nazism was a mortal threat to the United States. He denounced anti-Semitism, proposed the Evian Conference in 1938 to help refugees, and, after the terror of Kristallnacht, was the only head of state to recall his ambassador from Berlin.

And he did this in a time when anti-Semitism in the United States was far more prevalent and virulent than it is today. Gunnar Myrdal, the Swedish expert on race relations, wrote in his great book *An American Dilemma* that American anti-Semitism in these years "probably was somewhat stronger than in Germany before the Nazi era." FDR's New Deal was called the "Jew Deal." His advisers—Felix Frankfurter, Henry Morgenthau, Jr., Sam Rosenman, Ben Cohen—were under constant attack because of their race. The onetime national hero Charles Lindbergh denounced the Jews as one of the groups trying to bring America into war.

Moreover, America was still mired in the Great Depression. With millions out of work, Congress and the trade unions were not disposed to look favorably on the entry of new competitors in the job market. The anti-Semitism of the day infected lower echelons in the State Department and impeded the issuance of visas. FDR had to deal with the world as it was.

He did what he could. The PBS film claims that he was indifferent to the Wagner-Rogers Bill of 1939 seeking the admission of German children in excess of the immigration quota. The authoritative *Eleanor and Franklin* (1971) by Joseph Lash, himself a Jew, provides a very different account. Roosevelt gave the bill a green light and offered advice on congressional strategy. But the bill was headed for certain defeat. The "File No Action" scrawl—not by FDR, incidentally—on an informal congressional inquiry about the bill referred to the inquiry, not to the bill. The idea that FDR was indifferent to the fate of the children, Joseph Lash writes, is "an unjust accusation." (Joe Lash is dead, but his widow, Trude, says that "FDR did not have an anti-Semitic bone in his body.") America admitted more refugees than any other country. When war broke out in Europe and some isolationists followed Lindbergh in blaming the Jews, FDR well understood that it would be fatal to let the war be defined as a war to save the Jews. He knew that he must emphasize the large and vital interest all Americans had in stopping Hitler, and that is what he did. And he knew that winning the war was the only way to save the people in the concentration camps.

In January 1942, Nazi anti-Semitism entered a new phase—the program of extermination called the Final Solution. Later that year reports of the new horror began to trickle out of Germany. A generation that remembered the phony atrocity stories of World War I regarded such reports with initial skepticism. Bill Moyers once asked William Shirer, who knew the Nazis better than most Americans, what he had thought when told that a whole people were being systematically obliterated. Shirer replied, "I couldn't believe it. . . . I did not get the story, really, until the war-crimes trials at Nuremberg. The Holocaust was recognized as the Holocaust only after victory opened up the death camps."

The PBS film implies that if only the U.S. government had pursued a different course, millions of European Jews could have been saved. In fact, opportunities for rescue were extremely limited until the tide of war began to turn toward the Allies, and Allied victory could not be assured until a cross-channel invasion succeeded. When the valiant Henry Morgenthau, Jr., told Roosevelt about State Department foot-dragging on rescue possibilities, FDR, five months before D-Day, promptly established the War Refugee Board. Had the board been established while the Germans still had a chance to win the war, it could have done little in the way of rescue.

Should the Allies have bombed the death camps or the railroads leading to them? Bombing rail tracks, the United States discovered by 1943, had little effect; tracks were repaired in 24 hours. Precision bombing was far from reliable with the primitive bombsights of half a century ago; even our smart bombs today turned out not to be so smart as Pentagon publicists made out during the Gulf War. The best use of Allied bombing—and the best way to save the people in the death camps—was to bring the war to its quickest end.

Lucy S. Dawidowicz, scholar of the Holocaust and author of *The War against the Jews* (1975), concluded that "military power . . . was the only way the United States could have saved the European Jews, not by negotiating with Hitler or by bribing his satellites." FDR, more than any other person, deserves the credit for mobilizing the forces that destroyed Nazi barbarism.

And if Americans wonder how their parents and grandparents could have stood aside half a century ago when the Nazis were said to be slaughtering the Jews of Europe, let them ask themselves why they stand aside today when their TV sets leave no doubt that the Serbs are slaughtering the Muslims of Bosnia. Righteousness is easy in retrospect.

An Amplification

William J. vanden Heuvel

The response to Professor Arthur Schlesinger, Jr.'s, article generally reflects four concerns:

1. *The prewar immigration policy of the United States:* From the beginning of the Hitler era (1933), understanding the Nazi fanaticism against the Jews, Franklin and Eleanor Roosevelt identified themselves with efforts to assist the persecuted. Eleanor Roosevelt, for example, was a founder in 1933 of the International Rescue Committee, which became the major nonsectarian refugee agency in America and which had a heroic role in assisting and resettling Jewish immigrants and refugees in America. Professor Gerhard L. Weinberg, a noted historian of World War II, points out that the United States, itself decimated by unemployment and hostile to all immigration, "accepted about twice as many Jewish refugees as the rest of the world put together: about 200,000 out of 300,000. . . ."[1]

2. *The fate of the passengers of the SS "St. Louis":* The S.S. *St. Louis* sailed from Hamburg, Germany, to Cuba in May 1939, some months before World War II broke out and almost three years before the beginning of the death camps. Other ships had made the same journey, and their passengers were disembarked successfully. Financial and other negotiations with the Cuban government (in which American Jewish agencies were participant) broke down despite pressure from the American government on the Cuban government to honor the original understanding.

Secretary of State Cordell Hull, Secretary of the Treasury Henry Morgenthau, Jr., and others tried various means to avoid the harsh reality of the immigration laws (such as an attempt to land the passengers as "tourists" in the Virgin Islands), but they were not successful in the face of a Congress that strictly monitored and controlled the immigrations laws. Congressman Samuel Dickstein (D, N.Y.) was chairman of the Subcommittee on Immigration. There is no record of his efforts that I am aware of in this matter. Despite the legal inability of the United States to accept the passengers of the SS *St. Louis* as immigrants, the State Department and its overseas representations were significantly helpful in resettling them. None of the passengers of the SS *St. Louis* were returned to Nazi Germany. They were all resettled in democratic countries—the United Kingdom, France, the Netherlands, Belgium, and Denmark.

3. *The bombing of Auschwitz:* James H. Kitchens III and Richard Levy (in chapter XIII of this book) provide new scholarship on this long-festering issue. No serious historian claims that bombing Auschwitz would have saved lives. The Nazis showed until the very end of the war that they did not need Auschwitz or the other "death camps" to murder the defenseless Jews. They had killed 1.5 million Jews before the first death camp was operable in late 1942. Auschwitz was closed in October 1944 as the Nazis tried to cover their murderous tracks in the face of advancing Soviet and Allied armies. They continued to murder Jews by shooting and every other barbaric means at their disposal.

At the very least, Jewish leadership in America and in the world was divided on the question of bombing Auschwitz. The World Jewish Congress asked that Auschwitz not be bombed. The Jewish Agency never made such a request to the War Department. No bombing request was put to President Roosevelt by any of the Jewish organizations, the War Refugee Board, the War Department, or anyone else. Many Jewish leaders were close friends of President Roosevelt, including Rabbi Stephen Wise—an acknowledged leader of the American Jewish community who had frequent access to the president as a family friend and counselor.

There are those like Professor David Wyman who dismiss the moral dilemma posed by the proposed bombing of Auschwitz. That dilemma was certainly a factor for those who had to make the bombing decisions. ". . . It is not easy to think that a rational person would have made such a recommendation" (to bomb Auschwitz).[2] Professor Wyman's thesis that attributes the Allied avoidance of death-camp bombing to callousness, insensitivity, and even anti-Semitic prejudice is an unsubstantiated calumny against men at least as honorable, humane, and honest as Professor Wyman.

4. *The establishment of the War Refugee Board (WRB):* The WRB should have been established sooner. There should have been some governmental entity whose sole concern was the plight of Europe's Jews. In 1943, a Senate resolution was introduced calling upon the president to establish such a board. At that time, and throughout the war years, there was a profound division in the Jewish community regarding what should be done and how it should be done. The split in many ways reflected the division between Menachem Begin (the Likkud) and David Ben-Gurion (the Mapai) regarding the creation and purposes of Israel. The Jewish spokesman for the Senate resolution was Peter Bergson, who was believed to be connected to the Stern gang that was carrying out terrorist activities against the British in Palestine. The Zionists led by Rabbi Wise were profoundly opposed to Bergson and his colleagues, such as Ben Hecht. They urged the president not to support Bergson although Eleanor Roosevelt did meet with him to discuss his proposals.

Secretary of the Treasury Henry Morgenthau, Jr., went to President Roosevelt in January 1944 and urged the immediate creation of the WRB to provide a voice for Jewish interests separate from the State Department. Roosevelt agreed immediately, and within days the WRB was created. It is doubtful whether such a body could have been significantly effective before the winter of 1944. In February 1944, Hitler tried to remove Admiral Horthy, the Regent ruler of Hungary, which had until that time essentially protected its Jewish population from the Nazi murderers. Hitler sent the infamous Adolf Eichmann to Hungary to pursue the extermination of the Jews. Hundreds of thousands were saved, in large part because of WRB interventions, which included retaining the services of Raoul Wallenberg, enlisting and supporting the efforts of neutral embassies such as Sweden and Switzerland to give safe haven, and sending personal messages from President Roosevelt to the Hungarian government promising to hold its officials personally accountable for the protection of the Jews from the Nazis.

There was still a year to go in the war but with the success of D-Day (June 1944) the defeat of the Nazis was foreseeable. The full might of the Allied armies would continue to be engaged in brutal battle (the Battle of the Bulge began in December 1944). Once the European mainland was conquered and occupied by Nazi armies in June 1940, President Roosevelt and British Prime Minister Winston Churchill were in full agreement that the Nazi barbarism could be stopped only by the total and complete destruction of Hitler and his forces. Roosevelt and Churchill had issued a proclamation in the name of the United Nations on 17 December 1942 in response to the Riegner cable and other information, warning the Germans that they would be held individually accountable for their treatment of the Jews.

Notes

1. Gerhard L. Weinberg, *The Foreign Policy of Hitler's Germany,* vols. I and II (Chicago: University of Chicago Press, 1970, 1980).
2. James H. Kitchens III, "The Bombing of Auschwitz Reexamined," *Journal of Military History* 58 (April 1994), 233-265.

The Holocaust, Auschwitz, and World War II

INTRODUCTION

The search for global accomplices was started in the late 1960s largely by American writers. One of the first was journalist Arthur Morse,[1] who expressed exasperation at what he considered narrow histories focused only on the murderers and their victims. "It is as if there were no other world, as if two circling antagonists, one armed, the other unarmed, inhabited an otherwise vacant planet."

In Morse's version, the planet wasn't vacant, but—except for the conflict between the Germans and the Jews—inhabited by nations at peace. These idle countries were fully capable but completely unwilling to carry out a universally agreed upon plan to rescue the victims.

His portrayal of World War II and the Holocaust as two distinct and separate events that did not occur on the same planet became an essential component of the search for accomplices. Once this spatial relationship was established, it was not difficult to dismiss the anti-Hitler coalition's war against Germany as a trivial response to Germany's war against the Jews.

As this approach took hold, the war in which over sixty million were killed, millions more were wounded or displaced, and vast treasures drained was downsized to little more than footnotes to the Holocaust. The Allied nations, which mobilized their entire countries and put over forty million men and women into uniform to fight across the globe, could be dismissed as mere bystanders. It began to be possible to imagine that the war the United States and Britain fought against Germany was not only unrelated, but even antithetical, to rescuing the Jews from slaughter by the Germans and their fellow executioners.

By the mid-1980s, authors David Wyman and Monty Penkower had concluded that the Jews were "abandoned" because they were "expendable," and, at the very least, this was an unforgivable moral failure by Franklin Roosevelt.[2] By then, World War II had all but vanished from much of Holocaust history. As Lucy Dawidowicz[3] took note, in Wyman's chapter criticizing the U.S. War Department and its military operations, the only reference to D-Day is buried in a footnote.

This anomaly was recalled at a June 1994 Franklin and Eleanor Roosevelt Institute–sponsored conference in the Netherlands coinciding with D-Day activities. Several Dutch pointed out that even with the Allied armies of liberation surrounding the Netherlands, they could not rescue eighty thousand Dutch who were starved to death by the occupying German forces.

The question of bombing the gas chambers and crematoria at Auschwitz-Birkenau and the rail lines leading to them has long been at the center of the debate over culpability in the Holocaust. There is almost no agreement on any of the central points. In a paraphrase of the question repeated throughout the Watergate hearings: What did the Allies know and when did they know it?

For over 15 years, Wyman has been the accepted expert on the case against the Allies for their refusal to bomb Auschwitz. He has maintained that (1) Auschwitz and the rail lines should have been bombed; (2) it was tactically possible to bomb them; (3) had they been bombed, many lives, perhaps hundreds of thousands, would have been saved; and (4) the United States and Britain, knowing all of this, refused to bomb the Auschwitz facilities and then dissembled in their reasoning.

In 1981, Martin Gilbert[4] argued that the Allies did not know Auschwitz was a death camp until the summer of 1944. However, in a paper he presented to a symposium at the Air and Space Museum in April 1993,[5] Richard Breitman contends that the Allies were aware of the mass exterminations at Auschwitz in 1943.

Breitman seems to accept that from a moral standpoint, Auschwitz *should* have been bombed. That is, even if Jewish inmates would have been killed during the raid, it would have diminished the Germans' ability to continue the exterminations. As to whether it *could* have been bombed, Breitman demurs. "I will leave it to the military experts to discuss the logistics and feasibility of the bombing."

James H. Kitchens III, a military historian, and Richard Levy, an independent scholar, take on the challenge. Kitchens challenges Wyman's methodology and competence, faulting him for a lack of knowledge about military operations and his incomplete and superficial use of sources. These have combined, the author concludes, to elevate Auschwitz from an item of minor speculation after the war, to one of intense divisiveness.

Wyman's shortcomings, Kitchens suggests, are replicated by many of the reviewers who greeted Wyman's thesis with high approval. While they may have been experts on refugee policy, religious history, or the Holocaust, Kitchens charges, they knew little about the intricacies and efficacy of air power.[6]

What has been lost in the debates, Levy observes, is the original basis for proposing that any of the death camps should be bombed: to impede the slaughter. The reason it was rejected was because British and American military authorities did not believe that was an attainable objective. Levy also emphasizes that no Jewish leader at the time believed strongly that Auschwitz should have been bombed, and many were strongly opposed.

He further argues that the Germans had shown they did not lack resourcefulness when it came to different ways to kill the Jews. The absence of the crematoria would not have spared the inmates who survived the bombing, and to disrupt rail traffic for perhaps only a few days would not have left the Germans without ways to dispose of those destined for Auschwitz. Thus, Levy considers bogus the claim that bombing would have saved hundreds of thousands of, or any, lives.

The debate over bombing Auschwitz may never be settled. But perhaps we are completing another cycle. The first Holocaust histories focused on the Germans and the Jews, the murderers and their victims and the extermination of the Jews as a central part, if not the central point, of the German's prosecution of the war. But there are signs that after over 25 years, the hunt for the guilty has led us too far afield. In a speech delivered at the U.S. Holocaust Memorial Museum in Washington shortly after the Hyde Park Conference, Gerhard Weinberg, author of the highly acclaimed *A World at Arms: A Global History of World War II*,[7] expressed concern about assigning guilt to the Allies. After years of focusing on those who failed to save the Jews, he cautions, those with a fixation on rescue attempts "should not divert all attention from those primarily responsible for the killing: the killers." This was precisely the approach that drove Morse to despair.

To Weinberg, it seems odd how rarely "the Allied victory [which] restricted Germany's program" to exterminate the Jews is even mentioned in works on the Holocaust. Instead of attacking the Allies for their failure to rescue the Jews, Weinberg suggests, attention should be drawn to the fact that "the Allies saved about two-thirds of the globe's Jews from the fate the Germans intended for them."

Gilbert has also stressed the correlations between World War II and the Holocaust. He points out that the period "during which the most Jews were being killed coincided with the period of maximum German military superiority and corresponding Allied military weakness."[8] Bernard Wasserstein, in *Britain and the Jews of Europe, 1939-1945*,[9] also makes a similar connection, citing British intelligence reports that in December 1943—at a time when the Germans were still staging fierce counterattacks against the Allied forces in Italy—90 percent of Poland's 3.3 million Jews were dead. By the following spring, with D-Day still weeks away, the majority of Jews in Germany, Austria, and numerous other European nations were also dead.

Gilbert might have added another disturbing observation. In several instances, Allied victories in their campaign to destroy the Third Reich led not to a diminution of persecution against European Jews but, as in the cases of Italy and Hungary, to an even greater catastrophe for them.[10]

This might be construed as vindication of FDR's insistence that the quickest way to halt the slaughter in Europe was to defeat Hitler and end the war. However, some Holocaust historians have been dismissive of this strategy, implying it ignored the plight of the Jews or was even a ruse intended to justify inaction as the annihilation continued. To this, Weinberg points out, "It might be worthwhile to consider how many more Jews would have survived had the war ended even a week or ten days earlier" or how many more would have died had it gone on for a week or ten days longer.

Holocaust historiography is not unique in its susceptibility to cycles. Various stages of Holocaust history are remarkably similar to the historiography of the Cold War, which has also been dominated by the countervailing forces of "guilt" versus "context." Both in the case of the Cold War and the Holocaust—at least in the hands of American historians—versions sharply critical of U.S. policy surfaced first and soon became practically the official version. And in both the Cold War and the Holocaust, even those who sought to mitigate the case against Roosevelt often felt their own credibility required them to embrace his critics's severest charges.

World War II had barely ended before histories appeared attacking Roosevelt for his dealings with the Soviets. For nearly a half century, one school of critics has with, if anything, increasing ferocity branded him naive and blundering for appeasing Joseph Stalin at Yalta and for abandoning the captive nations to the Soviet Empire.

At the same time that Roosevelt was characterized as uncomprehending of the evils of Stalin and the Soviet Union, many Holocaust historians were portraying him as cold and indifferent, a frivolous man who, incapable of comprehending the reality of the Nazi horrors, abandoned the Jews.

The Hyde Park Conference neither started nor ended a cycle. But along with the most recent writings of a number of historians, it allows us to see a decided change in the way Roosevelt, the Holocaust, and World War II are being portrayed.

Notes

1. Arthur Morse, *While Six Million Died: A Chronicle of American Apathy* (New York: Random House, 1967).

2. David Wyman, *The Abandonment of the Jews: America and the Holocaust, 1941-1945* (New York: Pantheon Books, 1984)

3. Lucy S. Dawidowicz, "Could the U.S. Have Rescued the European Jews from Hitler?" *This World* (fall 1985), 15-30.

4. Martin Gilbert, *Auschwitz and the Allies* (New York: Holt, Rinehart and Winston, 1981).

5. A symposium titled "The Bombing of Auschwitz: Should the Allies Have Attempted This?" was held 30 April 1993 at the National Air and Space Museum of the Smithsonian Institution, Washington, D.C.

6. James H. Kitchens, III, "The Bombing of Auschwitz Reexamined," *The Journal of Military History* 58 (April 1994), 233-265.

7. Gerhard L. Weinberg, *A World at Arms: A Global History of World War II* (Cambridge: Cambridge University Press, 1994), 909.

8. Gilbert, *Auschwitz and the Allies*, 339-341.

9. Bernard Wasserstein, *Britain and the Jews of Europe, 1939-1945* (New York: Oxford University Press, 1979).

10. Gilbert, *Auschwitz and the Allies*.

11

Allied Knowledge of
Auschwitz-Birkenau in 1943–1944

Richard Breitman

When we get into hypothetical questions in history—what could have been done—we have to start out by examining what was done. Then we can look at what was considered at the time, but not done, and the reasons why it was not done. Then we might look at what was technically and politically feasible, given what was known at the time. Then and only then can we proceed to discuss what should have been done. Lastly, we might want to consider what could have been done, given what we know in hindsight.

With regard to the proposals for bombing the death factory at Auschwitz-Birkenau, we know generally what happened in Washington. The one government agency that considered and, with reservations, promoted bombing of the gas chambers and crematoria at Auschwitz-Birkenau was the War Refugee Board. Created in January 1944, it was given the mission of taking all measures within American policy to rescue victims of enemy oppression in imminent danger of death. But this mission was restricted in certain respects after contacts between the British government and the War Department in Washington. The War Department declared: "It is not contemplated that combat units of the armed forces will be employed for the purpose of rescuing victims of enemy oppression unless such rescues are the direct result of military operations conducted with the objectives of defeating the armed forces of the enemy."[1] This initial mandate, or restriction of an initial mandate, made the War Refugee

Board quite reluctant to pose requests to the military for missions such as the bombing of Auschwitz, and it clearly allowed the War Department and other military authorities to remain uninterested in conducting any such operations. Apart from the problems of mandate and jurisdiction, the War Refugee Board did not have the full cooperation of other agencies of the American government. It had limited clout and leverage. So, to a certain extent, we are looking today at a possibility that was politically (or bureaucratically) difficult, if not impossible, in 1944 for reasons that we may decide were good reasons or for reasons that we may decide were not good reasons.

But I would like to go back to our sequence of issues, to stress one, and then to pose an answer. How much did interested parties during World War II actually know about Auschwitz-Birkenau and when? It is, after all, unrealistic to expect any government to bomb any site unless it has specific intelligence about what is taking place there. The availability of information about Auschwitz-Birkenau would allow us to judge whether bombing might have been possible under different political circumstances and, if so, when.

Some historians have maintained that until the middle of 1944 the West knew little of Auschwitz-Birkenau as an extermination camp for Jews. In his 1981 work *Auschwitz and the Allies,* Martin Gilbert stated this argument most directly:

> From the first week of May 1942 until the third week of June 1944 the gas chambers at Auschwitz-Birkenau had kept their secret both as the principal mass murder site of the Jews of Europe and also as the destination of so many hundreds of deportation trains from France, Holland, Belgium, Italy, Greece, and elsewhere.[2]

Gilbert suggested that the West knew of Auschwitz earlier, but mainly as a concentration camp for Poles. At the end of his study, however, Gilbert conceded that a few reports of Auschwitz as a killing center for Jews did leak out, but he contended that none of them made an impact.[3]

Historian David Engel, now at New York University, in his two-volume study of the Polish government in exile, adopted part of Gilbert's argument but gave it a new twist. The Poles actually had some information about Auschwitz-Birkenau as a center for the extermination of Jews but consciously decided not to publicize it much, if at all.[4] Engel thus agreed with Gilbert that Auschwitz-Birkenau was not properly exposed, but he portrayed London and Washington's lack of knowledge as part of deliberate Polish policy.

I am not in a position here to discuss Engel's broader argument about the thrust of the policies of the Polish government in exile—only the narrow issue of whether the Poles obtained and transmitted information about Auschwitz. The issue of how secret the Nazis were able to keep their extermination camps is, even apart from the consideration of American and British knowledge, a matter of some historical import.

Actually, the Polish government in exile did receive and pass on to the United States and presumably also to Britain, a series of items about Auschwitz-Birkenau, especially during 1943 and early 1944. Some of this information has been declassified and is available to scholars, but I would bet that there is more, relevant material, especially in London, that is still classified.

Nonetheless, I have uncovered enough material in the archives to, let us say, inform adequately a hypothetical official of the War Refugee Board pondering the "Final Solution of the Jewish question"—how and where it was being implemented and what might be done to stop it. Such a hypothetical official with access to information available in other government agencies, as well as Jewish organizations, would have been able to find out the centrality of Auschwitz-Birkenau and might have begun thinking and planning to do something about it.

The Directorate of Civilian Resistance in Poland reported on 23 March 1943 that there was a new crematorium disposing of about three thousand persons per day in Auschwitz-Birkenau, and that most of them were Jews.[5] This report was very close to what postwar reconstruction would establish as the actual situation at that time. Crematorium IV had begun to operate on 22 March—one day earlier—and Crematorium V would start up about two weeks later. Together they had the capacity to deal with three thousand bodies per day.

The 23 March report was sent from Stefan Korbonski in underground Poland to London. I was not able to establish whether the Polish radio station in London known as SWIT broadcast it, but in April 1943 a Polish bulletin called *Poland Fights* summarized what was known about Auschwitz-Birkenau and included some of the 23 March report as well as other information. Through the middle of 1942, according to this publication, there were 63,340 prisoners registered at Auschwitz-Birkenau, but also another 22,500 persons who had arrived at the camp and had not been registered, but were simply liquidated. Among the unregistered were 4,000 Poles, 10,000 Jews, and 8,500 Soviet POWs. Also included was another estimate that 57,000 people had died at Auschwitz-Birkenau of illness, exhaustion, or execution.[6]

The degree of accuracy in these statistics is not what concerns us here. In this report and in ones I will mention shortly, there are underestimates and some overestimates. What matters is whether the thrust of the data and the reports provided enough information to alert the West to the general scope of the killing operation at Auschwitz-Birkenau.

On 18 April 1943, the day before the Warsaw Ghetto uprising began and the Bermuda Conference on refugee problems opened, a Polish underground courier[7] drafted a long report in London about his experience in Poland and Europe during the period November 1941–October 1942. There are some errors in this report, and some perhaps overly optimistic comments about the relationship between Poles and Jews in Poland, but there is also detailed information about Auschwitz. It is largely consistent with the earlier information from March and April 1943, and, although the report was written slightly later than the earlier ones, its observations are from an earlier period before the completion of the new crematoria.

The author explains:

> I lived in Oswiecim [Auschwitz] for a number of weeks. I know the conditions well, because I investigated them. . . . I had the most detailed information of what is going on there from people [Polish prisoners] who were freed. When I left Oswiecim at the end of September [1942], the number of registered prisoners was over 95,000. . . . Among the latter [unregistered were] 20,000 Russian prisoners of war who were brought there in the summer of 1940 [1941] as well as masses of Jews brought there from other countries. The POWs died from starvation. Jews were exterminated en masse.
>
> On the basis of information I collected and on the spot, I can ascertain that the Germans applied the following killing methods. a) Gas chambers: the victims were undressed and put into those chambers where they suffocated; b) Electric chambers: Those chambers had metal walls. The victims were brought in and then high-tension electric current was introduced; c) The so-called Hammerluft system. This is a hammer of the air (presumably some sort of air pressure killing). d) Shooting, often killing every tenth person.

The author claimed that the first three methods were the most common. Obviously, there were false elements and deductions in this account gathered from a variety of sources. Nonetheless, the courier left little doubt that large numbers of Jews were being gassed at Auschwitz-Birkenau:

> Gestapo men stood in a position which enabled them to watch in gas masks the death of the masses of victims. The Germans loaded the corpses and took them outside Auschwitz by means of huge shovels. They made holes where they buried the dead and then they covered the holes with lime. Burning of victims by means of electric ovens was seldom applied [in this period]. This is because in such ovens only about 250 people could be burned within twenty-four hours.

This Polish courier met in London with Dr. Ignacy Schwarzbart, a member of the Polish National Council and a representative of the World Jewish Congress. On 27 April, Schwarzbart sent a report about this meeting and this document to the Representation of Polish Jews in the United States within the World Jewish Congress. He asked his recipients to keep the information strictly confidential. But the American government had this information, too, because its Censorship Office inspected all transatlantic mail, summarized relevant and useful information, then sent it on its way.[8]

Some information reached American government agencies more directly. On 18 May 1943, Polish military intelligence in London prepared a report on conditions in Poland that was sent by diplomatic pouch to Washington; a copy in Polish was given to the Joint Chiefs of Staff in June. Again there was updating of information regarding Auschwitz-Birkenau, this time from new underground sources. The total number of people killed at Auschwitz-Birkenau through December 1942 was now said to be 640,000-650,000 Poles, 26,000 Soviet POWs, and 520,000 Jews. There was now mention of the huge new crematorium already at work, consuming about 3,000 persons per day.[9] This was hardly ignoring the fate of Jews at Auschwitz-Birkenau!

Another Polish military intelligence report came out in December 1943, reaching London at the end of January 1944. The author was a Polish woman, code-named Wanda, who had apparently also written about Auschwitz-Birkenau earlier. She was said to be completely reliable. Her report was given to the American liaison to the Allied governments in exile and to the American military attache in London, with the request to give it as wide publicity as possible. Copies were sent to OSS (Office of Strategic Services) London and eventually to Washington. Wanda claimed that through September 1942, 468,000 nonregistered Jews had been gassed at Auschwitz-Birkenau. Then during the next eight months, 60,000 Jews had arrived from Greece, 50,000 from Slovakia and Bohemia-Moravia, 60,000 from Holland, Belgium, and France, as well as 11,000 others. Ninety-eight percent of the recent arrivals were gassed. So Wanda's grand total as of early June 1943 was 645,000 Jews gassed.

She described the processes of selection and killing:

Each convoy arriving at Auschwitz is unloaded. Men are separated from women and then packed haphazard in a mass. Children and women are put into cars and lorries and taken to the gas chamber in Brzezinka. There they are suffocated with most horrible suffering lasting ten to fifteen minutes, the corpses being thrown out through an aperture and cremated. Before entering the gas chambers, the condemned must be bathed. At present, three large crematoria have been erected in Birkenau-Brzezinka for 10,000 people daily which are ceaselessly cremating bodies and which the neighboring population call "the eternal fire."

Wanda also mentioned that the overwhelming majority of Gypsies from Greece and southern France were gassed immediately.[10]

This flow of information during 1943 and 1944, only part of which I have described here, casts a new perspective on the now well-known stories of three escapees from Auschwitz during 1944. Two Slovak Jews, Rudolf Vrba and Alfred Wetzler, escaped in April and gave their information to Jewish officials, and a Polish major escaped a bit earlier but took longer to get his account out. So two detailed reports of the facilities and operations at Auschwitz-Birkenau reached the West more or less simultaneously toward the end of June 1944 and both were widely circulated by, among others, Gerhart Riegner. These reports did get a lot of attention in Washington, including at the War Refugee Board.

Outside the War Refugee Board, the attention was not always positive; some tended to question the credibility of the reports, but that is another story.[11]

These mid-1944 reports were the most detailed and most accurate ones yet, though they were not completely accurate. Despite Martin Gilbert's dramatic rendition of Vrba and Wetzler suddenly exposing the secret of Auschwitz-Birkenau,[12] however, their account was not, or should not have been, a sudden shock to intelligence analysts, who would have or should have seen the earlier reports discussed in this chapter. Not that the intelligence analysts had an easy time. There were, of course, plenty of inaccurate reports about Auschwitz-Birkenau. All intelligence work involves sifting out the wheat from the chaff, the good from the bad, and certainly it would have been possible for someone to go through the data and come out with mistaken ideas about Auschwitz-Birkenau. What I have done here is to present the better sources.

Still, there was enough generally accurate information about Auschwitz-Birkenau to preclude the argument that the Allies did not bomb the camp because they got the necessary information too late. Gilbert's claim that the Allies could not have responded to Auschwitz-Birkenau for the first two years of its existence because of lack of knowledge will not stand in the light of new evidence.[13] In actuality, if there had been the political will and agreement among the various agencies involved, the planning of a bombing raid could have begun in early 1944. Implementation could occur only if and when Allied bombers located in Italy could reach Upper Silesia. I will leave it to the military experts to discuss the logistics and feasibility of the bombing.

I would like to make a final observation about the significance of a bombing raid on the gas chambers and crematoria. The broader question here is: Do we allow moral considerations to influence the determination of military objectives? The answer given to that in 1944 was no. The answer given to that question today might or might not be different.

NOTES

1. War Refugee Board to American Embassy, London, 9 February 1944, copy in Edmund R. Stettinius Papers, War Refugee Board Folder, University of Virginia. Partly reprinted in David S. Wyman, *The Abandonment of the Jews: America and the Holocaust 1941-1945* (New York: Pantheon Books, 1984), 291.
2. Martin Gilbert, *Auschwitz and the Allies* (New York: Holt, Rinehart and Winston, 1981), esp. 339-340.
3. Ibid., 340.
4. David Engel, *Facing a Holocaust: The Polish Government in Exile and the Jews, 1943-1945* (Chapel Hill: University of North Carolina Press, 1993), 287n121: "The Polish government had long been in possession of information pointing to Auschwitz as a primary center for killing Jews, but it had not given such reports wide publicity." Engel's first volume, *In the Shadow of Auschwitz: The Polish Government in Exile and the Jews, 1939-1942* (Chapel Hill: University of North Carolina Press, 1987), 202, was even stronger: "The news [of Jews being gassed in large numbers at Auschwitz-Birkenau] may thus not have been altogether suppressed, but it was certainly so deeply buried and downplayed that only the most careful and thorough of readers would have noticed it at all, and hardly anyone would have attached to it any particular importance."
5. S. [Korbonski] cable to the Polish radio station SWIT, in London 23 March 1943, cited by Engel, *Facing a Holocaust*, 231n122.
6. Nazi Black Record, Record Group (RG) 165, Poland 6950, from *Poland Fights*, 5 April 1943, National Archives (NA).
7. Tentatively identified as Jerzy Salski by Engel, *Facing a Holocaust*, 209n109.
8. Schwarzbart to Representation of Polish Jews, World Jewish Congress, 27 April 1943, Schwarzbart Papers, M2 535, Yad Vashem, Jerusalem. I am grateful to Shlomo Aronson for sending me a copy of this cover letter. For the full document, see Censorship Report, 5 May 1943, RG 226, Entry 191, Untitled Folder, NA.
9. Joint Chiefs of Staff (JCS) Memo 334, 18 May 1943, Polish Liaison (Washington), Folder 30, RG 218, NARA.
10. Military Attaché (London) Report 907, 17 March 1944, RG 165, Poland 6950, NA. Also F. W. Belin to William L. Langer, 10 April 1944, RG 226, Plain

182   *RICHARD BREITMAN*

Number File 66059, NA. Engel, *In the Shadow,* 287nl21, mentions a 15 September 1943 cable from Wanda about Birkenau.

11. Richard Breitman and Alan M. Kraut, *American Refugee Policy and European Jewry, 1933-1945* (Bloomington: Indiana University Press, 1987), 201-202.
12. Gilbert *Auschwitz and the Allies,* 192-239.
13. Ibid., 340. Newly declassified signals intelligence passed to the British prime minister in September 1942 indicates that more than eight thousand people died at Auschwitz during the month of August 1942. See "Nazis Wanted British Troops as Guards at Death Camps," *The Times* (London), 27 November 1993.

12

The Bombing of
Auschwitz Reexamined

James H. Kitchens III

Word of this essay by James H. Kitchens III on the bombing of Auschwitz was circulating through historical circles months before it first appeared in April 1994. Kitchens challenges Wyman's thesis head on and faults him for superficial research and understanding of the issues related to the proposal to bomb Auschwitz.

One of the most curious—even bizarre—legacies of the Holocaust is the question of whether the Allies could, and should, have used their air power to destroy the gas chambers and crematoria at Auschwitz and the rail net feeding them. For a decade or so, it has been argued that the camp's location and layout were well known and that the installations and rails vital to its operations could have been easily and precisely neutralized from the air, had not insensitivity, indifference, and even antipathy prevented it. Critics, on the other hand, argue that aerial bombing of Auschwitz or its vital railroads was technically infeasible and militarily chimerical. So where in the cross fire does the truth lie? Though the past cannot be changed, the answer is consequential because the alleged failure to act inculpates the Allies' high commands, governments, and even peoples in collective guilt for the deaths of innocent millions. Professional historians, too, have a stake in the answer, because dissection of the bombing problem reveals unsettling deficiencies in the investigation, determination, and assignation of this culpability. Indeed, few dialogues in modern historiography have been so charged with subjectivity and so encumbered by irrelevancies; few have suffered so much from intellectual insularity and from ineffective colloquy. The following comments explore the genesis of the bombing idea and its seminal expressions, identify its premises, and demonstrate that operational constraints rather than prejudice prevented Allied authorities from bombing Auschwitz.

The initial inspiration for bombing of concentration camps or railroads to counter the Holocaust may be traced to early summer 1944, when the dimensions and import of Adolf Hitler's Final Solution first began to be appreciated in the West.[1] In mid-May 1944, the Slovak Orthodox Rabbi Dov Weissmandel, horrified by the incipient deportation of hundreds of thousands of Hungarian Jews to Auschwitz, begged the Allies to block the movement by bombing the Kosice-Presov rail line.[2] Sent surreptitiously from Bratislava to Switzerland and thence to Jewish leaders in New York, Weissmandel's message reached the U.S. War Refugee Board on 18 June. On 2 June, Yitzak Gruenbaum, chairman of the Rescue Committee of the Jewish Agency, independently sent an analogous suggestion to the War Refugee Board.[3] Later in June, the World Jewish Congress in Switzerland proposed that "the camps at Auschwitz and Birkenau and especially the buildings containing the gas-chambers and crematoriums, . . . as well as the sentries around the railings and the watch-towers and the industrial installations should be bombed from the air."[4] Despite explicit firsthand descriptions of Auschwitz's horrors received later in the summer, however, the Allies turned a deaf ear to pleas for aerial intervention. In late June 1944, the U.S. War Department rejected the Kosice-Presov rail-bombing plea on the grounds that it was impractical and would require diversion of too many essential resources; in August, the British Air Ministry also refused aerial rescue operations, citing poor intelligence, hazards and high casualties, and dubious results.[5] Thus, no German concentration camps were deliberately attacked from the air before war's end, and no discernible efforts were made to single out deportation railroads for special attacks.

Following the war, whatever questions there may have been about Allied inaction long lay inchoate, in part because of popular satisfaction with victory, in part because of document classification, and in part because even those who had urged bombing during World War II had recognized it as a desperate, symbolic gesture at best.[6] At the same time, however, the Holocaust's dimensions not only became fully known but increasingly became the focus of conscience-wrenching inquiry. This inquiry did not always produce satisfaction, especially where causation and responsibility were concerned. Within this context, the possibility that air power could have saved thousands of innocent lives may occasionally have made cocktail chitchat during the late 1940s and the 1950s, but it remained nothing more than grist for casual speculation until a school of collective guilt began to emerge in the late 1960s. The new tilt toward global responsibility for Nazi atrocities was signaled by Arthur D. Morse's *While Six Million Died: A Chronicle of American Apathy* (1968), which asserted that American authorities had been apathetic bystanders to the Holocaust.[7] Eight years later, historian John Morton Blum adopted a more temperate, dispassionate, and scholarly version of this theme in his *V Was for Victory: Politics and American Culture during World War II*.[8]

Against this backdrop, in May 1978 David S. Wyman, professor of history at the University of Massachusets, published a startling article entitled "Why Auschwitz Was Never Bombed" in the American Jewish Committee's magazine *Commentary*.[9] The title told all: Wyman proposed to disclose how the camp could have been bombed but was not. Two months later, in the July issue, several letters pro and con turned up, thus igniting a controversy that spread to other periodicals in the ensuing months. Some of these commentators went even further than Wyman. For example, Roger William's article "Why Wasn't Auschwitz Bombed?" in the 24 November 1978 issue of *Commonweal* was subtitled "An American Moral Tragedy," which phrase epitomized its theme.[10] Williams, then senior editor of *Saturday Review,* wrote that "at Auschwitz alone, almost half a million Jews died *after* the U.S. had acquired the ability to prevent their deaths there" and that, since the inmates were doomed anyway, "the bombing should have been done for larger symbolic reasons."[11] For the next five years, the issue bubbled like the mud pots of Yellowstone, percolating but not quite erupting into the national arena. In 1981, for example, Martin Gilbert presented his *Auschwitz and the Allies,* a sober and professional book that carefully chronicled Allied intelligence about Auschwitz but that also uncritically deduced that the camp could, and should, have been bombed.[12] Two years later, the American Gathering of Jewish Holocaust Survivors in Washington, D.C., prompted Morton Mintz to ask again, in the *Washington Post,* "Why Didn't We Bomb Auschwitz?"[13]

Despite spasmodic publicity in the early 1980s, the bombing question really did not catch the public eye until late 1984, when Wyman incorporated a refined and annotated version of his *Commentary* article into a weighty monograph titled *The Abandonment of the Jews: America and the Holocaust, 1941-1945*.[14] Here Wyman argued that during World War II the United States had neglected several potential rescue measures, such as earlier establishment of the War Refugee Board; greater pressure on Germany to release the Jews; a freer refugee policy in the United States and abroad; support for a Palestinian homeland; concentrated broadcast warnings; and offers of ransom. The failure to energetically pursue such measures amounted to deliberate and callous abandonment of the Jews.[15]

In Chapter 15, "The Bombing of Auschwitz," Wyman integrated the camp- and railroad-bombing question into his larger thesis by positing that the Allies had contributed to the Holocaust's toll by refusing to smash the Nazi genocide apparatus at Auschwitz from the air. Essentially, the 19-page chapter was a footnoted version of the author's earlier *Commentary* article. As early as April 1944, Wyman postulated, the Allies had aerial photographs of the Auschwitz-Birkenau concentration camp, and additional evidence became available during May and June through the detailed report of two escapees, Rudolf Vrba and Alfred Wetzler.[16] When combined, these sources supposedly made clear the exact location, number, and dimensions of the camp's gas chambers and crematoria. Despite this intelligence, American bombing of the nearby I. G. Farben works at Monowitz,[17] and the repeated entreaties of European and American Jewish leaders to attack the facilities and the railroads feeding them, however, the U.S. War Department and British authorities did nothing. According to Wyman, American heavy-bomber flights over the camp, Frantic shuttle missions to Russia,[18] and relief missions to Warsaw demonstrated that heavy-bomber attacks on Auschwitz were eminently feasible without diversion of military resources, and, even if not, he reasoned, B-25 medium bombers, P-38 fighter-bombers or British D. H. 98 Mosquitoes could have performed the mission. Yet in June 1944, the U.S. War Department declared such attacks would be an impractical diversion:

> The War Department is of the opinion that the suggested air operation is impracticable for the reason that it could be executed only by diversion of considerable air support essential to the success of our forces now engaged in decisive operations. . . . It is considered that the most effective relief to victims of enemy persecution is the early defeat of the Axis, an undertaking to which we must devote every resource at our disposal.[19]

This no-bomb policy permitted the killing at Auschwitz to continue unhindered, costing tens, even hundreds, of thousands of lives until the camp ceased operations late in 1944. The author had, it appeared, amply documented these points in 80 chapter footnotes and supported them with appropriate bibliographic references.

Abandonment of the Jews received considerable attention and wide acclamation following its release by Pantheon Books in November 1984. On 6 November and again on 24 December, the *New York Times* published plausive articles about Wyman and his research, and on 16 December A. J. Sherman favorably reviewed *Abandonment of the Jews* for the paper's book review supplement. Perhaps boosted by this publicity, *Abandonment of the Jews* made the *New York Times Book Review*'s "best-sellers" list on 17 March 1985 and on four ensuing dates, rising to number 13 of 15 nonfiction titles on 31 March.[20] Subsequent reviews were almost universally positive,[21] the History Book Club later made it one of its monthly selections, and it was released in a paperback edition. Total sales ran to over eighty thousand. In short, the book became everything that an academic could dream of.

Largely because of its scholarly trappings and popular reception, but also in part because of its spectacular inferences, Wyman's thesis quickly gained a broad following. In fact, a veritable school of opinion predicated on his views and nurtured by brooding retrospection has arisen since 1984. Thus entrenched, Wyman himself has shown no inclination to revise his thinking on the subject, as his final words on the bombing of Auschwitz in Macmillan's 1990 *Encyclopedia of the Holocaust* indicate. The U.S. War Department's June 1944 refusal to bomb Auschwitz was, he concludes, "no more than an excuse for inaction."[22] Today this conviction is widespread and has been incorporated into several recent Holocaust histories.[23] The U.S. Holocaust Memorial Council subscribes to it—Wyman has served as adviser to the group[24]—and in mid-April 1990, just when the issue was again being debated in letters to the *Washington Post,* a pseudojudicial proceeding in Israel found the United States Army Air Force (USAAF) guilty of failure to save thousands of innocent lives by not bombing the death camps.[25]

As early as 1978, however, Wyman's bombing thesis excited some challenges. A few weeks after publication of the professor's initial *Commentary* article, Milton Groban, a former Fifteenth Air Force B-24 navigator-bombardier,[26] wrote the magazine to point out why gross inaccuracy made using heavy bombers against Auschwitz impractical without enormous casualties within the camp. Moreover, Groban asserted, bombing the facility would have been very costly in men and machines and might have only distracted, but not significantly impaired, the Nazi killing. Viewing the matter only from his own combat experiences in B-24s, Groban did not comment on sending medium, light, or dive bombers against Auschwitz, nor did he elucidate the requirement for, and costs of, a systematic anti-camp and rail campaign.[27]

After the initial exchanges in *Commentary* faded, further criticism of the Wyman thesis was muted until after publication of *Abandonment of the Jews* in 1984. Even then, the rigorous review process that often sieves out errors in historiography failed Clio's cause when academic specializations and disciplinary insularity among reviewers permitted marked deficiencies in Chapter 15 to slip through without notice. On the one hand, most reviewers of *Abandonment of the Jews* were schooled in refugee or religious history or Holocaust studies and apparently knew little about air power;[28] on the other hand, none of the country's handful of professional historians of air power seem to have noticed the book or to have publicly critiqued its camp-bombing thesis. Thus, the Holocaust-studies community and that of air-power history passed like ships in the night, and it was left to Richard Foregger, a Minnesota anesthesiologist and amateur historian, to become the first to systematically controvert Wyman's propositions. The physician's "The Bombing of Auschwitz," a well-documented 13-page article in the summer 1987 issue of *Aerospace Historian,* refuted most of Wyman's assertions about camp and rail bombing.[29] This quarterly, however, was published by the Air Force Historical Foundation, which to some may have tainted its objectivity. It was also something less than a formal academic forum, and it had a readership of less than five thousand, mostly aviation enthusiasts. Despite Foregger's evident scholarship and critical thinking, therefore, there is no evidence that his rebuttal penetrated the Holocaust-studies community; if it did, it prompted no perceptible responses from that community in either *Aerospace Historian* or the national press[30] and has not been cited in many, if any, post-1987 Holocaust histories. Since 1978, therefore, the Wyman thesis has remained for many a convincing explanation of why the Allies did little or nothing to derail the Holocaust from the air.

As conceived by Wyman and adopted by Gilbert and other historians, then, the camp-bombing proposition originated in the groves of academe, and a critical analysis of it properly begins with its chief disciple's perspective and sources. A member of the Society of Friends and a 1966 graduate of Harvard, Wyman joined the University of Massachusets history faculty in the same year. In 1968, his doctoral dissertation was published as *Paper Walls: America and the Refugee Crisis, 1938-1941,*[31] a study of the United States's prewar attitude toward Jewish refugees. Wyman found that it was shaped by unemployment, nativistic nationalism,[32] and anti-Semitism, factors that found expression in executive and legislative policy such as limited immigration quotas.

Wyman's second book, *Abandonment of the Jews,* built on these perspectives, themes, and conclusions and extended them through the World War II period. In particular, Wyman carried forward his view that public policy, presumably fashioned and driven by democratic process, was responsible for abandonment of the Jews between 1941 and 1945. He neglected, however, a crucial difference between the prewar era of *Paper Walls* and that of *Abandonment of the Jews:* a state of total war not of the Allies' choosing. Prior to 1941, though war was clearly on the horizon, the United States was ostensibly neutral; American diplomatic and public-policy options were unfettered by overt hostilities. After December 1941, America had to focus on mobilization of its wealth, manpower, allies, and world opinion in a global struggle to bring down the Axis powers. U.S. shipping, for example, was stretched to the limit to meet the needs of war; U.S. foreign policy had to take into account the posture of the Arab world vis-à-vis any Zionist settlements in Palestine. In such a setting, ultimate victory depended almost exclusively on mustering, then applying, brute force to break the Hitlerian regime; military options for rescuing large numbers of Nazi victims from fortress Europe before its fall were severely circumscribed. Given the irrational character of Nazism, its intransigence, and the occupation of most of Europe until after mid-1944, air power assumed overwhelming importance in any effective construct for salvation of the Jews. Air power, after all, was the sole means of projecting military power deep into the enemy's heartland. For these reasons, the camp-bombing question is highly germane to Wyman's overall thesis. Yet, it is exactly here in the realm of air power, far from prewar mores, immigration quotas, socioeconomic attitudes, public debate, or legislative mandate that the public-policy perspective carried over from *Paper Walls* dramatically changes character.

Not surprisingly, Wyman based *Abandonment of the Jews* largely on ethnic and sociopolitical sources and personal papers; considering the criticality of the bombing question to the book's thesis, its air power bibliography is astonishingly anemic. Of five books on air-power, two are elderly USAAF and Royal Air Force (RAF) official histories: the first 30 years old; the second 20 years old by 1981, 3 years before the publication of *Abandonment of the Jews*.[33] The age factor is particularly significant in such sources because over time the declassification of documents makes them obsolete; one instance of this is mentioned below in connection with the AZON (Azimuth Only) bomb (an early type of guided weapon). Of other books cited, one is a buff's book,[34] one an examination of the Poltava Affair,[35] and one a 1963 melange of unannotated articles and extracts about diverse aspects of the European air war.[36] Not a single reference to the B-17, B-24, B-25 or P-38 is listed, even though the combat capabilities and tactical employment of these machines are quintessential to the bombing dialectic.[37] Wyman's remarks about the D. H. 98 Mosquito are scarcely better supported, resting on nothing but Birtles's pictorial history—a far cry from C. Martin Sharp and Michael J. F. Bowyer's definitive 494-page treatment of the machine[38]—and on one apparently misunderstood letter from an RAF Air Historical Branch archivist. Some tangible consequences of this faulty documentation of the Mosquito will be seen shortly. The *Abandonment of the Jews* bibliography includes nothing on German air defenses, nor are any works on Ploesti raids listed, even though the experiences of the Fifteenth Air Force against this target usefully illuminate the camp-bombing problem. Finally, not a single article entry out of 58 seems to relate to aircraft, air power, air leaders, or air operations per se, although 2 essays do address aerial photo intelligence about Auschwitz. Of 10 unpublished works, none treat air power; of 24 pamphlets and booklets, just one, the Fifteenth Air Force's *Historical Summary: First Year of Operations* (1944), documents that Air Force's operations.[39] Primary sources are even weaker. The bibliography, for example, simply lists the United States Air Force Historical Research Center (USAFHRC) as an institution, and nothing indicates which of the facility's files were actually examined. In fact, there is strong inferential evidence that the author never visited the center, or that, if he did, he overlooked or ignored dozens of entries in its finding aids.[40] Nowhere does one find citations to the center's vast holding of original unit histories, intelligence reports, operational analyses, bombing-accuracy studies, airfield files, and orders of battles that are critical to analyzing the camp-bombing problem.[41] The center's 250-roll microfilm collection of Mediterranean Allied Air Force (MAAF)[42] operations and intelligence files are nowhere cited. Some vague references to mission reports on microfilm are scattered among Chapter 15 footnotes, but these are not clarified in the bibliography, and one is left to guess what and where these are. Moreover, no mention is made of the National Archives' immense Record Group (RG) 18, Records of the USAAF, which contains perhaps 80 percent of mission reports surviving today. The bibliography does list the National Archives' RG 243, Records of the Strategic Bombing Survey (USSBS), but readers are not told that the USSBS says nothing about bombing Auschwitz or that, in fact, the survey's reports offer solid evidence *against* the feasibility of such attacks. In any case, there are but four citations to the USSBS in Chapter 15, all to area maps or photo interpretation reports of the I. G. Farben works. Similarly, Wyman cites no materials from the RAF's Air Historical Branch or to AIR files at the Public Record Office, even after Gilbert pointed the way to these in *Auschwitz and the Allies,* nor are air-power-related citations from the Imperial War Museum in Britain, the Bundesarchiv and Militararchiv in Germany, the Hoover Institute for War, Peace, and Revolution, or other repositories included. Fewer than ten references to the Carl Spaatz Collection in the Library of Congress do not offset these deficiencies.[43]

Taken together, Wyman's scholarly interests, research foci, and superficial documentation go far toward explaining the formulation of his bombing thesis. For the historian of refugee policy, the failure to bomb Auschwitz fits comfortably a pattern of prejudice he believes existed before 1941 and persisted in 1944; pervasive indifference, insensitivity, and antipathy within the cabinet, the War Department, and even among the American people are sufficient to explain why Auschwitz was never bombed, especially since American aircraft were overflying the camp and could have struck it with few, if any, collateral casualties. Gross misconceptions about air power—common among those outside the military sciences—together with an uncritical reliance on Wyman's work, help explain how post–*Abandonment of the Jews* Holocaust historiography has perpetuated the bombing idea. An objective look at targeting possibilities, available intelligence, operational constraints, and the realistic allocation of military resources, however, shows that the effective use of air power against Auschwitz is a chimera having little to do with War Department policies, indifference, military ineptitude, or negative ethnic attitudes.

Immediately it must be pointed out that from Wyman's 1978 article onward it has never been clear exactly what targets should be included in the camp-bombing question. Wyman himself ostensibly focused on destruction of the four gas chambers and crematoria at Auschwitz-Birkenau but did not mention the gas chamber/crematorium at Auschwitz I ("Main Camp").[44] The Birkenau buildings were relatively soft targets of brick construction, each about 1 or 1.5 stories with large portions sunk below ground level. Their narrow aerial profile, however, made them quite difficult targets. The largest pair, Crematoria II and III, measured 321 feet (99 m) long by 32 feet (10 m) wide,[45] about the size and proportion of a highway bridge. Dispersion and proximity to camp housing posed even graver problems. The four Birkenau buildings were grouped in two loose pairs along the camp's western edge. About 800 yards (750 m) separated the northwestern pair from the nearer of two at the southwestern corner. All four gas chambers and crematoria were within 300 yards (275 m) of camp housing.[46] About 1.5 miles southeast of them was the older single gas chamber and crematorium of Auschwitz I, making a total of five discrete, widely spaced objectives within the Auschwitz complex whose destruction could have conceivably impeded the extermination process there.[47]

Adherents of camp bombing from Wyman onward have consistently maintained that Allied leadership possessed enough, and sufficiently exact, intelligence about these five Auschwitz buildings to mount the kind of attack necessary to safely destroy them. Two types of evidence for this are usually cited: photos derived from USAAF reconnaissance over the I. G. Farben Monowitz complex ("Buna") near Auschwitz and the report of escapees Vrba and Wetzler. It is true that images of Birkenau appeared on aerial photographs as early as April 1944, but as Dino Brugioni and Robert Poirier have pointed out, the death camp appeared only accidentally and was wholly incidental to the interpreters' work.[48] None of them was tasked to look for concentration camps; their prints and viewing equipment were primitive; none of them had the experience or interpretation guides to make the images speak intelligibly; few, if any, of them had access to other types of intelligence or to Fifteenth Air Force's overall air campaign. Brugioni has further noted that during May–August 1944 the Mediterranean Allied Air Forces' strategic assets were concentrated on the oil campaign, meaning that the MAAF photo interpreters were concentrating on known oil-producing facilities such as Monowitz and Blechhammer at the expense of other types of targets. During July and early August, the MAAF's focus also shifted to the forthcoming invasion of southern France. Under these circumstances, it is not surprising that Auschwitz's true nature passed unnoticed under the photo interpreters' stereoscopes. In the context of overall intelligence appreciation, it also should be noted that there was no historical precedent for genocidal installations like Auschwitz and that before the end of 1944, at least, the Allies lacked enough solid intelligence about the Final Solution to adequately comprehend its hideous import.[49]

Bombing advocates maintain, however, that, when combined with aerial photographs, the Vrba-Wetzler report should have precipitated immediate and decisive action from Washington or London. Close analysis reveals why the report's timing and contents prevented this from happening. As Gilbert depicts them, Vrba and Wetzler were both young men whose administrative duties and lengthy survival within Birkenau gave them an extraordinary perspective on the camp's horrors, which they determined to preserve through memorization and eventual escape. Between 7 April and 10 April 1944, their determination met with success, and on 25 April their report reached Jewish underground figures in Slovakia, who tried to get it out to Budapest, Switzerland, the Vatican, and Istanbul. For various reasons, the text was delayed, and a telegraphic summary did not reach the War Refugee Board in Washington until 24 June and the British Foreign Office until 4 July. The full 25-page text with a 5-page summary did not get to London until 26 July, by which time it was too late for any action to save the Jews of Hungary.[50]

Even after 26 July, the full Vrba-Wetzler report had minimal utility for military intelligence purposes. On the surface, the report appears to be a sickening revelation about what was going on in Auschwitz, and so it was. But, in fact, as intelligence collateral for analyzing the camp as a precision bombing target, the report had severe limitations. Neither escapee was a trained observer, and their 1.5-page description of Birkenau's crematoria was almost exclusively concerned with the ghastly details of operation rather than militarily useful targeting data such as building structural design, materials, foundations, and the like necessary for the selection and placement of ordnance. Potential low-flying hazards such as high-tension wires and radio transmission towers were nowhere mentioned, and chimneys and forested areas were only vaguely indicated. Flak guns—Birkenau itself had none—were nowhere mentioned. The escapees' report did not even estimate the gas chambers' and crematoria's outside dimensions, nor did it reliably locate them on the ground. Maps included with the report contained at least one error that could have puzzled those seeking to correlate the report with aerial photographs: The summary stated that the *northeast* end of the camp could be distinguished by the high smokestacks of four crematoria, when in reality these chimneys were located at the opposite, or *western*, side of the camp.[51] Moreover, as Foregger relates, a sketch map of the Auschwitz area that reached the British Foreign Office on 22 August was grossly inaccurate: "Neither the Auschwitz II camp at Birkinau [*sic*] nor the gas chambers and crematoria could be located with the map. A Plaster of Paris model to show the relative size, shape and location of the gas chambers and crematoria [necessary for attacking air crews] could not be correctly constructed with this sketch map."[52] Finally, expert photo interpreters might, with enough time and effort, have correlated aerial photographs with the Vrba-Wetzler report, but the authors themselves remained in Slovakia, inaccessible for person-to-person debriefing or clarification of the information they had provided.

In sum, the militarily useful intelligence available to the Allies about Auschwitz came late and was much shakier than Wyman suggests. Photo interpreters could not have reasonably been interested in the camp before being alerted to it, and this alert could not have been put out before receipt of the summary of the Vrba-Wetzler report on 4 July. Even under utopian conditions, with an instant appreciation of Auschwitz's vulnerability from the air and a resolute determination to attack, it would have taken another two to three weeks for the Central Intelligence Unit in England to be notified, then for the photographs to be retrieved, studied, and related to whatever other data could be had. A comparison with the complete Vrba-Wetzler text, of course, could not have been started before about mid-July. Further photo reconnaissance to verify and refine target assessment, probably at low altitudes, then would have been ordered, consuming a further week or more, depending on weather, availability of photo aircraft and crews, and losses or failures. So, even with the best will and under optimal conditions, it is unreasonable to think that sufficient intelligence to properly assess the Auschwitz-Birkenau buildings as targets could have been in hand before early to mid-August 1944. The next step, planning and training for, and execution of, an exacting combat operation *with forces on hand* in the Mediterranean, could not have reasonably consumed less than a week; transfer of specially qualified units within, or to, the theater for the raid would have taken longer. As a comparison, the spectacular 18 February 1944 Mosquito attack on Amiens prison—an infinitely better known, simpler, and closer target than Auschwitz with unmistakable life-and-death urgency—had taken approximately three weeks from receipt of the French resistance request to execution; bad weather had delayed the mission by only one day.[53]

Presuming adequate intelligence about Birkenau and Auschwitz I, their nature and location still would have presented insurmountable obstacles for precision bombing. One major problem was sheer range. The Auschwitz complex lay about 620 miles from Fifteenth Air Force heavy-bomber bases around Foggia and approximately 525 miles from the Adriatic island airfield on Vis, operational after 2 May 1944. Thus, Auschwitz was barely within the theoretical range of B-25 medium bombers, P-38 fighter-bombers using an external drop tank, and D. H. 98 Mosquito light bombers. Simple distance, however, was inseparably intertwined with factors of terrain, tactics, winds and weather, useful bomb load, air defenses, and crew performance. Sweeping in a great crescent from Albania to Switzerland, the Alps and Carpathian ranges presented tremendous obstacles to the penetration of central Europe from Italian bases. To attack Auschwitz via a direct route out of either southern Italy or Vis would have required crossing the Dalmatian Alps, ranging above five thousand feet, and the Tatras of Slovakia-Slovenia, also ranging over five thousand feet. Flying heavily escorted in formation above the highest ridges, heavy bombers had no difficulty with the mountains, but a low-level attack by medium or light bombers or fighter-bombers would have been much more difficult. To avoid detection by German air defenses, total radio silence and very low altitude would have been necessary. What would today be termed a med-lo-hi or a lo-lo-hi mission—meaning a medium altitude approach to target, low altitude run in and bomb release, high altitude return to base, or a low altitude approach to target, etc.—also would have demanded a zigzag approach through treacherous valleys filed with navigational hazards and wind shear. Such an approach raised fuel consumption, precluded tight defensive combat box formations, and fatigued crews. Long range demanded extra fuel, and extra fuel came only at the expense of bomb load and thus more aircraft; in the case of P-38s, for example, just one bomb per aircraft could be carried with one drop tank.

Using Vis Island for staging as Wyman suggests also would have had grave limitations. Built under German noses, the three-thousand-foot Vis airstrip[54] was a primitive, precarious, and clandestine toehold created as an advanced landing ground for close fighter support and supply of Yugoslav partisans. It had only one runway and 18 hardstands; fuel, maintenance, ground support and air defenses were minimal; and it did not even receive all-weather pierced steel planking until October 1944. A handful of aircraft might have used the island for refueling on a return to Italy, but any number would have meant dangerous congestion and a tempting target. Worst of all, any landing or takeoff accident could have blocked the single runway and closed the field to following aircraft.[55]

German air defenses have received relatively little attention in the bombing debate.[56] There were no flak guns at Auschwitz I and Birkenau, but 79 heavy guns defended the I. G. Farben works at Monowitz, 4.5 miles away, and wheeling formations of heavy bombers over Birkenau could hardly have avoided this defensive umbrella.[57] Even small-arms fire from the guards could have been effective against low-level attackers, especially P-38s and Mosquitoes with liquid-cooled engines. The Luftwaffe's fighter defenses in the Balkans were not nearly as strong as in Germany, but Y-stations and at least three early-warning radars directly opposite Bari, Italy, provided the Jagdfliegerfuhrer Balkan's (Director of Fighter Planes for the Balkans) headquarters in Belgrade with ample electronic intelligence.[58] Located directly under any bomber attack directed northward, the Jagdfliegerfuhrer Balkan in mid-1944 could have called on a minimum of 30 Bf 109G fighters from II./JG51, III./JG77 and II./JG301 for interception. Another 25 Bf 109Gs of Hungarian Fighter Group 101 were based at Veszprem, north of Lake Balaton and directly under the approach to Auschwitz.[59]

On arriving in the target area, attackers would have faced a dispersed, dauntingly complex objective consisting of five widely spaced buildings (four at Birkenau, one over a mile away at Auschwitz I) that would have had to be identified and attacked in concert with little loiter time and no release error. In making such attacks, weather also would have played a part. The atmosphere over mountainous Balkan terrain was likely to be more turbulent than over the sea or the northwest European plain. Accurate precision bombing would have required perfect visibility, yet over southern Poland such weather was unusual and its prediction problematical. How, then, have bombing adherents proposed to attack the Auschwitz complex?

One proposal, high-altitude raiding by four-engined heavy bombers of the Fifteenth Air Force based around Foggia, can immediately be discounted. It is true that some of these aircraft could have been diverted from formations attacking the Monowitz synthetic fuel/rubber plant during August 1944, or they could have been sent on a dedicated raid. B-17s and B-24s, however, cruised at 180 to 190 miles per hour and were designed to bomb from fifteen thousand to thirty thousand feet. Unfortunately, from these heights the pickle barrel placement required to hit chosen buildings without collateral damage was utterly impossible, a fact made crystal clear by the USSBS (which Wyman cites) and countless other sources. Normal bomb patterns from the heavies extended hundreds of yards from the aiming point, and it was quite common for bombs to fall a mile or more away from the target.[60] On 15 April 1945, for example, the Eighth Air Force's 467th Bombardment Group achieved that air force's most accurate bombing of the war. In striking a coastal artillery battery in

France—a pinpoint target not unlike the gas chambers or crematoria—B-24s from the 467th managed to put just 50 percent of their bombs within a 500-foot radius around the guns. This was accomplished only with long experience, a 15,000-foot drop altitude, near-perfect weather, and no resistance. If this was the best that heavy bombers could do, what would average bombing have done to the exterminations camps' inhabitants?

Bombing advocates have consistently minimized the casualties that might have resulted from bombing Auschwitz. Wyman avoided any estimate, but in 1978 Williams ventured that "there would have been inmate deaths, *perhaps dozens of them*" (italics mine).[61] In fact, without too much speculation, it is possible to calculate what casualties a heavy bomber raid on Birkenau would have caused. In November 1944, the 1st Operation Analysis Section of Fifteenth Air Force reported on the relationship between altitude and bombing accuracy based on Mediterranean theater experience. The Fifteenth's calculations showed that under good conditions, the Circular Error Probable (CEP) at 15,000 feet for B-17s was 500 feet and that for B-24s about 515 feet. Put another way, *under absolutely optimal conditions,* one-half of the bombs dropped would have fallen at distances greater than 500 feet from the aiming point. The northern pair of gas chambers and crematoria at Birkenau were about 650 feet from the nearest huts; the southern pair were about 300 feet away. Using Gilbert's scale diagram of Birkenau with aiming points in the center of each target building,[62] it can be conservatively estimated that 25 to 30 percent of bombs dropped from 15,000 feet would have fallen within camp housing areas. According to the Paskuly edition of Commandant Rudolf Höss's memoirs, Birkenau held about 36,000 people on 4 April 1944 and upwards of 135,000 in August.[63] If, then, one hundred B-17s and B-24s bombed and each dropped eight 500-pound bombs, approximately 160 to 200 of the 800 would have exploded in densely populated housing areas, within which there was no air-raid protection whatsoever and no place to flee. Assuming five deaths by each errant missile, a minimum of five hundred to a thousand deaths could reasonably have been expected, with a realistic possibility of as many as two thousand to three thousand under adverse circumstances.[64]

One does not have to rely on theoretical modeling, however, to know what a heavy-bomber raid on Auschwitz might have done. On 24 August 1944, the USAAF's Eighth Air Force carried out Operation No. 568 against a V-2 guidance works and an armament factory adjoining Buchenwald concentration camp at Weimar, Germany. The setting was as analogous to Auschwitz as history permits: The grounds of one target ran along the camp fence, the other was a few hundred yards away. Backed by precise intelligence, including the factory shift schedule, 129 B-17s dropped 303 tons of bombs in near-perfect conditions, obliterating the objectives. Despite good knowledge of the target and much-above-average accuracy, however, 315 prisoners were killed, 525 seriously wounded, and 900 lightly wounded.[65] Neither *Abandonment of the Jews* nor any subsequent Holocaust historiography mentions this Buchenwald attack.

A more attractive variation on four-engine bombing that Wyman did not mention, quite possibly because his old and inadequate sources did not suggest it,[66] was employment of the VB-1 AZON bomb, an early type of guided weapon. The 301st Bomb Group of the USAAF actually tested such devices in the Mediterranean theater between April and July 1944, finding better overall accuracy than with conventional bombs. Unfortunately, the 301st also found that the AZON was quite unreliable: Half of the bombs went wild, some hitting 850 feet from their mark.[67] Other guided weapons of the time were no more successful and would have offered no significant advantages over conventional bombing techniques.

Dismissing the possibility of accurate high-altitude raids, would it have been possible to send B-17s and B-24s at very low levels to achieve surprise and accuracy? Presumably, such a mission would have been of the hi-lo-hi variety,[68] with the aircraft maintaining defensive formations and high altitudes on the way to Auschwitz, then descending to a few hundred feet north of the Tatras to run in to their targets, then climbing back to high altitude for the return to base. Even with strict radio silence, however, it is doubtful that such tactics would have achieved surprise, owing to radar and visual observation during the approach over the Adriatic. Moreover, USAAF heavy-bomber crews lacked the specialized doctrine, experience, and training necessary to execute the precise bombing of designated buildings from very low altitudes. Used in such a way, the elephantine Fortresses and Liberators would not only have failed, they might well have been decimated, as in fact happened on the low-level Ploesti raid of 1 August 1943 when plane losses reached 30 percent; on the day after, Brigadier General Uzal Ent, chief of IX Bomber Command, had just 33 B-24s fit to fly, out of 178 sent to Ploesti.[69] Not surprisingly, the USAAF never again tried using large formations of heavy bombers at low levels.

Lest the 1 August 1943 Ploesti operation be thought an aberration, a fluke of bad luck, one should also consider RAF Bomber Command's strike against the M.A.N. diesel engine works at Augsburg. This raid, in fact, bears the closest resemblance to a hypothetical low-level Auschwitz raid of any actual mission of the European air war. On 17 April 1942, the RAF dispatched 12 Lancasters in daylight across northern France to attack a single building, the main engine assembly shed within the M.A.N. diesel engine factory complex. Like Wyman's theoretical Auschwitz raid, planning for the M.A.N. mission was partly based on the interrogation of a prisoner who provided details for a sketch map of the plant; unfortunately, the engine construction building was marked in the wrong position. The raid involved a round trip of 1,250 miles, almost exactly the same distance as from Foggia to Auschwitz and back; it was conducted in daylight and at treetop height; there was even some mountainous country between Mulhouse and Lake Constance. Of the strike force of 12, only 5 bombers, all damaged, returned to their bases; 8 bombers dropped 17 bombs, 5 of which failed to explode. Two buildings, neither of which was the intended target, were substantially damaged.[70] The miserable results of this raid helped persuade the RAF that the Lancaster should be used exclusively in high-altitude night operations, which remained the pattern for the rest of the war.

Though again conjecture precludes surety, B-25 medium bombers likely would have suffered the same fate and achieved the same results as heavies. Normally operating from six thousand to fifteen thousand feet, these aircraft were markedly faster than the heavies (but much slower than single-engine fighters) and had a bombing accuracy that was somewhat better. With modest bomb loads and ideal conditions, the aircraft might have reached Auschwitz at the very limit of their endurance.[71] But like the Fortresses and the Liberators, B-25s wholly depended on swarms of fighters and the mutual defense found in tight combat box formations for protection. With these mass formations, surprise was highly improbable; without them, prohibitive losses could have resulted. In either case, considerable resources would have been tied down. MAAF's Twelfth Air Force never had more than three groups of B-25s,[72] and after mid-April 1944 all three were concentrated in Corsica in support of operations in central and northern Italy and especially for the forthcoming invasion of southern France.[73] Even assuming technical and tactical suitability, utilization of these B-25s for an Auschwitz raid would have required deployment of at least one group with support equipment and personnel to southern Italian bases, a withdrawal from other missions of about 60 aircraft for a minimum period of a week, depending on weather and other factors.

Wyman's suggestion that "a small number of Mitchell medium bombers, which hit with surer accuracy from lower altitudes, could have flown with [one of the heavy-bomber] missions to Auschwitz"[74] manifests an ignorance of B-25 characteristics and tactics: The airplane's engines had only two-stage mechanical superchargers, giving their best performance at about thirteen thousand feet with a practical operating ceiling of about eighteen thousand feet. Moreover, the 30 miles per hour cruising speed differential between heavy bombers and B-25s would have imposed impossible problems of station keeping, fuel consumption, and fighter cover while the B-25s were accompanying B-24s and B-17s. Had B-25s been tasked for Auschwitz, they would have had to fly independently, with whatever fighter escort was available; that the Twelfth Air Force never used these aircraft for long-distance raids into southern Germany and Austria is a strong indicator of their unsuitability for such missions.

It is true that the Allies were occasionally able to carry out surgical stabs at well-known, high-priority targets, and bombing advocates have usually cited this kind of operation as optimal for raiding Auschwitz. Typically, it is suggested that twin-engined Lockheed P-38 fighter-bombers or De Havilland D. H. 98 Mosquitoes could have bombed selected camp buildings with precision and surprise. The P-38 model is based on an actual Fifteenth Air Force operation against the Ploesti oil refinery on 10 June 1944, when the USAAF's 82nd Fighter Group sent 46 of its planes covered by another 48 from the 1st Fighter Group some 600-plus miles to dive bomb selected buildings in the Romana Americana works. Each plane carried one thousand-pound bomb and one 300-gallon drop tank. The 82nd's pilots reported that they had to dive through dense smoke—artificial cover thickened by bomb blasts—and had had considerable trouble in locating their targets. Ultimately, the raid achieved modest success, with about half of the objectives being damaged or destroyed, but the refinery resumed operations eight days later.[75] The raid's cost was appalling: 8 aircraft, or 17 percent, of the 82nd's planes were lost, compared with an average Eighth Air Force heavy-bomber loss at this time of about 5 percent. The escort lost an additional 14 planes, or 18 percent.[76] Perhaps pondering this sobering box score, the Fifteenth Air Force never again tried such a long-range dive-bombing mission, though it continued to hammer the Ploesti refineries with heavies until August 1944.

Of all of the tactics for camp attacks, however, it is a daring surgical strike by De Havilland D. H. 98 Mosquito bombers that has attracted the most attention. In 1984, Wyman wrote that "the most effective means of all for destroying the killing installations would have been to dispatch about twenty British Mosquitoes to Auschwitz."[77] In comments on Foregger's article in *Aerospace Historian,* ex-USAAF pilot Robert H. Hodges claimed that the author had "distorted the history of DH 98s on low-level missions" and went on to assert how several of these raids demonstrated the potential for an Auschwitz operation.[78] On the surface, the Mosquito's potential indeed might seem impressive. Capable of carrying a ton of bombs at nearly 300 miles per hour close to the ground, the all-wood Mosquito was one of World War II's wonder planes. Highly versatile, it was built in over two dozen versions and performed well in many roles. Its most impressive—though not necessarily most important or successful—operations were a handful of split-second treetop attacks on high-priority pinpoint targets in Western Europe conducted between September 1942 and March 1945. The five most daring of these were undoubtedly the raid of 18 February 1944 against Amiens prison; that of 11 April 1944 against the Dutch Population Registry in the Hague; that of 31 October 1944 against the Aarhus, Denmark, Gestapo headquarters; that of 31 December 1944 against the Oslo, Norway, Gestapo headquarters; and that of 21 March 1945 against the Gestapo headquarters in Copenhagen, Denmark. In the famous Amiens operation, 19 D. H. 98 F. B. Mk. VIs flying as low as 15 feet breached the prison walls and released 258 resistance fighters, many of whom were later recaptured and shot; over 100 others were killed by the bombs or while escaping.

The similarity of the dramatic Mosquito operations to the problem of attacking Auschwitz's gas chambers and crematoria, however, is vague at best, and in a close comparison, Auschwitz emerges as a well-nigh invulnerable target. All of the notable low-level Mosquito raids from England were conducted across the North Sea or relatively flat northwest Europe, and none had to contend with navigating long mountainous stretches while flying at maximum range. Few, if any, of the special Mosquito raids attacked more than one building, while there were *five* discrete objectives at Auschwitz. Mosquito fighter-bombers had no defensive armament and could not dogfight with interceptors: Flying unescorted, they relied solely on surprise and lightning speed for success. These advantages would have been very hard to achieve and maintain while attacking multiple objectives with a force of perhaps 40 aircraft, and in fact even the later special low-level Mosquito operations in western Europe were escorted by P-51 Mustangs. Thus, the idea that the Mosquitoes could fly over 620 miles in radio silence, cross the Alps in some semblance of cohesion at low altitude, then sneak through German air defenses with enough fuel to make a coordinated precision attack on five targets and return home beggars belief.

Ironically, the astonishing standards of flying that characterized special Mosquito operations put further limitations on the possibility of such operations out of Italy. In *Abandonment of the Jews,* Wyman asserts that "at least 44 Mosquitoes (and probably more) were stationed at Allied air bases in Italy in June 1944."[79] His authority for this is a letter from archivist Eric Munday of the RAF Historical Branch. But, in fact, as MAAF orders of battle at the USAF Historical Research Center show, all 44 of these Mosquitoes were N. F. (night fighters) Mk. XII and XIII (108 and 256 Squadron) and Mk. IX and XVI photo reconnaissance aircraft (60 South African Squadron), which could carry no bombs.[80] Furthermore, no Mosquito fighter-bombers were stationed in the Mediterranean in the summer of 1944, and none could be moved there. There were good reasons for this. The USAAF had no *Mossie* (Mosquito) fighter-bombers, and, though after mid-1944 the RAF had six or seven squadrons available in Great Britain, it entrusted only four squadrons with the most exacting missions against Gestapo headquarters and prisons.[81] These units, all concentrated in 140 Wing, were Nos. 21, 464, 487, and 613 Squadrons. Their elite crews were priceless human assets, made all the more so by continuous demand and high losses.[82]

During 1944-1945, 140 Wing typically employed from 6 to 20 aircraft against single-building targets on its most demanding low-level strikes. About one-third of the force was usually launched as a reserve. If one assumes a strike force of just 8 aircraft to destroy each target at Auschwitz, a strike force of 40 aircraft, or two full squadrons, would have been required. In 1944-1945, this amounted to one-half of the very best Mosquito fighter-bomber crews in Britain. Had such a force been transferred to the Mediterranean theater for a death-camp raid, numerous sorties against NOBALL (V-1 rocket) sites, barges, petroleum-oil-and-lubricant depots, roundhouses, airfields, power stations, and other German military installations would have been sacrificed, and some of the special pinpoint humanitarian missions might have been delayed or given up. How many innocents—some of them Jews—in occupied countries would then have perished because Gestapo headquarters or the Dutch Central Population Registry might have gone unattacked? Such agonizing questions of asset allocation lay at the heart of military science, and Allied air leaders probably had them in mind when they responded negatively to pleas for an attack on Auschwitz-Birkenau in mid-1944.

Diversions of heavy bombers, B-25s, P-38s, or Mosquitoes with attendant losses could perhaps have been justified had the probability of success been higher. No one then could, or can now, accurately predict how much damage might have been inflicted on the gas chambers and crematoria at Auschwitz, or how much effect the destruction would have had on the Final Solution. Based on parallel USAAF and RAF experiences during the war, however, the author believes that in any type of operation, destruction or heavy damage to 50 to 60 percent of the structures would have represented the most that could be hoped for on one mission, thus follow-up raids—a mini-campaign—would have been required to assure complete success.

The tragic side effects of bombing on the camps' populations are much easier to envision. Dazed, debilitated, and disoriented, most escapees would have quickly been rounded up. While the able-bodied would have been forced to pick up the casualties and repair the damage, trains destined for the two camps would have been diverted to Mauthausen, Belsen, Buchenwald, or any of the Reich's 20-odd other camps. The rate of genocide at Auschwitz might have been slowed for a few days or a few weeks, but no one can calculate what impact this might have had on the Holocaust. More certainly, it can be said that any low-level air raid on Auschwitz-Birkenau would have been a one-shot proposition because the camps would have been easy to defend against precise low-altitude strikes. Cheap passive defenses like decoy buildings, barrage balloons, and smoke pots, together with a few 20 mm flak guns, would have sufficed to prevent any further intrusions.

Although Wyman hesitates about trying to bomb railroads serving the extermination camps, other bombing adherents have advocated it.[83] But as Foregger pointed out in 1987, a successful line-cutting campaign requires day-in, day-out attacks over the entire system that serves a selected area—in this case, all of occupied Europe. Unless all routes are simultaneously interdicted and remain cut, alternative routes, repair gangs, and make-do will largely negate the effort. Thanks to their Operations Analysis Sections, Allied air staffs knew this resources-results equation with great exactitude.[84]

In fact, despite the immense difficulty and modest rewards of strategic rail-cutting, the USAAF did try repeatedly to disrupt the Reich's transportation system. Contrary to some assertions that rail lines and rolling stock were never attacked,[85] Freeman's *Mighty Eighth War Diary* lists no fewer than 145 missions by the Eighth Air Force that included attacks against marshaling yards from the France-German border eastward.[86] In addition, the Fifteenth Air Force's effort from Italy, though as yet untabulated, probably nearly doubled the Eighth's pounding. Even through the marshaling yards at Bingen, Hamm, Frankfort, Munich, Salzburg, Linz, Landshut, and elsewhere were turned into moonscapes, the Germans, relying heavily on forced labor, managed to keep some lines open. What happened in the camps and on the battlefronts, therefore, occurred *in spite of* bombing, and what might have happened with different priorities remains entirely speculative.[87]

Two other vital observations about the bombing question cannot be overemphasized: Attacking Auschwitz might have been illegal under international law, and it would certainly have been morally dubious. Under the Hague Convention of 1907 (Hague, IV), Article 25, "the attack or bombardment, by whatever means, of towns, villages, dwellings, or buildings which are undefended is prohibited."[88] The U.S. War Department's Basic Field Manual FM 27-10, *Rules of Land Warfare,* issued in 1940, quoted the Hague rule verbatim and specifically noted that with the phrase "by whatever means," signatories meant that bombardment of these undefended localities from balloons or airplanes was prohibited. It also gave three examples of "defended places."[89] Only by torturing the third example, "a place that is occupied by a combatant military force," could Auschwitz-Birkenau have qualified as a legitimate target for bombardment.

Legality aside, bombing Auschwitz also becomes a radically different problem if casualties within the camp are disregarded. This would have made operations by B-17s and B-24s technically feasible, for example. Yet, the underlying dilemma is as plain today as 50 years ago: Would it be moral to kill a minimum of several hundred internees in trying to save others—with no assurance of success—and, if so, what tragic ratio would have been acceptable? Ultimately, this is a philosophical or theological dilemma, not a historical one, and it is not the historian's duty to resolve it. Arguments, however, that camp inhabitants would have died anyway, or that the symbolism of bombing would have justified it, or that some within Auschwitz might have welcomed death from the air appear specious. In general, Allied leaders were convinced that the innocent should be spared if possible and, weighing out the possibilities, acted accordingly.[90] When ULTRA intelligence officer and later Supreme Court Justice Lewis F. Powell was questioned on this specific point in 1985, he stated that "I am perfectly confident that General [Carl] Spaatz would have resisted any proposal that *we* [italics Powell's] kill the Jewish inmates in order temporarily to put an Auschwitz out of operation. It is not easy to think that a rational person would have made such a recommendation" (to bomb Auschwitz).[91]

Looking back from 1995, the bombing of Auschwitz emerges as a peculiar and peculiarly difficult, historical conundrum. No bombing took place, and asking why decades later has as yet produced only conjecture. The Wyman thesis attributes the Allied avoidance of death-camp bombing to callousness, insensitivity, and even anti-Semitic prejudice in high circles. These attitudes were, Wyman believes, evident in prewar America and persisted after 1941, ultimately producing the abandonment of the Jews to their fate. Clearly, a major part of any historian's task is to find and describe meaningful patterns in the chaos of events and, if possible, to establish causative links between possible motives and observed facts. The writer is not expert in refugee and immigration policy, modern anti-Semitism, or Holocaust studies: It is in nowise his purpose here to debate *Abandonment of the Jews's* overall thesis. To date, however, the Wyman school has adduced only inferential and circumstantial evidence that Auschwitz remained inviolate because of indifference or outright antipathy for the plight of European Jews. Corollary proof derived from social attitudes, refugee policy, or diplomatic posturing is wholly insufficient to establish the contentions in *Abandonment of the Jews's* Chapter 15 and of the bombing school in general. This is especially true considering the poverty of documentation offered in *Abandonment of the Jews,* as well as that of subsequent commentators. More—much more—than inference is required. It is incumbent upon bombing advocates to describe precisely how Auschwitz might have successfully been attacked, given the capabilities of aircraft and airmen in mid-1944; their availability for the mission(s); the anticipated losses; the probable results; and the implications for conduct of the war. The most convincing pro-attack argument would be a hypothetical raid scenario analogous to operations that actually occurred, or a credible model based on operational realities. No bombing advocate has yet constructed such a paradigm, and available evidence indicates that one cannot be.

The author suggests that whatever was said or not said, felt or not felt, about camp bombing among Allied politicians and bureaucratic organs in 1944 was, and is, largely irrelevant to what happened, or could have happened. In the instance of Auschwitz, military policy was driven by availability of intelligence, operational possibilities, asset allocation, the rules of war, and conventional morality. Any Allied option to frustrate the Holocaust from the air was illusory, a fact so unmistakably obvious to contemporary commanders that it was taken for granted and warranted little policy discussion. Inaction may have been colored by ethnic attitudes, but it was ultimately dictated by the immutable exigencies of intelligence, operational considerations, weapons-system performance, and available resources. From their own experience and that of their staffs, senior air commanders knew that attempting to bomb Auschwitz would have diverted resources from vital military, industrial, and even humanitarian targets; might have entailed heavy Allied casualties; would have had vague or ephemeral success; would have posed grave legal and moral questions; and would to some degree have prolonged the war. Target committees, the Joint Chiefs of Staff, the War Department, and senior civilian officials also knew that their air-power assets were finite and imperfect and they acted accordingly, even if some of their justifications were not always highly articulate. The author believes, therefore, that an awareness of operational limits, not ethnic motives, best explains the failure to bomb Auschwitz. Allied leaders made the mistakes that all humans do, but the available evidence suggests that avoidance of death-camp bombing out of prejudice was not one of them.

NOTES

1. It is, of course, true that information about the annihilation of European Jews began to seep out of Europe by various channels during 1941-1942. This information, however, was quite fragmented, was transmitted orally, and usually could not be substantiated by documents, photographs, signals intercepts, or other means of conventional military intelligence. As Walter Laqueur perceptively points out, the credibility of German mass murder at this time was also seriously impaired by public recollection of how German atrocity reports from World War I had been debunked during the 1920s and 1930s. Walter Laqueur,

The Terrible Secret: Suppression of the Truth about Hitler's "Final Solution" (New York: Little, Brown, 1980).

2. The Kosice-Presov line was a key north-south segment of track leading northward out of Hungary over which Jews deported from Budapest to Auschwitz most likely would have traveled. Kosice lay in northern Hungary, while Presov lay almost due north in Slovakia. For a map of the Hungarian and Slovakian rail nets pertinent to the Weissmandel message, see Martin Gilbert, *Auschwitz and the Allies* (New York: Henry Holt, 1981), 247.

3. Ibid., 209, 216-217, 219-220, 236-237, 245. Because Gilbert treated the bombing idea as but one element in the unveiling of Auschwitz's horrors, his narration of its initial development is somewhat discontinuous. Despite the complexities of narration, however, *Auschwitz and the Allies* remains the most thorough account of the origins of the bombing idea and its reception during the World War II period.

4. Ibid., 246.

5. David S. Wyman, *The Abandonment of the Jews: America and the Holocaust, 1941-1945* (New York: Pantheon Books, 1984), 292; Bernard Wasserstein, *Britain and the Jews of Europe, 1939-1945* (Oxford, England: Clarendon Press, 1979), 308-320; Gilbert, *Auschwitz and the Allies,* 299-311.

6. On 1 July 1944, Leon Kubowitzki, head of the Rescue Department of the World Jewish Congress, wrote to the U.S. War Refugee Board to oppose proposals to bomb Auschwitz. Any bombing, Kubowitzki thought, would itself kill Jews held in the camp and would offer an opportunity for the Germans to make a propaganda advantage of such deaths. Gilbert, *Auschwitz and the Allies,* 256, citing letter of 1 July 1944, War Refugee Board, Measures Directed towards Halting Persecutions, F: Hungary No. 5., Franklin D. Roosevelt Library (FDRL), Hyde Park, N.Y.

7. Arthur D. Morse, *While Six Million Died: A Chronicle of American Apathy* (New York: Random House, 1968). See especially Morse's remarks on 383. Morse did not introduce the bombing issue, nor did he inculpate Allied military authorities in responsibility for the German genocide.

8. John Morton Blum, *V Was for Victory: Politics and American Culture during World War II* (New York: Harcourt, Brace, Jovanovich, 1976), 172-181.

9. David S. Wyman, "Why Auschwitz Was Never Bombed," *Commentary* 65 (May 1978), 37-49. The article was unannotated, but at the end the author provided a list of principal archival sources consulted. In a follow-on letter published in the July 1978 issue, Wyman offered to furnish a full set of footnotes in exchange for photocopy costs and a self-addressed, stamped envelope.

10. Roger M. Williams, "Why Wasn't Auschwitz Bombed? An American Moral Tragedy," *Commonweal* 105 (24 November 1978), 746-751.

11. Ibid., 750.
12. See, for example, Gilbert's surprising conclusion in *Auschwitz and the Allies*, 341, that in the summer of 1944 "the American government possessed a great deal of information about Auschwitz, including both its location and its function, *together with the technical ability to bomb both the railway lines leading to the camp and the gas chambers in the camp itself*" (italics mine).
13. Morton Mintz, "Why Didn't We Bomb Auschwitz?" *Washington Post*, 17 April 1983. Alan Brinkley, "Minister without Portfolio," *Harper's*, February 1983, 31-46, is a miniature biography of John Jay McCloy, influential special assistant to Secretary of War Henry Stimson, that includes a lengthy passage on McCloy and the Holocaust.
14. Wyman, *Abandonment of the Jews*.
15. Wyman summarized 12 potential rescue measures under the heading "What Might Have Been Done," 331-334.
16. The Vrba-Wetzler report has been published in full in David S. Wyman, ed., *America and the Holocaust*, vol. 12, *Bombing Auschwitz and the Escapees' Report* (New York: Garland, 1990), Document 1: "The Extermination Camps of Auschwitz (Oswiecim) and Birkenau in Upper Silesia," 3-44.
17. The I. G. Farben works at Monowitz were approximately 2.5 miles east of Auschwitz town and about 3 to 4 miles east of the Auschwitz or Birkenau concentration camps. The Monowitz factory complex produced synthetic oil and rubber and became the object of repeated Allied bombing during the summer of 1944. Monowitz had a separate slave labor camp attached, which was not part of the Auschwitz-Birkenau facility.
18. Frantic was the cover name given to long-range United States Army Air Force (USAAF) strategic bombing operations that used Russian bases at Poltava, Mirgood, and Piryatin, all east of Kiev, as staging points. Under the Frantic plan, bombers that normally would have bombed their objectives and returned to bases in England or Italy would instead land in Russia, where they would receive ordnance, fuel, and maintenance. It was not envisioned that these Frantic bases would become permanent homes for heavy-bomber groups or their fighter escorts. The first Fifteenth Air Force Frantic mission was carried out on 2 June 1944; D-Day in France delayed the first such Eighth Air Force operation until 21 June. Frantic missions continued throughout the summer of 1944 but were eventually discontinued for various reasons.
19. Wyman, *Abandonment of the Jews*, 292, quoting O. P. D. D/F (Hull to C. A. D.), 26 June 1944, Record Group (RG) 165(1), National Archives (NA).
20. See *New York Times*, 4 November 1984, and 24 December 1984, *New York Times Book Review*, 16 December 1984, 1, 16; 17 March 1985, 42; 24 March 1985, 38; 31 March 1985, 34; 7 April 1985, 22; 28 April 1985, 36.

21. In addition to the *New York Times Book Review,* 16 December 1984, 1, 16, see reviews in *Library Journal* 1 (October 1984), 1848; *Nation,* 239 (15 December 1984), 656-657; *Commentary* 72 (April 1985), 70-75; *American Historical Review* 90 (December 1985), 1294-1295; *Choice* 22 (April 1985), 1220; *Journal of American History* 72 (June 1985), 186-187.

22. *The Encyclopedia of the Holocaust* (New York: Macmillan, 1990), see "Auschwitz, Bombing of" by David S. Wyman, 119-121. See also Wyman's defense of his previous assertions in a letter to the *Washington Post,* 21 April 1990.

23. For example, Leni Yahil writes in *The Holocaust: The Fate of European Jewry, 1932-1945* (New York: Oxford University Press, 1990), 639: "Research has shown that the refusal of the American and British air forces to bomb these installations (Auschwitz and Birkenau) stemmed from their disinclination to be involved with rescue actions per se." For her two-page passage "No Bombing of Auschwitz-Birkenau," Yahil's footnotes 20, 21, 22, and 23, 638-639, cite only Wyman's Chapter 15 from *Abandonment of the Jews* and Gilbert, *Auschwitz and the Allies.* See also Michael R. Marrus, *The Holocaust in History* (London: University Press of New England, 1987), 193-194, and Michael Berenbaum, *After Tragedy and Triumph: Essays in Modern Jewish Thought and the American Experience* (Cambridge, England: Cambridge University Press, 1990), 9, 82.

24. See Executive Director Sara J. Bloomfield's letter to the *Washington Post,* 24 March 1990, in which she states that "the United States and its allies, fully aware of the murder factories in Poland, failed to act and *even declined to bomb the death camps, though the knowledge and the opportunity existed"* (italics mine). *The Directory of American Scholars,* vol. 1, *History* (New York: R. R. Bowker, 1982). "Wyman, David S.," 847, lists him as a special adviser to the council.

25. *New York Tribune,* 23 April 1990.

26. Equipped with a mix of B-17 Flying Fortresses, B-24 Liberators and escort fighters, the Fifteenth Air Force made up the USAAF's strategic bombing force in the Mediterranean theater of operations (MTO) after the spring of 1944. By May, it was operating several hundred heavy bombers and fighters from a complex of bases around Foggia on the eastern coast of southern Italy. Though slightly younger as an organization, the Fifteenth Air Force grew to become comparable in size, striking power, and effectiveness with the USAAF's Eighth Air Force, which operated out of England after August 1942.

27. The letter is in *Commentary* 65 (July 1978), 10-11.

28. Richard S. Levy, reviewer for *Commentary,* was an associate professor of history at the University of Chicago and a specialist in anti-Semitism, Jewish history, immigration history, and Holocaust studies; Leonard Dinnerstein, reviewer for the *Journal of American History,* was professor of history at the University of Arizona and a specialist in American Jewish history; Jonathan D. Sarna, reviewer

for *Library Journal,* was an assistant professor of history at Hebrew Union College and a specialist in American Jewish history; B. Kraut, reviewer for *Choice,* was an associate professor of Judaica at the University of Cincinnati and a specialist in modern Jewish history and modern Judaism. See *Directory of American Scholars,* vol. 1, *History.*

29. Richard Foregger, "The Bombing of Auschwitz," *Aerospace Historian* 34 (summer 1987); 98-110.

30. Two commentaries on Foregger's article did subsequently appear in *Aerospace Historian,* but neither came from the Holocaust-studies community or from academic historians. Both included a number of digressions from the basic questions, and neither added anything substantive to the basic Wyman-Foregger dialogue. See Robert H. Hodges, "The Bombing of Auschwitz: A Clarification," and Michael G. Moskow, "The Bombing of Auschwitz: A Reply," in *Aerospace Historian* 35 (summer 1988); 123-126, 127-129.

31. Amherst, Mass: University of Massachusets Press, 1968.

32. Wyman defined "nativistic nationalism" as an attitude held by patriotic and veterans groups that reflected pride in "100 percent Americanism," a sentiment that he thought manifested a certain antialienism. Many nativistic nationalists sought to limit immigration, if not to deport aliens, as deleterious to the American body politic.

33. Wesley Frank Craven and James Lea Cate, eds., *The Army Air Forces in World War II,* vol. 3, *Europe: ARGUMENT to V-E Day, January 1944 to May 1945* (Chicago: University of Chicago Press, 1951); Charles Webster and Noble Frankland, *The Strategic Air Offensive against Germany, 1939-1945,* vol. 3 (London: HMSO, 1961).

34. Philip Birtles, *Mosquito: A Pictorial History of the DH98* (London: Jane's, 1980).

35. Glenn Infield, *The Poltava Affair* (New York: Macmillan, 1973).

36. James F. Sunderman, ed., *World War II in the Air: Europe* (New York: Franklin Watts, 1963).

37. Sunderman's *World War II in the Air: Europe* contains elementary tables of USAAF aircraft characteristics in an appendix. These tables, however, are far from adequate for assessing the aircraft in question. No information, for example, is presented about the B-25J models that equipped the USAAF's Twelfth Air Force squadrons in the Mediterranean theater in 1944.

38. C. Martin Sharp and Michael J. F. Bowyer, *Mosquito* (London: Faber and Faber, 1967). Although older than Birtles's book, *Mosquito* is a much more detailed and informative work containing 23 appendices and a detailed text with important data not found in Birtles. Michael J. F. Bowyer's *2 Group RAF: A Complete History, 1936-1945* (London: Faber and Faber, 1974) also could have enlightened Wyman about special Mosquito operations analogous to camp attacks, and

Philip J. R. Boyes's *Bomber Squadrons of the RAF*, new ed. (London: Macdonald and Jane's, 1976) could have furnished order-of-battle data about Mosquito units, but neither is cited.

39. There are also indications that Wyman selectively used the sources he does cite: The RAF Bomber Command's 17 April 1942 operation against the M.A.N. diesel engine works at Augsburg, for example, had many similarities to one mode of assault on Auschwitz and is described at length in Webster and Franklin's official history, *Strategic Air Offensive* (London: H.M. Stationary Office, 1961), yet it is not noted in *Abandonment of the Jews*.

40. Most, but not all, of the USAF Historical Research Center's files are duplicated on 16 mm microfilm at the Office of Air Force History, Bolling AFB, Washington, D.C., and it is conceivable that Wyman or a proxy performed research there. If that were the case, however, there is no bibliographic statement in *Abandonment of the Jews* to suggest it.

41. The United States Air Force Historical Research Center (USAFHRC) is a direct reporting unit of Headquarters USAF in Washington, D.C. Its collections originated with the institution of a USAAF historical program in 1942; files collected at the Pentagon during the war, together with unit histories up to that point, were moved to Maxwell (Air Force Base in Montgomery, Alabama) in the late 1940s to support research and education at the Air University. Today the center holds approximately sixty million pages of documents on approximately three linear miles of shelving, of which approximately one-third to one-half treat the World War II period.

42. The Mediterranean Allied Air Forces (MAAF) was a joint USAAF-RAF command of the Mediterranean theater that controlled all of the Allied air-power assets there. the MAAF's major elements included the Fifteenth and Twelfth Air Forces and several large constituent elements from the RAF such as 205 Group and the Balkans Air Force. The Historical Research Center's MAAF microfilm collection reproduces the MAAF Headquarters files from formation of the force in 1943 to approximately late 1944.

43. An examination of the Spaatz documents cited in Wyman's Chapter 15 footnotes 34, 40, 41, 49, 57, 62, and 75 reveals that these are uniformly correspondence, cables, and minutes of staff meetings and not the war plans, studies, reports, and operational records upon which General Carl Spaatz (commander in chief of the U.S. Strategic Air Forces in Europe) and General Ira C. Eaker (commander of Allied air forces in Italy) based their opinions and decisions. Thus, this selection of sources from personal papers also reflects Wyman's focus on bombing policy rather than the operational constraints surrounding policy.

44. See Wyman, *Abandonment of the Jews*, 301-302.

45. An excellent plan drawing of Crematory and Gas Chamber III at Birkenau has
been published in Anna Pawelczynska, *Values and Violence in Auschwitz*, trans.
Catherine S. Leach (Berkeley: University of California Press, 1979), 31. Another
less detailed plan is in Rudolf Höss, *Death Dealer: The Memoirs of the SS
Kommandant at Auschwitz*, ed. Stephen Paskuly (New York: Prometheus Books,
1992). The Paskuly edition also contains several external and internal photographs of Birkenau's gas chambers and crematoria that are helpful in analyzing
them as bombing targets.

46. The maps and diagrams of Auschwitz provided in Gilbert, *Auschwitz and the
Allies*, 193 and 195, are indispensable references to the problem of the area's
camps as aerial targets. These maps and diagrams were published three years
before *Abandonment of the Jews* appeared. Diagrams of Auschwitz I ("Main
Camp") and of Birkenau are also available in Pawelczynska, *Values and Violence
in Auschwitz*, 26-27.

47. The large slave labor camp at I. G. Farben's nearby Monowitz works also killed
hundreds of thousands through overwork, disease, starvation, and other causes,
but presumably because it possessed no easily targetable gas chambers or crematoria and existed as a labor adjunct to the chemical works it was not included as
a potential target in Wyman's thesis.

48. Dino Brugioni, "Auschwitz-Birkenau: Why the World War II Photo Interpreters Failed to Identify the Extermination Complex," *Military Intelligence* 9
(January-March 1983), 50-55, and Dino Brugioni and Robert G. Poirier, *The
Holocaust Revisited: A Retrospective Analysis of the Auschwitz-Birkenau Extermination Complex* (Washington: Central Intelligence Agency, February 1979),
NTIS ST-79-10001, are indispensable for understanding the problem of interpretation and intelligence appreciation of the Auschwitz aerial photographs
made in 1944.

49. Two important pieces of evidence indicate just how little was known about the
Holocaust in Allied intelligence circles. USAFHRC 512.6162-1, 10 October
1944, "Axis Concentration Camps and Detention Camps Reported as Such in
Europe," British War Office (MI 14), 10 October 1944 (originally Secret,
declassified 22 September 1972) was a 105-page report that attempted to
summarize the concentration-camp intelligence then in hand. An examination
of this document, prepared at the highest levels of the wartime intelligence
apparatus, clearly shows that the Allies had no exact knowledge of the number
of camps the Germans were operating, where the camps were located, how many
internees there were, or to what overall purpose the detainees were being held.
This document is not included in Wyman's bibliography or notes. A footnote
in F. H. Hinsley et al., *British Intelligence in the Second World War*, vol. 3, pt. 2
(London: HMSO, 1988), 736, states that ULTRA—the most sensitive intelli-

gence available to the Allies from intercepted radio traffic—made scarcely any references to concentration camps. "There were," the authors note, "no Sigint [signal intelligence] references to the extermination camps" before April 1945 apart from "a few Police decrypts in the second half of 1944 and early 1945 about the movement into concentration camps of Jews from France, Hungary, and the Baltic states and about the use of camp inmates as forced laborers." The reason, of course, was that for clarity and security the Germans used land lines not subject to eavesdropping wherever possible.

50. Gilbert, *Auschwitz and the Allies*, 190-239; Wyman, *Abandonment of the Jews*, 288-296.

51. Several maps associated with the Vrba-Wetzler report have been published. Document 1, "The Extermination Camps of Auschwitz (Oswiecim) and Birkenau in Upper Silesia," November 1944, in Wyman, *America and the Holocaust*, vol. 12, *Bombing Auschwitz and the Escapees' Report*, reproduces three sketches from a copy in the Franklin D. Roosevelt Library, OF5477, War Refugee Board, German Extermination Camps—Auschwitz and Birkenau. Another sketch, taken from an original in the Public Record Office, is available in Foregger, "The Bombing of Auschwitz," 98-99.

52. Foregger, "The Bombing of Auschwitz," 108. The sketch map, titled "Topographical Sketch of the Concentration Camp at Oswiecim/Auschwitz," is reproduced in Foregger's article. It bears the notation "Drawn according to the description of a former prisoner of the camp."

53. Sharp and Bowyer, *Mosquito*, 241.

54. Vis airfield was lengthened to 3,600 feet in the autumn of 1944.

55. USAFHRC 638.01-1, 1943-1944, AAF Engineer Command, Mediterranean Theater of Operations (Prov.), "Airfields in the Mediterranean Theater of Operations"; USAFHRC 638.245, July-August 1944 and July 1945, HQ AAF Engineer Command Mediterranean Theater of Operations (Prov.), "Airfield Status Report," 1 July 1944. The July 1945 edition of "Airfield Status Report" has a small map of the airfield. For the absence of permanent combat units on the island, see USAFHRC 622.6318, January-December 1944, HQ MAAF, "Order of Battle-Mediterranean Allied Air Forces, Royal Air Force," monthly reports stating the duty stations of each Allied combat unit in the MTO. Vis's primitive, precarious, and clandestine existence is made clear from USAFHRC 622.011-1, MAAF Microfilm Project, Roll 272, Section 376, "Defense of Vis," and Section 377, "Use of Vis for Operation of Advanced Air Forces." In the latter, on 18 June 1944, RAF 242 Group specifically warned HQ MAAF about the dangers of aircraft making forced landings there. "Your A245 [message dated] 2 May," it advised, "is being continually ignored and situation on Vis is becoming increasingly intolerable. On 15 June 5 Liberators and 1 Lightning

landed there. This frequent landing and crash landing of heavy aircraft seriously jeopardizes operations and could easily lead to disastrous consequences."

56. Wyman made no effort to identify the Luftwaffe order of battle defending Auschwitz-Birkenau, and it is surprising that subsequent commentators such as Hodges and Moskow have largely ignored the question in favor of generalities about the effectiveness of the German fighter force in mid-1944.

57. For the figure of 79 guns around Monowitz, see the 5th Bombardment Wing's intelligence briefing for the wing's 20 August 1944 attack on the I. G. Farben works, in "Annex to Operations Order No. 671 for 20 August 1944," USAFHRC WG-5-HI, August 1944, Unit History, 5th Bombardment Wing, August 1944. German heavy-flak pieces ranged from 88 mm to 128 mm. The most numerous German antiaircraft weapon, the 88 mm Flak 36, had a maximum horizontal range of 16,200 yards (9.2 miles) and a maximum vertical range of 13,000 yards (7.3 miles). Thus, many pieces emplaced around Monowitz would have coincidentally covered most, if not all, of the Birkenau camp area.

58. An MAAF map of "Approximate *Freya* Location and Coverage—Western Mediterranean" dated 29 March 1944 shows three *Freya* radar sites, at Bar, Durazzo, and Fier, as positively located and a further four sites at Zara, Split, Dubrovnik, and Lesh, as known or believed to exist. These *Freya* radars operated on several frequencies in the A, B, C, D, and other bands; intruders could be detected at ranges from 12 miles for very low flying planes to 60 miles for those flying at eight thousand to ten thousand feet. By 31 May, the MAAF had also detected several other types of radars in the Dubrovnik area. This meant that German radars could track any aircraft flying at medium altitudes out of USAAF bases in southern Italy from a few minutes after takeoff all the way across the Adriatic. *Freyas* could also scan 360°, permitting a degree of tracking inland. Sites in the vicinity of Precko, Sinj, Banja Luka, Vukovar, and other locations permitted German fighter control to follow raids from Yugoslavia to southern Poland. As a rule of thumb, the lower an intruder's altitude, the more difficult tracking became, until, at altitudes of 200-250 feet or less, radar detection became nearly impossible. Sustained flight to avoid radar detection, however, would have imposed a variety of handicaps and hazards, and interception of voice radio communications always remained a possibility. USAFHRC 622.011, MAAF Microfilm Project, Roll 132, Section 194, "Radar Intelligence-Pt 1."

59. Documentation of the location of German fighter units in the Balkans and western Hungary at a given moment is quite difficult. In order to maximize its fighter assets, the Luftwaffe became adept at frequently and quickly moving its units from one airfield to another in a way unknown to the Allies; within a day's time, intercepting units might use one airfield as a home base but could be

ordered to leapfrog across considerable distances to concentrate against a perceived threat. Assessment of this kind of shifting defense is further complicated
by loss of at least 95 percent of the Luftwaffe's operational records at war's end.
I am greatly indebted to Henry L. de Zeng IV, a lifelong student of the Lutfwaffe
in the Balkans, for his invaluable assistance in documenting the German order
of battle from diverse published and archival sources.

60. USAFHRC 137.306-3, January 1943–May 1945, USSBS, Military Analysis
    Division Report No. 3, "A Study on the Bombing Accuracy of the USAAF Heavy
    and Medium Bombers in the ETO," 3 November 1945. This USSBS study
    found that the actual average circular error on ten target complexes in the study
    ranged between 825 and 1,175 feet. The average circular error of USAAF
    strategic bombers in Europe diminished from 3,400 feet in January 1943 to a
    rough average of 1,100 feet during 1944-1945. In the Fifteenth Air Force,
    approximately 30 percent of bombs fell within 1,000 feet of the aiming point
    during 1944-1945.

61. Williams, "Why Wasn't Auschwitz Bombed?" 751.

62. Gilbert, *Auschwitz and the Allies,* 195.

63. Höss, *Death Dealer,* 359, 363.

64. In an independent calculation made in 1983, Pierre M. Sprey, a weapons analyst
    in the office of the assistant secretary of defense, estimated that 135 bombers
    would have been necessary to destroy 50 percent of the gas chambers, crematoria,
    rail sidings and loot structure and that one-third of the 1,350 bombs dropped
    would have hit the prisoner barracks area. Mintz, "Why Wasn't Auschwitz
    Bombed?" *Washington Post,* 17 April 1983.

65. For details of the mission, see USAFHRC 520.332, 24 August 1944, "Eighth
    AF Mission Report [for Operation 568], 24 August 1944." Casualty figures are
    from "Die Toten des Bombenangriffs vom 24 August 1944," a written report
    of SS-Hauptsturm-fuhrer d.R. Gerhard Schiedlausky, medical officer at Wei-
    mar, to Chef des Amt D III of the WVHA Berlin-Oranienburg dated 27 August
    1944, attached to a 1 October 1991 letter from Squadron Leader Booker's letter,
    together with the SS report. This is on file at USAFHRC, Inquiries Branch,
    internal reference file "Buchenwald." A copy is also in the author's possession.

66. Craven and Cate, eds., *The Army Air Forces in World War II,* make one brief
    reference to AZON in vol. 3, *Europe: ARGUMENT to V-E Day,* 728. This
    scarcely acknowledges the existence of AZON bombs and says nothing about
    their technology or MTO testing. The reason for this is almost certainly the
    cloak of security surrounding guided weapons at the time Craven and Cate were
    writing (1951, in the case of vol. 3); largely because of such security considera-
    tions, the Fifteenth Air Forces's report on the accuracy and effectiveness of
    AZON bombs was not declassified until 1972. See USAFHRC 670.310-1,

JAMES H. KITCHENS III

Fifteenth AF, Operations Analysis Section, "AZON Bombing-Fifteenth AF," 2 October 1944, declassified by Executive Order 11652 on 10 March 1972. Such security considerations also help explain why Sunderman, *World War II in the Air: Europe,* makes no mention of the weapon. There was no reason for Infield to mention AZON in connection with Poltava, and the USSBS says little, if anything, about the bomb, probably because as a weapon in development it played no significant part in the strategic air war.

67. USAFHRC 670.310-1, Fifteenth Air Force, Operations Analysis Section, "AZON Bombing-Fifteenth Air Force," 2 October 1944. I am also indebted to Dr. Kenneth A. Werrell and Ernest Helton for access to their findings on AZON bombing presented in a forthcoming unit history of the 301st Bomb Group and to David Friday, whose Auburn University MA thesis in history deals with the wartime development and testing of AZON.

68. A hi-lo-hi mission would have entailed a *high*-altitude approach to the target, a *low*-altitude run-in and bomb release, and a *high*-altitude return to base.

69. James Dugan and Carroll Stewart, *Ploesti: The Great Ground-Air Battle of 1 August 1943* (New York: Random House, 1962), 222.

70. Webster and Frankland, *Strategic Air Offensive,* vol. 1, *Preparation,* 441-443.

71. The range of the B-25Js operated by Twelfth Air Forces's 57th Bomb Wing in the summer of 1944 was 1,350 miles with three thousand pounds of bombs. Adverse winds, a zigzag route, navigational errors, or other factors might well have caused critical fuel shortages, even allowing for the possibility of emergency landings on Vis.

72. During the summer of 1944, Twelfth Air Force B-25s totaled 192 aircraft in 310th, 321st and 340th Bomb Groups under the 57th Bomb Wing. All of these B-25J models had a theoretical range of 1,350 miles with a bomb load of three thousand pounds. USAFHRC 622.6318, July 1944, HQ MAAF, Order of Battle-Mediterranean Allied Air Forces, Royal Air Force, as at 31 July 1944, 9-10.

73. Kenn Rust, *The Twelfth AF Story* (Temple City, Calif: Historical Aviation Album, 1975), 35.

74. Wyman, *Abandonment of the Jews,* 303.

75. USAFHRC 622, 424-426, August 1943–August 1944, HQ MAAF, Ploesti Records Obtained in Roumania.

76. USAFHRC GP-82-HI(FI), June 1944, 82nd Fighter Group Unit History June 1944, 2; USAFHRC GP-1-HI(FI), June 1944; 1st Fighter Group Unit History June 1944, 2.

77. Wyman, *Abandonment of the Jews,* 303.

78. Robert H. Hodges, "The Bombing of Auschwitz: A Clarification," *Aerospace Historian* 35 (summer 1988), 124. The *Aerospace Historian* simply described

Hodges as "a former USAAF pilot." There is no indication that he had any flying time in Mosquitoes or had any personal familiarity with the aircraft.

79. Wyman, *Abandonment of the Jews*, 303n. 63.

80. USAFHRC 622.6318, January-June 1944, HQ MAAF, Order of Battle-Mediterranean Allied Air Forces, Royal Air Force, as at 30 June 1944, 15-16, 18, 22. Although one cannot be certain, it is doubtful that Munday, a long-serving and highly experienced archivist at the Air Historical Branch, misinformed Wyman. The author believes it more probable that Wyman, not especially familiar with the complexities of the Mosquito family, simply asked Munday how many D. H. 98s were present in the Mediterranean theater in June 1944, and the archivist correctly replied with a gross total of 44.

81. In an unusual break with normal mission assignments, No. 627 Squadron, a target-marking unit from 3 Group, Bomber Command, executed the 31 December 1944 strike against the Gestapo headquarters in Oslo, Norway. So far as the author can determine, this was the only such operation ever mounted by this squadron. Sharp and Bowyer, *Mosquito*, 369.

82. Between 3 October 1943 and 26 May 1944, 2 Group Mosquitoes carried out 155 day-bombing operations and about 1,600 sorties; 464 Squadron executed 78 sorties between 21 and 30 June and 421 sorties between 1 October and 31 December 1944. Operational losses for D. H. 98 Mosquito F. B. Mk. VIs (the type used by 140 Wing) averaged 8 percent per month for the 16 months between January 1944 and April 1945; losses reached 20 percent during February 1945. Sharp and Bowyer, *Mosquito*, 235-259; Bowyer, *2 Group RAF*, 355-415, 473-477.

83. See, for example, Williams's statement that "a strong case can be made for the feasibility and effectiveness of bombing several targets connected with the Hungarian episode of the Final Solution: Auschwitz . . . and the rail lines leading to it; [and] the Budapest railroad yards." Williams, "Why Wasn't Auschwitz Bombed?" 746.

84. For example, in the spring of 1944, the Operational Research Section of IX Bomber Command reported that a 250-pound general-purpose-bomb crater on a single-track railroad would take about 6 hours to repair, and that of a 100-pound bomb 3.5 hours. Out of a box formation of 18 aircraft, 5.2 hits with 100-pound bombs and 3.1 hits with 250-pound bombs might be expected. "The total hours delay thus produced by a single attack of 18 Marauders loaded with 30 100 lb bombs will be 5.2 x 3.5 = 18.2 hours, and loaded with 14 250 lb bombs it will be 3.1 x 6 = 18.6 hours. These are the hours of daylight delay [in rail traffic]. British experience is that repair cannot be made at night. The delay per mission of 18 planes may be, therefore, taken as 24 hours regardless of whether 100 lb or 250 lb bombs are carried." The report concluded, "It is seen that, if the present bombing accuracy is to be expected

in these operations, about 1.1 attacking boxes are required per line cut if 100 lb bombs are used, or about 1.4 attacking boxes per line cut if 250 lb bombs are used." HQ IX Bomber Command, Operational Research Section, "Railway Networks as Joint Objectives for the IX Bomber Command and IX Air Support Command," 18 March 1944, in USAFHRC 534.02, March 1944, History of IX Bomber Command. Bridges were tougher but more rewarding targets. In July 1944, the 1st Operations Analysis Section of Fifteenth Air Force stated: "The probability of obtaining a successful hit on a bridge depends to a marked degree upon its size and construction." It calculated that 36 aircraft (one bomb group) each carrying ten 500-pound bombs had a 19 percent probability of one hit on a bridge 20 x 300 feet; a 46 percent probability on a bridge 30 x 600 feet; and a 76 percent probability on a bridge 30 x 1,400 feet. In effect, to be reasonably sure of *damaging* a 30 x 1,000 foot bridge (100 percent probability of one hit), about two bomb groups (50 to 65 aircraft) would have to be dispatched. Absolute certainty of *destroying* the structure would have required many more aircraft. See HQ IX Bomber Command, 1st Operations Research Section, "Effect of Size and Construction of a Bridge on Probability of Obtaining a Successful Hit," in USAFHRC 670.310-1, Fifteenth AF, Operational Analysis Reports, 1944-1945.

85. See Michael A. Baker's letter to the *Washington Post,* 14 April 1990, in which he writes: "Most critics of the 'no-bomb' policy toward the camps agree that the camps were difficult targets. Their criticism is that the infrastructure of rail lines, rolling stock, etc., was never attacked. . . . Destroying the transport used by the SS could have saved many who were shipped to the camps in the final year of the war while denying the German army much of its needed transport."

86. Roger A. Freeman, *Mighty Eighth War Diary* (New York: Jane's, 1981).

87. The best source on the air war against German transportation remains USAFHRC 137.312, 20 November 1945, USSBS, Transportation Division, "The Effects of Strategic Bombing on German Transportation." The 90-page report contains 99 exhibits, including maps, tables, photographs, and graphs.

88. Department of State, "Laws and Customs of War on Land" (Hague, IV) 18 October 1907, *Treaties and Other International Agreements of the United States of America, 1776-1949,* vol. 1, 648.

89. War Department, *Rules of Land Warfare,* FM 27-10 (Washington: GPO, 1 October 1940), 12. The three examples of "undefended places" given in the manual are: (1) a fort or fortified place, (2) a town surrounded by detached forts, the whole considered as fortified, and (3) "a place that is occupied by a combatant military force or through which a force is passing."

90. See Ronald Schaffer, *Wings of Judgment: American Bombing in World War II* (Oxford, England: Oxford University Press, 1985). Air war Commanders H. H. "Hap" Arnold, Carl Spaatz, Ira Eaker, James Doolittle, George Anderson,

Elwood Quesada, Curtis LeMay and Lewis Brereton and their staffs were well aware of the moral implications of strategic bombing, and, although some of them drifted toward acceptance of Douhetian ideas as the air war in Europe progressed, few, if any, lost a repugnance for the killing of wholly innocent civilians.

91. USAFHRC K239.0512-1754, Oral History Interview with Lewis F. Powell dated 26 February 1985. The interview includes subsequent clarifications requested by Chief of Air Force History Dr. Richard Kohn, and Powell's statement is included in these supplementary comments. Major General Carl Spaatz commanded the U.S. Strategic Air Forces in Europe (USSTAF) between 6 January 1944 and 3 June 1945. Lewis F. Powell served as a staff intelligence officer with the Army Air Forces. He was trained in ULTRA at Bletchley Park, England, during February and March 1944, and in April and May 1944 he toured operational commands in the Mediterranean theater. In May 1944, he became special security representative to headquarters, U.S. Strategic Air Forces in Europe, and in August 1944 he became chief of operational intelligence of the USSTAF. These wartime experiences gave Powell an insider's view of high-ranking Allied air commanders and the intelligence that was available to them.

13

The Bombing of Auschwitz Revisited:
A Critical Analysis

Richard H. Levy

After the manuscript for this book was put into production, Richard Levy, the author of this chapter, received the "provisional and partial translation of the minutes of the meeting of the Executive of the Jewish Agency held June 11, 1944" chaired by David Ben-Gurion.

During this meeting, in a discussion on rescue, Isaac Gruenbaum, the head of the Rescue Committee of the Jewish Agency, proposed that the Allies be urged to bomb death camps in Poland such as Auschwitz and Treblinka. The Executive members were overwhelmingly opposed (11-1) to this proposal. The discussion ends with Ben-Gurion stating "the view of the board is that we should not ask the Allies to bomb places where there are Jews."

At the time he was writing this chapter, Mr. Levy knew of Gruenbaum's proposal. And he knew that Gruenbaum's "colleagues" had opposed this proposal. But Levy mistakenly thought this referred to Gruenbaum's colleagues on the Rescue Committee. Upon receiving the June minutes, he realized the "colleagues" were those on the far more important Executive. We have tried to clarify this point in the text.

Mr. Levy obtained a copy of the minutes in Hebrew from the Zionist Archives in Jerusalem; this copy, along with a translation of agenda item #2, was faxed to him in America. He has since had the document translated from

the Hebrew by several different sources. No substantive errors were found from
the "provisional translation" he received with the original document. The
translation is partial in that the discussion covering items #1 and #3 on the
agenda are not included.
  The translation of agenda item #2 appears following the source notes
for this chapter.

INTRODUCTION

Starting in May or June,* the American and British governments were asked to
bomb the deportation railways in Hungary. Later, they were asked to bomb the
gas chambers and crematoria at Auschwitz-Birkenau. The requests were made
in a desperate effort to explore every possibility of helping those Hungarian Jews
who had not yet been murdered. Most of the requests originated with Jewish
organizations. In the event, the Hungarian railways were not bombed as or when
requested, and the gas chambers and crematoria were not bombed at all. There
is a strongly held moral view that the failure of the Allies to bomb either target
was at best callous and at worst amounted to complicity in the murderous crimes
of the Nazis.
  The subject was first brought to the attention of the public in 1961, when
a document from Chaim Weizmann's archives was introduced by the prosecution into the Adolf Eichmann trial in Jerusalem.[1] As this document was
intended for the British rather than the Americans, its disclosure resulted in
several articles in the British press,[2] but apparently none in the United States.
There was also a short discussion in Parliament,[3] during which the prime
minister promised to consider the publication of the relevant British documents. This was eventually done, though not, perhaps, very promptly. References to the nonbombing and the moral criticism of this omission were rare
from about 1963 until 1978, when David Wyman's article "Why Auschwitz
Was Never Bombed" was published.[4] (A modified version of this article
appeared as a chapter in his 1984 book, *The Abandonment of the Jews: America
and the Holocaust.*)[5] In Wyman's view, the failure to bomb the gas chambers
and crematoria at Auschwitz-Birkenau (or the Hungarian railways) was merely
one aspect of a larger American culpability. For reasons that it would be
interesting to examine, this view fell on extremely fertile soil. Since 1978,

---

* All calendar dates in this chapter, for example, "April" or "6 July," refer to 1944
unless otherwise indicated.

references to the failure to bomb Auschwitz can be found in many places, invariably coupled with expressions of righteous indignation, outrage, or shame. Very little analysis critical of Wyman has been undertaken, although Frank Brecher[6] and Lucy Dawidowicz[7] made sweeping attacks on his ideas. Richard Foregger[8] and James H. Kitchens III[9] criticized him on technical grounds, using journals not normally read by students of the Holocaust. A subsequent paper by Foregger[10] addressed some of the operational questions. This chapter aims to expand the technical criticism and to integrate it with some of the broader issues. It will be seen that Wyman is wrong in many important respects.

THE EARLY PROPOSALS

The Nazis must have used every railway line in occupied Europe to deport Jews to the extermination camps in the east, especially Auschwitz, from the beginning of 1942. Yet the suggestion that the deportations could be stopped by bombing railway lines does not seem to have surfaced until mid-May, by which time more than five million of the ultimate six million murders had already been committed. On 16 and 23 (or 24) May, two short coded telegrams were sent to Isaac Sternbuch, the representative in Switzerland of the Union of Orthodox Rabbis.[11] They relayed urgent appeals originating in Hungary[12] for the bombing of the Hungarian railways.

Among a host of contributory reasons, two in particular help explain why the suggestion to bomb railway lines surfaced at that particular moment and not before. These were conditions in Hungary and the increasing power of the Allied bomber offensive. In April, Hungary contained the last intact Jewish community in occupied Europe, amounting to some 750,000 people. Starting in mid-April, the Hungarian Jews were subjected to a systematic concentration, to be followed by deportations. While the destination of the deportees was at first known only to be somewhere in Poland, the true meaning of deportation was all too clear to the authors of the railway-bombing appeals. Also, Hungary being a nominally independent state, there was some communication with the outside world. Budapest contained many foreign legations.

At the same time, the Allied bomber offensive was finally in full swing. The British Royal Air Force (RAF) and the United States Army Air Force (USAAF) had reached essentially full strength and were pounding targets in Germany and occupied Europe. The USAAF in particular had, since about the turn of the year, established bases at Foggia in southern Italy from which it was able to attack many hitherto unreachable targets in southern and eastern

Germany, Austria, southern Poland, Romania, and Hungary. Of these targets, the most important were the oil and aircraft industries. Beyond their tangible accomplishments, the bomber fleets, which could be seen flying over all parts of the Nazi empire, had become, by this point in the war, the clearest harbinger of Allied victory. There was, however, a very large gap between what the bombers achieved and what their capabilities were imagined by various parties to be. No effort was made in public to play down the power of the bombers; on the contrary, contemporary USAAF propaganda stressed the precision of their attacks. But even with access to the best available intelligence, some officers in command of the bomber forces exhibited a notable propensity to exaggerate their capabilities. Like Herman Göring before them, some were convinced that air power alone could win the war. If opinions of this kind were current among these officers, who can blame the Jews of Hungary or their friends in Switzerland and elsewhere, desperate for help from any source, for believing that the bombers could help them?

The routes by which the earliest appeals to bomb the Hungarian railways reached the British and American governments were many. The telegram of 16 May referred specifically to the RAF, and its message should have been delivered to the British government. While it is not known whether this happened, it is certainly the case that the Jewish Agency was in frequent contact with the British government at this time. On 2 June, at the request of Isaac Gruenbaum, who was chairman of the Rescue Committee of the Jewish Agency, L. C. Pinkerton, the U.S. consul-general in Jerusalem, sent a telegram addressed to the War Refugee Board (WRB) in Washington,[13] which reached the State Department on the same day. Weizmann was at the British Foreign Office in London on 2 June and met Anthony Eden on 7 June.[14] On 18 June, Jacob Rosenheim of the New York office of Agudath Israel, upon receipt of a message from Sternbuch in Switzerland, addressed letters to high American government officials; his appeals were relayed to the WRB. Wyman claims that the message from Sternbuch to Rosenheim was delayed by American censorship.[15] This claim is irrelevant since Gruenbaum's telegram of 2 June carrying a similar appeal had long since reached Washington. Wyman does not comment on the apparent lack of action in response to Gruenbaum's appeal.

Martin Gilbert has shown in great detail how the fact that Auschwitz was the only destination of the deportees was not known until the end of June. Thus, the message sent by Pinkerton to the WRB at Gruenbaum's request referred only to "the railways between Hungary and Poland." Rosenheim also referred only to "Poland." Wyman misquotes this proposal when he wrongly refers[16] to "Rosenheim's proposal to bomb rail points between Hungary and Auschwitz...." Toward the end of June, however, and from that time forward, the appeals all sought the bombing of the gas chambers and crematoria at Auschwitz, usually in combination with the Hungarian railways. There could be no clearer indication of the exact time at which details of the extermination camp at Auschwitz precise enough to support a bombing appeal reached the West. The first appeal of this kind to reach the U.S. government came on 24 June, addressed to the WRB in Berne.[17] A similar appeal reached the Foreign Office in London on 27 June.[18] Moshe Shertok (head of the Jewish Agency's political department) and Weizmann repeated the request to the Foreign Office in London on 30 June[19] and to Eden himself on 6 July.[20] The Czech government in exile relayed appeals that reached the British Foreign Office on 4 July and the War Refugee Board in Washington on 14 July.[21] Wyman says only that "starting in early July, appeals for Air Force action to impede the mass murders increasingly centered on destruction of the Auschwitz gas chambers."[22]

INITIAL REACTIONS

The WRB, under its executive director, John W. Pehle, seems to have acquired a virtual monopoly on the transmission of the appeals to the War Department, where its designated contact was Assistant Secretary John J. McCloy. Pehle's attitude was therefore of critical importance. Pehle apparently did nothing with Gruenbaum's appeal of 2 June, but Wyman recounts Pehle's reaction to Rosenheim's appeal of 18 June as follows:

> On June 21, Pehle transmitted the request to the War Department. Three days later, he discussed it with McCloy. Pehle himself expressed doubts about the proposal, but asked that the War Department explore the idea. McCloy agreed to look into it.[23]

This is inadequate. A serious attempt to find out why the requested bombing was never done should, above all, pay attention to contemporary efforts to think about the feasibility and efficacy of the requested operations. In a Memorandum for the Files,[24] written on the same day (24 June) that he saw McCloy, Pehle noted how he had told McCloy that "I wanted to mention the matter to him for whatever exploration might be appropriate by the War Department." But, Pehle added, "I had several doubts about the matter." He said he doubted:

> (1) whether it would be appropriate to use military planes and personnel for this purpose; (2) whether it would be difficult to put the railroad line out of

commission for a long enough period to do any good; and (3) even assuming that these railroad lines were put out of commission for some period of time, whether it would help the Jews in Hungary.

Having expressed these doubts, Pehle had gone on, as he himself noted, to make it "very clear to Mr. McCloy" that he was not, "at this point at least, requesting the War Department to take any action on this proposal, other than appropriately to explore it."

Thus, McCloy was not given a ringing endorsement of the appeal to bomb the Hungarian railways, a fact that Wyman fails entirely to bring out. Pehle's first doubt raised a question that both he and McCloy must have known very well could have been settled only by President Roosevelt. His second and third doubts could, however, be given professional consideration at the War Department.

The WRB was established by President Roosevelt on 22 January and functioned with some success in a number of spheres. These included the facilitation of negotiations at the fringes of occupied Europe, bribery of corrupt officials, handling of messages, transmission of funds, and many other such useful activities. It is understandable that the bombing appeals originating with Jewish and other organizations in Europe were passed to the WRB. It is less clear that the WRB was the appropriate governmental agency to respond to them, and Pehle's doubts underline the point. Wyman[25] quotes a legalistic discussion about the language of the paragraph in the executive order that established the WRB. The paragraph in question charged the War Department (among others) with executing WRB programs. Wyman appears to believe that the language meant that the War Department was required to mount an operation to bomb the Hungarian railways or Auschwitz, merely because the WRB had a program calling for it. Pehle certainly knew better. Such an interpretation of his mandate would have prejudiced General Dwight D. Eisenhower's operational command of the U.S. forces in the European theater of operations (ETO) and would have been roundly dismissed. Neither McCloy nor anyone else at the War Department had the authority to order Eisenhower to undertake specific operations. On operational matters, Eisenhower was subject only to orders from President Roosevelt, the commander in chief.

With the arrival in Washington of the earliest appeals for the bombing of the gas chambers and crematoria at Auschwitz, Benjamin Azkin of the WRB wrote an interoffice memo[26] dated 29 June that amounted to a sustained attempt to argue in favor of such bombing. But the strongest statement he felt able to make on the likely efficacy of the bombing was that the destruction of the "physical installations" at Auschwitz and Birkenau "might appreciably slow down the systematic slaughter at least temporarily." Misquoting this memo, Wyman has Azkin writing "would" instead of "might."

Leon Kubowitzki, head of the Rescue Department of the World Jewish Congress, met with the WRB on 28 June[27] and wrote to it on 1 July. He was opposed to the bombing of Auschwitz, arguing that the destruction of the "death installations cannot be done from the air, as the first victims would be the Jews who are gathered in these camps." Kubowitzki also argued that "such a bombing would be a welcome pretext for the Germans to assert that their Jewish victims have been massacred not by their killers, but by the Allied bombing." Medoff[28] tells us that on 27 June a columnist for the Yiddish daily *Morning Journal* criticized the proposal on the grounds that a raid on the death camps would result in the accidental killing of inmates.

We also know of a remarkable instance in which an appeal to bomb the death camps was suppressed.[29] Gruenbaum reported (on 7 June) that when he met with Pinkerton on 2 June he had asked the latter to transmit to Washington an appeal to bomb "the death camps in Poland." (Note the plural and the absence of any mention of Auschwitz). Foreshadowing Kubowitzki's arguments, Pinkerton remarked: "Will this [i.e., bombing the death camps] not cause the deaths of many Jews? And will not German propaganda claim that the Americans are participating in the extermination of the Jews?" He then declined to transmit the request to bomb the death camps unless it was made in writing. What prompted Pinkerton to impose this condition is not known. Perhaps he had an idea of what, in fact, would happen next. In Gruenbaum's words:

I was forced to consult with [my Executive of the Jewish Agency] colleagues and they all expressed their opinion that we should not request a thing like that because Jews might get killed in the death camps! I explained to them that in such places all the Jews are about to be killed. They didn't listen to me. They do not want to take such a responsibility upon themselves. They prefer not to prevent mass murder for fear that Jews will be killed by bombs.

Gruenbaum's disgust at being a minority of one on the Executive of the Jewish Agency is plain. The JA then made no request of Pinkerton, and therefore no appeal to bomb the death camps was transmitted from Jerusalem to Washington. Indeed, nothing further on the subject of bombing either the railways or the death camps was heard from the Jewish Agency in Jerusalem until 13 September. On that date, with or without the concurrence of his committee and acting in response to reports that more deportations from Budapest to Auschwitz were imminent, Gruenbaum telegraphed Shertok in

London, suggesting that five Hungarian railways and Auschwitz itself should be bombed.[30] Shertok evidently passed this telegram on to the British government. There were, in fact, no renewed deportations from Hungary to Auschwitz (though deportations from many other places did continue), and two of the five railways that Gruenbaum listed were already largely in Soviet hands. In 1961, Gruenbaum told a reporter[31] that he had sent telegraphic appeals for bombing to Joseph Stalin, Winston Churchill, and Roosevelt; any such telegrams would clearly have been sent over the objections of his committee, and I am not aware that any copies of them have been found in Churchill's papers, Roosevelt's papers, or in the Zionist Archives. The Jewish Agency in London did revert to the subject of bombing, as will be seen.

Even though the views of Kubowitzki, the columnist for the *Morning Journal,* and all of Gruenbaum's colleagues might, with hindsight, be judged wrong, they were obviously sincerely held. In his paper, Wyman relegates Kubowitzki's opinion to a footnote. In his book, it doesn't appear at all. But he does say[32] (without citing any sources) that unidentified Jewish leaders in Europe and the United States, assuming the use of heavy bombers and the consequent death of some inmates, wrestled with the moral problem involved. Most, according to Wyman, concluded that loss of life under the circumstances was justifiable.

Wyman makes no reference to the overwhelming rejection of Gruenbaum's bombing proposal. Were Wyman's unidentified Jewish leaders aware that "some inmates" might mean many thousands? Does "most" refer to a large or a small majority? The issue was still divisive in 1978.[33]

Here, then, are a number of contemporary views. Pehle had serious doubts; Azkin approved of the bombing but was extremely cautious about its probable efficacy; Kubowitzki, the columnist for the *Morning Journal,* and all of Gruenbaum's colleagues (on the Executive of the Jewish Agency in Jerusalem) were opposed. Gruenbaum himself was in favor but was silenced by his own committee. It appears that no one was willing and able to argue the case that the bombing would be feasible, effective, and proper.

THE FEASIBILITY OF RAILWAY BOMBING

In London, Weizmann and Shertok (representing the Jewish Agency) read an Aide-Memoire comprising six paragraphs to Eden on 6 July.[34] The sixth and last paragraph contained five suggestions. The fifth and last suggestion was that the railway line leading from Budapest to Auschwitz and the death camps at Birkenau and other places should be bombed.

It is not clear why Weizmann and Shertok were free to take a position opposed (so far as bombing the camps was concerned) to the position of the Executive of the Jewish Agency in Jerusalem. There is no indication that the committee in Jerusalem ever changed its collective mind and some that it did not. Perhaps wartime communication difficulties were to blame, perhaps it was simple bureaucratic muddle, or perhaps it was that Weizmann handled the British government from London while the American government was handled from Jerusalem.

In any event, the request was made, and Eden reported on the meeting to Churchill on the same day. On the next day, 7 July, Churchill responded favorably to the bombing request, writing "Get anything out of the Air Force that you can." Accordingly, still on 7 July, Eden wrote to the secretary of state for Air, Sir Archibald Sinclair, asking him to examine the feasibility of stopping the operation of the death camps by bombing the railway lines leading to Birkenau.[35] Sinclair was also asked to examine the feasibility of bombing the camps themselves. On 15 July he replied, in part:

> You wrote to me on 7th July to ask if anything could be done by bombing to stop the murder of Jews in Hungary. I entirely agree that it is our duty to consider every possible plan that might help, and I have therefore examined: (a) interrupting the railways. . . . I am advised that (a) is out of our power. It is only by an enormous concentration of bomber forces that we have been able to interrupt communications in Normandy; the distance of Silesia from our bases entirely rules out our doing anything of the kind.[36]

When Rosenheim's railway-bombing appeal was delivered by Pehle to the U.S. War Department, McCloy replied on 26 June:

> The War Department is of the opinion that the suggested air operation is impracticable for the reason that it could be executed only by diversion of considerable air support essential to the success of our forces now engaged in decisive operations.[37]

Wyman is persuaded that this language is nothing more than an evasive brush-off. Yet McCloy's opinion, somewhat ponderously expressed, is clearly supported by Sinclair and his advisers. McCloy would not have felt free to provide the supporting detail from experience in Normandy to Pehle. Among the many other competent authorities that could be cited in support of these professional opinions on the prospects of saving Hungarian Jews by railway bombing, one of the most authoritative must be that of Marshal of the Royal

Air Force Sir Arthur Harris, wartime head of RAF Bomber Command. Harris was never consulted about bombing Auschwitz or its railways during the war, but in a 1962 interview he concluded:

> In the light of all these factors, I personally fail to see how the cutting of the relevant rail lines to Auschwitz could have achieved any effective result except for a few days, unless a totally impracticable (numerically) effort was applied virtually continuously to that end.[38]

At the time of this interview, Harris was clearly unaware of Sinclair's letter cited above. Wyman accepts the same point of view:

> In the case of railroad lines, the answer is not clear-cut. Railroad bombing had its problems and was the subject of long-lasting disputes within the Allied military. Successful cutting of railways necessitated close observation of the severed lines and frequent rebombing, since repairs took only a few days. Even bridges, which were costly to hit, were often back in operation in three or four days.[39]

The only question one can have about this statement is how Wyman can describe the situation as "not clear-cut." Preventing the Hungarian deportations by bombing railways was quite simply beyond the power of any conceivable force that the Allies could have brought to bear. To understand more clearly why this was so and was perceived at the time to be so, we need only to study the furious debates (in which Harris was an active participant) over the use of air power to deny the use of the railways in northwest France to the Nazis in the period after D-Day.[40] After protracted and heated arguments, a very large part of all of the air forces (strategic and tactical, American and British) based in Britain was committed to the so-called Transportation Plan. Devised by Solly Zuckerman, it called for attacks not only on key lines and bridges, but also on rail yards, sidings, stations, sheds, repair shops, roundhouses, turntables, signal systems, locomotives, and rolling stock. Under the plan, the attacks took place continuously for many weeks both before and after the invasion. The prevailing view at the time was that anything much less than a program as broad as this was effectively a waste of time and effort. This view would certainly have been familiar, if not to McCloy personally, then at least to his advisers. Postwar hindsight fully vindicated the contemporary views.[41]

The discussions leading to the adoption of the Transportation Plan were naturally carried on in secret. The conclusions could not have been known to Gruenbaum, Sternbuch, Rosenheim, and others. Nor, in all probability, were they known to Pehle. The desperation of the prospective victims in 1944 is wholly understandable, as is the eagerness of those not in danger to consider all possible means of assistance. The professional evaluations provided by Sinclair and McCloy were nevertheless correct, as Wyman himself acknowledges.

THE END OF THE HUNGARIAN DEPORTATIONS

It is possible, with hindsight, to compare the chronology of the actual Hungarian deportations with the chronology of the consideration given to the railway-bombing proposals. The facts are, indeed, tragic. The deportations started on 15 May. By 7 June, 289,357 Hungarian Jews had been deported.[42] By 17 June, the total had risen to 340,162; by 30 June, to 381,661; and by 9 July, to 437,402. Pressure on the Hungarian government resulted in the deportations being halted on 8 July, with the last transports arriving at Auschwitz on 11 July. When the deportations stopped, the Hungarian provinces had lost essentially all of their Jews, but in and around Budapest there remained between 200,000 and 350,000 Jews, depending on whose figures one believes. On 18 July, the news that the Hungarian deportations had ceased reached London, where it was widely publicized.[43]

It can be seen that the discussions among Rosenheim, Pehle, and McCloy (18-26 June) and still more the discussions among Shertok, Weizmann, Eden, Churchill, and Sinclair (6-15 July) were far too late to affect the outcome, even if anything had been possible. In addition, the timing of these discussions vividly illustrates the complete absence of any up-to-date intelligence on which particular railways out of Hungary were being used at any given moment. This problem alone would have made it very hard to conduct effective military operations.

Wyman concedes some merit to the argument that railway bombing after 8 July would not have helped.[44] Then he refers[45] to the possibility that deportations from Budapest might have been resumed and to a further appeal for bombing the railways, which came from Hungary in late August when renewed deportations from Budapest appeared imminent. Ignoring entirely his own views about the problems of railroad bombing, Wyman suggests that the "War Department could have agreed to stand ready, if deportations had resumed, to spare some bomb tonnage for those two railroads, provided bombers were already scheduled to fly near them on regular war missions." He apparently believes that only two railroad routes were available between Budapest and Auschwitz. Operationally speaking, his plan is bizarre. If the bombers were to be assigned the mission of bombing specific railroads, what difference would it have made where their previously scheduled war missions would have taken them? The vague reference to "some bomb tonnage" entirely avoids the hard questions of the minimum tonnage that might have been expected to do any good and the maximum that might have been "spared." In this way, Wyman continues, "the United States could have demonstrated concern for the Jews." He feels that cuts in the rail lines "would have been of some help, even if the bombing had to be sporadic." Wyman does not explain why the concern of the United States would have been demonstrated by standing ready to bomb two Hungarian railroads, if they were used, while it continued to do nothing at all about the numerous other railroads that were used to bring victims to Auschwitz from all of occupied Europe (except Hungary) until November. He says that fifty thousand were gassed there between 7 July and 20 August. Finally, Wyman observes that on 13 September, 324 American heavy bombers flew within six miles of one of the railways that might have been used for deportations, and that a total of 2,700 American heavy bombers flew within easy reach of both railways between July and October. This observation shows only that Wyman can't (or won't) distinguish between the undoubted ability of the bombers to fly over a railroad and their very limited ability (which he himself has described) to interrupt it by dropping their bombs. Furthermore, if every single one of the 2,700 heavy-bomber missions to which Wyman refers had been redirected to the railways that might have been used for deportations (but were not), the average of about 27 missions a day would have been wholly inadequate to the purpose of interrupting them.

For whatever reason, the Hungarian government did, in fact, stop the deportations on 8 July. Many efforts were made to exert the influence necessary to achieve this aim. Among these was pressure from the Swedes, the Swiss, the Vatican, and others[46] (all encouraged by the British and the Americans). Formidable warnings were broadcast by the British Broadcasting Corporation (BBC)[47] on 5, 6, and 11 July to all of those involved in the deportation of Jews to the death camps, and Gilbert appears to credit these broadcasts with having saved more than a hundred thousand.[48] But, according to Raul Hilberg,[49] the strongest point made by Hungarian Prime Minister Dome Sztójay in a meeting on 5 July with German Minister and General Plenipotentiary Edmund Veesenmayer was the following: Hungarian counterintelligence had intercepted and deciphered three secret teletype messages sent by the U.S. and British missions in Berne to their governments. These messages dealt with the fate of the deported Jews and suggested the bombing and destruction of destination points and railroad lines, "target bombing of all collaborating Hungarian and German agencies—with exact and correct street and house numbers in Budapest." This kind of bombing was, of course, well beyond the power of the Allies. Nevertheless, Hilberg says:

> History plays strangely with its participants. The Jewish relief committee in Budapest had sent these requests to Berne to be transmitted through diplomatic channels to the Allied capitals, where no action was taken on them. But fate had intervened. The Hungarians in their eagerness had intercepted the messages and had thereupon frightened themselves to death.

A different interpretation of the same event is given by Gilbert,[50] who suggests that these telegrams, which were sent from Berne on 26 June, were leaked to the Hungarians rather than intercepted and deciphered by them. He also says that the leakage was accomplished by the simple device of sending the messages *en clair*,[51] thus offering the amusing picture of Hungarian counterintelligence claiming to have deciphered uncoded messages. If Gilbert is right, the individuals who conceived and authorized the idea of leaking these messages to the Hungarians should be remembered as unsung heroes. Bernard Wasserstein[52] says that it was the Germans who intercepted the British message and that they drew it to the attention of the Hungarian government.

The effectiveness of the threatened use of force depends upon the credibility of the threat, and the threat contained in the leaked telegrams was no exception. Accordingly, it was, intentionally or unintentionally, greatly strengthened by the Allied bombing campaign in general and by the Allied bombing of Hungary in particular. Looking now at the actual bombing of Hungary, Hilberg[53] refers to two raids on Budapest at the end of June. Mario Fenyo[54] reports that Hungary was raided on 13 and 17 April; 5 and 11 May; 2, 13, 14, and 26 June; 2 July; "and so on." The raid on 2 July was on a scale comparable to the major raids directed against German cities in the same period. Additional massive raids took place on 14 and 30 July. Gilbert[55] describes the raid of 2 July as "an unusually heavy American bomber attack on the marshalling yards of Budapest;" Wesley Craven and James Cate say that "712 B-17s and B-24s bombed Budapest, which contained oil refineries, aircraft factories, and railway targets."[56] Curiously, Hilberg makes no mention of the raid of 2 July, nor does it figure in his account of Veesenmayer's report on his meeting with Sztójay, which took place only three days later.

Clearly, the effect of the leaked telegrams would have been much reduced without the actual bombing (especially the heavy raid of 2 July on Budapest) that underlined the threats that the messages contained. It is not known whether there was any coordination between the bombing raids on Hungary and the leakage of the telegrams. Perhaps it was no more than a happy coincidence.

The deportation railways were not bombed as, or when, requested. This does not constitute proof that "no action was taken." It can be argued that (even though it was indirect) the most effective possible use of air power was made and that it was made in a timely way. With the help of the actual bombing of Hungary, the total cessation of deportations was brought about. The 200,000 to 350,000 Jews concentrated in Budapest were spared deportation to Auschwitz. In terms of lives saved, this was a far more valuable result than any that could possibly have resulted from the short-lived interruption of a few provincial railway lines.

One last point concerning the bombing of the Hungarian railways needs to be made. In the article on the city of Debrecen, the *Encyclopaedia Judaica* makes the following claim: "About 7500 persons were deported up to June 26-28 1944; some to Auschwitz, and the rest—because the railway lines had been destroyed by bombing—to Austria."[57]

The texts cited in support of this assertion are not available to me, and I am somewhat doubtful of the claim; after all, if the victims could be deported to Austria, why could they not be deported to Auschwitz via Austria? Hilberg[58] refers to a request on 7 June from the mayor of Vienna for the assignment of Hungarian Jews to labor-starved factories in the Viennese area. Some 18,000 were sent, most of whom survived. It would seem more logical to assign the survival of the 7,500 persons from Debrecen to the influence of labor shortages in Austrian factories rather than to difficulties in transporting them to Auschwitz caused by the bombing of the Hungarian railways. However, it would be interesting to follow up this unique lead; clearly, someone ascribes the survival of some Jews directly to the bombing of the Hungarian railways.

OTHER REACTIONS

We have seen how, when the first appeals to bomb the gas chambers and crematoria at Auschwitz were made, Azkin, while approving of the idea, was able to offer only a highly conditional view of its likely efficacy, while Kubowitzki, all of Gruenbaum's colleagues, and the columnist for the *Morning Journal* opposed the idea outright. Wyman misquoted Azkin, omitted Kubowitzki in his book, and made no reference to Gruenbaum's colleagues or the columnist for the *Morning Journal*. He also made little or no reference to the contemporary evaluations of Weizmann and Shertok, of Sinclair (who had a reputation for sympathy with Zionism),[59] or of the Czech government in exile, all of which we shall now examine.

Weizmann and Shertok made their bombing proposal to Eden on 6 July. Eden[60] wrote to Sinclair on 7 July, saying: "Dr. Weizmann admitted that there seemed to be little enough that we could do to stop these horrors, but he suggested that something might be done to stop the operation of the death camps by bombing. . . ." Five days after the meeting, on 11 July, the Jewish Agency in London prepared a note[61] that expressed a rather different view about the proposed bombing of the death camps. This note was prepared very soon after its topic had been discussed with Eden. It represents the most closely argued contemporary Jewish viewpoint available to us. The note said:

> The bombing of the death camps is . . . hardly likely to achieve the salvation of the victims to any appreciable extent. Its physical effects can only be the destruction of plant and personnel, and possibly the hastening of the end of those already doomed. The resulting dislocation of the German machinery for systematic wholesale murder may possibly cause delay in the execution of those still in Hungary (over 300,000 in and around Budapest). This in itself is valuable as far as it goes. But it may not go very far, as other means of extermination can be quickly improvised.

This is certainly consistent with the view ascribed by Eden to Weizmann: "little enough that we could do to stop these horrors." But the note then went on to say: "The main purpose of the bombing should be its many-sided and far-reaching moral effect." It then detailed this moral effect under five headings.

The note itself is not addressed to anyone at all, nor is it signed. But Gideon Hausner[62] describes it as "Weizmann's urgent plea to bomb Auschwitz." Abba Eban[63] also ascribes it to Weizmann. Wasserstein[64] quotes Chaim Barlas[65] (director of the Immigration Department and representative of the JA and the World Jewish Congress), who says that it was a "Memorandum from M. Shertok to the British Foreign Office" but does not say how he knows this. Norman Rose[66] quotes from the note, and ascribes its views ("little practical value") directly to Weizmann and Shertok. On the other hand, Gilbert[67] does not offer any opinion as to who prepared the note, nor as to who approved it, nor as to whom it was sent. The document has apparently not been recovered from British files. There is no indication that the British ever considered an operation expected to achieve little more than a "many-sided and far-reaching moral effect." They considered only whether "anything could be done by bombing to stop the murder." It is of some interest to know whether Weizmann and Shertok kept their view of the "main purpose of the bombing" to themselves; they might have done this in the belief that it would be much harder to persuade the British to undertake an operation whose main purpose was to be its "moral effect." It seems entirely possible that neither the note, nor the view it expresses on the main purpose of the bombing, was ever transmitted to the Foreign Office.

The note itself says that "a detailed description of the two camps [Auschwitz and Birkenau], contained in a report submitted to Allied Governments and published by the Jewish Telegraphic Agency, is attached" and that this report was "received since the original suggestion for bombing was made." The copy of this report recovered from British files was not attached to the Jewish Agency note. It was received at the Foreign Office[68] from the Czechoslovak Government in exile on 4 July. It contains appeals to bomb the crematoria and the railways leading to Auschwitz.

The narrow focus of the note on the plight of the three hundred thousand Jews in Budapest is also revealing. We now know, of course, that at about the same time Jews were being deported from Lodz, Greece, Italy, and elsewhere to Auschwitz, where they were gassed.

Whatever was done with this note, Sinclair held the same view that it expressed. He replied to Eden on 15 July: "It might be ineffective and, even if the plant was destroyed, I am not clear that it would really help the victims."[69]

Another appeal to bomb the camps was transmitted by the World Jewish Congress to the WRB on 8 or 9 August at the request of Ernest Frischer (Chairman of the Czech Jewish Party, 1935-1939) of the Czech government in exile in London. Frischer wrote:

> I believe that destruction of gas chambers and crematoria in Auschwitz by bombing would have a certain effect now. . . . Germans might possibly stop further mass exterminations. . . . Bombing of railway communications in this same area would also be of importance.[70]

The individual who forwarded this request to the WRB and the War Department was the same Kubowitzki who had argued against bombing the camps on 1 July. Kubowitzki did not in any way indicate that he had changed his mind and now endorsed the proposal. (There is evidence[71] to suggest that he had not changed his mind as late as the end of November, after the gassing at Auschwitz had stopped. In a speech he gave at that time, he stated that Auschwitz should be attacked in force either by the underground or by Allied paratroopers). His letter of transmission (". . . submit for consideration . . . an excerpt from a message dated July 29") suggests that he was taking care of an obligation in the most perfunctory way possible. McCloy's reply on 14 August was predictable. He probably knew Kubowitzki's views; if he did not, the tone of Kubowitzki's letter of transmittal would have suggested them. To his previous letters on this subject, McCloy now added a comment about the doubtful efficacy of the proposed operation. In expressing such doubts, he aligned himself with Azkin, Kubowitzki, Weizmann, Shertok, Frischer, Pehle, Sinclair, the columnist for the *Morning Journal,* and all of Gruenbaum's colleagues in the Jewish Agency in Jerusalem. Gruenbaum himself appears to have had no doubts but was silenced by his colleagues.

BOMBING AUSCHWITZ: LIKELY EFFECTIVENESS

Clearly, many people thought about the likely efficacy of bombing the gas chambers and crematoria in 1944. However, nearly all of the written material now available is limited to expressions such as "might appreciably slow down the slaughter, at least temporarily," or "Germans might possibly stop further mass exterminations," or ". . . even if the plant was destroyed, I am not clear that it would really help the victims." In fact, the only specific comment that goes beyond this kind of opinion can be found in the Jewish Agency note: the dislocation of the German machinery would be "valuable as far as it goes, but it may not go very far, as other means of extermination can be quickly improvised." We must now examine the question of efficacy from the entirely different standpoint of hindsight. Based upon what is now known, does it appear that bombing the gas chambers and crematoria would have been more effective than was believed at the time?

As good a place as any to start the retrospective evaluation of the likely effectiveness of bombing the gas chambers and crematoria is to note that Wyman hasn't even been able to count them correctly. He says that there were four of each.[72] He quotes Olga Lengyel[73] approvingly but doesn't seem to have absorbed the message of the title of her book *Five Chimneys.*[74] Uwe Adam[75] says that two gas chambers and crematoria were located in Auschwitz I ("Main Camp") at some distance from Auschwitz II (Birkenau); one is described as experimental, having been used as early as 3 September 1941, while the other was used until October 1942. Leni Yahil[76] says that in May "the pace of the extermination process was set at an unprecedented level, using all five crematoria—including No. I, which had been in use before the four main crematoria, equipped with gas chambers, had been built in the first half of 1943." To complicate matters further, Adam lists a total of ten gas chambers that were active at various times in Auschwitz II. Of these, four were in "Bunker 2" and were kept in service until the autumn of 1944. According to J. C. Pressac,[77] between May and the beginning of July 1944, some 200,000 to 250,000

Hungarian Jews were annihilated in the gas chambers and incineration furnaces of Crematoria II and III, the gas chamber and five incineration ditches of Crematoria V, and the gas chamber and incineration ditch of Bunker 2/V. This last was formed from the original four small gas chambers of Bunker 2 by removing the internal walls, making the count seven, the number mentioned by Foregger.[78] The remaining two gas chambers at Auschwitz II, according to Adam, were in Bunker 1. They were "subsequently demolished," he says, without giving a date. There is some ambiguity in all of this information. For instance, is Yahil's Crematorium I to be identified with the gas chamber at Auschwitz I, or with the modified gas chamber in Bunker 2/V? And Pressac is clear that main gas chamber IV was not used at this time, which contradicts Yahil. But the degree of ambiguity cannot alter the facts that the four main gas chambers were not the only ones available and that at least one of the other ones was in use at this time.

It is excusable that, for lack of intelligence, only the four main gas chambers and crematoria could have been targeted in 1944. I have found no contemporary reference to the others. One of the sketches reviewed by Foregger[79] shows Auschwitz I ("Main Camp"), but the one or two gas chambers located there are missing. Hausner[80] quotes Weizmann as saying to Eden: "Four crematoria are active daily in Auschwitz." It is inexcusable, however, that Wyman missed these essential details in 1978, although he is not alone in making this mistake. It is a remarkable fact that the entire postwar literature on the possible bombing of Auschwitz appears to contain only two papers in which the authors do not assume without discussion that Gas Chambers and Crematoria II, III, IV, and V constituted a complete list of the relevant targets. The exceptions are Kitchens and Foregger[81] (who, after covering this important ground, says without further comment that "the target was the four installations containing gas chambers and crematoria at the west end of the Birkenau camp"). An air raid destroying only the four main gas chambers and crematoria at Auschwitz II would have left intact the operating gas chamber and incineration ditch of Bunker 2/V, as well as up to four additional gas chambers divided between Auschwitz I and Auschwitz II.

This is no mere quibble. The enormous gassings of Hungarian Jews, at a rate of 10,000 or even 12,000 a day, ran from about mid-May until the abrupt termination on 8 July of the Hungarian deportations (which was known in London on 18 July). The last Hungarian transport arrived at Auschwitz on 11 July. According to Wyman,[82] gassings from 7 July until Auschwitz was closed in November amounted in all to about 150,000—that is to say, an average rate of perhaps 1,300 a day, little more than 10 percent of the previous rate. Thus, before 7 July, the killing operations were at full capacity, and even fell behind.

While improvisation was always possible, bombing Gas Chambers and Crematoria II, III, IV, and V in this period would certainly have caused some disruption. The same bombing after 7 July would scarcely have inconvenienced the murderers. The dates on which the earliest appeals to bomb the gas chambers were received were reviewed above; the first week in July can be taken as representative. How soon after the first appeals could an attack have been planned and executed?

Knowing that there was an extermination camp at Auschwitz that might be bombed was one thing; locating and identifying the gas chambers and crematoria with sufficient precision so that an air raid could be launched was quite another. Foregger[83] has analyzed in great detail the topographical information to be found in various sketches, one of which was made available to the Foreign Office on 22 August and the others published by the WRB on 7 November. These sketches differ from each other and from reality in numerous ways that would have made targeting even the four main gas chambers very doubtful. They were based on escapees' reports, but none of the escapees was available in England, and the original reports had been copied and translated into various languages by an unknown number of hands. One sketch, for example, has the camp misplaced with respect to the river Sola and is missing main-line and spur railways. According to Robert Hodges,[84] one of the escapees disowned one of the sketches supplied to, and reproduced by, Foregger. This in no way reduces the confusion. On the photographic side, pictures of Auschwitz II[85] were taken accidentally, but they could not be identified at the time for what they really were. At the very least, a special-purpose aerial reconnaissance mission would have been needed, and, even if that had been flown, it is hard to see how the exact targets could have been pinpointed without the possibility of interviewing one of the escapees. Kitchens[86] has carefully considered the matter and concluded that "it is unreasonable to think that sufficient intelligence to properly assess the Auschwitz-Birkenau buildings as targets could have been in hand before early to mid-August." Among the many other factors besides adequate intelligence that would have been necessary before the bombing mission could have been flown, one was the necessity of placing the matter before President Roosevelt for decision, after the intelligence had been gathered and feasibility determined. There never was the slightest chance that the gas chambers could have been bombed before 7 July; some time in the second half of August would have been the earliest possible time, and, in my opinion, even that is optimistic.

Even if by some miracle all of the gas chambers had been destroyed, including those whose existence was unknown, Milt Groban[87] has pointed out just how easy it would have been to improvise more. He also reminds us that at Babi Yar, the Nazis shot 33,000 Jews in just two days (29-30 September 1941). At Majdanek, on 3 November 1943, during what the SS euphemistically called a "harvest festival," 18,000 Jews were machine-gunned in front of the ditches that they had been made to dig to serve as their own graves.[88] Compare these figures with an average of 1,300 gassings a day at Auschwitz after 7 July. Albert Speer,[89] in a 1972 interview, said that if Auschwitz had been bombed, the SS would have reverted to the system of shooting-commandos, which the Einsatzgruppen had used in Russia. As if to support both Speer and Groban, but referring presumably to the period before 7 July, William Shirer[90] says that in the summer of 1944, when the rate of killing at Auschwitz resulted in the gas chambers falling behind, the SS resorted to mass shootings in the Einsatzkommando style.

At the same time, the transports also exceeded the capacity of the crematoria. To cope with the bodies:

> Oberscharführer Moll was working full steam. He employed four Jewish Sonderkommandos in four shifts, a total force of between 1500 and 2000 men. Eight pits were dug, each about four by sixty yards in size. . . . Although the corpses burned slowly during rain or misty weather, the pits were found to be the cheapest and most efficient method of body disposal.[91]

Hindsight of this kind fully supports the most skeptical opinion of the likely efficacy of bombing Auschwitz. Undeterred by the chronological facts or by the availability of alternatives, Wyman espouses a very robust view to the contrary. He says flatly: "There is no question that bombing the gas chambers and crematoria would have saved many lives."[92] However, he also offers the following:

> Without gas chambers and crematoria, the Nazis would have been forced to reassess the extermination program in light of the need to commit new and virtually non-existent manpower resources to mass killing.[93]

If Wyman had the chance to express his views in 1944, the first of these two statements would surely have been questioned. In fact, it was questioned in 1978 by Groban.[94] In response, Wyman took refuge in a disclaimer—"I did not claim that mass killing would have been impossible without Auschwitz"[95]—and pointed to the second statement above. But if mass killing was possible without Auschwitz, Wyman cannot possibly maintain that, "no question," bombing would have saved many lives. He has, therefore, effectively disavowed the first statement, and all he now claims is that the Nazis would have been forced into a reassessment. Is that the best case he could have urged upon McCloy or Roosevelt? Most observers, including Dawidowicz,[96] agree that the Nazis gave a very high priority indeed to the Final Solution, even when labor and transport were desperately short. The reassessment of which Wyman writes might, of course, have required some improvisation as the Jewish Agency suggested, but only to the extent of 10 percent of the original capacity for gassing. Wyman's 1978 disavowal of the robust view is nowhere to be found in his book, published six years later. As noted, Wyman also says that 150,000 Jews were gassed at Auschwitz after 7 July. He adds:

> If, instead, the earliest pleas for bombing the gas chambers had moved swiftly to the United States, and if they had drawn a positive and rapid response, the movement of the 437,000 Jews who were deported from Hungary to Auschwitz would most likely have been broken off and additional lives numbering in the hundreds of thousands might have been saved.[97]

Here Wyman seems to imply (the robust view again) that the 150,000 Jews gassed after 7 July would have been saved by bombing the gas chambers at that time and, furthermore, that an additional 437,000 Jews might have been saved by earlier bombing of the gas chambers. This is a new claim, and it is chronologically impossible by a wide margin.

BOMBING AUSCHWITZ: OPERATIONAL CONSIDERATIONS

Despite the serious errors already uncovered, the weakest part of Wyman's work still remains to be analyzed. This is the operational aspect of bombing the gas chambers and crematoria. Before examining Wyman's ideas on this subject, we must discuss two more details from Sinclair's letter to Eden of 15 July. Commenting on the possible use of RAF Bomber Command to bomb Auschwitz, he wrote: "Bombing the plant is out of the bounds of possibility for Bomber Command, because the distance is too great for the attack to be carried out at night."[98]

This would seem to be a final statement from the point of view of Bomber Command. The aircraft of Bomber Command, which were all based in England, were lightly armed and depended on darkness for their ability to penetrate the German defenses. The distance that could be covered during the hours of darkness, after the month of March, ruled out bombing beyond a range corresponding roughly to that of Berlin. Sinclair might well have mentioned other problems such as the absolute range (which must have been near the limit of what was then possible) or the considerable difficulty that would have attended finding such a small target in the dark. Perhaps he did not feel it necessary to offer more than one convincing reason in his letter.

Interviewed after the revelations at the Eichmann trial in 1961 on the possibility of bombing Auschwitz, Group Captain Leonard Cheshire, V. C., a highly decorated hero of RAF Bomber Command, said: "It would have had to be done by Lancasters and so would have had to be a night operation."[99] Cheshire thus excluded the use of any RAF aircraft type other than the heavy Lancaster bomber. He went on to say that "on a moonlit night, going in low, we could have bombed it accurately," but it appears that he was not aware, when making this statement, that the raid was requested only in the summer of 1944. He refers to a plan (which was not carried out) to drop Christmas presents in December 1943 to British prisoners of war in a camp near Breslau about 100 miles northwest of Auschwitz. But in a 1982 interview, in which he was clearly told that bombing Auschwitz would have taken place in the summer of 1944, he said: "You are asking a lot at this extreme range in knowing we have to get ourselves out without full cover of night—because it's summer now."[100] In both interviews, Cheshire displays a wholly admirable willingness to attempt the operation if requested or ordered, but the higher command of the RAF was simply unwilling to order missions that required flying heavy aircraft over enemy territory in daylight. Indeed, Deputy Commander-in-Chief of the Mediterranean Allied Air Force Sir John Slessor[101] was even reluctant to order missions at night except for the last and first quarters of the moon—that is, when there was little or no moonlight.

Sinclair dealt with Eden's request within the Air Ministry in London. It was unnecessary to ask questions of Bomber Command in the field. Bomber Command's available range at any season was well known at the ministry. Yet when Weizmann's request was made public in 1961, there was much surprise[102] that the head of Bomber Command, Sir Arthur Harris, had never been asked about it and knew nothing of it. Some comments made in the 1960s seem inappropriate now that Sinclair's letter has been published. In a 1962 interview,[103] Harris said that his responsibility was the tactical operation of the RAF bombers, including the selection of targets from the limited group laid down in their strategic directives—a selection that was governed almost entirely by the weather, tactical feasibility, and the extent of darkness as affecting range. Thus, Sinclair (or his advisers), Cheshire and Harris all refer to darkness as affecting the reach of Bomber Command, which was, therefore, unable to attack Auschwitz in the summer of 1944.

After ruling out the use of the RAF, Sinclair pointed out:

that an attack on Auschwitz might be carried out by the Americans by daylight, but it would be a costly and hazardous operation. It might be ineffective, and, even if the plant was destroyed, I am not clear that it would really help the victims. There is just one possibility, and that is bombing the camps, and possibly dropping weapons at the same time, in the hope that some of the victims may be able to escape. We did something of the kind in France, when we made a breach in the walls of a prison camp, and we think that 150 men who had been condemned to death managed to escape. The difficulties of doing this in Silesia are, of course, enormously greater, and, even if the camp was successfully raided, the chances of escape would be small indeed.[104]

"Something of the kind" is a reference to a raid on a prison at Amiens in February using 19 RAF Mosquito bombers. This raid,[105] which was coordinated with the French resistance, breached the walls of a small prison building and was intended to allow the escape of some members of the French resistance being held by the Gestapo for execution. It was known even when Sinclair wrote that the raid had achieved only mixed results. At Auschwitz, no local coordination was possible, and knowledge of at least some of the extremely elaborate arrangements[106] put in place by Heinrich Himmler in February 1943 to guard against mass breaks during air raids would have been available and discouraging.

Sinclair was not suggesting that Mosquitoes could be used against Auschwitz, but rather that the USAAF might employ some of the tactics that had been used by Mosquitoes over Amiens. In his 1978 article, Wyman made no mention of Amiens or Mosquitoes. Lawrence Blum,[107] however, in a 1978 letter to the editor, mentioned both and went on to say that the Mosquito was "the aircraft most capable of success." Wyman accepted this suggestion with alacrity, commenting that:

> requests for bombing the gas chambers and the deportation railways were also
> made of the British government, which, like the US government, refused
> without giving any real consideration to the proposals.[108]

This shows that Wyman cannot have read Sinclair's reasoned letter of 15 July. Following Blum's suggestion, Wyman obtained[109] a letter from the Air Historical Branch of the Ministry of Defence in London, assuring him that at least 44 Mosquitoes (and probably more) were stationed at Allied air bases in Italy in June. Thus reinforced, he wrote in his book:

> The most effective means of all for destroying the killing installations would
> have been to dispatch about twenty British Mosquitoes to Auschwitz, a

project that should have been possible to arrange with the RAF. This fast fighter-bomber had ample range for the mission, and its technique of bombing at very low altitudes had proven extremely precise.[110]

In his 1961 statement quoted above, Cheshire, who flew Mosquitoes as well as Lancasters during the war, ruled out the use of Mosquitoes for an attack on Auschwitz. Unfortunately, he did not give a detailed reason, and the subject has attracted much uninformed comment. The use of Mosquitoes for an attack on Auschwitz was also discussed by Dawidowicz,[111] Foregger,[112] Hodges[113] (who claims to have contributed to the Wyman book in the categories of aerial bombing and flak defenses), Kitchens,[114] and others. Several sound arguments against the possibility of using Mosquitoes for bombing Auschwitz are advanced, and others could be adduced. But none of these authors seems to have noticed the elementary point that, notwithstanding Wyman's blunt statement to the contrary, the Mosquito simply did not have sufficient range to bomb Auschwitz. The whole discussion is, therefore, entirely beside the point. It is likely that the Mosquito's inadequate range was the reason Cheshire flatly ruled out its use.

There were two versions of the Mosquito of interest.[115] The photo-reconnaissance version carried 760 gallons of fuel, giving it a still air range of 1,500 or 1,600 miles. It carried cameras, but neither bomb racks nor bombs. Using Italian bases, it was used for several high-altitude reconnaissance missions over Auschwitz in 1944. The bomber version had a maximum fuel load of 539 gallons "with a useful operational load" (that is, bombs) but could carry two 50-gallon drop tanks at the expense of its bomb load. This gave it a still air range of 1,430 miles but a maximum operational radius of only 535 miles. Wyman's egregious error appears to arise from failing to understand the difference between the still air range and the maximum operational radius, as the following examples will show.

An attack on a Gestapo HQ in Oslo was made in September 1942.[116] The planes refueled at Sumburgh in the Shetland Islands inbound and probably outbound, too. The distance from Sumburgh to Oslo is 415 miles, the operational track distance is given as 1,100 miles. Incidentally, John Terraine[117] says that this raid destroyed the wrong building. A raid on a Gestapo HQ in Aarhus, Denmark, on 31 October 1944 is cited by Martin Sharp and Michael Bowyer[118] and also by Hodges.[119] The distance from Mosquito bases near Norwich to Aarhus is 415 miles. The operational track distance is given as 1,235 miles. As it seems unlikely that the Mosquitoes started off any farther from their target than necessary, they must have made some considerable detours en route, perhaps for reasons of tactical surprise. A final example is the raid on Berlin,[120] about 500 miles distant, on 30 January 1943. The operational track distance averaged 1,145 miles. Sharp and Bowyer list about 200 Mosquito day-bombing raids undertaken in 1942 and 1943; not one involved a target 600 miles from base.[121] Even though all of western Austria (but not Vienna) was within 620 miles of Mosquito bases in England, 418 Squadron did not raid Austria until it began operating from St. Dizier in France on 30 September, "at last bringing Austria into [its] sphere of operations."[122] The distance from St. Dizier to Eferding, which 418 Squadron raided, is 440 miles. The distance from St. Dizier to Auschwitz is 620 miles. In contrast, as Wyman accurately states, the distance from Foggia to Auschwitz is 620 miles. The operational track distance would inevitably have been considerably greater, perhaps 1,400 miles or more. I have found no instance of a Mosquito bombing attack at this distance. On 12 October, two Mosquitoes used a newly captured airport at Iesi near Ancona in Italy to mount a raid on two airports in Czechoslovakia.[123] What facilities and armaments were available at this airport is not known, but the distance from Iesi to Auschwitz is about 500 miles, just within Mosquito bombing range. At the beginning of November, Himmler ordered the gassings at Auschwitz stopped. Yahil[124] says that the last large-scale gassing took place on 3 November. So much for Wyman's "most effective means of all" and "ample range."

Wyman also offered two other operational possibilities. He proposed that Mitchell medium bombers could have flown with one of the missions to Auschwitz.[125] The Mitchell was, by the standards of the day, unarmed and obsolescent. It was not used, in 1944, on deep-penetration daylight raids over enemy territory. The Mitchell, Wyman wrote, could have "hit with surer accuracy from lower altitudes." The heavy bombers, he added, bombed from twenty thousand to twenty-six thousand feet, and "complete accuracy was rarely possible from such heights." Why does he think they stayed so high, if it affected their accuracy? Could it have been the flak, deadly at "lower altitudes"? Were the Mitchells immune to flak?

Wyman also stated that an even more precise alternative would have been to use P-38s: "A few Lightning (P-38) dive-bombers could have knocked out the murder buildings without danger to the inmates at Birkenau."[126]

His basis for this belief is that some P-38s were used as dive-bombers in a raid against Ploesti on 10 June. On this raid, say Craven and Cate,[127] 36 P-38s were used as dive-bombers, and a further 39 as escorts. Of 75 planes, 23 were lost. Do 75 planes constitute more or less than "a few"? Three refineries received partial damage, and the experiment was not repeated. The refineries were much larger than the proposed targets at Birkenau. Wyman gives the distance for this mission as 1,255 miles, but the straight-line distance from Brindisi to Ploesti is 515 miles. This may well indicate yet more confusion between straight line and operational track distances. However, Wyman's sudden concern for the inmates does him credit.

Wyman's discussion of the German defenses is bizarre. Enemy fighter opposition was negligible, he says; while it certainly varied from day to day and from place to place, the claim that it was negligible in the period of interest is flagrantly inaccurate. Groban[128] and Kitchens[129] discuss the subject carefully, and a graphic instance is recorded by Sharp and Bowyer,[130] who describe a photo-reconnaissance mission from Italy on 15 August that was intercepted by a Nazi Me 262 jet fighter.

Taking a broader view of the foregoing, it can be seen that, 40 years later, Wyman has come up with three innovative techniques (Mosquito bombers, Mitchell bombers at moderate altitudes, P-38s) by means of which very small targets deep in enemy-controlled territory could have been destroyed by bombing, using the weapons available to the Allies in 1944. While the gas chambers and crematoria at Auschwitz surely constituted one such target, it could hardly have been the only one worthy of attention. If Wyman's innovative techniques make sense, it is much to be regretted that the Air Force commanders of the day did not have access to his counsel or think of his ideas themselves. The war might have been significantly shortened thereby.

BOMBING AUSCHWITZ: FURTHER OPERATIONAL CONSIDERATIONS

There was, in fact, just one way in which the Allies could have destroyed the killing installations at Auschwitz. It was the same one available for the destruction of the industrial installations in Auschwitz—namely, the use of the heavy bombers of the United States Fifteenth Air Force, based in Italy, with fighter escorts, for good-weather daylight raids. Such a raid might have been undertaken in combination with a raid on the nearby industries, but it would have required the detailing of a certain number of the bombers to drop their bombs on the gas chambers and crematoria. The number would have to have been such as to give an adequate probability of achieving the desired destruction, while bombing from the usual high altitudes even though, as Wyman says, "complete accuracy was rarely possible from such heights."[131] Groban[132] describes the techniques in use at the time; it would not be unfair to describe them as plastering the targets with bombs.

With the clear understanding that a second raid might be required if subsequent photo reconnaissance so indicated, a very rough estimate of the number of bombs required can be made as follows: The fraction of the bombs dropped by the Fifteenth Air Force that fell within one thousand feet of the target grew from 32 percent in June to 50 percent in August.[133] From Gilbert's layout of Birkenau, the gas chambers and crematoria numbered II to V each occupied about thirty-five thousand square feet.[134] This is roughly 1 percent of the area of the circle one thousand feet in radius within which half of the bombs fell. Thus it would have required 200 bombs to obtain a good probability of at least one direct hit. The buildings were of solid construction, and the gas chambers were largely underground,[135] suggesting that 500-pound bombs would be required. If one direct hit was enough, about 50 tons of bombs would have been required to put out of action each gas chamber and its associated crematorium. Although there were more, the available intelligence pointed to only four gas chambers and crematoria, numbered II, III, IV, and V, suggesting 200 tons of bombs in all. Gas Chambers IV and V were only 500 feet apart, so some reduction might have been possible. (Gas Chamber I was in a different camp entirely,[136] known as Auschwitz I ("Main Camp"). There were also other gas chambers at Auschwitz II. The mere existence of these other gas chambers, to say nothing of their exact locations, was not known at the time.) The synthetic-oil plant at Auschwitz absorbed 1,336 500-pound bombs (300 tons in all) on 20 August. The intelligence report[137] on the results of this raid was disappointing. It said: "The damage received is not sufficient to interfere seriously with synthetic fuel production, and should not greatly delay completion of this part of the plant." A further raid was judged necessary, and 235 tons were dropped on the same plant on 13 September.[138] Bombing the gas chambers would have diverted resources equivalent to one or both of these raids. This estimate substantially agrees with Kitchens,[139] and if this seems high, it will help to remember that essentially the same calculation would apply to a railway bridge or any other small target. Perhaps this is why heavy bombers were not used against such targets. Nahum Goldmann's (Zionist Emergency Council) estimate[140] of a few dozen bombs is far too low.

As a final note, it is worth thinking about the fact that if 200 tons of bombs had been aimed at the four gas chambers numbered II to V, about 100 tons would have landed more than one thousand feet away from them. A glance at the layout provided by Gilbert[141] suggests that many of the huts housing the inmates would have been hit. Recalling how crowded these huts were, there can be no doubt that many inmates would have been killed or injured. Kitchens[142] gives a version of Gilbert's layout, with typical bombing accuracies overlaid; his shaded areas of various sizes show the areas within which one-half of the bombs could be expected to fall, the other half being scattered outside. Without detailed technical information, this was why Kubowitzki and all of Gruenbaum's colleagues objected to the whole idea, and it is why Field Marshal Sir John Dill worried about the deaths of "thousands of prisoners."[143] Foregger[144] quotes weapons analyst P. M. Sprey, who estimates that 135 bombers delivering 1,350 500-pound bombs would have destroyed half the targets, while a third of the bombs would have hit the prisoner barracks area; that bombs would have fallen on the railway spur line where hundreds of freight cars packed with prisoners sometimes sat; and that bombs would have fallen into the "Canada" storage warehouse where prisoners worked. Roger Williams's 1978 estimate[145] of "perhaps dozens" of inmate deaths is far too low. The question plainly worried Wyman, too, as he favored the P-38s solely on the grounds of diminished danger to the inmates.[146] But he did not say how many thousands of inmate deaths would have been acceptable to him in such a raid.

After the war, some survivors (including one[147] who was an inmate in the Gypsy camp, only 600 feet from one of the crematoria) indicated with great feeling that they wished the camp had been bombed. Paradoxically, we probably owe our knowledge of this opinion to the fact that it was not. In any event, as this opinion could not have been known at the time in London, Washington, or Jerusalem, it seems very hard to castigate the participants in the debate (Kubowitzki and all of Gruenbaum's colleagues, for instance) for not wishing to accept the responsibility of assuming it.

To end this account of the operational factors relating to the bombing of Auschwitz, we note that some authors believe that the other extermination camps operated by the Nazis should also have been bombed. This was never possible inasmuch as Kulmhof (Chelmno), Belzec, Sobibor, Majdanek (Lublin), and Treblinka had all effectively ceased operation before the end of 1943—that is, before the Fifteenth Air Force was established at Foggia. In any event, the effective range of both the Fifteenth in Italy and the Eighth in England was limited by the range of the fighters that escorted the bombers to and from the target. These fighters could not reach Warsaw from either base, showing that the other death camps could not have been bombed in 1943 or 1944. Russian cooperation, which was grudgingly given in one instance (see chapter XI), would have altered this situation. Given these facts, the state of Allied intelligence concerning the other camps is hardly relevant. It is presumably coincidental that in 1944 the Nazis concentrated their killing operations in Auschwitz, the only one of the extermination camps within operational range of the USAAF.

BOMBING AUSCHWITZ: COMMAND CONSIDERATIONS

Wyman clearly believes that the failure to bomb Auschwitz or its railways was a culpable error, yet he is somewhat coy on the subject of who precisely was to blame. His favorite target would appear to be McCloy. Yet, as we have seen, McCloy was not in the chain of command and had no authority to order any actual operations.

Although McCloy was undoubtedly a man of considerable influence, his claim (in an interview after the war) that only the president could order such an operation— "I couldn't order a soldier from 'A' to 'B'"—is entirely accurate.[148] In a letter to the editor of *Commentary*,[149] Aaron Lerner sums the situation up very well: Wyman has told a story without including the main characters. Lerner asks why Roosevelt was mentioned only in passing. To fill the gap in Wyman's narrative, the chain-of-command issue needs to be reviewed.

The Fifteenth Air Force, based in Italy, was, as we have seen, the only weapon capable of striking at Auschwitz. At the time in question, the chain of command for the Fifteenth Air Force ran from its commander, General Ira C. Eaker, through General Carl Spaatz, commander in chief of the United States Strategic Air Forces in Europe, to General Eisenhower, the supreme commander. General Eisenhower received broad directives from the combined Chiefs of Staff, sitting as a committee, but was subject to direct operational orders only from the commander in chief, President Roosevelt.

At what level in this chain might an order have been issued for the highly political operations favored by Wyman? Eaker was far too low down to contemplate such a thing on his own authority. We have an interesting example[150] from the end of June (with the Allies struggling in the Normandy beachhead) that shows how much latitude Spaatz and Eisenhower thought they had over the choice of bombing targets. Spaatz was concerned about what he saw as numerous mistaken diversions that were imposed on his bombers, but he obeyed orders. Referring to the weather over Germany, he requested Eisenhower to release his bombers from operations against the V-1 launching sites in France ". . . on the few days which are favorable over Germany." In reply, Eisenhower directed his deputy to inform Spaatz that the priority for attacks on the launching sites would have to stand regardless of the weather over Germany. This exchange shows just how little latitude Spaatz had in targeting his bombers, and how little variation from agreed aims Eisenhower was willing to permit.[151]

It remains, therefore, to consider the role of Roosevelt himself; the proposal to use large military forces for a political operation belonged properly on his desk and nowhere else. In his book, Wyman cites an exhaustive search by *Washington Post* reporter Morton Mintz in 1983, which showed that the bombing proposals almost certainly did not reach Roosevelt. Wyman does, however, cite one letter[152] of 24 July to Roosevelt (from the Emergency Committee to Save the Jewish People of Europe) calling for bombing the deportation railways and the gas chambers. Nothing came of this overture. Roosevelt, without whose approval the operation could never have taken place, was never pressed. The problem was surely not one of access.

Azkin[153] of the WRB was one of the few who seems to have understood the chain-of-command problem. Better late than never, he urged WRB Executive Director Pehle on 2 September to go directly to Roosevelt with the proposal. Pehle did not do this. We are not told why; it might have been the natural disinclination of a civil servant to go outside the normal chain of command, which tied him to McCloy in the War Department. But then again, perhaps Pehle still had the doubts he had expressed on 24 June, and did not feel able to urge the operation in unequivocal terms.

If McCloy is to be faulted, his fault must lie in having failed to go to the president himself. If his judgment was wrong in this respect, however, the omission need not have been fatal to the operation, as many other people and organizations had access to the president and could have urged it on him. In fact, the operation would have had the best chance of being carried out if, as happened in London, it had descended from the political to the military level with an accompanying expression of enthusiasm qualified only by concern about its feasibility.

Among those who could have addressed the president were all of those who had urged him to create the WRB. Perhaps the very creation of this nonmilitary organization made it harder for them to go around it on the bombing question. With the head of its Rescue Committee, Kubowitzki, opposed to the bombing, however, the World Jewish Congress could hardly have joined such a lobbying effort.

The Jewish Agency in Jerusalem sent two telegrams to Roosevelt[154] on 11 July, once again using the facilities of the consul-general, Pinkerton. The proposal to bomb Auschwitz was being most actively considered at just this moment, and the Jewish Agency was anxious for action from President Roosevelt. But the action it desired had nothing to do with bombing Auschwitz or its railways, for these topics were not even mentioned in either telegram. The Jewish Agency wanted Roosevelt to approve negotiations with the SS concerning ransom payments for Hungarian Jewish lives. The lack of interest in the proposal to bomb Auschwitz exhibited by the Jewish Agency in Jerusalem was entirely consistent with the position taken earlier by its Rescue Committee. But the fact that the telegrams were addressed directly to President Roosevelt shows that the Jewish Agency in Jerusalem knew perfectly well which decisions were outside the authority of the WRB. It is just coincidental that the telegrams to Roosevelt were sent on the same day that the Jewish Agency in London prepared its rather discouraging note on the proposal to bomb Auschwitz.

Finally, Churchill might have addressed himself directly to Roosevelt, as he did later in a somewhat similar situation. We have seen that he took a favorable view of the operation, if it were feasible, on 7 July. But Sinclair's finding that the operations were impossible for the RAF but might be possible for the USAAF does not seem to have reached Churchill, and he played no further part in the matter.

Sinclair's finding, however, did lead to another way in which the proposals reached Spaatz and might conceivably have been forwarded to Roosevelt though, in fact, they were not. The circumstances were as follows: Neither the Jewish Agency in Jerusalem (for reasons of policy) nor Weizmann in London (for unknown reasons) ever requested the Americans to bomb Auschwitz. But Weizmann's request to the British did reach Sinclair, who concluded his letter to Eden of 15 July by writing:

> Nevertheless, I am proposing to have the proposition put to the Americans, with all the facts, to see if they are prepared to try it. I am very doubtful indeed whether, when they have examined it, the Americans will think it possible, and I do not wish to raise any hopes. . . . [155]

Sinclair was as good as his word, and on 26 July it was reported[156] that the matter was to be raised with Spaatz "when he is next in the Air Ministry." After this was done, apparently on 2 August, Spaatz was reported to have been "most sympathetic." It is unlikely that the geographical information given to Spaatz at that time went beyond what was contained in Eden's letter of 7 July to Sinclair— namely, the words "death camps at Birkenau in Upper Silesia." Weizmann and Shertok evidently did not spontaneously offer whatever precise details on the "death camps at Birkenau" they may have had on 6 July when they placed their bombing requests before Eden, or at any later time. As previously noted, for instance, the Jewish Agency note of 11 July refers to a detailed description of the two camps (Birkenau and Auschwitz) in a report emanating from Czech underground sources, a report "received since the original suggestion for bombing was made." The note states that the report is attached. Yet there is no indication that the note, with or without its attached report, was ever delivered to the British. Did it not occur to Weizmann, a scientist by training, that before Auschwitz could be bombed more intelligence than "death camps at Birkenau in Upper Silesia" would be needed? In the circumstances, the proposal was placed before Spaatz with almost no supporting detail, and it was entirely natural for him to ask the British to provide the additional intelligence without which a "most sympathetic" attitude could not possibly have been turned into a military operation. It is, therefore, no surprise to find out that on 3 August the chairman of the Joint Intelligence Committee, William Cavendish-Bentinck, noted:

> The Air Staff are anxious to obtain more precise details regarding the locality of this "death camp" at Birkenau. It may be within ten miles or more of that

place. Unless the Air Staff can be given an exact pinpoint of this camp the airmen will experience difficulty in finding it.[157]

If the chairman knew that the air staff wanted this intelligence in order to assist with the evaluation of an American operation (a British one having been ruled out on solid technical grounds since 15 July), he did not say so in his note. Subsequently, several British bureaucrats dealt with the matter. The memoranda that they left behind show clearly that they wrongly assumed that a British operation was contemplated. Writing long after the war, Wasserstein[158] and Gilbert[159] both missed this error. Wasserstein, in particular, assumes that a British operation was still being contemplated and was undermined by these bureaucrats, who in the event sidetracked Spaatz's request in a highly discreditable manner.

The intelligence available in London at that time, if it had been spontaneously supplied by Weizmann or Shertok, or if it had been obtained by the British bureaucrats, was not in good shape. Foregger[160] has shown in considerable detail just how confusing and inaccurate it was.

As a result of bungling by the Jewish Agency as well as by the British civil service, Spaatz never received such intelligence as was available. But if he had received the intelligence he wanted, and if his staff had succeeded in interpreting it, the most that could have happened was that, in mid- or late August, the proposal to bomb Auschwitz would have gone from him to Eisenhower and from Eisenhower to Roosevelt. It would likely have carried a sympathetic note and a negative recommendation.

There was thus no shortage of people who could have placed these matters before Roosevelt, where they properly belonged. But there was a critical shortage of people (Jews and non-Jews, civilian and military) who believed in the proposed operations with sufficient passion to see that they were, in fact, considered by the president.

OPERATIONS UNDERTAKEN IN THE RELIEF OF WARSAW

Operations were undertaken by both the RAF and the USAAF in August and September in a vain attempt to relieve the Polish Home Army, which had risen against the Nazis in Warsaw. The Red Army was already at the Vistula, but Stalin was apparently quite content to watch as the Nazis and the non-Communist Poles killed each other. These air force operations have been cited by Wyman[161] and many others as examples of what should have been done at

Auschwitz. There is, indeed, a rough parallel, but both the operational and the political details need to be examined.

The first operational point to note is that Warsaw and Auschwitz were both in Poland, Warsaw being 200 miles farther away from the Italian bases. The RAF[162] had only a relatively small number of planes capable of flying with useful loads from their bases in Italy to Warsaw. Some were, nevertheless, sent. Their mission was to drop supplies to the Home Army. Usually this involved prearranged dropping zones marked by light signals in open country behind the lines. Missing the target by half a mile on such missions would hardly have mattered. All of the missions took place at night, and even so Slessor was concerned not to send his planes out except in the last or first quarter of the moon, fearing attacks by German night fighters. By contrast, a night attack on Auschwitz would have been extremely difficult. Missing the targets by more than about 20 yards would have amounted to total failure. Finding the blacked-out extermination camp on a dark night would have been considered extremely difficult if not impossible. Herbert Loebel[163] writes that, in fact, the crematoria, going full blast, emitted bright red fiery plumes that might have been visible at night from 75 miles away. But Wasserstein notes:

> The danger of an air attack on Auschwitz later led to a cessation of the burning of bodies in open trenches at night as a consequence of protests by anti-aircraft units at the camp.[164]

Dino Brugioni and Robert Poirier[165] examined aerial reconnaissance photographs taken on 4 April, 26 June (on which date the massive gassings of the Hungarian Jews were under way), 26 July, 25 August, and 13 September and found no indication of smoke or flames emanating from the crematoria chimneys. Pressac[166] considers that the smoke and flames were not present at all times and that the absence of smoke or flames in the aerial photographs of 26 June, 25 August, and 13 September is coincidental, in that all three dates corresponded to temporary lulls in the activity. In any event, nothing was known on this subject where it counted, and, even if the chimneys had been emitting smoke and flame, it would still have been a very difficult job to strike them with the required precision. RAF operations to Warsaw cost 31 heavy bombers out of 181, and, according to Deputy Commander-in-Chief of the Mediterranean Allied Air Force Sir John Slessor, "achieved practically nothing."[167]

The bombers of the USAAF (which did not conduct night operations) could reach Warsaw from either Italy or England, but the escorting fighters, considered essential, could not. Before the USAAF could be employed, it was, therefore, necessary to make arrangements to refuel the bombers and fighters in territory controlled by the Russians. The Russians did not hurry to agree to such arrangements, but they were finally made, and the USAAF mounted an operation from England on 18 September. This operation was not expensive in terms of bombers lost, though it did tie up a considerable fleet for some time. Like the RAF operations before it, it "achieved practically nothing."

Another important distinction between the operations in relief of the Poles and the proposed bombing of the gas chambers and crematoria at Auschwitz was that the former in no way endangered the lives of those it was intended to help. Thus, there were no serious objections similar to those of Kubowitzki and Gruenbaum's colleagues to overcome.

The Warsaw operation is also of interest politically. Churchill[168] was pressed most vigorously by the Poles to help out, and he felt a strong impulse to assist. Warned that the RAF could accomplish very little, he nevertheless ordered it to make the attempt, and the RAF naturally obeyed orders. Told that the USAAF could do more, Churchill then persuaded Roosevelt to approve operations. (He didn't address Spaatz or Eisenhower. This was a political matter). Spaatz offered his advice:

> Notwithstanding the humanitarian aspects of the problem in Warsaw, it was clear to Spaatz and his staff that aerial delivery did not offer much promise of real relief to the Poles. . . . He was quite sure that the drops could never be massive enough or accurate enough to save the Poles.[169]

His biographer continues: "Once Spaatz had passed on information about the operational feasibility of the Warsaw airlift missions and his political superiors had ordered them to be carried out . . . ," which gives the reader a clear insight into the workings of the chain of command at this level and for this kind of operation.

Just as in the case of the Warsaw operation, Churchill also favored using the RAF to relieve Auschwitz if this was at all possible. He noted on 7 July: "Get anything out of the Air Force you can." For somewhat similar technical reasons, it turned out that the RAF was unable to do anything, but that the USAAF did have applicable capabilities. Here, however, the stories diverge, as Churchill never seems to have been informed of these facts and did not return to the subject. Had he known, would he have vigorously urged Roosevelt to intervene as he did in August on behalf of the Poles? We can never know for sure, but two facts may bear on the question. First, the general war situation was much less tense in August than it was in July, with the Normandy victory and the liberation of Paris and most of France in the past. Second, the only organization to have raised the question of bombing Auschwitz with the British was Weizmann's Jewish Agency. Relations between Weizmann and Churchill were cordial, and contacts between the Jewish Agency and the British government were frequent. But the question of bombing Auschwitz was at no time vigorously pressed by the Jewish Agency. The agency had another agenda, and Weizmann (unlike Wyman) thought that bombing Auschwitz would have little practical value.

PRE- AND POST-WYMAN
REFERENCES TO THE BOMBING ISSUE

In the vast literature dealing with the Holocaust, a very large number of the most respected authors have touched upon the subject of the bombing of Auschwitz and its railways. The following review will bring out the sorry fact that, without exception, all of these authors have seriously misrepresented the facts. To simplify the review, it will be helpful to start by listing the errors into which all of them have, in one way or another, fallen.

1. **Chronology.** Regardless of its practicability, the proposal to bomb the Hungarian railways was never brought to the attention of political and military circles in the West at any time before the use of these railways for deportations was practically over. Regardless of its efficacy, the proposal to bomb Auschwitz could not have been executed until mid- to late August, at least a month after the rate of killing had been drastically reduced by the ending of the Hungarian deportations.

2. **Contemporary opinion.** The wide array of contemporary Jewish opinion that, for one reason or another, argued against bombing Auschwitz, is for the most part ignored. Contemporary opinion in favor of bombing Auschwitz is frequently referred to, but citations are either misrepresented or totally lacking.

3. **Operational aspects.** An amazing collection of ignorant statements about bomber operations is offered, and illogical parallels with entirely different operations are put forward.

4. **Efficacy.** The postwar writings (as opposed to the contemporary voices) exhibit a wholly unjustified degree of certainty about what would have happened had Auschwitz been bombed. This covers both the immediate effects of an air raid and the likely Nazi actions following an attack.

5. **Innuendo.** In too many cases, questions of chronology, contemporary opinion, operational aspects, and efficacy are ignored, while odious

interpretations are offered tending to spread the guilt for the murders at Auschwitz beyond the murderers to the Allies.

With this preamble, we shall now look briefly at some representative examples. The only author I have found who refers to the nonbombing of the Hungarian railways before the publication in 1961 of Weizmann's papers at the Eichmann trial is Hilberg[170] (1961), who gives the subject a quarter of a page in a very long book. With no reference whatsoever to the efficacy of railway bombing, he concludes, "From the Allies, however, there was no response." Hilberg could claim that, when he wrote, the responses of the Allies were not yet a matter of public record.

One short newspaper article and several books published after the Eichmann trial use the material released there. The authors do not appear to have used the British documents on the subject, presumably because they were not available in time. The influence of the Weizmann papers shows clearly in that all of these authors discuss the omissions of the British with little or no reference to the Americans. The short article by S. B. Unsdorfer[171] appeared in 1962, while the books include Hausner[172] (1967), George Steiner[173] (1967), Eban,[174] (1968) and Katz[175] (1968). Unsdorfer's article is uniquely poignant in that he himself was at Auschwitz. It is also remarkable in that the author manages, in a narrow space, to make every one of the errors that have so badly marred all subsequent consideration of the matter. He associates the proposed bombing of Auschwitz with the period when "every single day 13,000 of your brothers are being led to their death." He makes no reference to contemporary Jewish opinion, although Weizmann's view ("little practical value") was available to him. He thinks that because "the guns of the guards in the watch-towers were directed towards the inside of the camp, not above it or beyond it, the camp could have been bombed easily by day or by night." If Auschwitz had been bombed, he says, "One thing is certain: a mass of nearly 200,000 inmates would have rushed the gates. No power on earth could have halted this human stampede." Unsdorfer's certainty cannot possibly be reconciled with the precautions taken by Himmler in February 1943 against just such a mass break. As one example, Himmler ordered that each camp should be divided into blocks, four thousand inmates per block, each block to be fenced in with barbed wire. Hilberg[176] says that this and the many other precautions ordered by Himmler were put into effect. Unsdorfer concludes with innuendo directed at the "leaders of the West" who, had they "only taken the trouble to give some real thought to the Jewish tragedy . . . could and would have found a way to help."

Hausner, the lawyer who prosecuted Eichmann, states: "The Jewish representatives repeatedly urged this course [i.e., bombing the extermination camps and the railway lines leading to them] in London, Washington and Moscow," but he cites only Weizmann. Hausner quotes some of the reasons in favor of bombing offered in Weizmann's note of 11 July, but he never tells his readers that Weizmann started by disclaiming much practical value for the bombing, whose main purpose would have been to achieve a "moral effect." He makes no mention of the considerable Jewish opposition to bombing the camps. He mentions Kubowitzki without indicating that he was opposed to bombing the camps.

Steiner, who wrote literary criticism, has seen fit to address the questions of bombing Auschwitz and its railways in a book otherwise devoted to problems of language and literature. He refers to the raid on Amiens in elegant language: ". . . as Mosquitoes, flying low, had broken wide a prison in France to liberate agents of the marquis." He has not worried himself about whether Mosquitoes could reach Auschwitz. His chronology exhibits the usual error, as he wishes the gas chambers had been bombed when nine thousand or ten thousand Jews were being exterminated each day. Then he asks "just when did the names Belsen, Auschwitz, Treblinka first turn up in Allied intelligence files?" But he doesn't answer his own question, preferring to jump straight to political conclusions. He does not appear to be aware of the Jewish opposition to bombing Auschwitz. The Jewish casualties that would have been caused by the bombing of Auschwitz are always justified by the necessity of destroying the gas chambers and crematoria. Horrifying as it was, the camp at Belsen had no such facilities, and I believe that Steiner is alone in suggesting that it, too, should have been bombed.

Eban quotes fairly from the Jewish Agency note of 11 July, ascribing it to Weizmann, but implies that the message in this note was transmitted to the Foreign Office. He reports that the request was rejected by the RAF "for technical reasons." His use of quotation marks suggests that he doubts the validity of these reasons and, assuming with no cited evidence that they were invalid, he draws broad and unfavorable conclusions about British policy. Like Hausner and Steiner, he does not appear to be aware of the Jewish opposition to bombing Auschwitz.

Katz makes the usual chronological error, mentions Weizmann's appeal without referring to Weizmann's doubts about the practical value of bombing Auschwitz, and, like Eban, uses quotation marks to imply doubts about the technical difficulties alleged by the British. He provides a map that is supposed to prove that trains from Budapest to Auschwitz could use only one particular routing; even Wyman thought that two routes were possible. He also makes much of the effort to relieve Warsaw.

Feingold[177] gave a brief discussion of the bombing question in his 1970 book. It was hoped, he says, that bombing the Hungarian railways might disrupt the fragile rail coordination required to get masses of people to Auschwitz, but he does not mention the highly relevant contemporary views on the likely efficacy of such bombing. Following Hilberg, he does say that the several air raids on Budapest during the last weeks of June caused the Budapest regime to frighten itself to death, but he cannot manage to credit these raids with having at the very least contributed to the ending of the deportations. He says that Kubowitzki joined in an attempt to convince McCloy of the need for "such bombing." What bombing? He seems to be referring to the bombing of Auschwitz, which Kubowitzki opposed. Then he adopts Weizmann's line and argues that bombing Auschwitz would have had a useful propaganda effect. But bombing for this purpose never seems to have been urged on either the American or the British governments. Finally, he believes that advantages would have been obtained if the contemporary raids against German cities were specifically identified as retaliation for Auschwitz. I do not believe that this course of action was ever seriously proposed.

Herbert Druks's comments on the subject[178] (1977) are just as confused. He says Weizmann believed that if the railways and camps were bombed, deportations and exterminations would be slowed down, if not stopped altogether. Did Weizmann really believe that the exterminations might be stopped altogether by bombing? No other author has made such an assertion. Druks then takes serious objection to the fact that a number of quite fantastic propositions were not carried out. These include propositions that: Allied parachutists (from Italy, it appears) liberate the camps; the Polish Home Army attack the camps and rescue the victims; the Russians be asked to dispatch paratroopers (did they ever conduct an airborne operation?) to seize the buildings and free the inmates; the Russians bomb the Hungarian railways (what sort of bomber force did the Russians have?). The desperation of those who made these requests at the time is understandable, but Druks's interpretation of the rejection of these far-fetched demands is not. Then he turns to British claims of technical difficulties and dismisses them by pointing to a number of unrelated military operations that were possible.

Wasserstein[179] in a 1979 book devotes 14 pages to the subject of bombing and has clearly studied the British sources on the subject. His conclusions are marred by his failure to recognize that, after the bombing of Auschwitz by the RAF was ruled out on solid technical grounds by Sinclair on 15 July, all subsequent British discussion of the subject was directed (unknown to the participants) to obtaining intelligence that could assist Spaatz in his evaluation of a possible American operation. Thus, the result cannot be seen as, in Wasserstein's words, "a striking testimony to the ability of the British civil service to overturn ministerial decisions."[180] British ministers could hardly decide upon USAAF operations. Wasserstein criticizes a Foreign Office communication based on the fact that the Hungarian deportations had stopped, but he quotes without criticism a section of the Jewish Agency note of 11 July that is similarly concerned only with the Hungarians. Finally, he refers to the moral significance of a raid on Auschwitz, as urged by Weizmann and Shertok. However, I doubt that an air raid on Auschwitz, which was expected to have little practical value but whose main purpose was to be its moral effect, was ever urged by Weizmann and Shertok upon the British government, which certainly never gave it serious consideration. So far as I am aware, such a raid was never at any time urged by anyone upon the American government.

After the publication of Wyman's article in 1978, references to the bombing are much more plentiful. First off the mark, in November 1978, was Roger Williams,[181] who does not refer to Wyman and may have written on the subject independently. Williams first tells us that Kubowitzki requested bombing or other military action, then that he actively opposed bombing the camps. He says, possibly quoting McCloy, that Rabbi Stephen Wise and Nahum Goldmann may have asked Roosevelt to order the bombing of Auschwitz. But Goldmann wrote to Gilbert[182] in 1980, saying that he remembered discussing the matter with McCloy and with Field Marshal Dill; it doesn't seem likely that Goldmann would have remembered these two interviews and forgotten one with the president of the United States on the same subject. Williams estimates without foundation, and then justifies, "perhaps dozens" of inmate deaths if Auschwitz had been bombed. He thinks that with Auschwitz inoperable, "the Führer might have neglected to take alternate steps needed to get the killing done." Then, like Wyman, Williams jumps from "might" to "would," saying that "if any of the suggested targets had been bombed, some and perhaps many lives would ultimately have been saved."

Yehuda Bauer[183] (1981) writes:

> The demand was also put forward—by Isaac Gruenbaum of JA and by Isaac Sternbuch of VH, both on June 2—to bomb Auschwitz and/or the railway lines leading to it. Others picked up the idea and it was presented to the western governments. The Americans rejected it on July 4 and the British followed on September 1, both arguing that there would be technical difficulties and that the diversion of the war effort to that particular mission could not be justified. That the Americans nevertheless bombed part of the Auschwitz complex in September and flew over and attacked other targets in the general area of Upper Silesia in July, August, and September was due to the presence there of the Buna artificial rubber factory and other military targets. It was very important to destroy the German capacity for making war goods; it was apparently less important to hamper their capacity for producing corpses.

Bauer casts aspersions on the Americans for failing to bomb the death camps and at the same time refers to Gruenbaum's correspondence (from which we learn that all of the members of the Executive of the Jewish Agency except Gruenbaum himself opposed bombing the death camps). Perhaps Bauer is telling us that hampering the German capacity for producing corpses was also not the top priority of the Executive of the Jewish Agency.

Also in 1981, Gilbert[184] produced an excellent chronology of the period, with much interesting documentation. On the whole, Gilbert refrains from making judgments and allows the facts to speak for themselves. But Gilbert, like Wasserstein, has missed the point that much British official discussion of the topic took place long after the use of the RAF had been ruled out and dealt only with obtaining intelligence information for Spaatz's consideration.

Randolph Braham[185] says, with no supporting analysis, that the reasons given by the British and the Americans for not bombing either the Hungarian railways or Auschwitz were "spurious" and "aimed to camouflage the Allies' resolve not to be deterred by considerations of morality in the pursuit of their national interests." He cites the aerial photographs of Auschwitz that were obtained at the time, without bothering to inform his readers that these photographs were not interpreted until 1979.

Monty Penkower[186] reports on Gruenbaum's meeting with Pinkerton, the U.S. consul-general in Jerusalem. He merely tells his readers that Pinkerton refused to transmit to Washington Gruenbaum's request to bomb the death camps. He does not tell his readers that Pinkerton's refusal was conditional, or that the condition was that the request be made in writing, or that Gruenbaum's colleagues refused to countenance any such request. He mentions a demand by the editor of the *Jewish Forum* that the Allies should bomb Budapest. The date of this demand was 2 July. He does not mention the fact that 712 American bombers bombed Budapest on 2 July, which just might have had something to do with the ending of the deportations.

Norman Rose[187] mentions the bombing issue in his biography of Weizmann. It is clear that Rose has read the Jewish Agency note of 11 July, and that he believes the note reflected the views of Weizmann and Shertok. But his version of the events is misleading. For example, if the Zionists believed that the main purpose of bombing Auschwitz was to have been its moral effect, why did they not say this to Eden? Rose should explain what could possibly be specious about the rejection of the railway bombing request at a time when the deportations were known to have ceased. And if, as he asserts, the British claims of "technical difficulties" were examined and found to be of "highly dubious validity," a citation would be helpful.

Michael Marrus,[188] writing in 1987, repeats Wasserstein's mistaken views about why the RAF did not bomb Auschwitz and explicitly follows Wyman's account of the American failure to bomb. He fails to note the critical operational differences between the operations undertaken in support of the Warsaw Poles and the proposed operation to bomb Auschwitz. But Marrus is redeemed by the attention he gives, in a short passage, to the facts that Kubowitzki opposed the bombing, that Weizmann and Shertok did not accord particular importance to the project, and that Shertok thought that it would achieve little practically, in the sense of saving lives. He notes that when Weizmann lunched with Churchill on 4 November, he did not even mention the request to bomb Auschwitz, concentrating instead on pressing Britain for a Jewish state.

Raphael Medoff[189] tells us that as late as the end of November, Kubowitzki's ideas on what to do about Auschwitz were that it should be attacked in force either by the underground or by Allied paratroopers. Thus, Kubowitzki does not appear to have changed his mind and favored bombing even at that late date.

Until 1987 there seems to have been nothing in print criticizing Wyman's view of the nonbombing of Auschwitz from a technical point of view. Authors writing after this date might have referred to Foregger,[190] but few of them can have been regular readers of *Aerospace Historian*.

Michael Berenbaum,[191] in a very thoughtful essay on a much broader topic, scatters unsupported remarks about the bombing—for example, "Bombs dropped everywhere but at Auschwitz." He badly misquotes McCloy's letter of 14 August and makes the usual chronological error. He also omits the fact that McCloy's letter was written to Kubowitzki, a known opponent of bombing the camps.

Yahil[192] devotes two pages of a long book on the Holocaust to the bombing question. In a single paragraph, she includes the Berne telegrams with their bombing threats (intercepted by German intelligence, she says), the heavy air raid of 2 July on Budapest (though wrongly including the British in this American operation), and the order from Miklos Horthy (Regent of Hungary 1919-1944, forced to abdicate to the Germans in October 1944) halting the deportations. Her summary combination of these events possibly implies a belief that they were connected. Gruenbaum's railway bombing appeal of 2 June is mentioned, but she says without a single citation that this and subsequent appeals to bomb the extermination camps continued "relentlessly" until October. This hardly does justice to the opposition from Kubowitzki and from Gruenbaum's colleagues, among others. The aim of bombing the gas chambers was to halt their operation, but she makes no mention of the Jewish Agency's 11 July opinion of the likely efficacy and main purpose of bombing Auschwitz: little practical value, but a moral effect. She is wrong in saying that British planes bombed Warsaw in support of the Polish uprising. She quotes Wyman's political reasons for the lack of action by the American military and says that the British failed to act for similar reasons. Thus, with almost no mention of the question of feasibility and none of the questions of efficacy or propriety, she draws broad political conclusions from the failure to bomb.

Brecher[193] (1990) is concerned with a rather general attack on Wyman's historiography, but he does make some remarks about the bombing question. He makes a wholly justified attack on Wyman's shallow approach to the military dimensions of the problem, but he is wrong when he says that the bombers that raided Buna were not escorted by fighters.

Comment on the bombing issue can even be found in a book by Alan Dershowitz,[194] who explicitly acknowledges his debt to Wyman. Dershowitz is a lawyer, not a historian. His talent for raising the temperature of debate is not matched by an equal devotion to presenting balanced views. Witness such statements as: "No American Jew in government—and there were many in high positions—even resigned in protest over the American refusal to bomb the rail lines to Auschwitz," and "Other proposals were more complicated, such as bombing the rail lines to the camps and even the gas chambers themselves. John McCloy, then a presidential adviser, was instrumental in preventing any humanitarian bombing designed to save Jewish lives on the grounds that all bombing decisions should be made on military grounds alone." Dershowitz has entirely missed the point. Resignations on matters of principle are invariably associated with very strongly held views. No American Jew in government came close to exhibiting the degree of conviction on the bombing, questions that would ordinarily precede a principled resignation. Can he name any himself? Did Wyman name any? McCloy doubted the efficacy of the bombing, and in this he had much company and no opposition. Dershowitz does not ask why those urging the bombing didn't bring the matter directly to the attention of President Roosevelt.

The Lapid Foundation of Jerusalem[195] held a "public trial" on the subject "Why Auschwitz Was Not Bombed," and a judgment was issued on 18 April 1990 by Professor Shimon Shetreet. The first half of the judgment is devoted to a legalistic analysis of the legal and moral duties of the Allies in connection with the bombing of the Hungarian railways and/or Auschwitz. While this analysis may be of interest to lawyers, it appears to be totally irrelevant to the issues, inasmuch as the British (explicitly) and the Americans (implicitly) accepted that there was a duty. Sinclair's letter of 15 July started out: "I entirely agree that it is our duty to consider every possible plan that might help," while McCloy's letters show that the Americans, too, considered various plans and did not reject them on the grounds that there was no duty to carry out a practical and acceptable plan. The Allies did not need a flock of lawyers to tell them where their duty lay. A ridiculous legalistic note was introduced at the public trial in which it was determined that only those arguments put forward by the Allies at the time could be considered as defenses. As this reduces the defense to unclassified letters written in wartime, it means that no information on intelligence, operational matters, related experience, Nazi defenses, bombing accuracy, and so forth, which was available to the authors of these letters, can be considered.

The judgment is extremely weak even on the defenses that were allowed. The question of whether and to what extent timely and accurate intelligence was available upon which an operation could be planned and executed is never mentioned. This was a particular problem in connection with railroad bombing, and here the judge has absurdly broadened the objectives to "the railroad tracks leading from the Jewish centers of Europe and primarily from Hungary, to the camp. . . ." The claim of diversion of resources is rejected as a defense, but there is no attempt to provide quantitative support for this judgment. The judge has determined that at least one serious attempt at striking at the death camp installations or the central railroad intersections would have been reasonable. Which one? When? How big an operation? As to the possibility of harming the inmates, the judge has decided that the balance weighs in favor of justifying the bombing due to the real possibility of saving "thousands of lives." (A press account of this affair has transformed thousands into millions).[196] Here, we note only Field Marshal Dill's somewhat more authoritative view that bombing would have killed thousands of inmates. The failure of Jewish organizations to press the bombing more vigorously is criticized, but the judge does not exonerate the Allies, who should apparently have consulted their lawyers and ignored Jewish opinion, for or against.

The guilty parties are poorly identified. They are apparently "world leaders and military commanders." No distinction is made between the British (who lacked the ability to bomb Auschwitz or railroads in Silesia) and the Americans, who might have bombed Auschwitz. All are found guilty, including, though to a lesser degree, the Australians, the New Zealanders, the Canadians, and the South Africans.

Two oral examples of Wyman's influence will further illustrate the appeal of his views. In 1979, not long after Wyman's article was published, Israeli Prime Minister Menachem Begin visited British Prime Minister Margaret Thatcher in London. He complained to her[197] that the wartime British government under Churchill had not ordered the bombing of Auschwitz. He could hardly have read the Jewish Agency note of 11 July or Sinclair's letter of 15 July and raised this issue. Unbriefed, Thatcher was not able to educate him.

Elie Wiesel[198] gave an emotional and affecting speech at the dedication of the U.S. Holocaust Memorial Museum on the 50th anniversary of the uprising in the Warsaw Ghetto, 22 April 1993. "Why weren't the railways leading to Birkenau bombed by Allied planes?" he asked, confident from having read Wyman or his followers that it was within the power of the Allies to interrupt these railways and thereby stop the murder.

CONCLUSIONS

It was beyond the power of any force the Allies could possibly have brought to bear to interrupt the Hungarian railways by bombing them as, or, when requested. This conclusion was reached by responsible British and American officials acting with the benefit of professional military advice. In spite of this, Allied bombers did play a significant and extremely valuable indirect role in persuading the Hungarian government to bring an end to the deportations on 8 July.

The British were unable to bomb the gas chambers and crematoria for sound technical reasons. From about the end of August (two months before the Nazis themselves stopped the gassings at Auschwitz), the Americans could have bombed these installations, but only by diverting substantial resources to the task and in a manner that would likely have resulted in death or injury to thousands of camp inmates. Among those who opposed bombing the camps for the latter reason were the head of the Rescue Department of the World Jewish Congress and all of the members, except the chairman, of the Rescue Committee of the Jewish Agency in Jerusalem. The bombing would also have required the approval of President Roosevelt. He was never seriously asked for such approval. It is likely that widely expressed serious doubts about the efficacy of the proposed operation discouraged many people from vigorously pressing the issue at lower levels or raising it with Roosevelt directly. Hindsight has amply confirmed that these doubts were well founded.

The reason that the issue has been resurrected is that in 1978 Wyman wrote that "there is no question that bombing the gas chambers and crematoria would have saved many lives."[199] This blunt assertion struck an extremely responsive chord in many quarters. In the same article, he also made the much weaker statement: "Without gas chambers and crematoria, the Nazis would have been forced to reassess the extermination program. . . ."[200] When pressed on the issue of efficacy, Wyman used the relative obscurity of the letters to the editor column to disavow the stronger statement: "I did not claim that mass killing would have been impossible without Auschwitz."[201] This did not prevent him from reprinting both statements but omitting the disavowal in his 1984 book.

ACKNOWLEDGMENT

The author wishes to acknowledge the encouragement generously offered by Professor Martin Gilbert, C.B.E., while this work was in progress. His encouragement and, in particular, his view that the work was of importance made it possible for me to see it through to its conclusion.

Notes

1. Gideon Hausner, *Justice in Jerusalem* (New York: Harper and Row, 1966), 243-244, 344-345. Prosecution Document T/1177 from the Eichmann Trial, Central Zionist Archives Z4/14870. This document shows Weizmann's pessimistic opinion of the practical value of bombing Auschwitz. Its relationship to the prosecution of Eichmann escapes me.
2. *The Guardian,* 31 May 1961; 3 June 1961; 7 June 1961. *Sunday Telegraph,* 4 June 1961. *Jewish Chronicle,* 16 November 1962; 14 December 1962; 11 January 1963.
3. *Parliamentary Debates,* Commons, vol. 642 (13 June 1961), 202-203.
4. David S. Wyman, "Why Auschwitz Was Never Bombed," *Commentary* 66 (May 1978), 37-46. See also Letters from Readers, *Commentary:* 66 (July 1978), 7, 10-12; 67 (September 1978), 24-25; and 67 (November 1978), 19-20.
5. David S. Wyman, *The Abandonment of the Jews: America and the Holocaust, 1941-1945* (New York: Pantheon Books, 1984).
6. Frank W. Brecher, "David Wyman and the Historiography of America's Response to the Holocaust: Counter-Considerations," *Holocaust and Genocide Studies* 5 (fall 1990), 423-446. See also Wyman's response in the same issue, 485-486.
7. Lucy S. Dawidowicz, "Could the United States Have Rescued the European Jews from Hitler?" *This World,* nos. 10-12 (fall 1985), 15. Reprinted under the title "Could America Have Rescued Europe's Jews?" in *What Is the Use of Jewish History* (New York: Schocken Books, 1992), ed. by Neal Kozodoy.
8. Richard Foregger, "The Bombing of Auschwitz," *Aerospace Historian* 34 (summer 1987), 98-110. See also two commentaries: Robert H. Hodges, "The Bombing of Auschwitz: A Clarification," and Michael G. Moskow, "The Bombing of Auschwitz: A Reply," in *Aerospace Historian* 35 (summer 1988), 123-126, 127-129.
9. James H. Kitchens III, "The Bombing of Auschwitz Reexamined," *Journal of Military History* 58 (April 1994), 233-266.

10. Richard Foregger, "Technical Analysis of Methods to Bomb the Gas Chambers at Auschwitz," *Holocaust and Genocide Studies* 5 (fall 1990), 403-421. See also *Holocaust and Genocide Studies* 6 (spring 1991), 442-443.

11. Martin Gilbert, *Auschwitz and the Allies* (New York: Henry Holt, 1982), 236-237. Both dates are given for the second telegram.

12. Raul Hilberg, *The Destruction of the European Jews* (Chicago: Quadrangle Books, 1961), 543.

13. Wyman, "Why Auschwitz Was Never Bombed," 38; Wyman, *Abandonment of the Jews*," 290; Gilbert, *Auschwitz and the Allies*, 219-220. Both books give the archival locations of this telegram and many other original documents.

14. Gilbert, *Auschwitz and the Allies*, 223.

15. Wyman, "Why Auschwitz Was Never Bombed," 38; Wyman, *Abandonment of the Jews*, 290; Gilbert, *Auschwitz and the Allies*, 236. The reference to American censorship does not appear in "Why Auschwitz Was Never Bombed."

16. Wyman, "Why Auschwitz Was Never Bombed," 39; Wyman, *Abandonment of the Jews*, 292; Gilbert, *Auschwitz and the Allies*, 237.

17. Gilbert, *Auschwitz and the Allies*, 246. The WRB in Berne had received information about Auschwitz a week earlier; that communication did not include a bombing appeal. It is not clear whether the WRB in Berne passed the 24 June request to bomb the gas chambers and crematoria on to Washington at that time. Wyman, "Why Auschwitz Was Never Bombed," 39; Wyman, *Abandonment of the Jews*, 294.

18. Gilbert, *Auschwitz and the Allies*, 251-252.

19. Ibid., 255.

20. Ibid., 269.

21. Wyman, "Why Auschwitz Was Never Bombed," 40; Wyman, *Abandonment of the Jews*, 295; Gilbert, *Auschwitz and the Allies*, 246, 262-265.

22. Wyman, "Why Auschwitz Was Never Bombed," 40; Wyman, *Abandonment of the Jews*, 295.

23. Wyman, *Abandonment of the Jews*, 291.

24. Gilbert, *Auschwitz and the Allies*, 238.

25. Wyman, *Abandonment of the Jews*, 292-293.

26. B. Azkin, memo of 29 June, Franklin D. Roosevelt Library (FDRL), Hyde Park, N. Y., cited in Wyman, "Why Auschwitz Was Never Bombed," 40; Wyman, *Abandonment of the Jews*, 295; Gilbert, *Auschwitz and the Allies*, 246-247.

27. Gilbert, *Auschwitz and the Allies*, 256.

28. Rafael Medoff, *The Deafening Silence: American Jewish Leadership and the Holocaust* (New York: Shapolsky, 1988), 152.

29. Gruenbaum, memorandum of 7 June, Central Zionist Archives S26/1232. Gruenbaum to Barlas, 21 June, Central Zionist Archives S26/1284. These items

were noted by Yehuda Bauer, *American Jewry and the Holocaust* (Detroit: Wayne State University Press, 1981), 496n31.

30. Gilbert, *Auschwitz and the Allies*, 314-315. Gilbert says that "news of yet more deportations from Hungary had begun to reach the Jewish Agency in Jerusalem, following the overthrow of Admiral Horthy, and the return of the Gestapo to Budapest." But the telegram from Gruenbaum that he cites says only that the newly installed Hungarian government had ordered the deportations to begin again, "daily transports . . . being prepared." The overthrow of Admiral Horthy and the return of the Gestapo to Budapest did not take place until the middle of October, a month later.

31. *The Sunday Telegraph,* 4 June 1961.

32. Wyman, "Why Auschwitz Was Never Bombed," 44-45; Wyman, *Abandonment of the Jews,* 302.

33. Milton Groban, a former Fifteenth Air Force B-24 navigator-bombardier, had his letter to the editor appear in *Commentary* 66 (July 1978), 10-11; Charles M. Bachman, Letter to the Editor, *Commentary* 67 (November 1978), 20.

34. Gilbert, *Auschwitz and the Allies*, 267-269.

35. Ibid., 271-272.

36. Ibid., 284-285.

37. Wyman, "Why Auschwitz Was Never Bombed," 39; Wyman, *Abandonment of the Jews,* 292; Gilbert, *Auschwitz and the Allies*, 238.

38. *Jewish Chronicle,* 16 November 1962.

39. Wyman, "Why Auschwitz Was Never Bombed," 42; Wyman, *Abandonment of the Jews,* 300.

40. For example: Solly Zuckerman, *From Apes to Warlords* (New York: Harper and Row, 1978), 217 ff.; David R. Mets, *Master of Airpower: General Carl A. Spaatz* (Novato, Calif.: Presidio Press, 1988), 199 ff.; Lord Tedder, G. C. B., *With Prejudice* (Boston: Little, Brown, 1967), 502 ff.; Wesley F. Craven and James L. Cate, eds., *The Army Air Forces in World War II,* vol. 3, *Europe: Argument to V-E Day, January 1944 to May 1945* (Chicago: University of Chicago, in conjunction with the U.S. Office of Air Force History), 72 ff.

41. Foregger, "Technical Analysis," 412-414.

42. Hilberg, *Destruction of the European Jews,* 547.

43. Gilbert, *Auschwitz and the Allies*, 286-287.

44. Wyman, "Why Auschwitz Was Never Bombed," 43; Wyman, *Abandonment of the Jews,* 300.

45. Wyman, *Abandonment of the Jews,* 300.

46. Gilbert, *Auschwitz and the Allies*, 266.

47. Ibid., 255, 265, 279-280.

48. Martin Gilbert, *Churchill: A Life* (New York: Henry Holt, 1991), 783.

49. Hilberg, *Destruction of the European Jews*, 549.
50. Gilbert, *Auschwitz and the Allies*, 266.
51. Gilbert, private communication, 22 March 1994.
52. Bernard Wasserstein, *Britain and the Jews of Europe, 1939-1945* (Oxford, England: Clarendon Press, 1979), 319-320.
53. Hilberg, *Destruction of the European Jews*, 537.
54. Marion D. Fenyo, *Hitler, Horthy, and Hungary* (New Haven: Yale University Press, 1972), 212.
55. Gilbert, *Auschwitz and the Allies*, 266.
56. Craven and Cate, *Army Air Forces in World War II*, 290.
57. *Encyclopaedia Judaica*, vol. 5, 1434-1435 (Jerusalem: Keter Publishing House Jerusalem, 1974). Article on Debrecen contributed by Dr. Alexander Scheiber, Budapest.
58. Hilberg, *Destruction of the European Jews*, 545.
59. Wasserstein, *Britain*, 312.
60. Gilbert, *Auschwitz and the Allies*, 272.
61. Ibid., 278 ff.
62. Hausner, *Jews in Jerusalem*, 243.
63. Abba Eban, *My People* (New York: Behrman House and Random House, 1968), 427.
64. Wasserstein, *Britain*, 310.
65. Haim Barlas, *Hatzalah Bi'yemi Hashoah* (Tel Aviv: Hakibbutz Hameuchad, 1975), 293-295.
66. Norman Rose, *Chaim Weizmann: A Biography* (New York: Viking, 1986), 394.
67. Gilbert, *Auschwitz and the Allies*, 278 ff.
68. Ibid., 262 ff.
69. Ibid., 285.
70. Wyman, "Why Auschwitz Was Never Bombed," 40; Wyman, *Abandonment of the Jews*, 295-296; Gilbert, *Auschwitz and the Allies*, 303.
71. Medoff, *Deafening Silence*, 160.
72. Wyman, "Why Auschwitz Was Never Bombed," 43; Wyman, "Abandonment of the Jews," 301.
73. Wyman, "Why Auschwitz Was Never Bombed," 45.
74. Olga Lengyel, *Five Chimneys* (Chicago: Ziff-Davis, 1947).
75. Uwe Dietrich Adam, "The Gas Chambers," in *Unanswered Questions*, ed. Francois Furet (New York: Schocken Books, 1989), 151.
76. Leni Yahil, *The Holocaust: The Fate of European Jewry, 1932-1945* (New York: Oxford University Press, 1990), 527.
77. J. C. Pressac, *Auschwitz: Technique and Operation of the Gas Chambers* (New York: Beate Klarsfeld Foundation, 1989), 253.

78. Foregger, "Technical Analysis," 403.
79. Foregger, "The Bombing of Auschwitz," 106.
80. Hausner, *Jews in Jerusalem*, 345.
81. Kitchens, "Bombing of Auschwitz Reexamined," 245; Foregger, "Technical Analysis," 403.
82. Wyman, "Why Auschwitz Was Never Bombed," 44; Wyman, *Abandonment of the Jews*, 304.
83. Foregger, "The Bombing of Auschwitz," 106-108.
84. Hodges, "The Bombing of Auschwitz: A Clarification," 125.
85. Dino A. Brugioni and Robert G. Poirier, *The Holocaust Revisited: A Retrospective Analysis of the Auschwitz-Birkenau Extermination Complex*, NTISUB/E/280-002 (Washington, D.C.: U.S. Department of Commerce, National Technical Information Service, February 1979). Dino A. Brugioni, "Auschwitz-Birkenau: Why the World War II Photo Interpreters Failed to Identify the Extermination Complex," *Military Intelligence* 9 (January 1983), 50-55.
86. Kitchens, "Bombing of Auschwitz Reexamined," 248-249.
87. Groban, Letter to the Editor, 10-11.
88. Gilbert, *Auschwitz and the Allies*, 162; *Encyclopaedia Judaica*, vol. 11, 794-795. Article on Majdanek contributed by Danuta Dombrowska, M.A., historian, Jerusalem.
89. Shlomo Aronson, cited in Dawidowicz, "Could America Have Rescued?" 173.
90. William L. Shirer, *The Rise and Fall of the Third Reich* (London: Secker and Warburg, 1960), 972.
91. Hilberg, *Destruction of the European Jews*, 629.
92. Wyman, "Why Auschwitz Was Never Bombed," 43; Wyman, *Abandonment of the Jews*, 301. The version in the book reads: "There is no doubt that destruction of the gas chambers and crematoria would have saved many lives."
93. Wyman, "Why Auschwitz Was Never Bombed," 44; Wyman, *Abandonment of the Jews*, 304.
94. Groban, Letter to the Editor, 10.
95. David S. Wyman, Reply to Letter to the Editor, *Commentary* 66 (July 1978), 12.
96. Lucy S. Dawidowicz, *The War against the Jews, 1933-1945* (New York: Bantam Books, 1986), 140-142.
97. Wyman, "Why Auschwitz Was Never Bombed," 44; Wyman, *Abandonment of the Jews*, 304. The 1978 "Why Auschwitz" article used 450,000 instead of 437,000. The lower figure agrees with Hilberg.
98. Gilbert, *Auschwitz and the Allies*, 285.
99. *Sunday Telegraph*, 4 June 1961.
100. Extract from taped interview with Martin Gilbert, 1982. Gilbert, private communication, 14 October 1993.

101. Sir John Slessor, *The Central Blue* (New York: Praeger, 1957), 615 ff.
102. Samuel Katz, *Days of Fire* (Garden City, N.Y.: Doubleday, 1968), 85-86. See also map facing 55.
103. *Jewish Chronicle,* 16 November 1962.
104. Gilbert, *Auschwitz and the Allies,* 285.
105. C. Martin Sharp and Michael J. F. Bowyer, *Mosquito* (London: Faber and Faber, 1967), 241-244, and photographs 96 and 97. Many more details of the Amiens raid, including further references, may be found in the *Jewish Chronicle* article cited in note 103 above.
106. Hilberg, *Destruction of the European Jews,* 584.
107. Lawrence H. Blum, Letter to the Editor, *Commentary* 66 (July 1978), 7.
108. Wyman's response to the above letter, *Commentary* 66 (July 1978), 11.
109. Wyman, *Abandonment of the Jews,* 409n63.
110. Ibid., 303.
111. Dawidowicz, "Could America Have Rescued?" 171.
112. Foregger, "The Bombing of Auschwitz," 108-109. In his 1990 article, "Technical Analysis," 403, Foregger includes the Mosquito in a list of aircraft types that could fly from Foggia to Auschwitz and return, but he does not assert that it could carry a useful bomb load over this distance.
113. Hodges, "The Bombing of Auschwitz: A Clarification," 124.
114. Kitchens, "Bombing of Auschwitz Reexamined," 258-261.
115. Sharp and Bowyer, *Mosquito,* Appendix 4, "Summary of Mosquito Variants," 393-400; Appendix 5, "Mosquito Operational Performance and Loads," 401-403.
116. Ibid., 192-193.
117. John A. Terraine, *A Time for Courage* (New York: Macmillan, 1985), 497.
118. Sharp and Bowyer, *Mosquito,* 254.
119. Hodges, "The Bombing of Auschwitz: A Clarification," 124.
120. Sharp and Bowyer, *Mosquito,* 198-199.
121. Ibid., 209-213.
122. Ibid., 351.
123. Ibid., 351.
124. Yahil, *The Holocaust,* 524, 727n72.
125. Wyman, *Abandonment of the Jews,* 303.
126. Ibid.
127. Craven and Cate, *Army Air Forces in World War II,* 283. Foregger, "Technical Analysis," 409, has also considered the P-38 raid on Ploesti as a model for an attack on the facilities at Auschwitz. In his view, the average error of this type of attack was such that it was not certain that one of the facilities could have been hit. He also says that there would have been inmate casualties.
128. Groban, Letter to the Editor, 10-11.

129. Kitchens, "Bombing of Auschwitz Reexamined," 251-252.
130. Sharp and Bowyer, *Mosquito*, 230.
131. Wyman, *Abandonment of the Jews*, 302.
132. Groban, Letter to the Editor, *Commentary* 66 (July 1978), 10.
133. Craven and Cate, *Army Air Forces in World War II*, 305-306.
134. Gilbert, *Auschwitz and the Allies*, 195.
135. Ibid., Caption to Figure 28.
136. Ibid., 46.
137. Ibid., 310.
138. Wyman, *Abandonment of the Jews*, 299. Craven and Cate, *Army Air Forces in World War II*, 642.
139. Kitchens, "Bombing of Auschwitz Reexamined."
140. Gilbert, *Auschwitz and the Allies*, 321. Gilbert quotes a 1980 letter from Nahum Goldmann containing the latter's recollections. There are many doubtful points in these recollections. Goldmann disliked the objection offered by "General" (actually, Field Marshal) Dill to the prospect of killing thousands of prisoners. Goldmann may have been unaware that this view was held by Kubowitzki and others at the time. Goldmann's "few dozen bombs" are also cited in Medoff, *Deafening Silence*, 159.
141. Gilbert, *Auschwitz and the Allies*, 46.
142. Kitchens, "Bombing of Auschwitz Reexamined," 255.
143. Gilbert, *Auschwitz and the Allies*, 321.
144. Foregger, "Technical Analysis," 408.
145. Roger M. Williams, "An American Tragedy: Why Wasn't Auschwitz Bombed?" *Commonweal* 105 (24 November 1978), 751.
146. Wyman, *Abandonment of the Jews*, 303.
147. Herbert Loebel, Letter to the Editor, *Commentary* 66 (July 1978), 7, 10; Letter to the Editor, *Holocaust and Genocide Studies* 6 (spring 1991), 442.
148. John J. McCloy, Quoted in an interview with Morton Mintz, *Washington Post*, 17 April 1983.
149. Aaron Lerner, Letter to the Editor, *Commentary* 66 (July 1978), 7.
150. Mets, *Master of Air Power*, 237.
151. Wyman, *Abandonment of the Jews*, 410n78.
152. Wyman, "Why Auschwitz Was Never Bombed," 40; Wyman, *Abandonment of the Jews*, 295.
153. Wyman, "Why Auschwitz Was Never Bombed," 40; Wyman, *Abandonment of the Jews*, 296; Gilbert, *Auschwitz and the Allies*, 312.
154. Gilbert, *Auschwitz and the Allies*, 277-278.
155. Ibid., 285.
156. Ibid., 300-301.
157. Wasserstein, *Britain*, 313.

158.   Ibid., 313-316. In a review of Wasserstein's book and in a subsequent exchange of correspondence (John P. Fox, *European Studies Review* 10, [January 1980], 138-146; and *European Studies Review* 10, [October 1980], 487-492), a sharp difference of opinion on the meaning of these 1944 British documents is aired. As the authors of the documents thought they were involved in the preparation of a British operation to bomb Auschwitz, it may be possible to draw conclusions about the motives of British civil servants and officers. But nothing that these people said or did could alter the fact that a British operation had been ruled out on solid technical grounds since 15 July, and only an American operation was being considered. If Sinclair had found a practical way for the RAF to bomb Auschwitz, the whole affair would obviously have started in mid-July, and not in August. The last half of July was spent, so far as this issue is concerned, waiting for Spaatz to visit the Air Ministry in London.

159.   Gilbert, *Auschwitz and the Allies*, 301-319.

160.   Foregger, "The Bombing of Auschwitz," 104-108.

161.   Wyman, "Why Auschwitz Was Never Bombed," 45; Wyman, *Abandonment of the Jews*, 305.

162.   Slessor, *The Central Blue*, 615 ff.

163.   Loebel, Letter to the Editor, (1978), 7, 10; Letter to the Editor, *Holocaust and Genocide Studies* 6 (1991), 442.

164.   Wasserstein, *Britain*, 319-320.

165.   Brugioni and Poirier, *The Holocaust Revisited*, 11.

166.   Pressac, *Technique and Operation*, 253.

167.   Gilbert, *Auschwitz and the Allies*, 319n2.

168.   Winston S. Churchill, *The Second World War*, vol. 6, *Triumph and Tragedy*, 113-128. (London: Cassell, 1954).

169.   Mets, *Master of Air Power*, 231.

170.   Hilberg, *Destruction of the European Jews*, 543, 549.

171.   S. B. Unsdorfer, "The Call That Went Unanswered," *Jewish Chronicle*, 14 December 1962.

172.   Hausner, *Jews in Jerusalem*, 243, 244, 345.

173.   George Steiner, *Language and Silence* (New York: Atheneum, 1967), 149, 150, 158.

174.   Eban, *My People*, 425, 427.

175.   Katz, *Days of Fire*, 85-86. See also map facing 55.

176.   Hilberg, *Destruction of the European Jews*, 584.

177.   Henry L. Feingold, *The Politics of Rescue: The Roosevelt Administration and the Holocaust, 1938-1945*. (New Brunswick, N.J.: Rutgers University Press, 1970), 256-257.

178.   Herbert Druks, *The Failure to Rescue* (New York: Robert Speller and Sons, 1977), 64-69.

179. Wasserstein, *Britain,* 307-320.
180. Ibid., 316.
181. Roger M. Williams, "An American Moral Tragedy," 746-751.
182. Gilbert, *Auschwitz and the Allies,* 321.
183. Bauer, *American Jewry,* 396-397, 496n31.
184. Gilbert, *Auschwitz and the Allies.*
185. Braham, Randolph L. *The Politics of Genocide* (New York: Columbia University Press, 1981), 1108-1112.
186. Monty Noam Penkower, *The Jews were Expendable.* (Chicago: University of Illinois Press, 1983), 190-191, 195.
187. Rose, *Chaim Weizmann: A Biography,* 394.
188. Michael R. Marrus, *The Holocaust in History* (London: University Press of New England, 1987), 192-194.
189. Medoff, *Deafening Silence,* 160.
190. Foregger, "The Bombing of Auschwitz," 104-108.
191. Michael Berenbaum, *After Tragedy and Triumph* (Cambridge, England: Cambridge University Press, 1990), 9, 82.
192. Yahil, *The Holocaust,* 638, 639.
193. Brecher, "Historiography," 429-430.
194. Alan M. Dershowitz, *Chutzpah* (New York: Little, Brown, 1991), 296.
195. The Lapid Foundation, Jerusalem, Israel. 18 April 1990. *Public Trial: Why Auschwitz Was Not Bombed.*
196. *New York City Tribune,* 23 April 1990. Story by Steven Rodan, correspondent.
197. Gilbert, private communication, 22 March 1994.
198. Elie Wiesel, Address at the Dedication of the Holocaust Memorial Museum in Washington, D.C., 22 April 1993. Supplied by Professor Wiesel, Boston University, Boston, Mass.
199. Wyman, "Why Auschwitz was Never Bombed," 43.
200. Ibid., 44.
201. Wyman's response appears in *Commentary* 66 (July 1978).

Translation of agenda item #2:

Provisional and partial translation of the minutes of the meeting of the Executive of the Jewish Agency held June 11, 1944.

Present: Ben-Gurion—Chair, Mr. Gruenbaum, Dr. Senator, Rabbi Fischman, Mr. Kaplan, Dr. Schmorek, Dr. Joseph, Mr. Schapira, Mr. Ben-Tzvi, Dr. Hantke, Dr. Granovsky, Mr. Eisenberg.

Agenda:
  1. Matters of rescue

2. Discussion of Mr. Gruenbaum with Mr. Pinkerton on matters of rescue
3. The department of immigrant absorption

Item 2, Discussion of Mr. Gruenbaum with Mr. Pinkerton on matters of rescue.

Mr. Gruenbaum: Sent to the members of the board a protocol of his discussion with the U.S. Consul General on matters of rescue. Among other things he (Gruenbaum) suggested that the Allies should bomb the communication lines between Hungary and Poland. If they destroy the railway line, it would be impossible to carry out, for a definite period of time, their vicious plans. Mr. Pinkerton promised to transmit the suggestion to the War Refugee Board.

Mr. Gruenbaum also suggested that airplanes of the Allies should bomb the death camps in Poland, such as Auschwitz, Treblinka etc. Mr. Pinkerton argues that if this were done the Allies would be blamed for the murder of Jews, so he asked for the suggestion to be put in writing. Mr. Gruenbaum promised to consult with his colleagues on the matter.

According to the news available, every day thousands of Jews are being murdered in the death camps. Only the "Ordung-Dienst" remain alive for a short period of time. They do not wait long before they kill the victims. Even if we assume that they will bomb the camps while there are Jews in them, and some of them will get killed, the others could disperse and save themselves. By destroying the buildings they will not be able to murder, by means of the techniques they use, for months. We have received news today that, in the course of ten days, 120,000 Jews were expelled from Hungary.

Ben-Gurion: We don't know what really is the situation in Poland, and it seems that we could not offer (propose) anything with regard to this matter.

Rabbi Fischman: Concurs with Ben-Gurion's opinion.

Dr. Schmorek: Here we hear that in Auschwitz there is a large labor camp. We cannot take upon ourselves the responsibility of a bombing which would cause the death of a single Jew.

Dr. Joseph: He too opposes the suggestion to ask the Americans to bomb the camps, and so to murder Jews. Mr. Gruenbaum does not speak as a private individual, but as the representative of an institution. He (Joseph) thinks that the institution to which we are linked should not suggest such a thing.

Dr. Senator: Concurs with the view of Dr. Joseph. It is regrettable that Mr. Gruenbaum spoke of it with the American Consul.

Ben-Gurion: The view of the board is that we should not ask the Allies to bomb places where there are Jews.

CONTRIBUTORS AND
CONFERENCE PARTICIPANTS

BERNARD BELLUSH is a professor of history at the City College of New York. His research specialty is Franklin D. Roosevelt and the New Deal era. His works include *Franklin D. Roosevelt as Governor of New York; Franklin D. Roosevelt: A Great American Liberal;* and *An Interpretation of Franklin D. Roosevelt.*

JOHN MORTON BLUM, the conference chairman, formerly was a Woodward Professor of History at Yale University. His books include *Joe Tumulty and the Wilson Era; The Republican Roosevelt; Yesterday's Children; The Promise of America; From the Morgenthau Diaries;* and *V Was for Victory.*

RICHARD BREITMAN is a professor of history at American University. He is the author of *German Socialism and Weimar Democracy; Breaking the Silence,* coauthored with Walter Laqueur; and *American Refugee Policy and European Jewry: Roosevelt and the Holocaust,* coauthored with Alan Kraut.

J. GARRY CLIFFORD, rapporteur of the conference, is a professor of political science at the University of Connecticut and coauthored *American Foreign Policy: A History.*

ROBERT DALLEK is currently in residence at The Queens College, Oxford, England, and is a professor of history at the University of California, Los Angeles. He is the author of *Democrat and Diplomat: The Life of William E. Dodd and FDR;* and *American Foreign Policy, 1932-1945.*

HENRY L. FEINGOLD is professor of history at Bernard Baruch College of the City University of New York. He is the author of *The Politics of Rescue: The Roosevelt Administration and the Holocaust, 1938-1945,* as well as numerous articles on the Holocaust that have appeared in *American Jewish History, Jewish Social Studies,* and elsewhere.

DORIS KEARNS GOODWIN is a noted lecturer and the author of *Lyndon Johnson and The American Dream; The Fitzgeralds and the Kennedys;* and *Franklin and Eleanor at War: The American Homefront during World War II.*

KAREN J. GREENBERG has written extensively on the Holocaust and is associated with the Soros Foundation.

JAMES H. KITCHENS III is an archivist at the United States Air Force Historical Research Center at Maxwell Air Force Base, Alabama. In addition to numerous other articles, he has published and given presentations on the Auschwitz bombing question.

WILLIAM KOREY served for many years as director of international policy research for B'nai B'rith. He has taught at Long Island University, City College of New York, and Columbia University. He is a prolific writer on human-rights issues, and his essays have been published in *Foreign Affairs, Foreign Policy,* the *Washington Quarterly, Commentary,* and elsewhere. He is the author of *The Promises We Keep.*

TRUDE LASH is chairman of the Eleanor Roosevelt Institute and a board member of the Franklin and Eleanor Roosevelt Institute. She is active in child-development and human-rights issues.

RICHARD H. LEVY is a retired nuclear engineer. Born in London, he was educated at Cambridge University (B.A. in mathematics) and at Princeton (Ph.D. in aeronautical engineering). He has worked in the defense and nuclear-power industries, published many scientific papers, and holds several patents. As far as history is concerned, he has the honor of having been described by Professor David S. Wyman as a verbose amateur.

CHARLES MAIER is a professor of history at the Center for European Studies at Harvard University. His research specialty is twentieth-century Western European history and recent U.S. diplomacy.

MICHAEL R. MARRUS is professor of history at the University of Toronto and a Fellow of the Royal Society of Canada. During recent years, he has concentrated on the history of European fascism and the Holocaust. He coauthored with Robert Paxton *Vichy France and the Jews* and is the author of *The Unwanted: European Refugees in the Twentieth Century,* and *The Holocaust in History.* He is the editor of *The Nazi Holocaust,* a 15-volume series reproducing 300 of the most important articles on Nazi genocide.

VERNE W. NEWTON has been the director of the Franklin D. Roosevelt Library since 1991. He is the author of *The Cambridge Spies* and the writer/producer of "Harry Hopkins: At FDR's Side," a PBS special.

ARTHUR SCHLESINGER, JR., until recently held the Albert Schweitzer Chair in the Humanities at the City University of New York and has twice won the Pulitzer Prize. His books include *The Coming of the New Deal; The Imperial Presidency; Robert Kennedy and His Times; Cycles of American*

History; and *The Disuniting of America.* He is chairman of the Franklin and Eleanor Roosevelt Institute.

CARL SCHORSKE is professor of history at Princeton University. He specializes in German history and the politics of the twentieth century. His works include *The Historian and the City; The Critical Spirit;* and *The Responsibility of Power.*

WILLIAM J. VANDEN HEUVEL, counsel to the law firm of Stroock and Stroock and Lavan and international adviser to the investment banking firm of Allen and Company of New York City, was the U.S. deputy representative to the United Nations and the U.S. ambassador to the European office of the United Nations in Geneva, Switzerland. Ambassador vanden Heuvel is president of the Franklin and Eleanor Roosevelt Institute.

BERNARD WASSERSTEIN is professor of history at Brandeis University and is the author of *Britain and the Jews of Europe, 1939-1945.*

Index

Breinigsville, PA USA
03 December 2009
228506BV00001B/2/P